From the Lighthouse to Monk's House

From the Lighthouse to Monk's House

A Guide to Virginia Woolf's Literary Landscapes

Katherine C. Hill-Miller

Duckworth

First published in 2001 by
Gerald Duckworth & Co. Ltd.
61 Frith Street, London W1D 3JL
Tel: 020 7434 4242
Fax: 020 7434 4420
Email: enquiries@duckworth-publishers.co.uk
www.ducknet.co.uk

A catalogue record for this book is available
from the British Library

ISBN 0 7156 2995 6

Typeset by Derek Doyle & Associates, Liverpool
Printed in Great Britain by
Bookcraft (Bath) Ltd, Midsomer Norton, Avon

Contents

For Fred and Chris

Acknowledgements

I am grateful to the copyright holders and their agents who have generously given me permission to quote from copyrighted works: to Nigel Nicolson, for permission to quote from the works of Vita Sackville-West, especially her *Knole and the Sackvilles;* to the Society of Authors as the literary representatives of the Virginia Woolf Estate, for permission to quote from Woolf's novels and short fiction. (Thanks to Jeremy Crowe at the Society.) Extracts from *The Letters of Virginia* Woolf, edited by Nigel Nicolson and Joanne Trautmann; from *The Diary of Virginia Woolf,* edited by Anne Olivier Bell; from *The Essays of Virginia Woolf,* edited by Andrew McNeillie; from *Moments of Being* by Virginia Woolf; from *The Complete Shorter Fiction of Virginia Woolf,* edited by Susan Dicks; and from *A Passionate Apprentice* by Virginia Woolf are all published by the Hogarth Press and reprinted by permission of the Estate of Virginia Woolf and The Random House Group Ltd. (Thanks to Catherine Trippett at Random House for facilitating my requests.) Thanks are also due to Stuart Clarke, who has allowed me to use parts of his *Mrs Dalloway* walk as the basis for my 'Clarissa and Septimus' walk.

I am indebted to the Research Committee at the C.W. Post Campus of Long Island University, which has consistently provided me with research time. Thanks are also due to Paul Sherwin and Mike Arons, who provided the sabbatical that allowed me to finish the manuscript, and to David Steinberg, who provided both logistical support and familial connections. I am especially grateful to the National Endowment for the Humanities, which gave this project its beginnings.

Almost all the participants in my NEH seminars have read and commented on versions of chapters at various stages, but special thanks must go to Idris Anderson, Peggy Cornelius, Nita Pettigrew, Joey Hill and Nancy Homer, who kept the intensity of those seminars alive when they shared their subsequent research at conferences. Jeff Rosinski took brilliant photographs of Woolf sites in England. Neither the NEH seminars nor this book could have happened without my seminar assistants: Liz Ranellone Fritz; Leslie Broder; and Chris Barnes, who single-handedly saved scores of people from being lost between St Ives and Carbis Bay, and between Regent's Park and the squares of Bloomsbury.

I am indebted to the staff of the C.W. Post library, and in particular to Diane

Podell, Gisela E. Miceli and Lewis Pisha. I am also grateful to James Caira, information officer at the British Museum's Reading Room; to Anne Thomson, archivist at the library of Newnham College, Cambridge; to Dorothy Sheridan at the University of Sussex library; and to Isaac Gewirtz, Curator of the Berg Collection of the New York Public Library.

James Bednarz, Marge Hallissy, Norbert Krapf and Dennis Pahl all provided advice on topics ranging from travel to this book's title. Susan Miller made a special trip into London to inspect the Cock Tavern. Edmund Miller advised me on George Herbert, and Janet Newkirk scoured the local history section in her Kensington library for information about sites associated with the Stephen family. Vanessa Curtis and Jasmyne King-Leeder provided information about Hyde Park Gate; Sue Fox kindly shared information about unpublished Leslie Stephen letters; Sue Bedford generously showed me around Talland House, where she lives. Annie Crowther deserves thanks for her gracious hospitality last June, as do Ten Gower and Malcolm Sherman, who also kindly provided information from their upcoming pamphlet about walks in Firle. Brenda Nichols and Grace McGrorty generously provided logistical help on a moment's notice.

I am especially indebted to colleagues and friends who read chapters and offered commentary. Rosemary Sumner corrected details about St Ives; Jonathan Steinberg, Fellow Emeritus of Trinity Hall and currently Walter H. Annenberg Professor of Modern History at the University of Pennsylvania, made me into a Cantabridgian. Nigel Nicolson provided support, friendship, and details about Knole that only he could know.

Warm thanks must go to the badger set, who spent hours collaborating with me. Stuart Clarke – an impeccable editor who knows more about Leonard and Virginia Woolf than they knew about themselves – read several chapters and improved them significantly. David Wilkinson drove indefatigably around St Ives and Sussex, maps at the ready, planning best routes and measuring distances. Stephen Barkway provided sage advice about luggers, about Sussex walks, and also drew the charming images that appear at the head of each chapter. Sheila Wilkinson has been a true partner in research for the last year. She has saved me from many Americanisms related to jogging, bowling and cricket stumps; she sent photos, books and notes across the Atlantic on a regular basis. Her careful historical research and wide knowledge of the Bloomsbury group have improved this book immeasurably.

Finally, last and best thanks must go to the people who have lived through this book on a daily basis. Thanks to my mother, Genevieve Bytner Hill, for reading drafts and always being the first to ask how the project was going; thanks to my father, M. Joseph Hill, whose clear prose style is still the model I emulate. I dedicate this book with love and gratitude to my son, Chris, who is a better writer than I am, and to my husband, Fred, who is as always a true feminist, a brilliant editor – and who understands more than anyone I know.

Introduction

'I do not know whether pilgrimages to the shrines of famous men ought not to be condemned as sentimental journeys. It is better to read Carlyle in your own study chair than to visit the sound-proof room and pore over the manuscripts at Chelsea.'

Virginia Woolf, 'Haworth, November, 1904'

'So that to know her, or any one, one must seek out the people who completed them; even the places.'

Virginia Woolf, *Mrs Dalloway*, 1925

Although Virginia Woolf worried about descending into sentiment when she visited the homes of famous writers, she enjoyed her literary tours immensely. She visited the Carlyles' home in Cheyne Row, Keats's house in Hampstead, the Brontës' parsonage at Haworth. She saw Swift's epitaph at St Patrick's Cathedral in Dublin, and concluded that Young Street, Kensington, expressed Thackeray's spirit perfectly. She admitted that literary pilgrimages were a guilty pleasure: she liked to choose a darkish day, 'lest the ghosts of the dead should discover us'.[1] But it was generally a pleasure that sparked her imagination, that gave her some new ideas about the writer and his work, and that forged a sense of her connection to the ghostly presence of vanished great minds. That sense of connection was a result of her delighted response to place.

1

And Virginia Woolf's delight in places is precisely the subject of this book: how she reacted to places, how she transformed places in her works, and how her lively evocations of literal places lie at the heart of some of her most important pieces of writing.

In fact, the first essay Virginia (then Stephen) wrote for publication was a travel piece. In 1904, when Virginia Stephen was twenty-two, she stayed for ten days in Yorkshire with Madge Vaughan and her husband, Will. Will Vaughan was Virginia's cousin through her mother's line and worked as headmaster of the Giggleswick School near Settle. Virginia was recovering from the bout of mental illness that had followed her father's death in February of 1904 and, following her doctor's usual orders to retire to a quiet spot, she left London to holiday in the country. While Virginia was at Giggleswick, she and the Vaughans made a pilgrimage to the Brontë family home at Haworth Parsonage. On the way to Haworth, Virginia carefully noted the countryside: the earth sheathed in 'virgin snow'; the houses lining the edge of the moor; the little clump of trees just outside the Parsonage itself. Once at Haworth, Virginia was deeply moved by the sight of Charlotte Brontë's thin muslin dress and small shoes, since their survival conjured up Charlotte Brontë's very presence: 'The natural fate of such things is to die before the body that wore them, and because these, trifling and transient though they are, have survived, Charlotte Brontë the woman comes to life.'[2] She was equally moved by Haworth's ancient churchyard, with its invasion of graves and crush of tall headstones. Like any good tourist, Virginia dutifully sent postcards to her friend Violet Dickinson. And then she sat down to write an account of her expedition for Mrs Lyttelton, editor of the Women's Supplement of the *Guardian*. After all, Virginia Stephen already knew that she wanted to support herself as a writer, and Haworth Parsonage seemed a good place to start.

This account of Virginia Woolf's first publication encapsulates several of the themes that came to characterise Woolf's life: her battles with mental illness; her tendency to alternate city life with country life; her lively sense of imaginative connection to people and authors who lived and died long before her time. It also suggests patterns that came to characterise Woolf's career as a writer: her determination to support herself by her pen; her habit of turning every experience she encountered into words; her gifts for visual detail and suggestive description. Most importantly, the story captures her delight in the expressive powers of a place, especially when that place was associated with an author.

To say that the idea of place is important to Virginia Woolf is to say the obvious: connection to a place is an inescapable fact of the human condition, and places are therefore an element or theme in the work of every novelist who ever picked up a pen. But the idea of 'place' occupies a special position in Woolf's work. Near the end of her life, when Woolf sat down to write her autobiography and to consider her development as a writer, she returned to very specific places and invested them with the power to expand – or to contract – the human spirit. In her essays about places, the idea of place acts as a fulcrum for the creative imagination. A place is the element that anchors memory. A place is continuous and solid, and therefore has the power to connect people to their pasts, and to the lives of people who have worked and died before them. Woolf discovers a sort of immortality in places, and it is in the idea of place that Woolf's fierce attachment to the natural world meets her urge towards transcendence: 'place' is the most solid of things, yet certain places inspire Woolf to a nearly mystical vision into the heart of reality.

Throughout her work, Woolf casts 'place' as being crucial to the activity of the creative imagination in a variety of ways. To begin with, an artist can't work until she has found her place – that is, until she has grounded and positioned herself in some fundamentally important way. For Lily Briscoe in *To the Lighthouse*, this positioning means finding the right spot in the Ramsay family's garden to complete her painting – a spot that looks towards Mrs Ramsay sitting in the window, but that also looks outward, over the sea and towards the lighthouse. For Orlando, finding her place means grounding herself in her vast home, furnishing it and making it her own, and then (finally) completing the poem that has lain close to her heart for three centuries. In *Between the Acts*, Miss La Trobe must ground herself in the continuity of the English countryside – and then in a pub – before she can write her next play; in *A Room of One's Own*, Mary Beton must acquire a room of her own with a lock on the door before she can write poetry. Even Clarissa Dalloway, who is an artist of human emotions rather than paints or language, must find her place before she can create: Clarissa walks the streets of London and finally returns to her Westminster home, where she throws the party during which she discovers herself.

In Woolf's eyes, 'place' is also crucial to the creative imagination as a stimulus: places provide material for the writer, or reveal some crucial fact that results in creative insight. In her essay 'Great Men's Houses', for example, Woolf's visit to the Carlyles' home at 5 Cheyne Row in London reveals a central fact that explains their famously difficult marriage and Carlyle's famously idiosyncratic habits: 5 Cheyne Row had no running water. As Woolf puts it, she enters the house and sees in a flash 'a fact that escaped the attention of Froude, and yet was of incalculable importance – they had no water laid on'.[3] Being at 5 Cheyne Row spurs Woolf to imagine how the lack of running water devastated the marriage and destroyed the wife: every drop of water had to be pumped, boiled and carried up three flights of stairs for Carlyle's bath; the stairs seemed 'worn by the feet of harassed women carrying tin cans';[4] Jane Carlyle ended her life with hollow cheeks, and with a look of bitterness and suffering in her face. As Woolf puts it, 'Such is the effect of a pump in the basement and a yellow tin bath up three pairs of stairs'.[5] Woolf's entire imaginative excursion about the Carlyles and their marital difficulties is a revelation occasioned by 'place' – when Woolf sees the Carlyles' home first hand, her visit results in creative insight into their life and marriage.

Woolf also insists that places stimulate the creative imagination simply by providing material. This idea is the main thrust of her essay 'Street Haunting', in which the narrator leaves her London house late on a winter's afternoon to walk to the Strand to buy a pencil. The fact that the narrator is in search of a pencil indicates that she is in search of material, and she finds her material in abundant supply on the crowded streets of London. As she walks along in the crush of people, her identity shifts in response to the place: she sheds her indoor self and becomes 'part of that vast republican army of anonymous trampers, whose society is so agreeable after the solitude of one's own room'.[6] When she enters Oxford Street, the objects in shop windows send her on long imaginative flights. A window filled with furniture makes her 'build up all the chambers of an imaginary house and furnish them at one's will with sofa, table, carpet'.[7] The window of an antique jewellery store holds a lovely string of pearls, and she imagines how her life would change if she wore them: 'It becomes instantly between two and three in the morning; the lamps are burning very white in the deserted streets of Mayfair ... There are a few lights in the bedrooms of great peers returned from the Court, of silk-stockinged footmen, of dowagers who have pressed the hands of statesmen.'[8] When she stops in a second-hand bookshop close to the Strand, the place makes her feel a vivid imaginative connection to 'the unknown and the vanished whose only record is ... this little book of poems'.[9] And as she heads for home, the places she passes evoke the people she has seen, so that she describes the imaginative release the streets of London give her: 'Into each of these lives one could penetrate a little way, far enough to give oneself the illusion that one is not tethered to a single mind, but can put on briefly for a few minutes the bodies and minds of others.'[10] By the close of 'Street Haunting', London's places have given the narrator an abundance of material; they have stimulated her to feats of literary creativity; they have connected her to vanished minds; and they have transported her beyond herself, into a state of union with other lives.

It is this last idea – place as a stimulus to experiences of connection, continuity and union with something beyond the confines of the single self – that is most important to Woolf's work. Woolf writes vividly about the importance of this aspect of 'place' in her essay 'The Moment: Summer's Night'. And since the concept of 'the moment' is so central to Woolf's work – the experience of 'the moment' appears in some form in all Woolf's novels, and is central to her autobiographical essays and to her ideas about the purposes of fiction – it is important to understand how experiences of 'place' lie at the heart of 'the moment'.

'The Moment: Summer's Night' is set in a garden in the country as night falls, with several people sitting outside at a table. (The literal location is no doubt Monk's House, the Woolfs' country home at Rodmell.) Woolf opens 'The Moment: Summer's Night' by recognising that 'the moment' is composed largely of visual and sense impressions: the feel of tired feet expanding into worn slippers; the cool evening breeze blowing gently over warm skin. But 'the moment' is not only a fleeting sensation; it is also something rooted and durable, and that timeless aspect of 'the moment' derives from place:

> But this moment is also composed of a sense that the legs of the chair are sinking through the centre of the earth, passing through the rich garden earth; they sink, weighted down. Then the sky loses its colour perceptibly and a star here and there makes a point of light. Then changes, unseen in the day, coming in succession seem to make an order evident. One becomes aware that we are spectators and also passive participants in a pageant. And as nothing can interfere with the order, we have nothing to do but accept, and watch.[11]

As Woolf sees it, part of the experience of 'the moment' is the sense of being completely rooted in a place – the sense that the legs of one's chair are weighted into the garden and sink to the centre of the earth. And this sense of being firmly tied to a place results, in turn, in a vivid feeling of historical continuity and connection – the feeling that the place connects the viewer to all of human life that unfolded on that spot before him. It is as if human life were arranged in a pageant, and being rooted to a place makes one 'aware that we are spectators and also passive participants in a pageant'.

As 'The Moment: Summer's Night' unfolds, 'place' assumes other roles in the experience of 'the moment'. It ties together the 'knot of consciousness'[12] around the table – that is, it connects the four people who sit together in the dark. Their talk leads to an imaginative flight about the lives of the villagers next door: one of the people speculates that the husband beats the wife every Saturday night. And then the dark place in the garden assumes a different, expectant aspect. The cows begin to low in the fields; the trees become heavy dark shapes – and the place and the dark combine to send the narrator outside herself, into an experience of union with something far transcending the single self:

> Then comes the terror, the exultation; the power to rush out unnoticed, alone; to be consumed; to be swept away to become a rider on the random wind; the tossing wind; the trampling and neighing wind; the horse with the blown-back mane; the tumbling, the foraging; he who gallops for ever, nowhither travelling, indifferent; to be part of the

eyeless dark, to be rippling and streaming, to feel the glory run molten up the spine, down the limbs, making the eyes glow, burning, bright, and penetrate the buffeting waves of the wind.[13]

This nearly mystical experience of transcendent union with things beyond the self is another staple of Woolf's work: her characters often crave a similar release from the confines of the self, and her journals and other autobiographical works contain descriptions of similar visionary experiences. The experience may take the form of a transcendent, momentary union with nature, or of a vision of something indisputably 'real' in the landscape around her. Sometimes – especially in her diaries – Woolf lacks the language to describe something so ineffable, and simply calls this intense vision 'it'. But these transcendent experiences of connection to something beyond the human personality, and of a resultant sense of the expansion and release of the self, always begin with some significant experience rooted in a specific place, and always produce the sense of connection to something timeless.

'The Moment: Summer's Night', then, defines 'place' as the nexus for two characteristically Woolfian experiences: a person's vivid sense of connection to the lives and minds of people who have gone before, and a person's sense of fusing with things outside the self, allowing an escape from the narrow confines of individual personality into something timeless. Both of these aspects of 'place' appear consistently in Woolf's novels. In *Orlando*, when the heroine lives in her vast house, she feels an intense connection to the building that sums up the lives of the people who have lived and worked there before her; she then makes herself part of the vast creative procession by adding her own anonymous touches to the house. In *Between the Acts*, Miss La Trobe's village pageant – rooted in the locales of Pointz Hall – vividly evokes the audience's connection to the procession of village life that unfolds on the stage, and that extends back to a time when prehistoric beasts roamed the grounds. In *A Room of One's Own*, the narrator understands that the quadrangles of Cambridge were once prehistoric swamps, until generations of kings and people worked to build a tradition (exclusive though it is) that connects the living past to the present. In *To the Lighthouse*, the characters' attachment to Mrs Ramsay and her place results in a moment of timeless vision as they sit gathered around the dinner table. In *Mrs Dalloway*, Clarissa's connection to place allows her to move beyond herself and to formulate her 'transcendental theory', in which she becomes part of the trees around her, and in which she can live on forever in the places that complete her.

From the Lighthouse to Monk's House examines five places and five books. Each chapter examines the way Woolf portrays a literary landscape in terms of her consistent ideas about the importance of places; but each chapter also tells the story of a place and the story of a work in her life. Chapter One, on *To the Lighthouse* and St Ives, examines Woolf's childhood summers in St Ives, and the effect of those golden summers on her subsequent writing; it also examines the way Woolf uses *To the Lighthouse* to realign herself and her work in relation to her parents – an act Woolf later defined as 'psycho-analysing' herself. Chapter Two, on *Mrs Dalloway* and London, discusses Woolf's love of London and the way London landscapes give Clarissa and Septimus timeless experiences of connection to things outside themselves; it also tells the story of Woolf's periodic battles with mental illness, and the way those struggles are reflected in the novel. Chapter Three, on Knole and *Orlando*, focuses on Woolf's love affair with Vita Sackville-West; it also examines the way Woolf came to portray Knole as an emblem of imaginative connection to the past, and discusses *Orlando* as an act of homage to Vita. Chapter Four, on Cambridge and *A Room of One's Own*, tells the story of Woolf's uneasy relationship with Cambridge University as one source of her feminism; it also discusses her portrayal of the historical continuity that Cambridge represents – a historical tradition that systematically excluded women. Chapter Five, on *Between the Acts* and Rodmell, discusses Woolf's loving relation to Monk's House and examines how the Sussex countryside gave her an enduring and consoling sense of connection to the past; it also tells the story of the early days of World War II, Woolf's last bout with mental illness, and her suicide in the River Ouse.

Each chapter of the book is divided into three sections. The first section tells the story of a place in terms of Woolf's life: how she felt about it, what she said about it, how it had an impact on her personality. The second section discusses the way Woolf uses the place as the basis for a work, and evokes and transmutes its physical geography and history. The third section guides the traveller on a tour of the place, interpreting specific aspects in terms of Woolf's life and work. *From the Lighthouse to Monk's House* is aimed at the audience Woolf cherished most – those whom Dr Johnson described as 'common readers' – and is an unabashedly hybrid work that combines literary biography, literary criticism and travel. I hope that *From the Lighthouse to Monk's House* will bring Woolf's landscapes and novels alive for the armchair traveller; I also hope that those readers who make the literary pilgrimage to Woolf's places will discover in these pages – and in the places themselves – some new insight into Woolf's work.

During her long career as a journalist, Virginia Woolf had occasion to write reviews of books like this one – books that, at least in part, described literary pilgrimages. Once, in a disapproving mood, she concluded that a book failed miserably because 'a writer's country is a territory within his own brain; and we run the risk of disillusionment if we try to turn such phantom cities into tangible brick and mortar'.[14] Woolf began her essay on the Brontës and Haworth Parsonage with an apology based on similar principles: 'I do not know whether pilgrimages to the shrines of famous men ought not to be condemned as sentimental journeys. It is better to read Carlyle in your own study chair than to visit the sound-proof room and pore over the manuscripts at Chelsea.'[15] But on other occasions, Woolf confessed that she herself had made such journeys, 'dozens of times', and even identified with the literary pilgrim who looked up 'earnestly at a house front decorated with a tablet', trying to 'conjure up the figure of Dr Johnson'. As Woolf put it, 'We cannot get past a great writer's house without pausing to give an extra look into it and furnishing it as far as we are able with his cat and his dog, his books and his writing table'.[16] Or, to put it another way – as Woolf put it in *Mrs Dalloway* – 'to know her, or any one, one must seek out the people who completed them; even the places'.[17]

CHAPTER ONE

St Ives and *To the Lighthouse*

'How anyone with an immortal soul can live inland, I cant imagine; only clods and animals should be able to endure it.'
Virginia Woolf to Violet Dickinson, 27 December 1909

'I see myself taking the breath of these voices in my sails and tacking this way and that through daily life as I yield to them.'
Virginia Woolf, 22 September 1940

I

When the Stephen family departed for a summer in St Ives in, say, 1889, it was an exhausting, hilarious, epic trek. They might leave Hyde Park Gate in the early morning, followed by two hansom cabs of luggage, books, toys and beach paraphernalia. It was a large group: Julia and Leslie Stephen; seven-year-old Virginia and her siblings Vanessa and Adrian (Thoby would come direct from Clifton once his term ended); Julia's older children Stella, Gerald and George Duckworth; two servants and a nanny. They boarded the train at Paddington by 10 a.m., rumbled through Bristol to Plymouth and Truro, and arrived in St Erth station at nearly 7 p.m. There they had precisely six minutes to transport themselves and their baggage across the track and onto the little branch line train for St Ives. (Lost dolls; crumpled food wrappers; discarded magazines; children rubbing their eyes with sleep.) Today's traveller will find the connection just as tight.[1]

Shortly out of the St Erth station, the landscape opens. The tracks run along the Hayle Estuary – at low tide, a mud flat – round a curve, and burst upon a vista of the sea, dominated by a lighthouse. The lighthouse sits, whitewashed and stark, on a cleft rock just visible at the horizon line. Built in 1859 to mark the dangerous reef just off Godrevy Island, Godrevy lighthouse even at a distance is a potent reminder of human determination and human frailty. These are, of course, two central themes in *To the Lighthouse*.

St Ives, Godrevy lighthouse and Talland House – the home where Virginia spent her childhood summers – are central to Virginia Woolf's life and work. The Cornwall landscape reappears consistently, and in addition to its centrality in *To the Lighthouse*, is especially important to *Jacob's Room* and *The Waves*. St Ives and Talland House shape Woolf's earliest memories; the sound of the sea reverberates through nearly all her novels. Woolf's obsessive images – the glimmer of silver fish, the beating of waves against the sand, sails puffing in the breeze – have their origins in her childhood summers on the Cornwall coast.

Leslie Stephen, Virginia's father, discovered St Ives and Talland House on a walking tour in 1881. The railway had come to St Ives in 1877; Woolf pictured her father, up at Tregenna four years later, munching his sandwiches, contemplating the bay, and deciding in his silent way that this village 'on the very toenail of England' would do for their summer holidays. Stephen was charmed by St Ives itself – it had changed little since the sixteenth century, it had no hotels or villas, and the bay was then, as Woolf put it, 'as it had been since time began'.[2] But Stephen was no doubt also charmed by Talland House, with its great windows opening onto the sea and its terraced front garden. He took Talland House on a long lease from the Great Western Railway; the family came for its first summer in 1882, when Virginia was six months old. They made the pilgrimage to St Ives every summer for the next twelve years, until Julia Stephen died in 1895.

When Woolf began her memoirs close to the end of her life, she was drawn back to the light and rhythmic sounds of Talland House:

> If life has a base that it stands upon, if it is a bowl that one fills and fills and fills – then my bowl without a doubt stands upon this memory. It is of lying half asleep, half awake, in bed in the nursery at St Ives. It is of hearing the waves breaking, one, two, one, two, and sending a splash of water over the beach; and then breaking, one, two, one, two, behind a yellow blind. It is of hearing the blind draw its little acorn across the floor as the wind blew the blind in and out. It is of lying and hearing this splash and seeing this light, and feeling, it is almost impossible that I should be here; of feeling the purest ecstasy I can conceive.[3]

Woolf remembered the shimmer of light against the white house and escallonia hedge, and the steep path to the beach – the walker looked down into gardens and directly onto the tops of apple trees. Woolf associated her first experiences of 'moments of being' with Talland House – once, when she heard of the suicide of a family friend; another time when she saw a flower by the front door in Talland House's garden and thought 'That is the whole'.[4] She remembered with great affection the view out over the bay from the 'Lookout Place' at the end of the Talland House garden:

> It was a large Bay, many curved, edged with a slip of sand, with green sand hills behind; and the curves flowed in and out to the two black rocks at one end of which stood the black and white tower of the Lighthouse; and at the other end, Hayle river made a blue vein across the sand, and stakes, on which always a gull sat, marked the channel into Hayle Harbour. This great flowing basin of water was always changing in colour; it was deep blue; emerald green; purple and then stormy grey and white crested. There was a great coming and going of ships across the bay. Most usually, it was a Haines steamer, with a red or white band round the funnel, going to Cardiff for coal. In rough weather, sometimes one would wake to find the whole bay full of ships that had come in overnight for shelter – little tramp steamers mostly, with a dip in the middle. But sometimes a big ship would be anchored there; once a battle ship; once a great sailing ship; once a famous white yacht. Then every morning the clumsy luggers went out, deep sea fishing; and in the evening there was the mackerel fleet, its lights dancing up and down; and the fleet returning, rounding the headland and suddenly dropping their sails. We would stand with mother on the Lookout place watching them.[5]

During the summer months, Virginia and Vanessa became tomboys: they climbed trees, scrambled over rocks, tore their dresses. They hunted for bugs; they played cricket. Virginia was so good at cricket that her brothers called her 'the demon bowler'. It was on the cricket lawn at Talland House that Virginia first met Rupert Brooke, who was then six years old.

But the greatest delight of the Stephens' St Ives summer was sailing, a treat indulged perhaps once every two weeks. Leslie Stephen hired a fisherman's boat; the fisherman came along to chat and steer. Once Leslie let Thoby sail the boat home; as Woolf remembered it, Thoby, 'flushed and with his eyes very blue, and his mouth set ... sat there, bringing us round the point, into harbour, without letting the sail flag'.[6] On another occasion, in September 1892, when Virginia was ten, some local friends walked to Talland House to invite Thoby and Virginia to accompany them on a trip to Godrevy lighthouse, 'as Freeman the boatman said that there was a perfect tide and wind for going there'. The older children made the day's sail but Adrian, aged nine, was kept at home. As young Virginia put it in that week's edition of the family newspaper: 'Master Adrian Stephen was much disappointed at not being allowed to go.'[7]

As befits a summer holiday, adult life at Talland House was shabby and simple. Nephews and grandmothers came and went; guests were invited on the spur of the moment, and if too many appeared, lodged at a hotel in town, taking their meals and afternoon naps on the lawn at Talland House. George Meredith, who immortalised Leslie Stephen in his novel *The Egoist*, was invited to stay. So were Henry James, the painters Edward Burne-Jones, G.F. Watts, John Everett Millais and the writer James Russell Lowell. (Lowell thought Julia was the most beautiful woman in the world.) Other guests were less famous, such as Mr Wolstenholme, a brilliant man who made a disastrous marriage and escaped into opium; or the guest who lost her brooch on the beach and had it cried through town by Charlie Pearce, the town crier. The first perhaps provided Woolf with the germ for Augustus Carmichael in *To the Lighthouse*; the second perhaps engendered Minta Doyle.

There were also more serious occupations for the long Cornwall summers. The children had daily lessons indoors, usually in the dining room, at a table overlooking the bay. Leslie Stephen wrote much of his *Dictionary of National Biography* at Talland House; he also wrote reviews and sent them up to London. And, feeling the affection he did for St Ives, Stephen became involved in its local affairs. In 1892, as vice-president of the St Ives Swimming and Sailing Association, Stephen presented the bronze medal of the Royal Humane Society to a fisherman who rescued a man from drowning. He and Julia were among the first members of the St Ives Arts Club, an association founded in 1890 to promote the artists' colony that sprang up at St Ives early in the 1880s. Stephen was elected president of the Arts Club in 1891. And during the General Election of 1892, he presided over at least one political meeting at the Guild Hall.[8]

Julia Stephen's daily schedule was less intellectual, but more gruelling. In addition to giving the children their lessons, she organised the meals and work of the house, tended to her guests, and spent many hours visiting the poor and sick in St Ives. One of Julia's main interests was nursing, which she approached with the fervour of a vocation. (However, Julia would never have considered it appropriate for a woman to engage in a profession outside the home.) In 1883, she wrote a small book called *Notes from Sickrooms*; when Woolf returned for a visit to St Ives many years later, she met people who tearfully remembered Julia's beauty and kindness. Julia was so appalled by the lack of consistent medical care for the poor in St Ives that she raised a subscription to engage a nurse for the town and advertised the project in a letter to the local St Ives newspaper in 1892:

The want of a certificated nurse for the sick poor of St Ives has long been felt. At Penzance, Marazion and Newlyn such nurses are worked with success and a committee of ladies is now formed in St Ives which undertakes to superintend the working of a nurse should funds be procured. The patients are required to pay nothing for the care they receive and all are nursed irrespective of creed or position.[9]

After Julia's death, this project was formalised, and the Julia Prinsep Stephen Nursing Association was set up in St Ives in her memory. It was still in operation in 1939.[10]

August in St Ives was always dominated by the annual Regatta, as it still is; September held the excitement of the pilchard boats. The entire Stephen family watched both events from the beach. Woolf remembered the Regatta as a scene from a French Impressionist painting:

> Every year, in August, the Regatta took place in the bay. We watched the Judges' boat take its station, with lines of little flags hung from mast to mast. The St Ives notables went on board. A band played. Wafts of music came across the water. All the little boats came out of the harbour. Then a gun was fired, and the races began. Off went the boats – the luggers, the pleasure boats, the rowing boats; racing round the different courses that were marked by flags round the bay. And while they raced, the swimmers got ready in a line on the Regatta boat for their races. The gun fired; they plunged and we could see the little heads bobbing and the arms flashing and heard the people shouting as one swimmer gained on another. One year our charming curly headed young postman (I remember the brown linen bag in which he carried letters) should have won; but he explained to Amy later 'I let the other chap win, because it was his last chance.'
>
> It was a very gay sight, with the flags flying, the guns firing, the boats sailing, and the swimmers plunging or being hauled back on board. A crowd of St Ives people gathered to watch in the Malakoff, that octagonal space at the end of the Terrace which had been built, presumably, in the Crimean War and was the only attempt that the town made at ornament. St Ives had no pleasure pier, no parade, only this angular gravelly patch of ground, set with a few stone seats upon which retired fishermen in their blue jerseys smoked and gossiped. The Regatta day remains in my mind, with its distant music, its little strings of flags, the boats sailing, and the people dotted on the sand, like a French picture.[11]

Woolf's association of the St Ives landscape with Impressionist painting is central to *To the Lighthouse*. Her reaction to the September pilchard boats is central to her work in another way.

September in Cornwall was Woolf's favourite time in her favourite place. 'All the months are crude experiments out of which the perfect September is made,'[12] she wrote; she was careful to set the action of *To the Lighthouse* in the month of September. The September pilchard harvest – Woolf waited for it every year of her childhood but saw it only once, in 1905, when she was twenty-three – gave her what became an obsessive image in her work: the image of the successful writer as a fisherman who nets, with words, the reality of small, gleaming, silver fish. Woolf describes landing the pilchards in an entry in her 1905 diary:

> When we came near we saw that the enclosed school was of a deep & unmistakeable purple; little spurts of water were flickering over the surface, & a silver flash leapt into the air for a second. We took up our places by the row of corks & waited; after a time the empty pilchard boats with their baskets drew up & let down a smaller net, called the tucking net, in the centre of the larger one, so that all the fish were gathered in a small compass. Now all the boats made a circle round the inner net, & the two boats who held the net gradually drew it up. The water within seethed with fish. It was packed with iridescent fish, gleaming silver & purple, leaping in the air; lashing their tails, sending up showers of scales.
>
> Then the baskets were lowered & the silver was scooped up & flung into the boats; it was a sight unlike any one has seen elsewhere, hardly to be described or believed.[13]

Woolf's novels and diaries are filled with fish that gleam silver and purple; her writers, like Bernard in *The Waves*, fling out 'nets of words' to capture 'six little fish that let themselves be caught while a million others leap and sizzle, making the cauldron bubble like boiling silver, and slip through my fingers'. Drawing fish from the sea's deep became a powerful and consistent image throughout Woolf's work – an image that suggests the unpredictability, surprise, and mystery of both the human experience and the artistic endeavour.

But even at the outset, Woolf's childhood paradise had its imperfections. The Stephen children spent the warm summer days free from most cares; Leslie Stephen did not. His work on the *Dictionary of National Biography*, which he undertook in 1882, was slow and exhausting – Woolf always said that the *DNB* cramped her younger brother Adrian in the womb. Further, *The Science of Ethics*, which Stephen saw as the book that defined his career as a thinker, was badly reviewed when it appeared in print. Stephen convinced himself that he was a failure. He went for weeks without sleep; he tottered on the verge of complete nervous collapse. He paced the lawn at Talland House, distracted and muttering under his breath; he exploded in anger if Julia spent too much money on household expenses, or if too many guests came to dinner. Worst of all in Woolf's eyes, he depended on his wife to rebuild his ego and to offer him an unending stream of sympathetic support. Many years later, looking back on the emotional turmoil that hung over Talland House like a cloud, Woolf concluded that her father often behaved like a child. The Stephen siblings sometimes felt they were sacrificed to his needs:

> Every afternoon we 'went for a walk'. Later these walks became a penance. Father must have one of us to go out with him, Mother insisted. Too much obsessed with his health, with his pleasures, she was too willing, as I think now, to sacrifice us to him. It was thus that she left us the legacy of his dependence, which after her death became so harsh an imposition. It would have [been] better for our relationship if she had left him to fend for himself. But for many years she made a fetish of his health; and so – leaving the effect upon us out of the reckoning – she wore herself out and died at forty-nine; while he lived on, and found it very difficult, so healthy was he, to die of cancer at the age of seventy-two.[14]

These habitual walks took Leslie and the children to all the sites and vistas around St Ives: to Trencrom, to Gurnard's Head, to the Huer's House overlooking the bay, to Knill's monument.

But Woolf's childhood at St Ives was also menaced in a much more serious way. If her earliest ecstatic memories of Talland House were associated with the light and sounds of the nursery there, her earliest terrifying memories were associated with Talland House's hall, and two specific objects in it: a mirror and a ledge. Woolf associated the mirror with her first memory of shame:

> There was a small looking-glass in the hall at Talland House. It had, I remember, a ledge with a brush on it. By standing on tiptoe I could see my face in the glass. When I was six or seven perhaps, I got into the habit of looking at my face in the glass. But I only did this if I was sure that I was alone. I was ashamed of it ... Let me add a dream; for it may refer to the incident of the looking-glass. I dreamt that I was looking in a glass when a horrible face – the face of an animal – suddenly showed over my shoulder ... Was I looking in the glass one day when something in the background moved, or seemed to move? ... I cannot be sure. But I have always remembered the other face in the glass, whether it was a dream or a fact, and that it frightened me.[15]

18

The shame and the brutish face Woolf connects with the hall mirror are perhaps explained by the fact that it was in this same hall she was sexually molested by her half-brother Gerald Duckworth – Virginia was then six or seven; Gerald eighteen or nineteen – who sat her on a ledge in Talland House's hall and fondled her.

Finally, though, St Ives and Talland House were much more the source of ecstatic than menacing memories. The summer in St Ives was, as Woolf put it, 'the best beginning to life conceivable. When they took Talland House, father and mother gave us – me at any rate – what has been perennial, invaluable'. Woolf's own description best evokes the sights, sounds and smells of St Ives and Talland House:

[N]othing that we had as children made as much difference, was quite so important to us, as our summer in Cornwall. The country was intensified, after the months in London to go away to Cornwall; to have our own house; our own garden; to have the Bay; the sea; the moors; Clodgy; Halestown Bog; Carbis Bay; Lelant; Trevail; Zennor; the Gurnard's Head; to hear the waves breaking that first night behind the yellow blind; to dig in the sand; to go sailing in a fishing boat; to scrabble over the rocks and see the red and yellow anemones flourishing their antennae; or stuck like blobs of jelly to the rock; to find a small fish flapping in a pool; to pick up cowries; to look over the grammar in the dining room and see the lights changing on the bay; the leaves of the escallonia grey or bright green; to go down to the town and buy a penny box of tintacks or a pocket knife; to prowl about Lanhams – Mrs Lanham wore false curls shaking round her head; the servants said Mr Lanham had married her 'through an advertisement'; to smell all the fishy smells in the steep little streets; and see the innumerable cats with their fishbones in their mouths; and the women on the raised steps outside their houses pouring pails of dirty water down the gutters; every day to have a great dish of Cornish cream skinned with a yellow skin; and plenty of brown sugar to eat with blackberries ... I could fill pages remembering one thing after another ... Suppose I had only Surrey, or Sussex, or the Isle of Wight to think about when I think of my childhood ... Oak apples, ferns with clusters of seeds on their backs, the regatta, Charlie Pearce, the click of the garden gate, the ants swarming on the hot front door step; ... Old Mr Wolstenholme in his beehive chair; the spotted elm leaves on the lawn; the rooks cawing as they passed over the house in the early morning; the escallonia leaves showing their grey undersides: the arc in the air, like the pip of an orange, when the powder magazine at Hayle blew up; the boom of the buoy – these for some reason come uppermost at the moment in my mind thinking of St Ives – an incongruous miscellaneous catalogue, little corks that mark a sunken net.[16]

Many of these incongruous, miscellaneous sights and smells can still be found in St Ives today. It is also the spot whose wonder, luminosity and terrors animate *To the Lighthouse*.

II

The geography of *To the Lighthouse* is dominated by three places: the interior spaces of the Ramsay family house, the garden in front of it that opens to the sea, and the lighthouse standing in the bay. These three places are, in turn, dominated by the three central characters of the novel: Mrs Ramsay; Lily Briscoe, the painter; and Mr Ramsay. Mr and Mrs Ramsay are loving, satirical, angry portraits of Julia and Leslie Stephen. Lily Briscoe, who hovers suspended between them, is in many ways Woolf's portrait of herself, struggling in middle age to grasp her parents' legacy.

As rooted as *To the Lighthouse* is in her Cornwall summers, Woolf transposes some spatial and temporal aspects of the novel. Just as Lily Briscoe is moved 'by some instinctive need of distance and blue'[17] before she can complete her painting, so Woolf is moved to set the action of her autobiographical novel at one remove from its literal sources in her childhood. She places the Ramsay's summer home far north, in the Hebrides, just off the Scottish coast. She also pushes the action of the first two sections of the book forward by more than a decade, so that the 'Time Passes' section can encompass World War I. These dislocations in time and space serve important artistic purposes. With the Ramsay house set on an island, rather than the mainland, Woolf can portray the house and its inhabitants being slowly eroded by the watery flux of time. With the action of the 'Time Passes' section of *To the Lighthouse* set to include World War I, Woolf can have Andrew Ramsay, the oldest son, die in a parenthesis, thus making an implicit political statement about the senselessness of war. One suspects that Woolf's spatial and temporal dislocations also serve a personal purpose for her, since *To the Lighthouse* is, after all, so much a book about gaining distance, and a perspective on one's past. But for all Woolf's deliberate transpositions of time and place, *To the Lighthouse* is still very much set in the last decade of the nineteenth century, on the Cornish coast, with its brilliant summer sun, its subtropical plantings of pampas grass, escallonia and jacmanna, and Talland House's windows overlooking the sea.

Woolf transforms the literal Cornish landscape in *To the Lighthouse* by abstracting the topography of St Ives and Talland House, and reducing them to their essential elements. In this respect, Woolf herself uses the same method she gives Lily Briscoe: Lily's painting reduces mother and child to a 'triangular purple shape'.[18] While some novelists evoke place by exhaustively enumerating the details and objects in it – in Joyce's *Ulysses*, the reader knows the titles of the books that lie upside down on a shelf in Leopold Bloom's bookcase – Woolf instead evokes Mrs Ramsay's places by painting the interior of Talland House in broad strokes, and by filling its rooms with her creative energies. Woolf shows Mrs Ramsay moving through three important interior spaces: the nursery, the drawing room and the dining room. She associates each of these spaces with some specific aspect of Mrs Ramsay's creative power – or creative failure.

After her dinner party, close to the end of the first section of *To the Lighthouse*, Mrs Ramsay ascends to the nursery to make sure that James and Cam, aged about six and seven, have fallen asleep. Of course they haven't. They are too excited by the crush of adults below; worse, the nurse has forgotten to move a pig's skull nailed to the wall. Cam can't sleep with the skull in the room; James screams if anyone touches it. Wherever the nurse places the lamp, the skull casts a shadow that terrifies Cam; James can't go to sleep unless the lamp is lit.

Mrs Ramsay, whose understanding of childish emotion is perfect, wraps her green shawl around the pig's skull. With the terrifying horns hidden, Cam falls asleep instantly. After checking to make sure his pig's skull hasn't been moved, James falls asleep too, comfortable in his six-year-old knowledge that he has got his way. This scene recalls one of Woolf's own childhood memories: the fact that she could never sleep with the nursery fire lit, while Adrian couldn't sleep with it put out. Julia Stephen solved the problem by hanging a towel over the fender to hide the fire's light from Virginia. More importantly, this scene reveals Mrs Ramsay's instinctive grasp of human emotion and action, and her

21

unerring ability to put people's feelings right. Mrs Ramsay is, above all, the epitome of motherhood.

Mrs Ramsay exerts even greater emotional power around her dinner table, as her guests sit in her dining room, eat her Boeuf en Daube, and look out over the lights flashing on the bay. When her guests first gather for the meal, everyone is dispirited and distracted: William Bankes is distant; Lily is preoccupied with her painting; Charles Tansley wants to insist that 'women can't write, women can't paint'.[19] Mr Ramsay becomes enraged when Augustus Carmichael asks for a second bowl of soup; even Mrs Ramsay herself wonders 'what have I done with my life?'.[20] But then the candles on the table are lit. And Mrs Ramsay, with her great creative powers in the realm of the human spirit, manages to calm feelings, engage loyalties, and merge the guests at the dinner party into a moment of intensely shared pleasure and perception, in which the passage of time seems momentarily to come to a halt:

> Now all the candles were lit up, and the faces on both sides of the table were brought nearer by the candlelight, and composed, as they had not been in the twilight, into a party round a table, for the night was now shut off by panes of glass, which, far from giving any accurate view of the outside world, rippled it so strangely that here, inside the room, seemed to be order and dry land; there, outside, a reflection in which things wavered and vanished, waterily.
>
> Some change at once went through them all, as if this had really happened, and they were all conscious of making a party together in a hollow, on an island; had their common cause against that fluidity out there ... Nothing need be said; nothing could be said. There it was, all round them. It partook, she felt, carefully helping Mr Bankes to a specially tender piece, of eternity; as she had already felt about something different once before that afternoon; there is a coherence in things, a stability; something, she meant, is immune from change, and shines out (she glanced at the window with its ripple of reflected lights) in the face of the flowing, the fleeting, the spectral, like a ruby; so that again tonight she had the feeling she had had once today, already, of peace, of rest. Of such moments, she thought, the thing is made that endures.[21]

This creative moment has its roots in Mrs Ramsay's ability to understand and sympathise with people; it is based on her motherly skill at resolving conflicting needs by submerging her own; it serves, in fact, as the emotional climax to the first section of the novel.

The third interior space Woolf associates with Mrs Ramsay – the drawing room window – is the most important. Woolf names the first section of her novel 'The Window'; the remaining two sections are entitled, respectively, 'Time Passes' and 'The Lighthouse'. Mrs Ramsay spends the greater part of her time in *To the Lighthouse* sitting at the drawing room window that opens onto the terrace, looking out over the bay. There, she simultaneously knits a reddish-brown stocking, plays with James, consoles her husband, and poses for Lily's painting.

As she sits at the window, Mrs Ramsay again displays her motherly skills: she amuses James by finding him a complicated picture to cut from a catalogue; she tells him he can make the trip to the lighthouse if the weather is fine the next day; she tries to shield him from disappointment when Mr Ramsay, the eternal rationalist, says the weather will be too rough to make the sail. But she also reveals the price exacted by her motherly skills. As Mr Ramsay paces up and down the lawn in front of the window, greedy for the sympathy that will restore his confidence, Mrs Ramsay gives him what he asks and nearly loses herself in the process:

> Mrs Ramsay, who had been sitting loosely, folding her son in her arm, braced herself, and, half-turning, seemed to raise herself with an effort, and at once to pour erect into the air a rain of energy, a column of spray, looking at the same time animated and alive as if all her energies were being fused into force, burning and illuminating (quietly though she sat, taking up her stocking again), and into this delicious fecundity, this fountain and spray of life, the fatal sterility of the male plunged itself, like a beak of brass, barren and bare. He wanted sympathy. He was a failure, he said. Mrs Ramsay flashed her needles. Mr Ramsay repeated, never taking his eyes from her face, that he was a failure. She blew the words back at him. 'Charles Tansley … ' she said. But he must have more than that. It was sympathy he wanted, to be assured of his genius, first of all, and then to be taken within the circle of life, warmed and soothed, to have his senses restored to him, his barrenness made fertile … Standing between her knees, very stiff, James felt all her strength flaring up to be drunk and quenched by the beak of brass, the arid scimitar of the male, which smote mercilessly, again and again, demanding sympathy … Flashing her needles, glancing round about her, out of the window, into the room, at James himself, she assured him, beyond a shadow of a doubt, by her laugh, her poise, her competence (as a nurse carrying a light across a dark room assures a fractious child), that it was real … So boasting of her

capacity to surround and protect, there was scarcely a shell of herself left for her to know herself by; all was so lavished and spent.[22]

Filled with the sympathy of her words, like 'a child who drops off satisfied',[23] Mr Ramsay regains his composure and walks off to watch the other children playing cricket. James is left, enraged, standing stiff between Mrs Ramsay's knees. Lily, watching Mr and Mrs Ramsay from a distance, thinks that she 'gave him what he wanted too easily'.[24] For her part, Mrs Ramsay sits like a closing flower, sinking in exhaustion upon herself.

Mrs Ramsay is perhaps most herself when, late in the day, she sits in the drawing room window entirely alone and watches the lighthouse's beam flash over the bay. Here she stops being a mother; here she attains complete privacy and becomes for a moment a 'wedge-shaped core of darkness' that knows no bounds:

> And that was what now she often felt the need of – to think; well, not even to think. To be silent; to be alone. All the being and the doing, expansive, glittering, vocal, evaporated; and one shrunk, with a sense of solemnity, to being oneself, a wedge-shaped core of darkness, something invisible to others ... And to everybody there was always this sense of unlimited resources, she supposed; one after another, she, Lily, Augustus Carmichael, must feel, our apparitions, the things you know us by, are simply childish. Beneath it is all dark, it is all spreading, it is unfathomably deep; but now and again we rise to the surface and that is what you see us by. Her horizon seemed to her limitless ... This core of darkness could go anywhere, for no one saw it. They could not stop it, she thought, exulting. There was freedom, there was peace, there was, most welcome of all, a summoning together, a resting on a platform of stability. Not as oneself did one find rest ever, in her experience (she accomplished here something dexterous with her needles) but as a wedge of darkness ... and pausing there she looked out to meet that stroke of the Lighthouse, the long steady stroke, the last of the three, which was her stroke, for watching them in this mood always at this hour one could not help attaching oneself to one thing especially of the things one saw; and this thing, the long steady stroke, was her stroke. Often she found herself sitting and looking, sitting and looking, with her work in her hands until she became the thing she looked at – that light, for example.[25]

For Mrs Ramsay, the lighthouse is an eye opening in the darkness, a light that evokes and illuminates the dark, impersonal, intensely private recesses of her personality.

Just as Woolf associates Mrs Ramsay with the interior spaces of the family's house, she associates Lily Briscoe with the garden. Lily is a painter and a summer visitor to the Ramsay household. She is middle-aged (forty-four years old at the end of *To the Lighthouse*), a spinster, and possessed of a plain face and 'little Chinese eyes'. Lily takes a daily turn in the garden with her friend William Bankes – Mrs Ramsay thinks that Lily and Bankes should marry – and together they contemplate the bay and lighthouse from a gap in the escallonia hedge:

> So off they strolled down the garden in the usual direction, past the tennis lawn, past the pampas grass, to that break in the thick hedge, guarded by red-hot pokers like brasiers of clear burning coal, between which the blue waters of the bay looked bluer than ever.
>
> They came here regularly every evening drawn by some need. It was as if the water floated off and set sailing thoughts which had grown stagnant on dry land, and gave to their bodies even some sort of physical relief. First, the pulse of colour flooded the bay with blue, and the heart expanded with it and the body swam, only the next instant to be checked and chilled by the prickly blackness on the ruffled waves. Then, up behind the great black rock, almost every evening spurted irregularly, so that one had to watch for it and it was a delight when it came, a fountain of white water; and then, while one waited for that, one watched, on the pale semicircular beach, wave after wave shedding again and again smoothly, a film of mother of pearl.[26]

This view becomes crucial at the moment Lily completes her painting.

During the first section of *To the Lighthouse*, Lily also shares the garden with Mr Ramsay, who paces up and down, up and down, muttering poetry under his breath and threatening accidentally to knock her painting off its easel. Lily's response to Mr Ramsay is ambivalent: he is a tyrant who misuses his wife and children; he is an unworldly man who, engaged as he is on a difficult quest for intellectual truth, must be judged by different standards from ordinary human beings. Lily's response to Mrs Ramsay is also ambivalent, though it sometimes verges on adoration: Mrs Ramsay is beautiful, fecund, and Lily above all wants to be united with her, 'like waters poured into one jar, inextricably the same, one with the object [she] adored'.[27] On the other hand, Lily knows that Mrs Ramsay cares 'not a fig for her painting',[28] and Lily resents Mrs Ramsay's highhandedness in insisting that 'she must, Minta must, they all must marry, since ... there could be no disputing this: an unmarried woman ... has missed the best of life'.[29]

In spite of her ambivalence towards both Ramsay parents, Lily is fundamentally in love with the Ramsay family and way of life. She struggles to understand the Ramsay marriage; she works to discern the many opposing forces it seems to embrace. Lily's physical position in the garden stresses the mediating role she plays: as she paints, she looks from the house's white wall dotted with jacmanna to the escallonia hedge, from the house to the sea, from Mrs Ramsay's window to the lighthouse, where Mr Ramsay sails. Lily's painting attempts to join opposites, too – the opposing forces of colour and form, of dazzling surface and unwavering structural balance:

> The jacmanna was bright violet; the wall staring white. She would not have considered it honest to tamper with the bright violet and the staring white, since she saw them like that, fashionable though it was, since Mr Paunceforte's visit, to see everything pale, elegant, semitransparent. Then beneath the colour there was the shape ... She could have done it differently of course; the colour could have been thinned and faded; the shapes etherealised; that was how Paunceforte would have seen it. But then she did not see it like that. She saw the colour burning on a framework of steel; the light of a butterfly's wing lying upon the arches of a cathedral.[30]

In its stylistic features, Lily's painting belongs to the Post-Impressionist school. Specifically, it seems to repudiate the work of James McNeill Whistler and model itself after the work of Vanessa Bell, Woolf's sister. Whistler visited St Ives in 1883; his taste for muted colours and etherealised shapes inspired a whole generation of St Ives artists who painted softly blurred views of beaches and the bay. But Lily refuses to paint in Paunceforte's style. She struggles to express her idiosyncratic vision – a vision that stresses muscular line and form, brilliant colour, and vigorous shapes and structure.

'The Window' section of *To the Lighthouse* ends with Mr and Mrs Ramsay sitting alone in the drawing room, reading. They discuss the events of the day; Mr Ramsay desperately wants Mrs Ramsay to say 'I love you'; instead she agrees with him that he and James won't make the sail to the lighthouse the next day. In the 'Time Passes' section of the novel, ten years fly by. As the empty house is taken over by weeds and nesting swallows, Mrs Ramsay dies in London, an event recounted in a parenthesis. The house trembles on the verge of ruin; a thistle grows between the stones in the larder floor. Suddenly, after ten years, the remaining remnant of the Ramsay family writes to the housekeeper to ask her to prepare the house: they plan a visit, and have left everything to the last minute. On a fine September evening, Lily Briscoe has her bag carried up to the house.

With Mrs Ramsay gone, the last section of the novel is dominated by Lily Briscoe, who works on the same painting in the same spot in the garden, and Mr Ramsay, who finally makes his journey to the lighthouse. He sails there with his children James and Cam, now aged sixteen and seventeen. As 'The Lighthouse' chapter begins, Mr Ramsay again paces back and forth in the garden. He is like a caged lion: with Mrs Ramsay dead, he is bereft, and his need for pity spills out inconveniently over the entire group. He is also angry. This time he is enraged because James and Cam aren't ready to leave for the lighthouse yet: Mr Ramsay is determined to make the sail his wife wanted for the children ten years ago; it's nearly eight o'clock and they'll miss the tide; James and Cam were supposed to be in the hall at half past seven. As Lily Briscoe paints on the lawn, she feels Mr Ramsay bearing down on her; she deflects his anger and need for pity by complimenting him on his fine boots – and she is astonished when her offhand compliment completely restores his good mood and composure. James and Cam eventually appear, lagging, sullen, silent. They will sail to the lighthouse, as their father insists, but they will defy him every step of the way: they have made a mutual pact 'to resist tyranny to the death'.[31]

In this grim mood, the fisherman's boat sets sail. As Mr Ramsay and Macalister, the fisherman, talk – three men drowned in a storm last winter; Macalister launched the lifeboat to save them – the mood subtly changes. The wind freshens; the 'boat was leaning, the water was sliced sharply and fell away in green cascades, in bubbles, and cataracts'.[32] Cam stares at the shore, where their house should be, and can't find it: from the vantage point of the bay, she sees their lives on shore in new perspective: 'She was thinking how all those paths and the lawn, thick and knotted with the lives they had lived there, were gone: were rubbed out; were past; were unreal, and now this was real; the boat and the sail with its patch.'[33] When her father asks her about her puppy, her anger vanishes and her pride in him comes to the surface: her father is brave and adventurous, she thinks; if her father had been here during the storm, he would have launched the lifeboat and saved men from drowning.

The sail to the lighthouse also gives James new perspective on Mr Ramsay. James takes the tiller with a scowl – he is determined not to let the sail pucker and flap, not to give his father a pretext to criticise him. As he steers for the lighthouse, James relives the scene on the terrace in which Mr Ramsay descends on James and Mrs Ramsay like an 'arid scimitar', greedy for sympathy. When the boat approaches the island and James sees the lighthouse at close range for the first time, he realises that his child's vision of the lighthouse was very different from his adult perspective. Then, the lighthouse was a 'silvery, misty-looking tower with a yellow eye, that opened suddenly, and softly in the evening'; now, it is 'stark and straight', and barred with black and white. James realises, with a start, that both visions of the lighthouse are true – that 'nothing was simply one thing'.[34]

James's recognition that 'nothing was simply one thing' allows him to begin to see Mr Ramsay in all his human multiplicity – not just as the tyrannical father he wants to strike to the heart with a knife, but also as a charming old man who sits reading as they sail; not just as a figure to be battled and resisted, but also as a man with whom James has much in common. The wind rises a second time; the sail fills and stiffens; James surmounts his anger and forgives his father. As they draw close to the lighthouse, Mr Ramsay for the first time reaches out to James with a compliment: ' "Well done!" James had steered them like a born sailor.'[35]

As they glide across the bay, Mr Ramsay also crosses a great emotional divide. On his journey to the lighthouse, he surmounts his grief for Mrs Ramsay, forges a new relationship with his children, and behaves towards them very differently from the way he would have ten years earlier. He compliments James on a sail well done; when he speaks to Cam, he deliberately subdues his need for female pity and tries to make her smile. As their boat approaches the spot near the lighthouse where three men drowned, Cam and James are afraid Mr Ramsay is going to burst into a fury of self-pitying passion, demanding that they console him for the loss of Mrs Ramsay. Instead, he behaves perfectly reasonably and asks nothing. Since Mr Ramsay does not demand his children's sympathy, of course that sympathy rises unbidden. Mr Ramsay completes his journey to the lighthouse; made young again, he springs lightly onto the rock:

> Mr Ramsay buttoned his coat, and turned up his trousers ... They watched him, both of them, sitting bareheaded with his parcel on his knee staring and staring at the frail blue shape which seemed like the vapour of something that had burnt itself away. What do you want? they both wanted to ask. They both wanted to say, Ask us anything and we will give it you. But he did not ask them anything. He sat and looked at the island and he might be thinking, we perished, each alone, or he might be thinking, I have reached it. I have found it; but he said nothing.
>
> Then he put on his hat.
>
> 'Bring those parcels,' he said, nodding his head at the things Nancy had done up for them to take to the Lighthouse. 'The parcels for the Lighthouse men,' he said. He rose and stood in the bow of the boat, very straight and tall, for all the world, James thought, as if he were saying, 'There is no God,' and Cam thought, as if he were leaping into space, and they both rose to follow him as he sprang, lightly like a young man, holding his parcel on to the rock.[36]

But the character who perhaps travels the greatest distance is Lily Briscoe. As she stands painting in the garden, looking from the house to the bay and back again, she thinks of herself as a sailboat voyaging on seas filled with life, experience and the Ramsays:

> One glided, one shook one's sails (there was a good deal of movement in the bay, boats were starting off) between things, beyond things. Empty it was not, but full to the brim. She seemed to be standing up to the lips in some substance, to move and float and sink in it, yes, for these waters were unfathomably deep. Into them had spilled so many lives. The Ramsays'; the children's; and all sorts of waifs and strays of things besides. A washer-woman with her basket; a rook; a red-hot poker; the purples and grey-greens of flowers: some common feeling held the whole.[37]

Lily's painting attempts to connect two opposing masses; as she works, she thinks again of the opposing forces in the Ramsay marriage. Lily is nagged by the meaning of the sympathy Mr Ramsay did not really need and she couldn't give; she wants to give him something now, but the answer eludes her whenever she thinks of Mrs Ramsay. Lily remembers all Mrs Ramsay's maternal perfections: her fecundity, beauty, and perfect goodness. She also remembers Mrs Ramsay's overbearing habits: her high-handedness, her insistence that all women must marry and have children, her dismissive attitude towards Lily's painting. Suddenly, as if Mrs Ramsay returns from the dead for an instant, someone sits in Mrs Ramsay's chair in the drawing room window and casts a triangular shadow on the steps. In a stunning moment of anguish, relief and recognition, Lily gives up her longing to have – and to be like – Mrs Ramsay:

> 'Mrs Ramsay! Mrs Ramsay!' she cried, feeling the old horror come back – to want and want and not to have. Could she inflict that still? And then, quietly, as if she refrained, that too became part of ordinary experience, was on a level with the chair, with the table. Mrs Ramsay – it was part of her perfect goodness – sat there quite simply, in the chair, flicked her needles to and fro, knitted her reddish-brown stocking, cast her shadow on the step. There she sat.
>   And as if she had something she must share, yet could hardly leave her easel, so full her mind was of what she was thinking, of what she was seeing, Lily went past Mr Carmichael holding her brush to the edge of the lawn. Where was that boat now? And Mr Ramsay? She wanted him.[38]

As Lily knows, this moment of insight – the moment at which she simultaneously gives up her need for Mrs Ramsay and her need to live up to Mrs Ramsay's expectations for her – is a function of distance. 'So much depends,' thinks Lily, 'upon distance: whether people are near us or far from us.'[39] The passage of time has given Lily distance, and a new perspective on both Ramsay parents. It is this sense of distance and closure that gives Lily the inspiration – and the image – to complete her painting. As she stares out at the lighthouse, where Mr Ramsay has by now landed, it comes to her:

> Quickly, as if she were recalled by something over there, she turned to her canvas. There it was – her picture. Yes, with all its greens and blues, its lines running up and across, its attempt at something. It would be hung in the attics, she thought; it would be destroyed. But what did that matter? She asked herself, taking up her brush again. She looked at the

steps; they were empty; she looked at her canvas; it was blurred. With a sudden intensity, as if she saw it clear for a second, she drew a line there, in the centre. It was done; it was finished. Yes, she thought, laying down her brush in extreme fatigue, I have had my vision.[40]

The line down the centre of Lily's painting is certainly her depiction of Godrevy lighthouse: Lily has completed her journey to the lighthouse as surely as Mr Ramsay has completed his. The line is also an image of Lily's stability and singular identity, an expression of the self-possession she has gained by the end of the novel. The line is just as surely an image of Lily's deliberate separation from the Ramsay family, an indication of the distance she has finally been able to achieve between herself and the Ramsays' powerful influence.

But the line down the centre of Lily's painting has autobiographical significance as well. Virginia Woolf wrestled with the ghosts of both her parents for many years. As she put it, 'I was obsessed by them both, unhealthily; but writing The Lighthouse laid them in my mind.'[41] Like Lily Briscoe, Virginia Woolf struggled against the troubling and seductive allure of her mother's version of Victorian womanhood; like Lily Briscoe, Virginia Woolf strove to live an unconventional life, a life defined by her work as an artist. In writing *To the Lighthouse* at the age of forty-four (Lily's age), Virginia Woolf revisited the places of her cherished childhood – St Ives, Talland House, St Ives bay, Godrevy lighthouse – in an attempt to repossess them, understand them, and then distance herself from them. When Virginia Woolf had Lily Briscoe paint a line down the centre of her canvas, it was a line that defined Woolf's own experience too: with it, she was finally able to draw the border between herself and the haunting spirits of her past.

III

St Ives today: Sights, Views, Excursions

ST IVES

St Ives has become much busier since the 1890s, when the Stephen family spent several months there every summer. It is a popular resort

31

town; unless one books well in advance, it can be difficult to find a room during the months of July and August. But the town still retains its uniquely Cornish charm: the sea air is bracing; the beaches are wide and soft.

St Ives takes its name from the Irish princess and missionary St Ia, who built an oratory on the site of the current parish church in the fifth century, after having reputedly sailed from Ireland on a leaf. In 1497 the village was still an obscure fishing port; Perkin Warbeck, pretender to the English throne, landed there with one hundred and fifty men in an attempt to foment a rebellion against King Henry VII. Eventually St Ives became the chief point of departure for Ireland from the west of England. It was incorporated as a municipality in 1639.

For many years, the three industries that supported the St Ives economy were fishing, mining and shipping. Pilchards swam into the bay and were harvested by the millions; tin was excavated from the Providence and Wheal Speed mines. During the mid-nineteenth century, two thirds of the world's copper supply was extracted from the mines of Cornwall. The natural richness of Cornwall's resources – at least underground and underwater – led to the growth of ports such as Hayle and Portreath. But the St Ives townsfolk always led rough, poverty-stricken lives. Stories abound of crowds of villagers following foundering ships along the rocky coast, waiting to claim the bounty of the cargo once the ships were smashed against the Cornish cliffs.

Though modern holiday villas have covered the hillsides overlooking the bay, the St Ives town centre still looks much as it did at the turn of the century, and the way Woolf speculated it must have looked for centuries before that:

The town was then much as it must have been in the sixteenth century, unknown, unvisited, a scramble of granite house crusting the slope in the hollow under the Island. It must have been built for shelter; for a few fishermen, when Cornwall was more remote from England than Spain or Africa is now. It was a steep little town. Many houses had a flight of steps, with a railing leading to the door. The walls were thick blocks of granite built to stand the sea storms. They were splashed with a wash the colour of Cornish cream; and their roughness was like the clot of cream. There was nothing mellow about them; no red brick; no soft thatch. The eighteenth century had left no mark upon St Ives, as it has so definitely upon every southern village. It might have been built yesterday; or in the time of the Conqueror. It had no architecture; no arrangement. The market place was a jagged cobbled open place; the Church was on one side; built of granite, ageless, like the houses; the fish market stood beside it. There was no grass in front of it. It stood flush to the market place. There were no carved doors, large windows, no lintels; no moss; no comely professional houses. It was a windy, noisy, fishy, vociferous, narrow-streeted town; the colour of a mussel or a limpet; like a bunch of rough shell fish clustered on a grey wall together.[42]

How to get there

By train: The train trip to St Ives takes about six hours; several trains leave Paddington station in London daily. The most direct route is the train to Penzance, with a change at St Erth; the layover is still approximately six minutes, as it was in Woolf's day. For train information and bookings, ring National Rail Enquiries at 08457 48 49 50 or check the Railtrack website at www.railtrack.co.uk. Information about accommodation is also available at the Britain Visitor Centre, 1 Lower Regent Street, London SW1 4NR (nearest underground stop: Piccadilly Circus).

The train is the recommended route to St Ives: once there, cars are a nuisance on the narrow streets and parking is very difficult. Most of the sights discussed here are best reached on foot. Buses frequently leave the Malakoff, the paved area above the train station car park, for nearby locations, including Zennor and Penzance.

St Ia's Church

The 'ageless' granite church that stands in the St Ives market square, with its large windows and uncarved doors, is dedicated to St Ia, the Irish saint who suffered martyrdom in AD450 at the hands of Theodoric, King of Cornwall, at the mouth of the Hayle River nearby. St Ives is named after her. Woolf and her brother sheltered from the rain in St Ia's church in 1905, and Woolf used the opportunity to turn St Ia's church into a symbol for the continuity and poverty of the St Ives community:

The other day as it rained A[drian] & I turned from the main street into the shelter of the Church. We looked for little more, but we found ourselves in a quaint but really beautiful old building, shaped something like a ship, it seemed, with a dark ceiling of oak, & strange old carvings wrought in the black pews & rafters. The sound of the sea might be heard by the congregation & there was something touching in the thought that generations of fisher folk had knelt here within the hearing of its voice & prayed for safety on its water, & prosperity in their fishing. There is more of quaintness, perhaps, than of beauty; as though the worshippers were poor people who could not afford much more ornament than a slab of graven slate when they died.[43]

Talland House

Talland House sits on a hill just above the town, overlooking the bay. It was built by the Great Western Railway in 1874; the Stephen family took the house on a long lease.

Though Talland House's grounds have been reduced in size since Woolf's time, one can still identify the cricket lawn and other features, and the house itself also looks much as Woolf remembered it just before she died:

> Our house, Talland House, was just beyond the town, on the hill. For whom the Great Western Railway had built it I do not know. It must have been in the forties, or fifties; a square house, like a child's drawing of a house; remarkable only for its flat roof, and the crisscrossed railing that ran round the roof; again, like something a child draws. It stood in a garden that ran downhill; and had formed itself into separate gardens, surrounded by thick escallonia hedges, whose leaves, pressed, gave out a very sweet smell. It had so many angles cut off, and lawns surrounded, that each had a name; there was the coffee garden; the Fountain – a basin with a funnel that dripped, hedged in with damp evergreens; the cricket lawn; the Love Corner, under the greenhouse, where the purple jackmanii grew – where Leo Maxse proposed to Kitty Lushington (I thought I heard Paddy talking to his son, Thoby said, overhearing the proposal). Then there was the kitchen garden; the strawberry beds; the pond where Willy Fisher sailed the little steamers he made with a paddle worked by an elastic band; and the big tree. All these different, cut off places were contained in that one garden of not more than two or three acres. One entered by a large wooden gate, the sound of whose latch clicking was one of the familiar sounds; up the carriage drive one went, under the steep wall of rock, sprinkled with the fleshy flowers of the mesembryanthemums; and then came the Lookout place, between the clumps of pampas grass. The Lookout place was a grassy mound, that jutted out over the high garden wall. There we were often sent to stand and to look out for the fall of the signal. When the signal fell it was time to start for

the station to meet the train. It was the train that brought Mr Lowell, Mr Gibbs, the Stillmans, the Lushingtons, the Symondses. But it was a grown-up affair – receiving friends. We never had friends to stay with us. Nor did we want them. 'Us four' were completely self-sufficient. Once when a child called Elsie was brought by Mrs Westlake to play with us I 'broomed her round the garden'. I remember scuffling her like a drift of dead leaves in front of me.[44]

The pampas grass and the high garden wall are still there, but Talland House's uninterrupted view of the bay and lighthouse no longer exists: the area around the house has been built over with hotels and other homes. This encroachment began even in the Stephens' day. As Woolf remembered it, 'just opposite the Lookout place a great square oatmeal coloured hotel appeared when we came down in July. My mother said, with her dramatic gestures, that the view was spoilt; that St Ives would be ruined ... then, a house agent's board appeared one October in our garden.'[45] (The structure that Julia Stephen found so offensive is now the Porthminster Hotel.)

But the bay and lighthouse can still be seen from many parts of Talland House's garden, and from most of the flats inside the house. The stone urns have been removed, but the visitor can still pace, in Mr Ramsay's footsteps, back and forth along the gravel terrace in front of the French windows.

How to get there
Coming up the hill from the train station via the A3074 (towards Carbis Bay), the visitor should make a sharp **right** turn just opposite the **Porthminster Hotel**. This turning leads directly into Talland House's car park – and car parks are a rarity in St Ives. For walkers, there is also a steep footpath from the train station up the hill to Talland House. This is probably the same footpath used by the Stephen family to meet people off the train.

Talland House has been divided into five luxurious holiday flats, and its current owners – Sue and Nigel Bedford – live on the ground floor. The Bedfords' home incorporates the Stephen family's parlour and the dining room where the famous dinner party took place. (The original staircase leading to the family bedrooms has been removed.)

35

Although the ground floor is a private home, the owners welcome Virginia Woolf scholars and enthusiasts and are happy to arrange visits to talk about the house's literary history. You can contact Talland House by post (Talland House, St Ives, Cornwall TR26 2EH), by telephone (01736 796 368), or by email (talland@fsbdial.co.uk).

The Woolf enthusiast who travels to St Ives should try to arrange a stay at Talland House. The five flats accommodate between two and six people each. Two of the first floor flats have balconies overlooking the bay and lighthouse; these flats incorporate the Stephen parents' bedroom and the children's nursery. Near the end of her life, Woolf recalled the details of these rooms vividly:

> But to fix my mind upon the nursery – it had a balcony; there was a partition, but it joined the balcony of my father's and mother's bedroom. My mother would come out onto her balcony in a white dressing gown. There were passion flowers growing on the wall; they were great starry blossoms, with purple streaks, and large green buds, part empty, part full.[46]

The flats at Talland House rent by the week during the high season; weekend rates are available at some other times of the year.

Tate Gallery, St Ives

The Tate Gallery opened this branch in 1993. Situated on the site of the old St Ives gasworks, at a spot overlooking Porthmeor Beach (frequented now by surfers), the Tate St Ives commands striking views of the sea, and is designed to integrate the sea's vistas into its interior viewing spaces. The building's architects have designed a very modern building that melds flawlessly with the older structures surrounding it. St Ives artists have lived and worked in this part of town for four generations, and the Tate St Ives both pays tribute to their work and evokes the shapes, light and atmosphere that inspired it.

The Tate St Ives does not house a permanent collection. Its displays change periodically, usually on an annual basis; the Gallery is devoted to modern art created in, or influenced by, Cornwall. Artists have travelled to Cornwall for its landscape and light since the eighteenth century. Bernard Leach established a pottery in the 1920s, and Barbara

Hepworth and Ben Nicholson came to work in St Ives at the outbreak of World War II. Since then, important figures such as Naum Gabo, Bryan Wynter and Patrick Heron have been associated with St Ives and the surrounding Cornwall communities.

The St Ives art colony had its real beginnings just about when the Stephen family took the lease of Talland House in 1882. James McNeill Whistler stayed in St Ives with two students – Mortimer Menpes and Walter Sickert – during the winter of 1883-4. Over the following decade, other painters travelled to St Ives or moved there to take advantage of its visual charm and light: by 1888, the number of writers and painters staying in St Ives had reached enough of a critical mass that the St Ives Arts Club was founded. Leslie and Julia Stephen were invited to be members; they readily accepted. The St Ives painter Bosch-Reitz painted Leslie Stephen in St Ives and exhibited the work at the Royal Academy. In 1891, Leslie Stephen was elected president of the St Ives Arts Club, but he never took office due to his ill health.[47]

This easy connection between the literary Stephen family and the painters of St Ives is hardly surprising. Julia Stephen, after all, came from a family long known for its association with painters. Julia's aunt Sarah Prinsep presided over a salon at Little Holland House, in London, that included G.F. Watts, Dante Gabriel Rossetti, William Holman Hunt and, sometimes, John Ruskin. Julia herself had posed for Edward Burne-Jones; she was also lovingly photographed by her aunt, Julia Cameron, who pioneered the use of the camera as a vehicle for visual aestheticism. Julia Stephen had grown up in a world of cultivated beauty; she had a good eye herself. So it is natural that, in *To the Lighthouse*, Mrs Ramsay can comment authoritatively on the painters working on the beach below her house:

But now, she said, artists had come here. There indeed, only a few paces off, stood one of them, in Panama hat and yellow boots, seriously, softly, absorbedly, for all that he was watched by ten little boys, with an air of profound contentment on his round red face gazing, and then, when he had gazed, dipping; imbuing the tip of his brush in some soft mound of green or pink. Since Mr Paunceforte had been there, three years before, all the pictures were like that, she said, green and grey, with lemon-coloured sailing boats, and pink women on the beach.[48]

Woolf probably had Whistler and his French Impressionist colleagues in mind when she described Paunceforte's work. Whistler rejected realism and vivid colour; he championed the tasteful expression of form in muted tonalities, unhampered by meaning or message. Many of Whistler's outdoor scenes are views over water, with titles that emphasise the musical, flowing sweep of their compositions: 'Symphony in Grey and Green: The Ocean'; 'Nocturne in Blue and Silver: The Lagoon, Venice'; 'Variations in Pink and Grey: Chelsea'. When he lived in St Ives during the winter of 1883-84, Whistler painted eighteen small pictures – views of the beach, fishing nets, herring boats, a village street. These paintings were done in the open air, 'on location', with Whistler standing outside and contemplating the scene that was his subject.

In *To the Lighthouse*, Lily Briscoe sets herself against Whistler's fashionable style. She refuses to tamper with the intense clarity of her vision of flowers blazing against a white wall: she will not paint everything 'pale, elegant, semitransparent',[49] as it has been fashionable to do since Mr Paunceforte's visit. She will not thin and fade her colours, or etherealise her shapes. Instead, Lily concentrates on the structural integrity of her canvas. Her colours will be bright and vivid, but her painting will have the solid, unmoving weight of sculpture:

> [T]he problem of space remained, she thought, taking up her brush again. It glared at her. The whole mass of the picture was poised upon that weight. Beautiful and bright it should be on the surface, feathery and evanescent, one colour melting into another like the colours on a butterfly's wing; but beneath the fabric must be clamped together with bolts of iron. It was to be a thing you could ruffle with your breath; and a thing you could not dislodge with a team of horses. And she began to lay on a red, a grey, and she began to model her way into the hollow there.[50]

Lily's painting takes its inspiration from the Post-Impressionist school, which was imported from the continent by Woolf's friend Roger Fry with his first Post-Impressionist exhibition in 1910. But what is most important about Lily's style is that it is her own: it is idiosyncratic; it yokes the opposing forces of line, shape and colour; it allows Lily to express her unique vision. In rejecting the Victorian impact of Whistler, Lily moves herself into her own future.

Since the Tate St Ives is devoted to contemporary art, the visitor will not see either Whistler or the Post-Impressionists there. But the Tate St Ives is a wonderful monument to the centrality of painting in the St Ives community. And as such it reminds the reader once more of the extent to which *To the Lighthouse* accurately reflects the cultural life of the place in which Woolf spent her youth.

How to get there
From the wharf, follow the pedestrian signs to the Tate Gallery. It is a short walk across the point to **Porthmeor Beach** – a total distance of perhaps a quarter of a mile.

The Lifeboat House and Memorial
St Ives has been a lifeboat station since 1840. In 1838, the story of Grace Darling captured the national attention. Grace Darling was the twenty-two-year-old daughter of the keeper of the Longstone Lighthouse, off the coast of Northumberland. During a fierce storm, Grace spotted a steamer wrecked on the nearby reef, and insisted that her father come with her to rescue the survivors – a feat they accomplished in the teeth of a gale, using a tiny, five-metre-long rowing boat. Grace Darling became a national heroine; the daring rescue – and the fact that it was done with all the wrong equipment – prompted a local Member of Parliament to petition the Royal National Lifeboat Institution for a lifeboat in St Ives. Since then, the bravery, self-sacrifice and skill associated with saving lives during fierce storms have been part of the St Ives marine mentality.

When James longs to sail to the lighthouse in the novel's first chapter, Mr Ramsay offers at one point to 'step over and ask the Coastguards'[51] about the upcoming weather report. This inquiry could have taken Mr Ramsay in one of two directions. He might have walked a short distance east along the coast road, towards Porthminster Point, to talk to the men at the Coastguard Station. Or he might have taken a short walk down the hill from Talland House to the lifeboat station, which in the 1880s and 1890s was located in a specially built structure close to St Ia's church. In the novel's closing section, Woolf provides this description of the Ramsay family's interaction with Macalister, a local fisherman whose boat they have hired to sail to the lighthouse, and who also mans the St Ives lifeboat in moments of crisis:

But now, when Macalister's boy had rowed a little way out, the sails slowly swung round, the boat quickened itself, flattened itself, and shot off. Instantly, as if some great strain had been relieved, Mr Ramsay uncurled his legs, took out his tobacco pouch, handed it with a little grunt to Macalister, and felt, they knew, for all they suffered, perfectly content. Now they would sail on for hours like this, and Mr Ramsay would ask old Macalister a question – about the great storm last winter probably – and old Macalister would answer it, and they would puff their pipes together, and Macalister would take a tarry rope in his fingers, tying or untying some knot, and the boy would fish, and never say a word to any one ... So they heard Mr Ramsay asking some questions about the great storm at Christmas. 'She comes driving round the point,' old Macalister said, describing the great storm last Christmas, when ten ships had been driven into the bay for shelter, and he had seen 'one there, one there, one there' (he pointed slowly round the bay. Mr Ramsay followed him, turning his head.) He had seen four men clinging to the mast. Then she was gone. 'And at last we shoved her off,' he went on (but in their anger and their silence they only caught a word here and there, sitting at opposite ends of the boat, united by their compact to fight tyranny to the death). At last they had shoved her off, they had launched the lifeboat, and they had got her out past the point – Macalister told the story; and though they only caught a word here and there, they were conscious all the time of their father – how he leant forward, how he brought his voice into tune with Macalister's voice; how, puffing at his pipe, and looking there and there where Macalister pointed, he relished the thought of the storm and the dark night and the fishermen striving there. He liked that men should labour and sweat on the windy beach at night; pitting muscle and brain against the waves and the wind; he liked men to work like that, and women to keep house, and sit beside sleeping children indoors, while men were drowned, out there in a storm. So James could tell, so Cam could tell (they looked at him, they looked at each other), from his toss and his vigilance and the ring in his voice, and the little tinge of Scottish accent which came into his voice, making him seem like a peasant himself, as he questioned Macalister about the eleven ships that had been driven into the bay in a storm. Three had sunk.

He looked proudly where Macalister pointed; and Cam thought, feeling proud of him without knowing quite why, had he been there he would have launched the lifeboat, he would have reached the wreck, Cam thought. He was so brave, he was so adventurous, Cam thought. But she remembered. There was the compact: to resist tyranny to the death.[52]

The lifeboat which would have been used during Woolf's childhood in St Ives was *The Exeter*, which operated off the St Ives beach from 1866 to 1899. This lifeboat carried a crew of rowers headed by a coxswain; it was launched off the beach from a carriage, with the help of assembled volunteers from the town. From a vantage point in front of the current lifeboat house, the visitor can still picture the difficulties Macalister describes: the terror of launching a boat in the face of a raging storm surf; the challenge of rowing into the teeth of the wind, out past the point to the place where wrecked ships lay foundering.

Perhaps most importantly, Macalister's story about lifeboats, storms, courage and men drowning sets the stage for the family reconciliations that take place at the end of *To the Lighthouse*. Cam, in a moment of insight, recognises her father's implicit bravery: 'had he been there he would have launched the lifeboat, he would have reached the wreck.'[53] And Mr Ramsay, in his instinctive identification with Macalister, begins to grasp the inevitability of loss and death as one aspect of nature's inexorable force.

How to get there
The new lifeboat house lies a short walk away from the market place, at the southern end of the wharf.

WALKS AND EXCURSIONS BEYOND THE TOWN CENTRE

Knill's Monument
This fifty-foot-high granite pyramid erected at the top of Worvas Hill dominates the St Ives countryside for miles: it can be seen from boats in the bay, from Trencrom, from most elevations in the area. The trek to Knill's monument was one of the Stephen family's habitual Sunday walks; Woolf herself often hiked to Knill's monument when she visited St Ives in subsequent years. A walk there in 1905 gave her the opportunity to reflect upon both the beauty of storms in Cornwall's granite hills, and upon the spontaneous allure of Cornwall's heat-heavy August afternoons:

At Knills monument I had to take my bearing, & repeated 'A blinding mist came down & hid the land!' & reflected how easily I might share

Lucy's fate. The delight of the country is that all moods of the air & the earth are natural, & therefore fit & beautiful. There is nothing incongruous about a wet day among the hills, as there is when decent streets & brick houses are exposed to the shock of an uncivilised storm. One may fancy even, a storm rejoicing among these granite hills when the wind & rain beat upon them as though they loved the conflict. But the sunny days give one, after all, a more spontaneous pleasure, the scents of the earth & the budding gorse are sucked out of them by the heat, & all the land glows with a mellow August radiance. The air becomes of a richly luminous quality; you see all things through an amber coloured medium.[54]

Woolf also saw Knill's monument as an emblem of the peculiarity of St Ives. The town had its unique customs and festivals; remote as it had been from the civilisation of urban London for so many years, St Ives had developed its own idiosyncratic traditions. One of them was the John Knill celebration, which Woolf remembered vividly:

Then once in every twelve years or so, old men and women over seventy danced round Knills Monument – a granite steeple in a clearing – and the couple who danced longest were given a shilling? half a crown? – by the mayor – Dr Nicholls, on that occasion, who wore a long fur trimmed coat.[55]

Woolf actually got most of the details of the ceremony wrong. The John Knill celebration takes place every five years, on 25 July; ten little girls dance around the base of the steeple, dressed in white frocks. The ceremony is organised under a trust set up by John Knill (1733-1811), a former smuggler turned lawyer, Collector of Customs, and eventually Mayor of St Ives.

Knill erected the monument as his mausoleum, although due to difficulties having the site consecrated, he was finally buried in London. Knill left a trust to finance a festival and procession every five years; he thus assured that his name and his monument would be remembered in perpetuity. Knill's trust stipulates that ten maidens under ten years old must march to his monument on St James's Day. The girls must be the daughters of seamen, fishermen, or tin miners; they are to be accompanied by a fiddler, by two widows over the age of sixty, and by various town dignitaries. Once at the monument, the girls dance around its base and then stop to recite the hundredth psalm. The mayor then gives each girl and widow a small cash award. In the early days of the ceremony, a cash award was also given to 'the married parents, of the like classes, who have brought up the largest family to the age of ten, without aid from the poor rate'. The Knill ceremony is a delightfully idiosyncratic St Ives custom; the last ceremony took place on 25 July 2001.

How to get there
If you happen to be in St Ives on 25 July during a year when the ceremony takes place, proceed to the Guildhall, usually at around 10 a.m. The first part of the ceremony is performed here; then the participants march and dance to Knill's monument.

On foot: (1½ to 2 hours) If you want to hike to the monument yourself, start your walk at the **Malakoff**, the paved area above the train station car park where the buses turn. From the Malakoff, turn *left* up the hill called the **Terrace**. Turn *right* at the first small street by the **Chy-An-Gerra Hotel**. Walk to the top of the street; turn *left*, and then immediately *right*, into **Talland Road**. Follow this road, bearing *left* until you reach **Belyars Lane** on the *left*. Turn into Belyars Lane and follow the road for one and a half miles to Knill's monument. To return to the Malakoff without retracing your steps, follow **Steeple Lane** down the hill. You will come out onto the main St Ives/Carbis Bay Road (A3074) by **Higher Tregenna Road**. Turn *left* down the hill, passing the **Tregenna Castle Hotel** on the *left*. Bear *right* at the roundabout past the **Porthminster Hotel** to return to the starting point. Following this route, it is about two miles from the Malakoff to Knill's monument, and just over a mile from Knill's monument back to the Malakoff.[56]

By car: From the **Malakoff**, take the A3074 (the **Terrace**) towards Carbis Bay. Pass the entrance to the **Tregenna Castle Hotel**; turn *right* at the **Cornish Arms Pub** onto **Higher Tregenna Road**. Make an immediate sharp *left* up **Steeple Lane**; keep bearing left on Steeple Lane to Knill's monument.

The Huer's House
The Huer's House is a building overlooking the sea at Porthminster Point (the headland between St Ives and Carbis Bay), from which look-

outs spotted shoals of pilchards as they swam into St Ives harbour. For Woolf, the Huer's House and the Cornish pilchard harvest became symbols both of frustrated expectation and of fulfilment – as she saw it, the St Ives fishermen waited for the pilchards for years, prepared for a great catch that stubbornly refused to materialise. When the fish finally swam into the bay in 1905, the event was a revelation, and Woolf recorded it with great relish.

Pilchards are herring – specifically, one variety of sardine. For centuries, pilchards migrated in huge shoals around the Cornish coast, spawning in the summer months and large enough to catch in autumn. St Ives fishermen netted pilchards in large seines slung between boats. They then salted the fish in barrels and exported fish and fish oil to spots as far away as Naples. Pilchard fishing was one backbone of the St Ives economy. Fortunes could be made or lost in a single catch; a broken net or an inaccurate placement of the seines might mean the difference between a comfortable winter and a hungry one.

But even by the time the Stephen family began to summer in St Ives, the pilchard industry had begun to grow unreliable. Whole seasons might pass without the fish appearing in the bay, and the St Ives locals felt the loss acutely. Pilchards were last landed on the St Ives beaches in 1908; lookouts were kept posted at the Huer's House for fourteen more years, but the lookouts were last paid and then vanished in 1922:

Every year, about the first week in September, we would cry 'The pilchard boats are out!' There they were being hauled down the beach, where they lay one behind another all the rest of the year. Horses were struggling to draw them over the beach. They were anchored near the shore, and looked like long black shoes, for each had a hood for the watchman at one end, and a great coil of net – seines they were called – at the other. The tarring of the pilchard boats was a regular occupation; and made the beach always smell slightly of tar. There they lay week after week and were still lying when we left in October, waiting for the Huer who sat at his telescope up in the white shelter on Carbis Bay point to sight a shoal. He sat there looking for a purple stain of pilchards to come into the bay and beside him was a great horn of some kind. Year after year the boats lay in the bay. The seines were never shot. The fishermen grumbled that the steam trawlers at Newlyn (perhaps) had disturbed the pilchards; and driven them out to sea. Once, though, as we sat at lessons we heard the Huer's cry – a long high clear hoot of sound. Then fishermen rowed out to the boats. We stopped lessons. The seines were shot. A dotted circle of corks floated here and there over the dark net beneath. But the pilchards passed out of the bay that time; and the seines were drawn in again. (It was in 1905, when we four took a lodging at Carbis Bay that the pilchards came. We rowed out early in the morning. The sea spurted and spat and bubbled with silver. A stranger in the next boat shovelled armfuls of that bubbling mass into our boat. 'Like some fresh fish for breakfast?' he said – everyone was excited and jubilant; and boat after boat was weighted down to the water line with fish. And we went down to the harbour and saw them packed. I wrote a description of it, and sent it to some paper; which rejected it. But Thoby told Nessa, who told me, that he thought I might be a bit of a genius.) All the years we were at St Ives the pilchards never came into the bay; and the pilchard boats lay there, anchored, waiting; and we used to swim out and hang onto the edge, and see the old man lying in his brown tarpaulin tent, keeping watch. The waiting pilchard boats was [sic] a sight that made father pish and pshaw at table. He had a curious sympathy for the poverty of the fisher people: a respect for fishermen, like his respect for Alpine guides. And mother, of course, got to know them in their houses; and went about, 'doing good' as Stella wished to have it said on her tombstone.[57]

Woolf's 1905 diary records the raw material she later turned into her rejected newspaper piece: she writes a wonderful description of the mechanics of the pilchard harvest, in which the men on the cliff next to the Huer's House direct the boats with megaphones and white signalling globes, while the lumbering pilchard boats in the bay struggle to interpret their commands.

How to get there
The Huer's House (also called the Baulking House) is best reached on foot: it is a lovely hike of about half a mile along the coastal path between St Ives and Carbis Bay. To find the path, walk down to **Porthminster Beach**, below the railway station. Follow the asphalt path *east* and up as it climbs beside lovely views over the bay. The Huer's House is a white structure on the walker's *right*. The same path can be followed further, all the way to **Carbis Bay** and **Lelant**. The walker can also leave the path at Carbis Bay to hike to **Trencrom**.

45

Trencrom

Trencrom hillfort is now a National Trust Property. It consists of a rocky hilltop, surrounded by a stone rampart dating to the Iron Age. Several hut circles can be found inside it. The hill affords spectacular views: eastward into central Cornwall and westward across both coasts. On clear days, St Michael's Mount is visible along the south coast of England, and on very clear days, one can even see as far as Lizard Point. Closer in, one can see Knill's monument and the Godrevy lighthouse. From its imposing vantage point, Trencrom hillfort guards the short overland passage between Hayle and Mount's Bay – a route used in ancient times to avoid the dangerous sail around Land's End.

Trencrom was a weekly Sunday afternoon destination for the Stephen family. In his youth, Leslie Stephen led mountaineering expeditions in the Alps; once a father, Stephen led his brood of children on long hikes around St Ives during the summer months. As a result, Virginia developed a passion for walking that perhaps exceeded even the typical English love of the pastime: she walked ceaselessly around London; country holidays were always punctuated by long tramps across fields.

When Virginia spent Christmas of 1909 alone in St Ives, she hiked to Trencrom on Boxing Day, and wrote to Clive Bell later from her room at the Lelant Hotel:

> One feels in the mood for phrases, as one sits by the fire, thinking how one staggered up Tren Crom in the mist this afternoon, and sat on a granite tomb on the top, and surveyed the land, with the rain dripping against one's skin. There are – as you may remember – rocks comparable to couchant camels, and granite gate posts, with a smooth turf road between them. Thinking it over is the pleasant thing. By writing to you I am sparing the 20 last pages of La Terre qui Meurt, for bedtime ... One gradually sees shapes and thinks oneself in the middle of the world.[58]

Virginia had also holidayed in St Ives with Adrian, Thoby and Vanessa in 1905, the year following Leslie Stephen's death. The Stephen children lodged at the Trevose View, in Carbis Bay, for half of August and all of September. Some of the details of this holiday were reimagined in *To the Lighthouse* twenty years later, but even in 1905, Woolf was already playing with the theme of the past seen through the eyes of the present. A walk to Trencrom provided her with one occasion for such rumination:

> Yesterday, for instance, we followed foot paths to Trencrom, which was, 11 years ago, our punctual Sunday walk. The brambles still stretch across it, & the granite blocks in the earth still bring you to your nose. At the corner we came to the Peacock farm, where the dunghill was as large as ever though there was no successor to the proud bird of old days. So, at every turn of the road, we could anticipate some little characteristic – a water trough – or a plank over the stream – which had impressed itself minutely upon our childish minds, & great was our joy when we discovered that our memory was right. To find these details unchanged, indeed, gave us a keener pleasure than to find the big hills in their places …
>
> Indeed every step of our walk might have been taken eleven years ago, & we should have found nothing to surprise our eyes. On the top of Tren Crom indeed, I was considerably surprised to see how large a view of the surrounding country was unfolded; moreover I had no notion that from this point you can see both sides of the coast at once; Hayle Harbour on the North, St Michael's Mount on the south, & all the long stretch of bay which ends in the Lizard point. But as these features of the landscape have not changed in eleven years, or in eleven hundred, the change must be in my point of view & not in the outlines of the earth.[59]

And six months before Woolf died, she remembered Trencrom from her writer's hut at Monk's House. It was the height of the Battle of Britain; bombs were dropping in the fields nearby. Woolf recalled the beauty of Trencrom, and her father's 'severe love of truth':

> The regular Sunday walk was to Trick Robin or, as father liked to call it, Tren Crom. From the top, one could see the two seas; St Michael's Mount on one side; the Lighthouse on the other. Like all Cornish hills, it was scattered with blocks of granite; said some of them to be old tombs and altars; in some, holes were driven, as if for gate posts. Others were piled up rocks. The Loggan rock was on top of Tren Crom; we would set it rocking; and be told that perhaps the hollow in the rough lichened surface was for the victim's blood. But father, with his severe love of truth, disbelieved it; he said, in his opinion, this was no genuine Loggan rock; but the natural disposition of ordinary rocks. Little paths led up to the hill, between heather and ling; and our knees were pricked by the gorse – the blazing yellow gorse with its sweet nutty smell.[60]

CHAPTER ONE

How to get there

On foot: This walk is best begun at the **Badger Inn**, which was known
as the Lelant Hotel in Virginia Woolf's day, and where Virginia Stephen
spent Christmas in 1909. (See Badger Inn on page 54-5.) The Badger
Inn is open at lunchtime from noon until 3 p.m. (last food orders taken
at 2 p.m.); one can lunch and then spend the afternoon walking.

Take the train from St Ives to Lelant. (Lelant is a request stop; it can
be requested only on certain trains. Check with the conductor before
you set out. And make sure not to confuse Lelant with Lelant Saltings.)
Walk two hundred yards uphill to the Badger Inn. After visiting the
Badger Inn, turn *left* out of the inn and follow the road until you reach
a small roundabout. Bear *right* towards **Nancledra**. Follow this road,
walking uphill until a *left* turn signposted to **Cripplesease**. (Do NOT
take the second turn on the left, even though it is signposted for
Trencrom.) Walk uphill for just over half a mile to the Trencrom car
park, passing **Flax Cottage** on the *left*. The National Trust car park is a
few hundred yards beyond Flax Cottage on the *right*, but the sign may
be obscured by foliage in the hedge. The path to the top of Trencrom
leaves from the car park. (From the Badger Inn to the Trencrom car
park is just over two miles.)[61]

For a much longer walk, one can hike east along the coastal path
from St Ives to Lelant rather than taking the train. Once at the Badger
Inn, follow the directions above. This route will add about four miles
to the walk. All walking paths to Trencrom are marked on Ordnance
Survey map 102.

By car: Follow the St Ives Road (A3074) to Lelant; the Badger Inn is
situated in **Fore Street**. From there, follow the same route described for
walkers. (Badger Inn telephone: 01736 752 181.)

A Sail to the Lighthouse

Godrevy lighthouse first showed its light on 1 March 1859. The
lighthouse marks the location of a dangerous reef called 'The Stones',
known locally by its Gwithian name 'The Nine Maidens'. The reef
consists of nine jagged peaks, each of which can be clearly seen at
certain low tides. Over the centuries, 'The Nine Maidens' have
claimed hundreds of lives. The earliest recorded wreck occurred in

January 1649, when the *Garland* – the boat carrying the belongings of the executed King Charles I to France – was driven across the reef, with the loss of sixty lives. Plans for a lighthouse at Godrevy were finally formulated after *The Nile* sank on 'The Nine Maidens' in 1854. In that tragedy, a seven-hundred-ton steamer en route from Liverpool to London failed to clear the reef. The boat sank almost immediately and all forty passengers aboard were lost. Nameless bodies washed ashore for days, as did the ship's cargo and other stores.[62]

This sort of tragedy was common along the Cornish coastline, which is characterised by a treacherous combination of hidden reefs and heavy seas – a combination that creates some of the most dangerous marine conditions found anywhere in England. The north coast around St Ives is also marked by extremely large tides and unpredictably high winds – winds which sweep in from the Atlantic, out of the west, with sudden and implacable intensity. Even today, a phone call to arrange a sail to the lighthouse is likely to elicit this immediate response: 'Yes, of course, if it's fine tomorrow.' The danger and unpredictability of the seas around St Ives add another stroke to Woolf's characterisation of Mr Ramsay: given the very real perils of setting sail, Mr Ramsay's caution about promising a trip to the lighthouse might be read in a more sympathetic light.

As the Ramsay family's boat sails toward the lighthouse, Cam fixes her eyes on the land they are leaving behind. But in a revealing Woolfian inversion of actual geography, Cam's description of the island they are leaving is in fact a very close literal description of the island they are sailing toward – the island on which Godrevy lighthouse sits. As they move out to sea, Cam looks back toward shore, searching for the Ramsay's house in the distance, and thinks:

> It was like that then, the island, thought Cam, once more drawing her fingers through the waves. She had never seen it from out at sea before. It lay like that on the sea, did it, with a dent in the middle and two sharp crags, and the sea swept in there, and spread away for miles and miles on either side of the island. It was very small; shaped something like a leaf stood on end. So we took a little boat, she thought, beginning to tell herself a story of adventure about escaping from a sinking ship. But with

the sea streaming through her fingers, a spray of seaweed vanishing behind them, she did not want to tell herself seriously a story; it was the sense of adventure and escape that she wanted ...[63]

As the Ramsay's boat sails farther away from shore, Cam's perspective slowly shifts: the sea seems more and more immense; the land lying in the distance upon the horizon seems small, vague, frail. This shift in perspective marks the change in Cam's attitude toward Mr Ramsay. But Cam's vision is also a very accurate description of the hills and terraces of St Ives, as seen from a boat far out in the bay:

> She gazed at the immense expanse of the sea. The island had grown so small that it scarcely looked like a leaf any longer. It looked like the top of a rock which some wave bigger than the rest would cover. Yet in its frailty were all those paths, those terraces, those bedrooms – all those innumerable things. But as, just before sleep, things simplify themselves so that only one of all the myriad details has power to assert itself, so, she felt, looking drowsily at the island, all those paths and terraces and bedrooms were fading and disappearing, and nothing was left but a pale blue censer swinging rhythmically this way and that across her mind. It was a hanging garden; it was a valley, full of birds, and flowers, and antelopes ... She was falling asleep.[64]

If Cam's gaze is fixed backward, on the receding shoreline that holds her home and family, James's gaze is fixed forward, on the lighthouse that has become their goal. As they make their final approach to the island, James and Cam both hear, with stunning clarity, the sound of the waves hissing around the reef and beating against the island's rocks:

> They had tacked, and they were sailing swiftly, buoyantly on long rocking waves which handed them on from one to another with an extraordinary lilt and exhilaration beside the reef. On the left a row of rocks showed brown through the water which thinned and became greener and on one, a higher rock, a wave incessantly broke and spurted a little column of drops which fell down in a shower. One could hear the slap of the water and the patter of falling drops and a kind of hushing and hissing sound from the waves rolling and gamboling and slapping the rocks as if they were wild creatures who were perfectly free and tossed and tumbled and sported like this for ever.
>   Now they could see two men on the Lighthouse, watching them and making ready to meet them.[65]

And James suddenly sees the stark, bare outline of Godrevy lighthouse in a new way: a way that underscores both Mr Ramsay's
resemblance to the lighthouse and James's growing identification
with his father:

> Mr Ramsay had almost done reading ... He sat there bareheaded with
> the wind blowing his hair about, extraordinarily exposed to everything.
> He looked very old. He looked, James thought, getting his head now
> against the Lighthouse, now against the waste of waters running away
> into the open, like some old stone lying on the sand; he looked as if he
> had become physically what was always at the back of both of their
> minds – that loneliness which was for both of them the truth about
> things.
>   He was reading very quickly, as if he were eager to get to the end.
> Indeed they were very close to the Lighthouse now. There it loomed up,
> stark and straight, glaring white and black, and one could see the waves
> breaking in white splinters like smashed glass upon the rocks. One could
> see lines and creases in the rocks. One could see the windows clearly; a
> dab of white on one of them, and a little tuft of green on the rock. A
> man had come out and looked at them through a glass and gone in
> again. So it was like that, James thought, the Lighthouse one had seen
> across the bay all these years; it was a stark tower on a bare rock. It satis-
> fied him. It confirmed some obscure feeling of his about his own
> character. The old ladies, he thought, thinking of the garden at home,
> went dragging their chairs about on the lawn. Old Mrs Beckwith, for
> example, was always saying how nice it was and how sweet it was and
> how they ought to be so proud and they ought to be so happy, but as a
> matter of fact, James thought, looking at the Lighthouse stood there on
> its rock, it's like that. He looked at his father reading fiercely with his
> legs curled tight. They shared that knowledge. 'We are driving before a
> gale – we must sink,' he began saying to himself, half aloud, exactly as
> his father had said it.[66]

But James's earlier description of the lighthouse is perhaps more
climactic, and more evocative of the unifying vision that marks *To the
Lighthouse*. When James first glimpses the lighthouse's stark outlines, he
balances his past against his present, night against day, female against male:

> 'It will rain,' he remembered his father saying. 'You won't be able to go
> to the Lighthouse.'
>   The Lighthouse was then a silvery, misty-looking tower with a yellow
> eye, that opened suddenly, and softly in the evening. Now –

51

James looked at the Lighthouse. He could see the white-washed rocks; the tower, stark and straight; he could see that it was barred with black and white; he could see the windows in it; he could even see washing spread on the rocks to dry. So that was the Lighthouse, was it?

No, the other was also the Lighthouse. For nothing was simply one thing. The other Lighthouse was true too. It was sometimes hardly to be seen across the bay. In the evening one looked up and saw the eye opening and shutting and the light seemed to reach them in that airy sunny garden where they sat.[67]

James's reflection provides two very accurate descriptions of Godrevy lighthouse as it still looks today: blurred and misty in the evening when seen from Talland House (and many other vantage points around St Ives); stark and imposing during daylight hours, when seen from a boat approaching by sea. Contemporary photographs of Godrevy lighthouse suggest that Woolf took pains to paint the lighthouse as a symbol of reconciled opposites: the lighthouse was entirely white in the 1890s, as it is today; but Woolf portrayed it as 'barred with black and white', perhaps to suggest a way in which opposites are brought together in the very pattern of its colours.

Most important, however, is the fact that James's dual vision of the lighthouse allows him to recognise that 'nothing was simply one thing' – an insight that sums up To the Lighthouse and underpins most of Woolf's other fiction. The lighthouse is a symbol of a journey completed – by the Ramsay family at sea and by Lily Briscoe at her easel. It is also a symbol of the completion of Woolf's own personal journey away from the orbit of her parents' lingering influence.

How to get there
The best way, of course, is to hire a boat and sail to the lighthouse. Several captains station men at the Wharf to engage passengers; one common tourist destination is Seal Island, but Godrevy lighthouse is becoming an increasingly popular journey.

The *Dolly Pentreath* is the most atmospheric of the boats to hire to sail to the lighthouse, and it is probably the St Ives boat most like the one hired by the Stephen family for their summer sails. Young Virginia

Stephen owned a model of a Cornish lugger, which she named *The Fairy*. One of her favourite memories was the time her toy lugger sank in the Round Pond in Kensington Gardens, to be rescued the following spring by a man dredging the pond.

The *Dolly Pentreath* is the first Cornish lugger to be built for seventy years. The boat was constructed by Mike Laity (the captain) and his family in 1993, from plans for an old lugger called *The Godrevy*. Dolly Pentreath was the last woman in St Ives who spoke only Cornish; she is an ancestor of the Laity family. The *Dolly Pentreath* makes a two-hour sunset cruise 'to the lighthouse', but the captain prefers a full boat when he makes the journey. To arrange a sail, phone 01736 796 080, or visit the Dolly's Boat House website at www.dollysboathouse.com.

The long tides in St Ives mean that a sail to the lighthouse must be timed precisely. At low tide, boats are beached in the harbour; keels stick in the sand and the boats tilt crazily. When the tide has fully ebbed, visitors can scramble around rocks and pools in the harbour, searching like Paul and Minta for shells and other treasures. The boat to the lighthouse will depart at high tide, probably from Smeaton's pier.

By car: The visitor can also drive ten miles outside St Ives to Godrevy point – the closest one can get to the lighthouse on land. Godrevy point is a National Trust site.

Take the coast road out of St Ives, past Carbis Bay and Lelant. Turn *left* at the roundabout. Turn *left* at a second roundabout signposted B3301 to Hayle. Proceed under the viaduct and turn *left*. Drive through Hayle; turn *left* at a small roundabout signposted Portreath and Gwithian on the B3301. After two miles, pass the **Gwithian Parish Church** on the *right*. A quarter of a mile further, cross over a narrow bridge and turn *left* towards the Godrevy Café and Godrevy (National Trust sign), where you can park in the National Trust car park. (There is a small fee.) Alternatively, continue down this narrow road for about half a mile and park in the field.[68]

Some other lodgings associated with Woolf
If you are unable to book a room at Talland House, there are many other charming hotels and lodgings in St Ives and Carbis Bay.

Arrangements can be made from London at the Britain Visitor Centre, 1 Lower Regent Street, London SW1 4NR (nearest underground stop: Piccadilly Circus). You can also phone the St Ives Tourist Board on 01736 796 297 (fax: 01736 798 309), or check the official St Ives website at www.stives-cornwall.co.uk. The following three hotels are associated with Virginia Woolf and her family.

The Tregenna Castle Hotel

The Tregenna Castle was built as a family estate in the latter part of the eighteenth century; it opened its doors as a hotel in August 1878, shortly after the branch line of the Great Western Railway was extended to St Ives. Leslie Stephen probably stayed at the Tregenna Castle Hotel in 1881, when he discovered St Ives and Talland House. Later, when Julia Stephen invited too many friends to holiday in Cornwall with them, some of the Stephens' guests had to find lodgings elsewhere in town – both Lily Briscoe and William Bankes find themselves in this situation in *To the Lighthouse*. Some of the Stephen family's overflow lodged themselves just up the hill at the Tregenna Castle Hotel; most notably, Henry James opted for the Tregenna Castle when he visited the Stephens in St Ives. (The Tregenna Castle Hotel, St Ives, Cornwall, TR26 2DE; telephone: 01736 795 254; fax: 01736 796 066.)

The Badger Inn

In 1909 Virginia Stephen suddenly decided to spend Christmas alone in St Ives, still the spot dearest to her in the world. Walking in Regent's Park on the morning of 24 December, it suddenly struck her 'how absurd it was to stay in London, with Cornwall going on all the time'.[69] It was already 12.30 p.m.; she barely caught the 1 p.m. train from Paddington and arrived in Cornwall late that night, without a coat, a chequebook, or glasses. On Christmas Day, she walked in the 'hot spring day' sun along the beach; she planned a hike to Trencrom, and then wrote to Vanessa from her room at the Lelant Hotel:

> I am so drugged with fresh air that I cant write, and now my ink fails. As for the beauty of this place, it surpasses every other season. I have the hotel to myself – and get a very nice sitting room for nothing. It is very comfortable and humble, and infinitely better than the Lizard or St Ives.[70]

On Boxing Day, Virginia listened to Christmas carols through her open window overlooking the bay:

> It is past nine o'clock, and the people still sing carols beneath my window, which is open, owing to the clemency of the night. I am at the crossroads, and at the centre of the gossip of the village. The young men spend most of the day leaning against the wall, and sometimes spitting. Innumerable hymns and carols issue from barns and doorsteps. Several windows, behind which matrons sit, are red and yellow, and a number of couples are wandering up and down the roads, which shine dimly. Then there is the lighthouse, seen as through steamy glass, and a grey flat where the sea is. There is no moon, or stars, but the air is soft as down, and one can see trees on the ridge of the road, and the shapes of everything without any detail.[71]

The Lelant Hotel has been renamed the Badger Inn. If you plan far enough in advance, the proprietor, Mrs Mary Allen, will try to accommodate you in the room Virginia was given in 1909. (The Badger Inn, Fore Street, Lelant, St Ives, Cornwall TR26 3JT; telephone and fax: 01736 752 181.)[72]

The Carbis Bay Hotel
In the spring of 1914, Virginia was recovering from a bout of mental illness when she and Leonard decided that a change of scenery would do them both good. They left London for Cornwall and stayed for three weeks in various lodgings around St Ives, Lelant and Carbis Bay. One of their hotels was the Carbis Bay Hotel, which has a private beach and rooms overlooking the bay and lighthouse. (Carbis Bay Hotel: St Ives, Cornwall TR 26 2NP; telephone: 01736 795 311; fax: 01736 797 677.)

FARTHER AFIELD

Zennor
Virginia often walked along the coastal paths west of St Ives during her visits to Cornwall and stayed several times in and around Zennor: at the Berryman's farm near Gurnard's Head in 1910; at Mrs Hosking's cottage (The Coastguards) at Ponion in 1921; with Ka and Will Arnold-

Foster at the Eagle's Nest for Christmas of 1926. Virginia called these paths 'the loveliest place in the world'.[73] The area around Zennor is remarkable for its stark landscape; it is also rich in literary associations with other authors: both D.H. Lawrence and Katherine Mansfield lived for a time near Zennor, and D.H. Lawrence wrote *Women in Love* in a cottage just outside the town.

In 1921, when Virginia and Leonard were staying in the tiny village of Ponion (only three houses; spelt on the Ordnance Survey 'Ponjou'), she described the view of Gurnard's Head and the granite beauty of Zennor to Saxon Sydney-Turner:

> Why do I always connect you with Zennor? Did we walk over here from Carbis Bay [in 1905]? I rather think you were carried off by Thoby tho to look for a raven on the cliff – which raven I saw yesterday, and two seals walloping on their backs off the Gurnards Head so near in that I could have swum out to them. Next holiday you must come here ... But the country – my dear Saxon. We are between Gurnards Head and Zennor: I see the nose of the Gurnard from my window. We step out into the June sunshine, past mounds of newly sprung gorse, bright yellow and smelling of nuts, over a grey stone wall, so along a cart track scattered with granite to a cliff, beneath which is the sea, of the consistency of innumerable plovers eggs where they turn grey green semi transparent. However when the waves curl over they are more like emeralds, and then the spray at the top is blown back like a mane – an old simile doubtless, but rather a good one. Here we lie roasting, though L. pretends to write an article for the Encyclopaedia upon Cooperation. The truth is we can't do anything but watch the sea – especially as the seals may bob up, first looking like logs, then like naked old men, with tridents for tails. I'm not sure though that the beauty of the country isn't its granite hills, and walls, and houses, and not its sea. What do you say? Of course its very pleasant to come upon the sea spread out at the bottom, blue, with purple stains on it, and here a sailing ship, there a red steamer. But last night walking through Zennor the granite was – amazing, is the only thing to say I suppose, half transparent, with the green hill behind it, and the granite road curving up and up. All the village dogs were waiting outside the church, and the strange Cornish singing inside, so unlike the English.
>
> I think a good deal about the Phoenicians and the Druids.[74]

D.H. Lawrence described Zennor in similar terms, as a 'tiny granite village' with a few houses and a church, all lying below 'lovely pale hills, all gorse and heather, and an immense peacock sea spreading all below'.[75]

Higher Tregerthen

In 1919, when the Woolfs were told they had to move out of their country house at Asheham, they took the lease of three cottages at Higher Tregerthen, just east of Zennor. They heard of the cottages from Katherine Mansfield, who had been introduced to them by D.H. Lawrence and his wife, Frieda. Though Katherine Mansfield told Virginia that Higher Tregerthen was 'the most divine place in the world',[76] the Woolfs never actually stayed at the cottages because they stumbled upon the opportunity to buy Monk's House at about the same time. They let the cottages temporarily to James and Alix Strachey; then Virginia had the idea that the Woolfs might share Higher Tregerthen with Ka and Will Arnold-Foster: 'The brilliant, if wild, idea has come into my head that we might arrange to share the three with you and Will … There are 7 rooms in all: and in the best country in all Cornwall, to my thinking … Monk's House makes it a little difficult to keep them, and yet I should feel desolated to let them go again.'[77] As it turned out, the Arnold-Fosters took The Eagle's Nest and the Woolfs let the lease of Higher Tregerthen lapse.

D.H. Lawrence had discovered Higher Tregerthen during World War I. He and his wife had fled to Cornwall to avoid the military hysteria of London, and to search out a way of life that was simpler, more genuine – and less expensive, since Lawrence's *The Rainbow* had just been prosecuted. Lawrence found the three vacant buildings a mile outside of Zennor, and a short distance above Tregerthen Farm; he described them to a friend in March 1916:

> There are three cottages, in a little knot, standing just under a hillside where enormous granite boulders are lodged among the gorse bushes, look as if they might roll down on us. It is all enormous granite boulders and gorse, above. Below, there are a few bouldery fields, with grey-stone hedges, then the sea. There is one farm in the hollow below. But all is rather windswept and grey and primitive. Yet it has a warm southern quality. When the sun shines, it is wonderful beyond words, so rich.[78]

57

The Lawrences lived at Higher Tregerthen for eighteen months, from March 1916 to October 1917; during which time Lawrence wrote *Women in Love*. At Lawrence's insistence, Katherine Mansfield and John Middleton Murry joined them for the spring of 1916, taking the cottage next to the Lawrence's – a cottage with a tower and seven rooms, and enough space for each of the Murrys to have a separate study. Lawrence assured Katherine that Higher Tregerthen was the perfect place for her to write, and Katherine in fact enjoyed 'a whole spring full of blue-bells one year with Lawrence'.[79] But the bleak surroundings and the Lawrences' marital quarrels soon drove them away; Katherine and Middleton Murry left Higher Tregerthen after just a few months' stay for less spectacular but more peaceful quarters near Falmouth. (In *Women in Love*, Gudrun Brangwen is based on Katherine Mansfield and Gerald Crich is based on Middleton Murry.)

The Lawrences stayed at Higher Tregerthen until October 1917, when they departed under much more dramatic circumstances. They had been viewed with suspicion by the locals from the minute they arrived in Cornwall. It was the middle of World War I, after all, and Lawrence was apparently an able-bodied man of military age. (Lawrence had failed his military medical examination, but he wasn't obviously ill.) Why wasn't he fighting for his country in France? Further, Frieda was German, and known to be related to Manfred von Richthofen, the famous 'Red Baron' of fighter pilot fame. (They were actually only distant cousins and had never met.) The Lawrences also had strange habits, such as receiving the *Berliner Tagesblatt* by post, and their house overlooked the sea. Then the Germans declared unrestricted submarine warfare along the Cornish coast in early 1917 and at first sank dozens of ships each week. When the Lawrences tarred a chimney, or hung curtains of different colours in their windows, or when they used a flashlight to go to their outdoor privy at night, they were suspected of sending secret signals to German U-boats.[80]

In August 1917, German submarines sunk two ships between St Ives and Land's End; in September, the toll rose to six, and vigilance along the coast rose to new heights. On 11 October, Higher Tregerthen was searched by the authorities while Lawrence was out, and papers and letters were taken away. The next morning the authorities reappeared, this time with an order for the Lawrences' expulsion: they were to leave Cornwall within three days, register with the police as soon as they found new quarters somewhere else in England, and stay out of all Class 2 prohibited regions – an area that comprised all coastal regions and every major port in the country. Stunned, the Lawrences took the train out of St Ives, through St Erth, and up to London seventy-two hours later. They never saw Zennor again.

Eagle's Nest

The Woolfs stayed with Ka and Will Arnold-Foster at Eagle's Nest for Christmas of 1926. Eagle's Nest is a large house, and still the chief landmark of the district; until recently, it was the home of the artist Patrick Heron. Since Woolf felt proprietary about this part of Cornwall, considering it almost her private landscape, she felt a pang of jealousy when the Arnold-Fosters took the house in 1921. She wrote in her diary: 'Yet what am I thinking of? That Ka has taken the Eagle's Nest, & that I wish it were mine.'[81]

Woolf described the Eagle's Nest as 'a large solid house, views from every window, water closets, bath rooms, studios, divine gardens, all scattered with Logan rocks'.[82] As she told Vita Sackville-West, the landscape around the Eagle's Nest was full of both beauty and surprise: 'You have never seen the Gurnard's Head? I should like to see you here – A tame raven taps at the window. We motor over the moors, so cold, like an 18th Century print – skeletons hanging on withered branches – Suddenly one dips into the valley, and finds rhododendrons, and palm trees, and St Michael's Mount riding out in a blue sea.'[83] But the Eagle's Nest was so frigid over Christmas 1926 that even the Woolfs were unable to stand 'the perishing cold', and they fled for home a day early.[84]

In 1927 the Arnold-Fosters lent Eagle's Nest to friends for five months. The father, Tom Heron, had temporarily relocated to Cornwall to run a business for a friend. His son Patrick – who spent his eighth birthday at Eagle's Nest – was tremendously impressed by the landscape and remembered seventy years later that he spent his time there drawing pictures of the garden, the sea and the rocks. Patrick Heron moved back to Cornwall as an adult and eventually purchased Eagle's

Nest. Heron was central to a group of modernist artists who assembled in and around St Ives; he also championed local environmental causes, such as preserving the landscape around Zennor.[85]

How to get there

By car from St Ives: Leave St Ives by the B3306 to Zennor. After approximately five miles, the turn to Zennor is on the *right*.

Higher Tregerthen and the Eagle's Nest are not open to the public. Eagle's Nest can be seen from the coast road, about a mile east of Zennor. Tregerthen Farm can be seen from the road below Eagle's Nest, but the Higher Tregerthen Cottages are hidden down a farm track.

The visitor should take time to walk in the village of Zennor, and from there along the coastal path. Tregerthen Cliff is owned by the National Trust.

By bus from St Ives: Buses leave for Zennor from the Malakoff on a regular schedule.

On foot: For a lovely hike, take the coastal path between St Ives and Zennor (Ordnance Survey map 102). This path was a favourite Stephen trek. The family wore good shoes; packed food, water and raingear; and then stopped to take in the views around Gurnard's Head: 'Here we spread out our tea, and that finished, walk home again in the dark. Last night it was dusk when we started, but we had to take a long look at the Gurnard's Head and the misty shapes beyond.'[86]

Though the walk looks short on the map, it is demanding: it totals about four miles as the crow flies, but in actuality becomes over six miles, because of the necessity of clambering up and down slopes. (The milestone at Carrick Du – on the first headland along the path from St Ives to Zennor – measures the distance at 6¼ miles.)

The visitor should set out along the coastal path from **Porthmeor Beach**. (Cars can be left in a car park there.) The path begins easily; it becomes very rough, but the views reward the effort: shifting views of Godrevy lighthouse behind, dizzying views over cliffs to the sea below. The visitor can make a ten-minute detour to Tregerthen cottages. (There is also a shorter high path which passes in front of Tregerthen cottages, but its views are not so spectacular. Yet Virginia Stephen loved this inland path to Zennor, too. As she wrote of it in 1905: 'It is a mistake to keep rigidly to the coast; strike inland & cross the hills, & then you will sight a broad ribbon of sea beneath you, & ships set like toys about it.'[87])

Once in Zennor, the visitor can find rest and refreshment at the Tinners' Arms – the setting for D.H. Lawrence's short story 'Samson and Delilah'. The visitor can return to St Ives by taxi or bus.

CHAPTER TWO

Mrs Dalloway and the streets of London

'London is enchanting. I step out upon a tawny coloured magic carpet, it seems, & get carried into beauty without raising a finger.'
                    Virginia Woolf's *Diary*, 26 May 1924

'London itself perpetually attracts, stimulates, gives me a play & a story & a poem, without any trouble, save that of moving my legs through the streets.'
                    Virginia Woolf's *Diary*, 31 May 1928

I

Nothing stimulated Virginia Woolf like the streets of London. She spent long afternoons walking through them, peering into windows and into people's faces, collecting copy. She might begin in Bloomsbury, at her house in Tavistock Square, and walk all the way to the City, where she could watch people streaming into and out of office buildings, and around St Paul's Cathedral. She might take a less ambitious stroll around the Georgian squares of Bloomsbury, making up stories about the people she passed. She might even walk all the way to the Tower of London, and then ride on the top of a double-decker bus back into

Central London. Wherever Woolf wandered, she drank in the views, the bustle, the noise of traffic, the vast spectacle of teeming humanity moving down narrow streets. London seemed emblematic of history, of vitality and beauty to her. The city landscape suggested possibilities for revelation, for connection, for continuity. Like Clarissa Dalloway, Virginia Woolf saw London as capable of expressing the very power of 'life itself'.

Woolf's London life began in Kensington, a suburb that had housed both her parents' families for more than fifty years. Her mother, Julia Jackson, had spent long hours with her aunt's Pre-Raphaelite friends at Little Holland House (in the street now renamed Melbury Road); later, Julia Jackson married the barrister Herbert Duckworth, and after his death moved with their three children to 22 Hyde Park Gate. Woolf's father, Leslie Stephen, was born in a house in Kensington Gore, lived in Kensington with his first wife, Minny Thackeray (daughter of the novelist William Makepeace Thackeray), and then moved after Minny's death to Hyde Park Gate, into the house next door to the widow Julia. Leslie Stephen brought with him his daughter, Laura, who had been born to Minny six years earlier. When Julia Duckworth and Leslie Stephen married in 1878, he and Laura moved into Julia's house. 22 Hyde Park Gate was therefore crammed with people while Virginia Stephen was growing up: her parents, the three Duckworth children, the four Stephen siblings, Laura (who exhibited mental difficulties), and seven or eight servants. The bedrooms were small; there was one bathroom. The house was dark, and Julia made its interior yet darker by covering the furniture in red velvet and painting the woodwork black. Hyde Park Gate itself was narrow – so narrow that Virginia could see their neighbour, Mrs Redgrave, readying herself for bed in her room across the way.[1]

The Stephen children spent much of their time in Kensington Gardens, one of whose entrances lay across Kensington Road from Hyde Park Gate. They usually walked twice a day in Kensington Gardens: up the Broad Walk, along the Flower Walk, to the Round Pond. They might skate on the Round Pond if the weather were cold enough, or sail boats, usually miniature versions of Cornish luggers they had brought home from St Ives. They often bought balloons from the squat old woman who sat by the gate opposite Gloucester Road, or sweets from a woman who kept a sweet shop in the white house near Kensington Palace. They bought the magazine *Tit-Bits* and read the jokes aloud to each other as they lay on the grass; they once nearly knocked over a woman as they raced their go-cart around a steep corner.[2]

It was in Kensington Gardens that Virginia remembered having two of the intense experiences of shocked perception that she came to call 'moments of being'. On one occasion, there was a puddle in her path, and, 'for no reason I could discover, everything suddenly became unreal; I was suspended; I could not step across the puddle ... the whole world became unreal.'[3] On another occasion, an idiot boy sprang into her path in the park, and she poured her whole bag of Russian toffee into his hand. Later that night the feeling returned as she sat in her bath: 'as if I were passive under some sledge-hammer blow; exposed to a whole avalanche of meaning that had heaped itself up and discharged itself upon me ... so that I huddled up at my end of the bath, motion-less.'[4] As a child, Virginia experienced these moments at St Ives, too: most memorably when she saw a flower and thought 'That is the whole'; more menacingly when the family received news of the suicide of a friend. These 'moments of being' – shocks of intense insight in which Virginia felt a sense of the meaning and connectedness of all people and things – became central to her writing. As she put it many years later, her 'shock-receiving capacity' was what made her a writer:

I hazard the explanation that a shock is at once in my case followed by the desire to explain it ... It is or will become a revelation of some order; it is a token of some real thing behind appearances; and I make it real by putting it into words ... It gives me, perhaps because by doing so I take away the pain, a great delight to put the severed parts together. Perhaps this is the strongest pleasure known to me. It is the rapture I get when in writing I seem to be discovering what belongs to what; making a scene come right; making a character come together. From this I reach what I might call a philosophy; at any rate it is a constant idea of mine; that behind the cotton wool [of daily life] is hidden a pattern; that we – I mean all human beings – are connected with this; that the whole world is a work of art; that we are parts of the work of art. *Hamlet* or a Beethoven quartet is the truth about this vast mass that we call the world. But there is no Shakespeare; there is no Beethoven; certainly and emphat-ically there is no God; we are the words; we are the music; we are the thing itself. And I see this when I have a shock.[5]

These shocks of perception – sometimes uplifting and sometimes terrifying moments in which a character senses a connection to a vast pattern – are a fundamental element in Woolf's fiction. They occur in some form in all of her novels: during the dinner party in *To the Lighthouse*; when Orlando sees the wild goose at the end of *Orlando*; at Hampton Court in *The Waves*. They are an exhilarating experience for Clarissa Dalloway, who senses her palpable connection to living things as diverse as trees and people. They are a frightening occurrence for Septimus Warren Smith, whose sense of connection to things outside himself is so intense that he feels his body tied by 'millions of fibres' that pull him painfully up and down.

But the intensity of moments outside, in Kensington Gardens, was counterpointed by the gloom of moments inside, in 22 Hyde Park Gate. The house itself seemed suffocating to Virginia. Its walls seemed permeated with conflicting family feelings; the place was tangled and matted with emotion. Part of Virginia's sense of suffocation resulted from the oppressive weight of the extended Victorian family and its stultifying social conventions. After Julia Stephen's death in 1895, as Virginia became an adolescent and then a young woman, her daily life was painfully divided. She spent her mornings doing precisely what pleased her: she immersed herself in the world of intellect; she read, wrote and studied Greek. But when tea-time came around, she was expected to be available to entertain Leslie Stephen's friends. Even worse, her half-brother George Duckworth expected her to accompany him on a round of social engagements late into the night. Virginia always found these evenings painful because she felt that she was socially inept: she didn't dance well enough; she shocked George's dowager friends when she talked about Plato's *Symposium*. But even worse was George Duckworth's excessive and histrionic physical attachment to Virginia. Under the guise of brotherly love, George sometimes crept into Virginia's darkened room as she was about to fall asleep, flung himself on her bed, and took her into his arms. As Virginia remarked many years later, the old ladies of Kensington and Belgravia would have been appalled to know that George Duckworth was not only brother to 'those poor Stephen girls; he was their lover also'.[6]

It was in this house that Virginia suffered her first two mental breakdowns, episodes she later associated with the conflicting emotions generated by Victorian family life. Julia Stephen died when Virginia was thirteen, and Virginia remembered being led into her mother's bedroom to kiss her goodbye. Julia's face felt cold and granulated, like kissing cold iron; even more terrifying, Virginia thought she saw a man sitting bent at the edge of her mother's deathbed. Shortly afterwards, she fell seriously ill: her pulse raced so quickly she could barely stand it; she became terrified of people and turned bright red if spoken to. The doctor prescribed rest and a simple life: four hours a day outside in the open air; no excitement; no lessons.[7]

Virginia's second mental breakdown occurred in 1904, shortly after Leslie Stephen's death. This time she heard voices urging her to commit desperate acts. Since she believed that these voices came from overeating, she starved herself. She raved at her three nurses, who had become fiendish interlopers; she mistrusted everything Vanessa did. Overwhelmed, Vanessa sent Virginia to stay with Violet Dickinson at her house, Burnham Wood, in Welwyn, Hertfordshire. As Virginia described it many years later, she lay in bed at Violet's house, listening to the birds in the bushes singing Greek choruses, and imagining that King Edward VII was hiding in the azaleas, using the foulest language imaginable.[8] It was at Violet Dickinson's home that Virginia made her first suicide attempt: she threw herself out of a window, but the window was not high enough for her to hurt herself seriously. In October 1904, recovering but still weak, Virginia went to stay with her father's sister, Caroline Emelia Stephen, in Cambridge.

By the time Virginia was well enough to return to London, Vanessa had disposed of 22 Hyde Park Gate. Laura had been sent to an asylum; George Duckworth had married and Gerald had moved into a bachelor flat. Vanessa had sorted, sold, torn up and burnt – and had looked at a London map for a location far away from Kensington. The four Stephen children settled on Bloomsbury, and 46 Gordon Square came into existence:

When one sees it today, Gordon Square is not one of the most romantic of the Bloomsbury squares ... But I can assure you that in October 1904 it was the most beautiful, the most exciting, the most romantic place in the world. To begin with, it was astonishing to stand at the drawing room window and look into all those trees; the tree which shoots its branches up into the air and lets them fall in a shower; the tree which glistens after rain like the body of a seal – instead of looking at old Mrs Redgrave washing her neck across the way. The light and the air after the rich red gloom of Hyde Park Gate were a revelation. Things one had never seen in the darkness there – Watts pictures, Dutch cabinets, blue china – shone out for the first time in the drawing room at Gordon Square. After the muffled silence of Hyde Park Gate the roar of traffic was positively alarming ... We had entered the Sargent-Furse era; white and green chintzes were everywhere; and instead of Morris wall-papers with their intricate patterns we decorated our walls with washes of plain distemper.[9]

After the gloom and darkened quiet of Hyde Park Gate, Gordon Square meant light, possibility, freedom. And in this account of her excited first reaction to the openness of Bloomsbury squares, Woolf uses two of the three major images that came to characterise her response to London cityscapes: windows and trees. The trees in Gordon Square were a positive revelation as they shot their branches in the air, or gleamed after the rain. And Virginia Stephen's perpetual view of old Mrs Redgrave through her window at Hyde Park Gate has given way to a view of the bright green of a Bloomsbury square – though a version of Mrs Redgrave will appear in *Mrs Dalloway* twenty years later.[10]

The change in location, décor, and views from windows was accompanied by a total change in social behaviour. The Stephen daughters were no longer obliged to pour tea for elderly relatives every day at four o'clock; they could paint and write without interruption. Virginia began to publish reviews; she also began to teach history and composition to working men and women at Morley College. The Stephen siblings decided that they could do without table napkins at dinner; they forgot to leave their visiting cards if they called on people. Most importantly, Thoby – who was reading for the Bar in London and missed his Cambridge friends – decided that he would be 'at home' to any friends who called at 46 Gordon Square on Thursday evenings. On Thoby's first Thursday, only Saxon Sydney-Turner came, so that Saxon, Thoby and the dog Gurth formed the entire party. But soon Thoby's other Cambridge friends began to frequent the Stephen household on Thursday evenings – Clive Bell, Lytton Strachey, Desmond MacCarthy

– and thus the Bloomsbury group was born. Thoby's Thursday evenings continued for almost two years, with the talk inevitably dominated by abstract questions concerning literature and philosophy, inspired by the Cambridge philosopher G.E. Moore. When Vanessa founded her Friday Club, young painters began to stream into Gordon Square as well.

The four Stephen children lived at 46 Gordon Square for a little more than two years. In late 1906, they travelled to Greece. On their return, Thoby was taken seriously ill with typhoid fever; he died on 20 November. Two days later, Vanessa accepted Clive Bell's proposal of marriage. Since Vanessa and Clive wanted to take over 46 Gordon Square, in early 1907 Virginia and Adrian leased 29 Fitzroy Square, a house still in Bloomsbury and still within walking distance of Vanessa and Clive. While she was living in Fitzroy Square, Virginia wrote for *The Times Literary Supplement* and continued to write reviews for the *Guardian*, a weekly newspaper for the clergy. She also began work on her first novel, *Melymbrosia*, which was finally published in 1915 as *The Voyage Out*. The move to Fitzroy Square introduced a number of new faces into the expanding group of Bloomsbury friends: Duncan Grant, Lytton Strachey's cousin, moved into a house at 21 Fitzroy Square; he was joined there by John Maynard Keynes, who had known Leonard Woolf and Adrian Stephen at Cambridge. E.M. Forster began to drift in and out of the Bloomsbury circle; Roger Fry met Clive and Vanessa, and embroiled all the friends in the controversy of the First Post-Impressionist Exhibition, which he organised in November 1910.

When the lease on 29 Fitzroy Square ran out in October 1911, Virginia and Adrian decided to take a larger house to share with friends in a communal arrangement. They settled on 38 Brunswick Square. Virginia would have the second floor to herself; Adrian would have the first. John Maynard Keynes planned to take the ground floor as a *pied-à-terre* for use when he was down from Cambridge; Duncan Grant could use the rooms as a studio in the meantime. All the old family friends and relatives from Hyde Park Gate days were scandalised by Virginia's shocking disregard for her reputation: how could she live in a house with unmarried men who were not family members? A horrified Violet Dickinson invoked the memory of Julia Stephen; George

Duckworth came all the way across town to beg Vanessa to dissuade Virginia from her foolhardy plan. He was not much comforted by Vanessa's observation that a provision existed if any real difficulties arose for Virginia: after all, she said, the Foundling Hospital was just next door.[11]

One of the unattached young men who moved into 38 Brunswick Square was Leonard Woolf, who took the top floor. Leonard had known Thoby Stephen, Lytton Strachey and Clive Bell at Cambridge, where Leonard had been admired for his probing mind and passionate convictions. Leonard was just back from seven years in Ceylon, where he had overseen the administration of a large colonial district. The cynical strength of the returning colonialist would come to play an important part in Woolf's novels: like Peter Walsh in *Mrs Dalloway*, Leonard Woolf was shaped after University by 'plains, mountains; epidemics of cholera; a district twice as big as Ireland; decisions he had come to alone'.[12] Virginia was drawn to Leonard's worldliness and pragmatic good sense; she was intrigued by her sense of something foreign about him: he was misanthropic; he was a Jew; his body trembled violently. Leonard was also extremely intelligent, and, as the close friend of her close friends, he was almost 'family'. Leonard was writing a novel, as Virginia was; he was even passionate about all the old Bloomsbury questions: when he visited Vanessa for tea, they argued about whether or not colour existed. Virginia was happy to spend an increasing amount of time with Leonard and she showed him one of her manuscripts. He told her that some day she 'might write something astonishingly good'.[13]

For his part, Leonard fell quickly and entirely in love with Virginia, and proposed marriage in January 1912. Virginia felt affection for Leonard, but she wasn't quite sure she wanted to marry him. She had had several skirmishes with her 'nerves' since her previous major breakdown in 1904, and had spent some time at Burley Park, a nursing home at Twickenham, where she was made to rest in a darkened room and offered large servings of wholesome food. Though Leonard's marriage proposal was attractive, it was also unsettling. Virginia returned to Burley Park for another rest cure shortly after Leonard proposed, and was released at the end of February 1912.

Back at Brunswick Square, Virginia and Leonard again saw each other every day. Every morning they sat down to write five hundred words in their respective rooms; then they might lunch together, or walk through adjacent Bloomsbury squares. Virginia was brutally honest with Leonard about her feelings. She wrote to him that the 'sexual side' of the relationship came between them – that she felt no physical attraction for him; that when he kissed her she felt no more than a rock. Yet she also told him that she wanted everything – 'love, children, adventure, intimacy, work' – and that they might have a marriage together that was 'a tremendous living thing, always alive, always hot, not dead & easy in parts as most marriages are'.[14] Virginia also confessed that she was overwhelmed by the extent to which Leonard cared for her, and that she was determined to care for him, too. On the strength of Virginia's letter, Leonard decided not to return to Ceylon and resigned from the Colonial Service. Finally, in May 1912, Virginia told Leonard that she loved him and wanted to marry him. Their wedding took place on 10 August, 1912, at the St Pancras Registry Office.

They honeymooned in Provence, Spain and Italy for six weeks, and found that Virginia was not inclined to sexual passion. Virginia said she found 'the climax immensely exaggerated';[15] when they came back to London, they pressed Vanessa for details of her first orgasm. Then they settled at 13 Clifford's Inn, in the City of London, a neighbourhood that bustled delightfully during the working week and fell silent over weekends. With Fleet Street, Fetter Lane, the Temple and Gough Square close by, they felt that their neighbourhood had been inhabited for hundreds of years by the likes of Chaucer, Shakespeare, Johnson and Boswell. They dined every night at the Cock Tavern, where people still remembered Tennyson. And they both resumed writing again, sitting near the open windows of their rooms, with a gentle rain of City smut settling over their pages.[16]

Leonard was working on a second novel; Virginia was rewriting *The Voyage Out* yet one more time. She finished it in February 1913 and Leonard delivered it to Gerald Duckworth's publishing firm on 9 March. It was accepted for publication a month later. Virginia corrected the proofs of *The Voyage Out* from May until June. In future years, correcting proofs would always distress her; this first experience pushed her to what she described many years later as 'acute despair'.[17] In July, she entered the nursing home at Twickenham yet once more, but when she was discharged in August, she was still teetering on the brink of collapse.

Once home with Leonard, the old hallucinations returned. Virginia blamed herself for her 'vile imaginations'.[18] She refused to eat; her body and everything associated with it seemed sordid and loathsome. She developed a horror of other people; she talked incoherently; she couldn't calm down enough to sleep. In the middle of September, Leonard left her in the care of a friend while he went to consult with doctors. He accidentally left behind an unlocked bag containing sleeping medications. Virginia took an overdose of veronal, fell unconscious, and nearly died.

With some respites, Virginia's illness continued for two more years, until the end of 1915. During that time, on the advice of doctors, the Woolfs moved out of central London to the quiet suburb of Richmond. They first stayed in lodgings at 17 The Green with a Belgian landlady called Mrs le Grys; then they leased half of a lovely Georgian building that had been broken into two separate houses. Their half was called Hogarth House and it was located on Paradise Road. *The Voyage Out* was finally published in March 1915, two months after Virginia's thirty-third birthday, but by that time Virginia had slipped again into 'the dark cupboard'[19] of her mental illness. As she recalled many years later, the dead seemed to speak to her from beyond the grave as she lay in bed at Hogarth House. A decade later, Virginia would pour all these incidents from her own mental illness – the suicide attempts, the hallucinatory voices of the dead, the loathing of things physical, the hatred and suspicion of strange people – into her characterisation of Septimus Warren Smith in *Mrs Dalloway*.

Virginia Woolf's illness was described by Leonard Woolf as manic depression; today's doctors might call it a bipolar affective disorder. But whatever diagnostic label one attaches to her condition, it is clear that contemporary doctors had few tools for treating it successfully. Dr George Savage, who had been her doctor since Hyde Park Gate, always insisted that the best medicine for Virginia was rest, quiet living, an ample diet, and absence from the boisterous social distractions of London. When Savage recommended that Virginia take a rest cure, it meant seclusion at Jean Thomas's nursing home in Twickenham, where she was kept in bed in a darkened room and not allowed to write. Dr Maurice Craig, the most eminent Harley Street psychiatrist of his day, prescribed something very similar. He insisted that Virginia needed to gain weight; he recommended that she eat large meals and avoid exercise to keep her weight up. Craig also recommended that Leonard and Virginia not have children, since the strain might be too great for her fragile mental balance. In 1922, when Virginia was beginning to conceive of *Mrs Dalloway*, the Woolfs visited another series of specialists who offered advice on Virginia's racing pulse and other physical ailments.[20] One of them, the great Dr Sainsbury, diagnosed the illness that Virginia was shortly to give to Clarissa in *Mrs Dalloway*: influenza and a tired heart. Then he shook Virginia's hand as they parted and said (in cadences Woolf was soon to give the terrifying Dr Bradshaw in *Mrs Dalloway*): 'Equanimity – equanimity – practise equanimity, Mrs Woolf.'[21]

Since this sort of medical advice was the best available, Leonard and Virginia followed it. One result was that, over the years, Leonard assumed the role of Virginia's guardian, the figure who managed her illness and controlled her schedule. It was Leonard who insisted that they leave parties if Virginia was becoming too excited; it was Leonard who vetoed visitors who might, in his judgment, interfere with Virginia's rest or peace of mind. Leonard encouraged Virginia to drink her milk; he insisted that she nap for a full half-hour after lunch. He made sure that she ate full meals; he sometimes made her lie down on the sofa. Leonard's behaviour towards Virginia is one of the continuing controversies animating discussion of her life. Some readers view Leonard Woolf as a controlling patriarch who misunderstood his wife entirely, and whose collusion with the medical establishment exacerbated her mental illness. Other readers view him as a loving husband who struggled to care for his wife using the best means at his disposal, and whose unwavering support provided the stability she needed to produce her greatest masterpieces. Virginia Woolf herself wrote about the 'inviolable centre' her marriage to Leonard provided, and said: 'If it were not for the divine goodness of L. how many times I should be thinking about death'.[22] Woolf portrays their relationship in the wary protectiveness that Richard Dalloway exerts over Clarissa's health in *Mrs Dalloway*; as Clarissa walks the streets of London, she is drawn back into her past with her husband, a past that is characterised by both enduring love and deep disappointments.

Virginia and Leonard Woolf lived at Hogarth House in Richmond for nine years, from 1915 until 1924. During that time, Virginia established herself as a serious writer by contributing essays to literary periodicals, by publishing short fiction, and by bringing out two novels, *Night and Day* and *Jacob's Room*. Leonard and Virginia founded the Hogarth Press, and were offered works as diverse as *Ulysses* and *The Waste Land*. (They published *The Waste Land* in 1923.) But once Virginia's health improved, she chafed at the isolation and inconvenience of 'suburban' Richmond. She often took the train to Sloane Square, and from there made the rounds from Partridge and Cooper's stationery shop in Fleet Street (her favourite place to buy pens), to Gordon Square, and then perhaps to a concert or a play. But she hated the distance between herself and her friends; she hated not being able to dash to the National Gallery to see a picture, or to the British Museum to check some fact; she hated the long train journey home. She persuaded Leonard that they should move back to Bloomsbury, and in January 1924 they bought a ten-year lease on 52 Tavistock Square.

Virginia was ecstatic at the idea of being back in central London, even as she recognised how good Richmond had been for her. Fifteen minutes after buying the lease to 52 Tavistock Square, she wrote:

London thou art a jewel of jewels, & jasper of jocunditie – music, talk, friendship, city views, books, publishing, something central & inexplicable, all this is now within my reach, as it hasn't been since August 1913, when we left Cliffords Inn, for a series of catastrophes which very nearly ended my life, & would, I'm vain enough to think, have ruined Leonard's. So I ought to be grateful to Richmond & Hogarth, & indeed, whether its my invincible optimism or not, I am grateful. Nothing could have suited better all through those years when I was creeping about, like a rat struck on the head.[23]

The Woolfs completed their move to Tavistock Square in March. They lived on the top two floors of the four-storey house; the solicitors' firm of Dollman and Pritchard continued to keep its offices on the ground floor and first floor. The operations of the Hogarth Press were moved to the house's large basement; a billiard room that had been extended into the garden became Virginia's writing room – 'The best study I've ever had.'[24] Virginia settled into a London routine that suited her entirely. She wrote every morning. Evenings were often taken up with cultural events or parties. And at some point most days she walked – to Red Lion Square with their dog Pinker; to Tottenham Court Road and Oxford Street on errands; to the British Museum or as far as the Tower of London. She often sat with Leonard or Vanessa in the garden at the centre of Tavistock Square. She explored the ancient streets of the City and walked along the Strand. She loved riding on the top of what she called her 'adorable omnibuses'.[25] The Woolfs lived in Tavistock Square until 1939, when they leased 37 Mecklenburgh Square. Eventually, the war drove them to spend most of their time in the country, at Monk's House in Rodmell.

All Woolf's excursions into the streets of London fired her imagination and provided her with copy for her books. One day in 1925, as Woolf walked around Tavistock Square, she made up *To the Lighthouse* 'in a great, apparently involuntary, rush'.[26] On one longer walk, when Woolf was writing *Mrs Dalloway*, she was taken with the aesthetic beauty and haunting impact of people simply living. Shortly thereafter, she gave Clarissa Dalloway a similar insight into the affecting potency of 'life itself':

> It was a beautiful clear November day, yesterday, when I went up & past our house … & the squares with their regular houses, & their leafless trees, & people very clearly outlined filled me with joy. Indeed, it was so lovely in the Waterloo Road that it struck me that we were writing Shakespeare; by which I mean that when live people, seeming happy, produce an effect of beauty, & you don't have it offered as a work of art, but it seems a natural gift of theirs, then – what was I meaning? – somehow it affected me as I am affected by reading Shakespeare. No: it's life; going on in these very beautiful surroundings.[27]

On some occasions, Woolf's walks through London gave her a nearly mystical insight into something even more abstract and powerful than what she came to call 'life itself': some sense of seeing into 'reality';

some vision so intense and inexpressible that, for lack of a better word, she called 'it'. This vision came to her once as she stood on Hungerford Bridge looking at the sky over the city.[28] It came to her another time as she looked at the sky while walking through Russell Square:

> Why is there not a discovery in life? Something one can lay hands on & say 'This is it?' ... Then (as I was walking through Russell Sqre last night) I see the mountains in the sky: the great clouds; & the moon which is risen over Persia; I have a great & astonishing sense of something there, which is 'it' – It is not exactly beauty that I mean. It is that the thing is in itself enough: satisfactory; achieved. A sense of my own strangeness, walking on the earth is there too: of the infinite oddity of the human position; trotting along Russell Sqre with the moon up there, & those mountain clouds. Who am I, what am I, & and so on: these questions are always floating about in me; & then I bump against some exact fact – a letter, a person, & come to them again with a great sense of freshness. And so it goes. But, on this showing which is true, I think, I do fairly frequently come upon this 'it'; & then feel quite at rest.[29]

At about the same time, Woolf described her sense of encountering this ineffable 'it' on the downs at Rodmell. It was an experience of start-ling insight into the heart of things: of the monumental reality of nature in the clouds and sky; of the oddity and contingency of the human condi-tion. It was an encounter that could be either terrifying or freeing, and that happened to Woolf most frequently when she was out of doors. The feeling was related to her childhood 'shocks' of perception in Kensington Gardens and at St Ives. And it was an experience that became crucial to Clarissa Dalloway's redemption at the end of *Mrs Dalloway*.

But most of the urban phenomena that gripped Woolf's attention as she explored the London streets were much more concrete, and even prosaic. She came to evoke the symbolic possibilities of the London cityscape using three repeated images: buses, trees and lighted windows. She was drawn to London's buses – she rode them everywhere, usually on the top deck, and always felt as if she were being carried into some adventure. The ride along Park Lane might remind her of the old days in Hyde Park Gate; by the time she arrived at Holborn, she was trans-ported by a sense of freedom.[30] Virginia and Leonard might take a bus to Richmond together. One such trip became an emblem of the 'immense success' of their life as a married couple, and made Virginia wonder if it was possible for anything to 'trouble this happiness'.[31] Woolf's imagination was equally stirred by the trees of London, which she described in many ways, all rapturous. Her most consistent image for London's trees compares them to a fine connective mist: 'The sun laid gold leaf over the trees & chimneys today. The willows on the bank were – what word is it? – soft yellow plumy, like a cloud; like an infinitely fine spray; something showery in it; & also grains of gold. I can't find the exact word.'[32] But Woolf's imagination was most fired by peering into lighted windows as she walked, especially during the winter months, when the lights went on early. She once said that 'a London winter is full of bright rooms, passages through dark streets to scenes of brilliancy';[33] on one April walk, she thought 'I was on one of my January walks, with lights lit at 3.30 in peoples bedrooms'.[34] Woolf devoted the whole of her essay 'Street Haunting' to an evocation of the powerful impact that London streets exert over the human imagination at a winter dusk. As the narrator walks through lighted squares, windows provide the central image in the essay:

> But this is London, we are reminded; high among the bare trees are hung oblong frames of reddish-yellow light – windows; there are points of brilliance burning steadily like low stars – lamps; this empty ground, which holds the country in it and its peace, is only a London square, set about by offices and houses where at this hour fierce lights burn over maps, over documents, over desks where clerks sit turning with wetted forefinger the files of endless correspondences; or more suffusedly the firelight wavers and the lamplight falls upon the privacy of some drawing-room, its easy chairs, its papers, its china, its inlaid table, and the figure of a woman, accurately measuring out the precise number of spoons of tea which – She looks at the door as if she heard a ring downstairs and somebody asking, is she in?[35]

In 'Street Haunting', Woolf's narrator peers into windows just after setting off from a Bloomsbury house late on a winter's afternoon. She has a vision of life going on in houses, framed and highlighted by windows. These same windows appear in *Mrs Dalloway* too, when Peter Walsh walks from Bloomsbury to Westminster on the way to Clarissa's party. And they recur in most of her novels in one form or another, from Jacob staring out of the windows of his Cambridge rooms in *Jacob's Room*, to the Pargiter sisters looking longingly from the windows of Abercorn Terrace in *The Years*.

Woolf poured all her passion for London and its urban vitality into the pages of *Mrs Dalloway*. Clarissa Dalloway might characteristically have said, as Woolf herself did, 'Oh the convenience of this place! And the loveliness too. We walk home … through the entrails of London. Why do I love it so much?'[36] Woolf's characters are revealed by their attachments to, or habitation in, very specific parts of town; they find that their imagination is kindled, as Woolf's was, by her favourite urban emblems of windows, trees and buses. Woolf knew that London itself perpetually stimulated her, and that her beloved city would give her 'a play & a story & a poem, without any trouble, save that of moving my legs through the streets'.[37] The best-known story London gave Virginia Woolf is *Mrs Dalloway*.

II

Just after Vita Sackville-West read *Mrs Dalloway* for the first time, she wrote to Virginia Woolf: 'One thing [*Mrs Dalloway*] has done for me for ever: made it unnecessary ever to go to London again, for the whole of London in June *is* in your first score of pages.'[38] Sackville-West's description of Mrs Dalloway's London is accurate: the novel portrays the city with a literal correctness reminiscent of Joyce's *Ulysses* and Dublin. But Woolf's portrayal of place in *Mrs Dalloway* is more than a masterpiece of evocative realism. Woolf uses her London locations, both interior and exterior, as metaphors for her characters' struggles with society and their own pasts. She associates London interiors with constriction and entrapment; her London exteriors – especially streets and parks – suggest expansion, independence, and experiences of intense perception and connection. Simultaneously, Woolf investigates the contiguous worlds of sanity and insanity, and of marriage and unconventional sexuality. As she does so, she emphasises the sense of continuity provided by a place, and uses *Mrs Dalloway* to orchestrate the symbolic objects she came to associate with the richness of her favourite London cityscapes: windows, trees and buses.

The major characters in *Mrs Dalloway* are very much defined by the places that produced them and the places where they currently live. Clarissa Dalloway, the novel's title character, spent her youthful summers in an elegant country house at Bourton and now lives in fashionable Westminster with her husband, a member of parliament. Peter Walsh – Clarissa's old love and a perennially rebellious outsider – was sent down from Oxford and then entered a career in colonial administration. This career took Peter far away from London, into the colonial backwaters of the Indian subcontinent; he has just returned from the East as the novel opens. Septimus Warren Smith, who emerges in *Mrs Dalloway* as Clarissa's alter ego, grew up in Stroud in Gloucestershire. But Septimus saw no future in Stroud for a poet, and so came to London, eventually settling after World War I into 'admirable lodgings off the Tottenham Court Road'.[39]

At the beginning of the novel, Clarissa Dalloway's Westminster house is a place that constricts her. Clarissa is fifty-two years old; she and her husband, Richard, have a seventeen-year-old daughter called Elizabeth. Clarissa is a society hostess, and, on the single June day in 1923 on which *Mrs Dalloway* is set, she is about to throw a party – a party so elegant that the Prime Minister has been invited. When Peter Walsh arrives on her Westminster doorstep unexpectedly from India, his presence sets Clarissa to re-evaluating her life. She relives her past and its possibilities, and wonders if she has made the right decisions in her marriage.

For Clarissa's marriage to Richard Dalloway is not entirely satisfactory. As Clarissa thinks about her youth, she realises that her days at Bourton, her parents' country home, suggested rich possibilities for her future. It was at Bourton that Peter Walsh proposed marriage to Clarissa; it was at Bourton that Clarissa experienced what she still regards, even at the age of fifty-two, as 'the most exquisite moment of her whole life'[40] – the moment when her rebellious friend Sally Seton kissed her squarely on the lips. Instead, Clarissa married Richard Dalloway, and her married life lacks these moments of passion. Richard cannot tell her that he loves her. Since Clarissa's illness – 'her heart, affected, they said, by influenza'[41] – Richard has insisted that they keep separate bedrooms. Though Clarissa actually prefers this arrangement,

she still feels trapped and confined by it. When she enters her attic
bedroom in the middle of the day, the interior arrangement of her
Westminster house – her narrow bed, with its tightly stretched white
sheets – becomes a symbol of the lack of physical passion in her
marriage, and for her fear that she does not possess the ability to feel
any emotion deeply:

> There was an emptiness about the heart of life; an attic room ... She
> pierced the pincushion and laid her feathered yellow hat on the bed. The
> sheets were clean, tight stretched in a broad white band from side to side.
> Narrower and narrower would her bed be. The candle was half burnt
> down and she had read deep in Baron Marbot's *Memoirs* ... For the
> House sat so long that Richard insisted, after her illness, that she must
> sleep undisturbed. And really she preferred to read of the retreat from
> Moscow. He knew it. So the room was an attic; the bed narrow; and lying
> there reading, for she slept badly, she could not dispel a virginity
> preserved through childbirth which clung to her like a sheet. Lovely in
> girlhood, suddenly there came a moment – for example on the river
> beneath the woods at Clieveden – when, through some contraction of
> this cold spirit, she had failed him. And then at Constantinople, and again
> and again.[42]

To the exterior observer, Clarissa seems a pinched and unhappy
middle-aged woman – a small, birdlike figure who has renounced
passion for the safety of social rank, and for the comforts of a conventional life in her stylish Westminster home.

But Clarissa's immersion in London street life reveals a very different
and expansive side of her personality. As she walks through the streets
and parks of London on her way to buy flowers for her party, Clarissa
responds passionately to the urban landscape around her – to its sights,
its sounds, its suggestiveness. The cacophony of London fills her with
joy; the chaotic scene evokes what Clarissa loves best about London: its
capacity to express 'life itself'. In a passage that brilliantly captures the
feel of central London, and that brims over with Woolf's own love for
the life and beauty inherent in her favourite cityscapes, Clarissa crosses
Victoria Street and thinks:

> For having lived in Westminster – how many years now? over twenty, –
> one feels even in the midst of the traffic, or waking at night, Clarissa was

positive, a particular hush, or solemnity; an indescribable pause; a suspense (but that might be her heart, affected, they said, by influenza) before Big Ben strikes. There! Out it boomed. First, a warning, musical; then the hour, irrevocable. The leaden circles dissolved in the air. Such fools we are, she thought, crossing Victoria Street. For Heaven only knows why one loves it so, how one sees it so, making it up, building it round one, tumbling it, creating it every moment afresh; but the veriest frumps, the most dejected of miseries sitting on doorsteps (drink their downfall) do the same; can't be dealt with, she felt positive, by Acts of Parliament for that very reason: they love life. In people's eyes, in the swing, tramp, and trudge; in the bellow and the uproar; the carriages, motor cars, omnibuses, vans, sandwich men shuffling and swinging; brass bands; barrel organs; in the triumph and the jingle and the strange high singing of some aeroplane overhead was what she loved; life; London; this moment of June.[43]

Clarissa's thoughts reproduce Woolf's own passion for the affecting power of the life of city streets – Woolf's sense that the beauty of the Waterloo Road suggested 'life: going on in these very beautiful surroundings', and that life in turn 'affected me as I am affected by reading Shakespeare'.[44] Equally importantly, Clarissa's thoughts reveal the depth of her own passion and feeling – the fact that she is, contrary to her private fears, capable of a keen response to everything around her, from the roaring sound of London's buses to the drunken women slumped on fashionable doorsteps. Clarissa Dalloway may experience emotional constriction inside her London house, but she feels spiritual enlargement in London's streets and parks, and on London's buses.

It is from the top decks of London buses, in fact, that Clarissa Dalloway, like Virginia Woolf, experiences some of her deepest feelings of freedom and happiness. When Clarissa rides on the top of a bus with Peter Walsh, she senses an intense connection to the urban landscape around her – a connection that ties her spirit to her place, and makes her feel immortal. As Peter Walsh remembers:

Clarissa once, going on top of an omnibus with him somewhere ... spotting queer little scenes, names, people from the top of the bus, for they used to explore London and bring back bags full of treasures from the Caledonian market ... But she said, sitting on the bus going up Shaftesbury Avenue, she felt herself everywhere; not 'here, here, here'; and she tapped the back of the seat; but everywhere. She waved her hand, going up Shaftesbury Avenue. She was all that. So that to know her, or any one, one must seek out the people who completed them; even the places. Odd affinities she had with people she had never spoken to, some woman in the street, some man behind a counter – even trees, or barns. It ended in a transcendental theory which, with her horror of death, allowed her to believe, or say that she believed (for all her scepticism), that since our apparitions, the part of us which appears, are so momentary compared with the other, the unseen part of us, which spreads wide, the unseen might survive, be recovered somehow attached to this person or that, or even haunting certain places after death ... perhaps – perhaps.[45]

Buses are a staple in Woolf's London fiction and the people who ride them – nearly always on the top deck – do so in a spirit of adventure and as a symbol of their openness to all that experience might offer. When Elizabeth Dalloway rides a bus up Whitehall and then along the Strand to Chancery Lane, she first feels that she has boarded a pirate ship, and then decides she wants to be either a doctor or a farmer – very unconventional career choices for a young woman of her class and time. Eleanor Pargiter in *The Years* feels that she is the youngest person on the bus when she rides it to her charity work in London slums; her ride along other London streets gives her a vision of the connection between the soaring spires of London churches and the pipes and drains that run beneath them. For Clarissa Dalloway, her ride on the top of one of Woolf's 'adorable omnibuses' cements her identity with the eternal bustle and life of London streets – she *is* Shaftesbury Avenue, and part of her will live on as long as Shaftesbury Avenue exists. To know her, Clarissa says, one must know the people and places she loves. Those places are part of her spirit; they complete her; they will express her life even after she is dead. Clarissa will live on in the people and the London cityscapes she adores; the bustle of London streets connects her to the pulse of 'life itself', and gives her immortality.

Clarissa also expresses her feelings of transcendence and immortality using the imagery of London's trees. Just as Woolf described London's trees as a fine connective mist – 'soft yellow plumy, like a cloud; like an infinitely fine spray; something showery'[46] – so Clarissa sees trees as emblems of a kind of connection that extends her life indefinitely. As she walks along Bond Street towards Hatchards, Clarissa concludes that she is part of the trees and people around her, 'being laid out like a mist between the people she knew best, who lifted her on their branches as she had seen the trees lift the mist, but it spread ever so far, her life, herself'.[47] Both the city trees and Clarissa's 'transcendental theory', as Peter Walsh calls it – an eccentric but sane idea of the way the human spirit survives in the objects to which it attaches itself – are echoed later in *Mrs Dalloway* by the mad imaginings of Septimus Warren Smith, the young man from Stroud who has been unhinged by his experiences in the trenches of World War I.

If Clarissa Dalloway frequents the fashionable haunts of Westminster and Bond Street, and experiences a sense of transcendent connection in images associated with London's buses and trees, her old suitor Peter Walsh is more at home in Regent Street and Bloomsbury, where he finds 'life itself' revealed through lighted windows. Peter, the returning colonialist who has lived outside the reach of London society for five years, visits Clarissa as soon as he returns from India. He brings the news that, at the ripe age of fifty-three, he has fallen in love with a very young married woman called Daisy. In reality, Peter is still passionately in love with Clarissa and bursts into tears in her drawing room. For her part, Clarissa still cherishes her old attachment to Peter, and his visit reawakens her sense of the passion that might have been hers if she had married Peter instead of Richard. Clarissa actually draws Peter to her and kisses him – she feels a flash of the old searing emotion and then struggles to suppress it. Clarissa spends the rest of her day thinking about her decision to marry Richard Dalloway and wondering whether she was right, thirty years earlier, to reject both Peter Walsh and Sally Seton for the safety of her current life. At the same time, Peter Walsh walks the streets of London, reliving the days at Bourton and his years of knowing Clarissa subsequently, and struggling to come to terms with the fact of Clarissa's rejection.

As soon as he leaves Clarissa's house, Peter plunges into the bustle and life of London's streets. He walks up Whitehall, noting the statues raised to the heroes of Empire – Nelson, Gordon, Havelock. He sees a troop of schoolboys disappearing in the direction of the Strand. As he crosses Trafalgar Square in the direction of Haymarket, he sees an 'extraordinarily attractive' young woman – and his temperamental unsuitability for an intimate relationship with Clarissa begins to be revealed. Peter follows the young woman through Cockspur Street, then through the crowds in Piccadilly and Regent Street, and finally across Oxford and Great Portland Streets, all the while watching the movement of her shoulders and thinking of her red lips. Simultaneously, Peter has his hand thrust in his trouser pocket, where he fingers the blade of the pocket knife he perennially carries. Peter's knife – and his stealthy encounter with the young woman – suggest why Clarissa chose Richard instead: the knife implies the threatening violence of Peter's repressed sexual passion, an ardour that frightened Clarissa with Peter's insistence that everything between them must be shared. Even Peter Walsh eventually realises that, in the old days, 'his demands upon Clarissa ... were absurd. He asked impossible things. He made terrible scenes'.[48]

But for all his flaws and emotional excess, Peter Walsh is a character capable of great understanding and insight. Later that evening, Peter walks from his hotel in Bloomsbury, near Bedford Place leading into Russell Square, all the way back down Whitehall to Westminster and Clarissa's party. As he walks through the long summer twilight – Mr Willett's summer time has been introduced since Peter's previous visit to England – Peter looks into windows, and at the beauty and richness of life that London's windows frame and highlight:

> For here he was starting to go to a party, at his age, with the belief upon him that he was about to have an experience. But what? Beauty anyhow. Not the crude beauty of the eye. It was not beauty pure and simple – Bedford Place leading into Russell Square. It was straightness and empti- ness of course; the symmetry of a corridor; but it was also windows lit up, a piano, a gramophone sounding; a sense of pleasure-making hidden, but now and again emerging when, through the uncurtained window, the window left open, one saw parties sitting over tables, young people slowly circling, conversations between men and women, maids idly looking out (a strange comment theirs, when work was done), stockings drying on top ledges, a parrot, a few plants. Absorbing, mysterious, of infinite richness, this life. And in the large square where the cabs shot and swerved so quick, there were loitering couples, dallying, embracing, shrunk up under the shower of a tree; that was moving; so silent, so absorbed, that one passed, discreetly, timidly, as if in the presence of some

sacred ceremony to interrupt which would have been impious. That was interesting. And so on into the flare and glare.[49]

As Peter walks towards Clarissa's party, London's windows give him a vision of what Woolf came to call 'life itself' – a vision of the beauty and mystery of people living unconsciously, viewed at a distance by a sympathetic observer. As Peter puts it on his stroll through the summer dusk, it is 'absorbing, mysterious, of infinite richness, this life'. It is the same vision of the beauty and richness of life that Woolf herself caught on all her walks around London, and that she described, using the imagery of London windows lighted at twilight, in her essay 'Street Haunting'. It is a vision that recalls Woolf's own memory of old Mrs Redgrave preparing herself for bed while Virginia Stephen watched her through the windows of 22 Hyde Park Gate. It is a vision that recalls Clarissa's passionate response to the life glimpsed on London streets, and that looks forward to the end of *Mrs Dalloway*, when Clarissa herself sees an old woman through a lighted London window. Finally, it is a moment whose passionate response to 'life itself' is counter-pointed to the last moment in the life of Septimus Warren Smith, who uses a window to throw his life away.

When Septimus Warren Smith first moved to London from Stroud to make a name for himself as a poet, he took lodgings off the Euston Road. He studied Shakespeare with Miss Isabel Pole at a London school for working men; when World War I broke out, Septimus was one of the first to enlist. Like Clarissa Dalloway, Septimus cherishes a passionate affection for a member of the same sex: just as Clarissa treasures the 'exquisite moment' of Sally Seton's kiss, Septimus developed a close emotional attachment to Evans, his commanding officer. But just before the Armistice, Evans is blown to bits in the trenches of France. Rather than responding with an excess of emotion, Septimus congratulates himself upon responding very 'reasonably': he feels nothing at all. He reacts indifferently as the last shells of the war explode around him; he is eventually billeted in Milan, in the house of an Italian innkeeper. There, he makes a fateful decision: 'to Lucrezia, the youngest daughter, he became engaged one evening when the panic was on him – that he could not feel.'[50]

Septimus Warren Smith's emotional situation closely parallels Clarissa Dalloway's – Woolf takes pains to portray Septimus as Clarissa's alter ego. Like Clarissa, Septimus is plagued by his fear that he can't feel enough; like Clarissa, Septimus has chosen a spouse who provides him with stability rather than passion. Septimus, however, slips over the edge into madness – he suffers from 'shell shock', or what today's medicine would call Post Traumatic Stress Disorder. As he sits on a bench in Regent's Park, waiting to walk to Harley Street to visit a doctor who might banish his terrifying hallucinations, Septimus thinks that the trees around him reveal a vast pattern to which his body is painfully connected:

> But they beckoned; leaves were alive; trees were alive. And the leaves being connected by millions of fibres with his own body, there on the seat, fanned it up and down; when the branch stretched he, too, made that statement. The sparrows fluttering, rising, and falling in jagged fountains were part of the pattern; the white and blue, barred with black branches. Sounds made harmonies with premeditation; the spaces between them were as significant as the sounds. A child cried. Rightly far away a horn sounded. All taken together meant the birth of a new religion.[51]

Septimus' sense of a transcendent pattern that connects him to trees is reminiscent of Clarissa's 'transcendental theory' – which makes her feel immortal and which she also associates with trees. But the difference is that Septimus' experience is painful, terrifying, and 'mad': he is so connected to the landscape of Regent's Park that 'red flowers grew through his flesh; their stiff leaves rustled by his head'.[52] These transcendent experiences of connection and insight, experienced by both Clarissa and Septimus, have their origin in Woolf's own childhood experiences in the parks of London – and specifically Kensington Gardens – when she stopped, shocked into perception by the seeming unreality of some event. These 'moments of being' made Woolf into a writer; these moments often gave Woolf a pleasurable sense of the connection and pattern behind things, which she then shaped into words. But these moments were also sometimes frightening, since they made her – like Septimus Warren Smith – 'passive under some sledge-hammer blow; exposed to the whole avalanche of meaning that had heaped and discharged itself upon me'.[53]

Woolf draws extensively on her own experience of mental illness for her portrayal of Septimus' symptoms – she confessed, in fact, that 'the mad part' of the novel 'tries me so much, makes my mind squint so badly that I can hardly face spending the next weeks at it'.[54] As he sits on a bench in Regent's Park, Septimus hears the birds singing in Greek and the dead speaking aloud – experiences that beset Woolf when she was in the throes of mental collapse at Burnham Wood, and at Hogarth House in Richmond. Like Woolf, Septimus becomes terrified of strange people; like Woolf, Septimus is racked with guilt. Like Woolf, Septimus begins to loathe his body and everything associated with physicality. And, like Woolf, Septimus threatens suicide. It is this threat that throws him into the path of the 'great' Dr Bradshaw.

Septimus and Rezia leave Regent's Park for their appointment with Bradshaw at noon. They walk out of the park, past Regent's Park underground station, and down Portland Place to Harley Street, where Bradshaw keeps his expensive offices. Woolf uses her portrayal of Bradshaw to caricature the frightening medical treatment she received from her own doctors: Bradshaw insists that Septimus must enter a nursing home in the country, where he will rest in a darkened room, isolated from his loved ones; Bradshaw insists that 'lunatics' such as Septimus must be forbidden to have children. Perhaps most terrifying, Bradshaw tells Septimus that he must practise 'proportion', and uses the same cadences as Woolf's Dr Sainsbury, who recommended 'Equanimity – equanimity – practise equanimity, Mrs Woolf.'

After their meeting with Bradshaw, Septimus and Rezia return to their Bloomsbury boarding house distraught. Bradshaw plans to take Septimus to his nursing home that night, but they vow that they won't allow any doctor to separate them. Septimus helps Rezia to make a hat for Mrs Filmer's daughter, and the simple creative act restores his mental balance: he no longer hears the voices of the dead; he no longer feels a painful physical connection to the landscape around him. Then Dr Holmes knocks on the door unexpectedly and Septimus, having regained himself, determines not to lose himself again. When Rezia leaves the room, Septimus walks to the window:

> There remained only the window, the large Bloomsbury-lodging house window, the tiresome, the troublesome, and rather melodramatic business of opening the window and throwing himself out ... Holmes and Bradshaw liked that sort of thing. (He sat on the sill.) But he would wait till the very last moment. He did not want to die. Life was good. The sun hot. Only human beings – what did *they* want? Coming down the staircase opposite an old man stopped and stared at him. Holmes was at the door. 'I'll give it you!' he cried, and flung himself vigorously, violently, down on to Mrs Filmer's area railings.[55]

In his last moment, Septimus's Bloomsbury window frames for him another vision of 'life itself' – the old man coming down the staircase opposite. This old man parallels the many people Peter Walsh sees framed in London windows as he walks to Clarissa's party. But, even though Septimus has regained a hold on his own life, and grasps – quite sanely – the lovely mystery of other lives seen through windows, he decides to throw 'life itself' away. Suicide is Septimus' only means of preserving himself; it is his only way of protecting himself from being remade in the image of Holmes and Bradshaw. For Septimus, his London window saves his integrity and provides a passage to freedom – his window is his escape from entombment in a darkened room at Bradshaw's nursing home. Septimus' Bloomsbury window frees him from the constrictions of interior space into the expanses of the exterior and impersonal – the freedom of death. So, although life is good and although Septimus loves life, he throws his life away, out of the window, onto the area railings beneath.

After Septimus Warren Smith throws himself out of his Bloomsbury window, the closing pages of *Mrs Dalloway* shift to Westminster and Clarissa's party. All Clarissa's friends have gathered there, including the two loves from her youth, Sally Seton and Peter Walsh. Sally Seton has married a manufacturer from Manchester and has five enormous sons; Peter Walsh's walk through London has given him a sense of perspective and a new openness towards Clarissa. Dr Bradshaw arrives at Clarissa's party late, explaining that he was detained because one of his patients committed suicide. Although Septimus Smith is not mentioned by name, the idea of death stops Clarissa in her tracks. She withdraws to a quiet room, looks out of her Westminster window, and considers the meaning of Septimus's suicide:

She [Clarissa] had once thrown a shilling into the Serpentine, never anything more. But he had flung it away ... A thing there was that mattered; a thing, wreathed about with chatter, defaced, obscured in her own life, let drop every day in corruption, lies, chatter. This he had preserved. Death was defiance. Death was an attempt to communicate; people feeling, the impossibility of reaching the centre which, mystically, evaded them; closeness drew apart; rapture faded, one was alone. There was an embrace in death.[56]

Clarissa recognises that Septimus' death embodies conflicting heroic impulses: his suicide is an act of senseless abandon, like throwing a coin into the Serpentine in Hyde Park; it is an act of defiance; it is an attempt at communication. But most importantly, Septimus' suicide is an effort to maintain an inviolable core of self – a self that Clarissa lets drop daily in 'corruption, lies, chatter'.

The perspective from her Westminster window allows Clarissa to understand Septimus's heroism, but it also gives her a transcendent insight into the human condition. Clarissa watches the sky over Westminster; then her gaze switches to an old woman preparing for bed across the way:

No pleasure could equal, she thought ... this having done with the triumphs of youth, lost herself in the process of living, to find it, with a shock of delight, as the sun rose, as the day sank. Many a time had she gone, at Bourton when they were all talking, to look at the sky; or seen it between people's shoulders at dinner; seen it in London when she could not sleep ... It held, foolish as the idea was, something of her own in it, this country sky, this sky above Westminster. She parted the curtains; she looked. Oh, but how surprising! – in the room opposite the old lady stared straight at her! ... It was fascinating to watch her, moving about, that old lady, crossing the room, coming to the window. Could she see her?[57]

The old woman Clarissa sees through her window recalls both the old man Septimus sees as he sits on his Bloomsbury window sill, and the various people Peter Walsh glimpses through lighted windows as he heads to Clarissa's party. Woolf gives Clarissa her own vision of 'life itself', glimpsed from a distance by a sympathetic observer – a vision that originated at Hyde Park Gate and expressed itself repeatedly as Woolf wrote about walking through London streets and peering into windows. But Clarissa simultaneously sees something even more abstract and powerful than 'life itself'. When Clarissa looks at the Westminster sky, which recalls the Bourton country sky, she senses something she can only call 'it' – some vision that affects her with a 'shock of delight', and gives her insight into both the monumental reality of nature and the oddity of the human condition. This same experience of some ineffable 'it' is the vision that periodically came to Woolf as she moved through London – most notably on Hungerford Bridge and while walking through Russell Square – and when she looked at the sky over Rodmell. It is a vision of the reality at the heart of things; it is an insight into whatever it is that is most moving about human beings and the way they live. It is a vision that propels Clarissa – unlike Septimus Warren Smith – away from her Westminster window and back into the life of her party. Thinking of Septimus' suicide, Clarissa decides that 'she must go back. She must assemble. She must find Sally and Peter. And she came in from the little room'.[58]

Once Clarissa returns to her party, she and Peter Walsh seek each other out. Peter Walsh's day of walking through London has provided him with new perspective and understanding: he has come to terms with Clarissa's rejection and has realised that, if they had married, the marriage would have failed. Peter has also realised that middle age deepens his power of feeling. When people are young, Peter remarks, they are much too excited to know people. But 'now that one was old, fifty-two to be precise ... now that one was mature then, said Peter, one could watch, one could understand, and one did not lose the power of feeling'.[59] Peter's bitterness is gone; he will be able to understand and accept Clarissa, and balance this acceptance against the depth of feeling he still has for her. The close of *Mrs Dalloway* does not portray the actual meeting between Peter Walsh and Clarissa Dalloway. Instead, the novel ends on a note of openness and anticipation as Peter prepares to encounter in a new way the woman he almost married thirty years earlier:

> What is this terror? what is this ecstasy? he thought to himself. What is it that fills me with extraordinary excitement? It is Clarissa, he said. For there she was.[60]

The note of openness, anticipation and excitement that closes *Mrs Dalloway* also sums up, of course, Clarissa's own personality, and her attitude towards the life that goes on around her. It is a life that Clarissa loves wherever she finds it, and she finds it especially in the streets and parks of London, and glimpsed through the city's lighted windows. In the pages of *Mrs Dalloway*, Woolf balances the constriction of city interiors against the expansive possibilities of London exteriors. She uses trees, buses, and windows – her favourite aspects of the London city scene – to suggest infinite possibilities for connection and revelation in London's landscape. Woolf's characters discover that London's streets give them ample material for moments of insight. And for Woolf, too, the wonder of London – her 'jewel of jewels'[61] – is that it continually provides her with both moments of insight and a startling connection to 'life itself'.

III

London today: Sights and walks

WALKING THROUGH *MRS DALLOWAY*'S LONDON

On the Wednesday in June 1923 on which *Mrs Dalloway* takes place, the major characters walk in various directions around London. Clarissa walks from her home in Westminster through St James's Park to buy flowers in Bond Street; Septimus Warren Smith and his wife Rezia begin in Bloomsbury near Tottenham Court Road, pass some time in Regent's Park, and eventually visit Dr Bradshaw in Harley Street. Peter Walsh walks from Clarissa's house all the way to Regent's Park; after lunch with Lady Bruton, Richard Dalloway walks along Bond Street with Hugh Whitbread. The following walk traces the steps of Clarissa Dalloway and Septimus Warren Smith.

Clarissa Dalloway's walk through London – like Septimus Smith's – is anchored in specific streets, parks and shops. As the characters walk, they notice an exterior landmark, or cross a particular street; Woolf then temporarily dispenses with exterior description to plunge the reader into the characters' consciousness – a technique Woolf refers to as her 'tunnelling process, by which I tell the past by instalments, as I have need of it'.[62] Woolf's use of her 'tunnelling process' means that she does not describe every step of her characters' paths. For example, Clarissa crosses Victoria Street at the beginning of *Mrs Dalloway*. As she crosses Victoria Street, she thinks about London, about the war's end, about the power of life. Clarissa then enters St James's Park, continues to think, and meets Hugh Whitbread. Since Woolf does not give the reader the precise path Clarissa follows from Victoria Street to St James's Park, the reader must deduce what streets Clarissa might have followed.

The first half of the following walk is based on the route reconstructed by Stuart Clarke. (This route is available on the website of the Virginia Woolf Society of Great Britain at http:/www.orlando.jp.org/vwsgb/index.html. The website is an indispensable tool for any traveller interested in Virginia Woolf: in addition to Stuart Clarke's *Mrs Dalloway* walk, the site provides a list of Virginia Woolf's London addresses, information about the Stephen family graves in Highgate, and a good deal of other useful material, including links to various websites associated with Virginia Woolf and the Bloomsbury group. Since it is updated regularly, travellers will want to check the site before leaving for London.) Depending on how often the walker stops to rest, read, have refreshments, or absorb the London atmosphere, this walk can take anything from thirty minutes to three hours. Peter Walsh walks from Clarissa's house in Westminster to Regent's Park (using a different route) – and the walk takes him fifteen minutes, with time included for a short nap on a park bench!

Clarissa and Septimus
The walk begins in **Dean's Yard**, next to Westminster Abbey. (The nearest underground station is Westminster.) Clarissa and Richard Dalloway live close to Dean's Yard: Richard enters Dean's Yard as he approaches his house on his way home from lunch with Hugh Whitbread at Lady Bruton's.

Leaving Dean's Yard, turn *left* into **Great College Street**, and then *right* into **Barton Street**. Woolf does not provide the exact location of the Dalloways' home. David Daiches deduces that the Dalloways lived in Great College Street; Jean Moorcroft Wilson suggests that they might have lived in Barton Street, since Virginia Woolf once saw a house in Barton Street which she much admired.[63]

At the end of Barton Street, turn *left* into **Cowley Street** and then *right* into **Great Peter Street**. Follow Great Peter Street to **Perkin's Rents**; turn *right* into Perkin's Rents. Continue along Perkin's Rents to **Abbey Orchard Street**, and from there to **Victoria Street**. It is as she crosses Victoria Street that Clarissa Dalloway experiences the power of 'life itself' in the London streets: she hears Big Ben strike; its leaden circles dissolve in the air; she thinks of what she loves most:

> In people's eyes, in the swing, tramp, and trudge; in the bellow and the uproar; the carriages, motor cars, omnibuses, vans, sandwich men shuffling and swinging; brass bands; barrel organs; in the triumph and the jingle and the strange high singing of some aeroplane overhead was what she loved; life; London; this moment of June.[64]

Cross Victoria Street into **Dean Farrar Street**. Continue into **Dartmouth Street**, and then turn *left* into **Queen Anne's Gate**. Where Queen Anne's Gate turns sharply left, turn *right* instead, and cross **Birdcage Walk** into **St James's Park**. As she enters St James's Park, Clarissa meets Hugh Whitbread 'coming along with his back against the Government buildings'. Clarissa is struck by the contrast between St James's Park and Victoria Street, and thinks of Peter Walsh:

> But how strange, on entering the Park, the silence; the mist; the hum; the slow-swimming happy ducks; the pouched birds waddling ... For they might be parted for hundreds of years, she and Peter; she never wrote a letter and his were dry sticks; but suddenly it would come over her, If he were with me now what would he say? – some days, some sights bringing him back to her calmly, without the old bitterness; which perhaps was the reward of having cared for people; they came back in the middle of St James's Park on a fine morning – indeed they did.[65]

Follow the path and cross the bridge over the lake; continue along the path to the **Mall**. Turn *left* and then *right* into **Green Park**, and continue up through Green Park along **Queen's Walk** on its eastern edge. As Clarissa walks through Green Park, she thinks of Peter Walsh and the many 'scenes' he made at Bourton. She soon reaches the top of Queen's Walk and stops to look at the traffic in Piccadilly, noting especially the buses: 'She had reached the Park Gates. She stood for a moment, looking at the omnibuses in Piccadilly.'[66]

At **Piccadilly**, turn *right*. Follow Piccadilly to the window of **Hatchards** (at number 187), passing the turning into Old Bond Street. As Clarissa walks along Piccadilly, she notes some of the buildings, thinks of London trees, and decides that some part of her will live on forever in the streets of London:

> Devonshire House, Bath House, the house with the china cockatoo, she had seen them all lit up once ... Did it matter then, she asked herself, walking towards Bond Street, did it matter that she must inevitably cease completely; all this must go on without her; did she resent it; or did it not become consoling to believe that death ended absolutely? but that somehow in the streets of London, on the ebb and flow of things, here, there, she survived, Peter survived, lived in each other, she being part, she was positive, of the trees at home; of the house there, ugly, rambling all to bits and pieces as it was; part of people she had never met; being laid out like a mist between the people she knew best, who lifted her on their branches as she had seen the trees lift the mist, but it spread ever so far, her life, herself. But what was she dreaming as she looked into Hatchards' shop window?[67]

In 1923, Devonshire House (the London address of the Duke of Devonshire) was immediately opposite Queen's Walk, between Stratton and Berkeley Streets; it has since been demolished.[68] Bath House, located at 82 Piccadilly, was in the 1920s the residence of Lady Ludlow. The 'house with the china cockatoo' belonged to the Baroness Burdett-Coutts and was located at 80 Piccadilly. The china cockatoo made this window one of the best-known in London, since thousands of people passed it every day; until she died in 1906, the Baroness used the cock-atoo to indicate that she was at home.[69] These residences are an indication of the social circle within which Clarissa aspires to move.

As Clarissa peers into Hatchards window, she reads the line from *Cymbeline* that remains in her thoughts for the remainder of the day. The rest of the books in Hatchards window represent an eclectic mix of reading – very much the sort of selection one is apt to find in Hatchards window today.

Retrace your steps along Piccadilly and turn *right* into **Old Bond Street**. As Clarissa proceeds up Bond Street – then as now one of the most fashionable shopping districts in London – she looks into windows and sees various goods: 'a Dutch picture ... one roll of tweed

94

in the shop where her father had bought his suits for fifty years; a few pearls.' She sees 'salmon on an iceblock' and then pauses for a moment 'at the window of a glove shop'. The glove shop might have been either A. Bide Ltd, Glovers (158A New Bond Street – on the left side of the street) or the London Glove Company (83 New Bond Street – on the right side of the street). The salmon on an iceblock was probably in the window of Gilsons Ltd, 121 New Bond Street (on the left side of the street).[70]

Clarissa finally pushes 'through the swing doors of Mulberry's the florists'.[71] Mulberry's is probably based on G. Adam and Co., florists and fruiterers to the King and the Prince of Wales, formerly located at 42 New Bond Street (on the right side of the street).[72] (In an amusing instance of life quite accidentally imitating art, the current shop located at 41-42 New Bond Street is called Mulberry's, although it sells high-end clothing rather than flowers.) As Clarissa chooses the flowers for her party that night, she hears a car backfire like a pistol shot.

> The violent explosion which made Mrs Dalloway jump and Miss Pym go to the window and apologise came from a motor car which had drawn to the side of the pavement precisely opposite Mulberry's shop window ... rumours were at once in circulation from the middle of Bond Street to Oxford Street on one side, to Atkinson's scent shop on the other, passing invisibly, inaudibly, like a cloud ...[73]

Atkinson's scent shop was located at 24 Old Bond Street.[74] (There is now a plaque on the north side of the building which reads: 'Atkinson's, founded 1799, has sold perfume and beauty products on this site since 1832.')

As you walk north along Old Bond Street and New Bond Street, you will pass the addresses discussed above in the following order: 24 Old Bond Street – former site of Atkinson's scent shop; 158A New Bond Street – former site of A. Bide Ltd., Glovers; 42 New Bond Street – former site of G. Adam and Co. florists and fruiterers to the King; 121 New Bond Street – former site of Gilsons Ltd, the fishmonger; 83 New Bond Street – former site of the London Glove Company. Note that Lady Bruton would have lived in this part of town; note also that just after Old Bond Street changes to New Bond Street, you will cross

Conduit Street – whose name changes to Bruton Street. Bruton Street, in turn, leads to Bruton Lane and Bruton Place.

The sound of the car backfiring marks the transition from Clarissa to Septimus Warren Smith: both Clarissa and Septimus hear the noise and look at the car. At this point, the narrative switches from Clarissa to Septimus; the walk through London now proceeds with Septimus and his wife, Rezia, who are on their way to their noon appointment with Dr Bradshaw. As the motor car proceeds towards Piccadilly and Buckingham Palace, Septimus and Rezia walk in the opposite direction, across Oxford Street and towards Regent's Park.

Cross over **Oxford Street**. Continue into **Vere Street**. Turn *right* at **Henrietta Place**; turn *left* into **Cavendish Square**; continue up **Harley Street** towards Regent's Park. (Dr Bradshaw's offices are located in Harley Street, but Septimus and Rezia are too early for their appointment, and enter Regent's Park to wait.) Cross **Marylebone Road**; continue along **Upper Harley Street** to the **Outer Circle**. Turn *right* into the Outer Circle and enter Regent's Park at the **Broad Walk**. Cross **Chester Road** to the northern half of the Broad Walk and take a seat on one of the park benches.

Septimus and Rezia sit on one of the benches 'in Regent's Park in the Broad Walk'.[75] Septimus looks at the trees and the sky, sees the sparrows fluttering, and hears the noise of traffic in the distance, all the while feeling as if he is connected by fibres to the trees and to his park bench. When Rezia leaves Septimus for a few minutes to walk to a fountain nearby, Septimus hears a sparrow perched on the railing opposite him singing in Greek. Then the figure of his dead comrade, Evans, materialises behind the black railings. Black wrought-iron railings still define the areas in this part of Regent's Park:

Men must not cut down trees. There is a God ... He waited. He listened. A sparrow perched on the railing opposite chirped Septimus, Septimus, four or five times over and went on, drawing its notes out, to sing freshly and piercingly in Greek words how there is no crime and, joined by another sparrow, they sang in voices prolonged and piercing in Greek words, from trees in the meadow of life beyond a river where the dead walk, how there is no death.

There was his hand; there the dead. White things were assembling behind the railings opposite. But he dared not look. Evans was behind the railings![76]

Rezia returns from her walk to the fountain and interrupts Septimus' hallucinatory vision of Evans. To follow Rezia's path, proceed to the north end of the Broad Walk, to the Ready-Money fountain. As she stands by the fountain, Rezia is gripped by her fear of loneliness, and her despair at Septimus' condition: 'I am alone; I am alone! She cried, by the fountain in Regent's Park (staring at the Indian and his cross).'[77]

The Ready-Money fountain was opened in 1869 and has recently been restored. Its brass tablet (now gone) explained that it was 'the gift of the Cowasjee Jehangheer Ready-Money, Companion of the Star of India, a wealthy Parsee gentleman of Bombay, for the protection enjoyed by him and his Parsee fellow-countrymen under British rule in India'. Woolf's reference to a cross probably evokes the shape of the entire structure, which recalls a market-square cross.[78]

Return to the area of Septimus' bench. Take one of the diagonal paths extending down the slope towards the London Zoo. Septimus insists that he and Rezia must get away from the people around them in the park; he points to chairs under a tree, down the long slope of the park, in the direction of the Zoo. He and Rezia walk there and sit in some chairs beneath a tree:

> Away from people – they must get away from people, he said (jumping up), right away over there, where there were chairs beneath a tree and the long slope of the park dipped like a length of green stuff with a ceiling cloth of blue and pink smoke high above, and there was a rampart of far irregular houses hazed in smoke, the traffic hummed in a circle, and on the right, dun-coloured animals stretched long necks over the Zoo palings, barking, howling. There they sat down under a tree.[79]

Rezia tries to call Septimus' attention to the troops of small boys with cricket stumps moving towards the green expanse of Regent's Park lawns. (These lawns are still used for organised play by schools in the area.)

Return to the **Broad Walk** and walk *right* (south), in the direction of Marylebone Road. While walking through the lower half of the Broad

Walk, after crossing **Chester Street**, note 'the stone basins, the prim flowers, the old men and women'[80] – the same scene viewed by Maisie Johnson after she asks Rezia for directions to Regent's Park tube station. Leave the Broad Walk and turn *left* into the **Outer Circle**. Turn *right* into **Park Square**, and then cross **Marylebone Road** into **Park Crescent**, noting Regent's Park tube station as you pass. Both Peter Walsh and Rezia see an old woman singing at the Regent's Park tube station.

Proceed along Park Crescent to **Portland Place**. As Septimus and Rezia walk down Portland Place, Septimus sees the street 'as if Portland Place were a room he had come into when the family are away'.[81] Turn *right* into **Devonshire Street**; return to **Harley Street**, where Dr Bradshaw's offices are located. Septimus' appointment is at noon; he and Rezia hear the leaden toll of Big Ben as they approach Dr Bradshaw's house somewhere along Harley Street. Harley Street is still filled with medical practices.

This is the end of the Clarissa/Septimus walk. The visitor may return to Westminster and other locations via the underground at the Regent's Park tube station.

A WALK THROUGH VIRGINIA WOOLF'S EARLY YEARS: KENSINGTON

This walk begins at the house where Virginia Woolf was born and follows the general route that Virginia Stephen and her siblings might have taken on daily excursions into Kensington Park. It also suggests a few detours of interest.

The walk begins in front of **22 Hyde Park Gate**. From the centre of London, take either the number 9 or number 10 bus (preferably riding on the top level, as Virginia Woolf would have), and alight at **Queen's Gate**. Hyde Park Gate is just to the west of Queen's Gate, opening off Kensington Road. (Hyde Park Gate is divided into two sections; this walk begins in the eastern half of Hyde Park Gate. The two streets were originally connected.)

22 Hyde Park Gate is not open to the public. It is now broken up into flats, and the blue plaque on the house indicates that it was the home of Sir Leslie Stephen.

Virginia Stephen was born at 22 Hyde Park Gate, in the first floor room (over what would have been the front sitting room) whose windows still overlook Hyde Park Gate.[82] She lived there from 1882 until just after her father's death in 1904. Leslie Stephen had moved to 20 Hyde Park Gate with his daughter Laura after his first wife's death; the widowed Julia Stephen already lived at 22 Hyde Park Gate with her three children from her first marriage. When they married, Leslie and his daughter moved into Julia's house. As the Stephen family grew with the addition of four more children, Leslie and Julia enlarged their property. They added two storeys to the top of the house and at least one addition to the back of the house. To save architect's fees, Julia herself sketched their plans for the builder. The result was a high, narrow house, which in the Stephens' time was divided into numerous small rooms.[83]

The basement of 22 Hyde Park Gate was home to the cook, Sophie Farrell, and as many as seven maids. The servants had a sitting-room in the basement but, as Woolf recalled many years later, 'Wild cats might have lived there. The basement was a dark unsanitary place for seven maids to live in. "It's like hell," one of them burst out to my mother as we sat at lessons in the dining room.'[84]

The ground floor of 22 Hyde Park Gate was the Stephen family's public area, where they lived and entertained, and where the children did their lessons at the dining room table. Woolf describes the first floor, where Leslie and Julia had their bedroom, as 'the sexual centre, the birth centre, the death centre of the house. [The Stephen parents' bedroom] was not a large room; but its walls must be soaked ... with ... all that makes the most private being of family life. In that bed four children were begotten; there they were born; there first mother died; then father died, with a picture of mother hanging in front of him.'[85]

The second storey had three bedrooms for Stella, George and Gerald Duckworth; the third storey contained the day and night nurseries for Virginia and her siblings. At the very top of the house were the servants' bedrooms and, most importantly, Leslie Stephen's study: 'the great study with its high ceiling of yellow stained wood.'[86] When Leslie Stephen worked in this room, Virginia and her siblings could hear him dropping books on the floor; it was to this room that Virginia came to talk to her father about her reading and to return the books he had given her – a ritual that, as Virginia Woolf recalled near the end of her life, made her feel 'proud and stimulated, and full of love for this unworldly, very distinguished and lonely man, whom I had pleased by coming'.[87] From the windows of the third floor nursery, Virginia Stephen could look across the narrow width of Hyde Park Gate to see old Mrs Redgrave preparing for bed in her room across the way in number 27.[88]

Before leaving Hyde Park Gate, note the house at number 24. After Stella Duckworth married Jack Hills in April of 1897, they moved to **24 Hyde Park Gate**, so that Stella wouldn't be too far away from the family and the father-in-law who still seemed to demand her care. But it was a tragically brief marriage. After Stella returned from her honeymoon ill, the doctors diagnosed peritonitis. The operation was put off for three months; she died after surgery on 19 July 1897.

As you leave Hyde Park Gate, notice the other blue plaques indicating the street's famous residents: Baden-Powell lived at number 9, Jacob Epstein lived at number 18, Enid Bagnold lived at number 29, and Winston Churchill lived at number 28.

Leave Hyde Park Gate and return to **Kensington Road**. Turn *left* (west) and walk along Kensington Road one block, to the other section of Hyde Park Gate. Leslie Stephen was born in 1832 in a house that probably stood on the site of what is now a block of flats called Broadwalk House. At the time of Stephen's birth, the house was numbered as part of Kensington Gore; it was subsequently renumbered as 42 Hyde Park Gate. So Stephen was born a few steps away from the spot where he died. Leslie Stephen's father moved his family to this area in 1829 and thus entrenched the Stephen clan in this part of Kensington for three generations. In his biography of his elder brother, Stephen described the Hyde Park Gate of his childhood:

The Kensington of those days was still distinctly separate from London. A high wall divided Kensington Gardens from the Hounslow Road; there were still deer in the Gardens, cavalry barracks close to Queen's Gate, and a turnpike at the top of the Gloucester Road. The land upon which South Kensington has since arisen was a region of market gardens, where in our childhood we strolled with our nurse along genuine country lanes.[89]

Continue along Kensington Road to the Palace Gate entrance to **Kensington Gardens,** just opposite the end of **Gloucester Road.** Woolf always remembered an old woman who sold air-balls (balloons) at the Palace Gate entrance to Kensington Gardens. (A second old woman sold nuts and boot-laces at the Queen's Gate entrance to the park, a few steps in the opposite direction along Kensington Road from Hyde Park Gate.) On their daily excursions to Kensington Gardens, the Stephen children would walk to the Palace Gate entrance, up the Broad Walk to the Round Pond, or perhaps along the Flower Walk, often comparing Kensington Gardens to St Ives. Woolf describes the daily routine best:

> Anemones, the blue and purple bunches ... always bring back that quivering mound of air-balls outside the gate of Kensington Gardens.
>
> Then we went up the Broad Walk. The Broad Walk had a peculiar property – when we took our first walk there after coming back from St Ives, we always abused it; it was not a hill at all, we said. By degrees as the weeks passed the hill became steeper and steeper until by the summer it was a hill again. The swamp – as we called the rather derelict ground behind the Flower Walk – had to Adrian and myself at least the glamour of the past on it. When Nessa and Thoby were very small, that is to say, it had been, they told us, a real swamp; they had found the skeleton of a dog there ... and we compared it, of course, with Halestown Bog near St Ives ... It was natural always to compare Kensington Gardens with St Ives, always of course to the disadvantage of London. That was one of the pleasures of scrunching the shells with which now and then the Flower Walk was strewn. They had little ribs on them like the shells on the beach. On the other hand the crocodile tree was itself; and is still there – the tree on the Speke Monument path; which has a great root exposed; and the root is polished, partly by the friction of our hands, for we used to scramble over it.[90]

Enter Kensington Gardens at the **Palace Gate** entrance and walk up the gentle slope of the **Broad Walk** to the **Round Pond.** Woolf remembered vividly 'the great day when my Cornish lugger sailed perfectly to the middle of the [Round] pond [in Kensington Gardens] and then with my eyes upon it, amazed, sank suddenly'. The following spring a man cleaning the pond pulled her lugger up from the bottom. She claimed the boat and ran home, delighted: 'Then my mother made new sails; and my father rigged it, and I remember seeing him fixing the sails to the yard-arm after dinner; and how interested he became and said, with his little snort … "Absurd – what fun it is doing this!" '[91]

After walking around the Round Pond, take the path towards **Lancaster Gate.** (This path runs north-east away from the Round Pond.) Stop at **Speke's Monument,** the red granite obelisk (visible in the distance from the Round Pond) dedicated to the memory of the explorer John Hanning Speke. Then head back south along the **Lancaster Walk,** passing G.F. Watts' statue of 'Physical Energy'. Watts was a family friend and lived with Virginia Stephen's great-aunt at Little Holland House.

From this location, it is a few steps to the **Serpentine** in Hyde Park. Virginia Woolf had vivid memories of 'being walked off my legs round the Serpentine by my father'.[92] For Clarissa Dalloway, the Serpentine recalls a moment of youthful abandon that her later life fails to match. When she hears of Septimus' suicide, Clarissa thinks: 'She had once thrown a shilling into the Serpentine, never anything more. But he had flung it away.'[93]

After walking to the Serpentine, return to the statue of 'Physical Energy', and continue along Lancaster Walk to the **Flower Walk,** which lies at the southern edge of the park, close to Queen's Gate and the Albert Memorial.

SOME OTHER KENSINGTON SITES ASSOCIATED WITH VIRGINIA WOOLF AND THE STEPHEN FAMILY

These sites are more widely scattered, so that a walk past all of them may take forty-five minutes to an hour. The visitor can begin at the Palace Gate entrance to Kensington Gardens.

6 Canning Place

To reach **6 Canning Place,** leave from the **Palace Gate** entrance of Kensington Gardens. Cross **Kensington Road,** and walk south down Palace Gate to **Canning Place.** Turn *right* into **Canning Place.**

6 Canning Place was the home of Clara Pater, Walter Pater's sister. Clara Pater was one of the first people to teach Virginia Stephen Latin and Greek.

After her brother's death, Clara Pater moved to 6 Canning Place. Beginning in 1898, Virginia took 'Miss Paters Intermediate Latin class, on Tuesdays at 2'[94] (offered in the Department for Higher Education for Women of King's College, Kensington); she began private lessons in Greek and Latin with Miss Pater in 1900. Virginia described the interior of Clara Pater's house as 'all blue china, Persian cats, and Morris wallpapers'.[95] Clara Pater was very involved in the cause of women's higher education in the late nineteenth century: she was instrumental in the founding of Oxford's Somerville College for Women in the late 1870s and early 1880s, and served as Somerville's vice-principal and first classics tutor. After her brother died, Clara and her sister moved to Kensington, where Clara Pater gave private lessons whenever their money ran thin. Clara Pater is probably the model for Julia Craye in Woolf's lesbian short story 'Moments of Being: "Slater's Pins Have No Points." '

16 Young Street

Return to **Kensington Road** from Canning Place by turning *right* (north) up **De Vere Gardens**. At Kensington Road, turn *left* (west) and walk past the end of **Kensington Gardens** to **Young Street**. (Kensington Road will become **Kensington High Street**.) At **Young Street**, turn *left* (south).

There is a blue plaque at **16 Young Street**, where William Makepeace Thackeray lived from 1846 to 1854. Leslie Stephen's first wife, Minny Thackeray, grew up here, along with her older sister, the novelist Anne Thackeray Ritchie. (After Thackeray's wife fell ill and was institutionalised, Anny and Minny lived with their grandparents in Paris until they were nine and eight years old respectively. Then they returned from Paris to Thackeray's new home in Young Street.) Thackeray wrote *Vanity Fair* at 16 Young Street; passing by it many years later, he joked to a friend: 'Down on your knees, you rogue, for here *Vanity Fair* was penned, and I will go down with you, for I have a high opinion of that little production myself.'[96]

Thackeray's daughter Anne went on to become a well-known Victorian novelist and was a frequent visitor to Leslie Stephen's home when Virginia was a child. Virginia had great affection for her 'Aunt

Anny', as she was always known. Virginia respected her aunt's stature as a novelist, especially since she knew from an early age that she too wanted to make her living as a writer; Virginia was also charmed by her aunt's great warmth and her eccentric personality. Anne Thackeray Ritchie appears as Mrs Hilberry – the gifted daughter of a famous writer, who can never quite finish her own monumental book – in Virginia Woolf's second novel, *Night and Day* (1919).

King's College, Kensington

Continue along Young Street to **Kensington Square**. The Department for Higher Education for Women of King's College, Kensington – where Virginia Stephen first took classes in Latin and Greek – was formerly located at numbers 11, 12 and 13 Kensington Square. (Number 13, where Virginia Stephen began studying in 1897, has since been replaced by a newer house.)

In 1878, a course of lectures for women was inaugurated at the Vestry Hall in Kensington under the auspices of King's College in the Strand. The lectures were so well attended that a larger hall was taken for the following year (at what is now 9 Hornton Street). In 1885, the King's College Department for Higher Education for Women was founded and housed in a rented building at number 13 Kensington Square. By 1908, the Department needed more space, and was incorporated into the University as King's College for Women, so numbers 11 and 12 Kensington Square were also taken over. Eventually, the entire operation moved to specially built premises on Campden Hill Road, where it still operates under the name of Queen Elizabeth College.[97] Queen Elizabeth College became part of King's College London in 1985.

Virginia Stephen began to study Latin and Greek in the Department for Higher Education for Women in 1897, at the age of fifteen. She worked with Dr George Warr, who was the translator of Aeschylus, and who was one of the founding members of the Department. By 1899, she was taking private lessons in the classics with Clara Pater.

Before leaving Kensington Square, note the blue plaques at number 17 (home of Charles Hubert Parry) and at number 18 (home of John Stuart Mill).

St Mary Abbott's Church

To reach St Mary Abbott's Church, return to **Kensington High Street** from Kensington Square by walking *north* along **Derry Street**. When you reach Kensington High Street, St Mary Abbott's Church will be directly across the road from you, on the north side, where the High Street intersects with **Kensington Church Street.**

Stella Duckworth and Jack Hills were married at St Mary Abbott's Church in 1897. But before the ceremony, Vanessa, Virginia and Adrian attended a service at St Mary Abbott's Church to hear their banns read – a ritual that irritated Virginia so much that she refused to kneel during the two-hour service. Virginia described Stella's wedding ceremony in her diary:

> Jack was there looking quite well and happy. Then at about 2:15 or 30, Stella and father came in – Stella walking in her sleep – her eyes fixed straight in front of her – very white and beautiful – There was a long service – then it was all over – and Stella and Jack were married.[98]

Little Holland House

Little Holland House was torn down in 1875, but it is worth a walk to the Melbury Road area to get a sense of this part of Kensington. To reach **Melbury Road**, continue to walk west along the Kensington High Street from St Mary Abbott's Church. Pass through the Kensington High Street shopping district; pass **Holland Park** and the Commonwealth Institute. Just after the Commonwealth Institute, turn *right* (north) into **Melbury Road**. As you walk up the hill, note the blue plaque commemorating the painter William Holman Hunt at 18 Melbury Road. Virginia also remembered being dragooned into a late night visit to this house with George Duckworth: though George found it to be a 'very *dritte* crowd', he insisted on taking Virginia to the Holman Hunts for 'another lesson in the art of behaviour'.[99] When Virginia entered, she found all their old family friends: the Stillmans, the Lushingtons, the Morrises, the Burne-Joneses. Holman Hunt, however, was so old by this time that he had no notion who anyone was.[100] Continue further up Melbury Road to number 14.

Little Holland House stood roughly on the location of number 14 Melbury Road, which is now a block of flats. Little Holland House was demolished in 1875 to build Melbury Road and thus open the area to more extensive development.

Little Holland House was the home of Virginia Stephen's great aunt, Sarah Prinsep, who moved with her husband to the rambling old farmhouse in 1850. Little Holland House quickly became known for the eclectic mix of politicians, writers, and artists who frequented Sarah Prinsep's 'Sunday afternoons': Gladstone and Disraeli; Thackeray and Tennyson; Holman Hunt, Burne-Jones, Woolner, Ruskin. The painter and sculptor G.F. Watts made his home with the Prinseps at Little Holland House for many years. When Julia Jackson – Virginia Woolf's mother – returned as a child from India with her mother, they lived for a time at Little Holland House. Throughout her life, Julia continued to visit her aunt and uncle there, and as a young woman became enmeshed in its artistic circle. Holman Hunt and Woolner both proposed to Julia; she was the model for the Virgin in Burne-Jones's *Annunciation* of 1879; she posed for a long series of intensely romantic photographs taken by her aunt, the pioneering photographer Julia Margaret Cameron.

The world of Little Holland House always carried an air of elusive, lost beauty for Virginia Woolf. She remembered that 'Once when we were children, my mother took us to Melbury Road; and when we came to the street that had been built on the old garden she gave a little spring forward, clapped her hands, and cried "That was where it was!" as if a fairyland had disappeared.'[101] Woolf herself always thought of Little Holland House as a 'summer afternoon world',[102] and pictured a garden filled with artists and writers, and her mother taking a group of visitors across the flowers to visit Watts in his studio.

6 Melbury Road

After Little Holland House was torn down, the first new house built along Melbury Road – at number 6 – was for G.F. Watts. Watts named his new home 'Little Holland House' in memory of the happy years he had spent with the Prinseps.[103]

From Melbury Road, two underground stations are easily accessible. You can retrace your steps along Kensington High Street to the **Kensington High Street** station. Alternatively, for **Holland Park** station, walk north along **Abbotsbury Road** to Holland Park Avenue; turn *right* (east) at Holland Park Avenue and continue a few blocks to the Holland Park station.

12 Holland Park Road, Leighton House

If you have any energy left, you might first want to make a fast visit to Leighton House. To reach Leighton House from 6 Melbury Road, return along Melbury Road toward the Kensington High Street. Turn *right* (west) into **Holland Park Road**; the Leighton House Art Gallery and Museum will be on your *right*.

Frederic, Baron Leighton of Stretton (1830-1896), President of the Royal Academy and consummate Victorian artist, lived and worked at this location for the last thirty years of his life. Leighton was part of the Little Holland House circle in its early days; he became good friends with the Prinseps' son Val – also an aspiring artist and eventual member of the Royal Academy – and was drawn to the Kensington location to be close to G.F. Watts. After Leighton moved into his new house in Holland Park Road in 1866, it became fashionable for other artists to settle there, and the entire area came to be known colloquially as the 'Leighton Settlement'.[104]

Leighton's home at 12 Holland Park Road is one of the earliest purpose-built studio houses in existence. It is especially notable for its exotic Arab Hall – a spot Woolf visited and much later confused with the setting of the Holman Hunts' home just around the corner.[105]

Leighton House is open Monday to Sunday from 11 a.m. to 5.30 p.m.; it is closed on Tuesdays and Bank Holidays. For more information about opening times, consult the website at: www.aboutbritain.com/leighton-houseartgallery.

A BLOOMSBURY WALKING TOUR

This itinerary provides a walking tour of the squares and houses associated with the Bloomsbury group. Though the Stephen siblings' first Bloomsbury home was at 46 Gordon Square, this itinerary begins in Fitzroy Square. The underground stop closest to Fitzroy Square is Warren Street. (This walking tour should take 1½ to 2 hours – without stops for refreshments.)

107

Fitzroy Square

29 Fitzroy Square

Virginia Stephen lived at 29 Fitzroy Square with her brother Adrian from 1907 to 1911. They vacated 46 Gordon Square so that Vanessa and Clive Bell could take over that house when they married. While living at 29 Fitzroy Square, Virginia Stephen nurtured the journalistic career she had begun in Gordon Square by writing reviews for both the *Times Literary Supplement* and the *Guardian*. She also began to write her first novel, *Melymbrosia*, which was eventually published as *The Voyage Out*. Virginia and Adrian revived the Thursday night gatherings that Thoby had begun at 46 Gordon Square, and a crowd of friends circulated through the house.

Virginia Stephen had the whole second floor of 29 Fitzroy Square to herself. She filled her drawing room with 'great pyramids of books, with trailing mists between them; partly dust, and partly cigarette smoke'.[106] (The cigarettes were also an emblem of Virginia's escape from Hyde Park Gate: in an essay on the centenary of Leslie Stephen's birth, she remarked that her father could 'rebuke a daughter sharply for smoking a cigarette – smoking was not in his opinion a nice habit in the other sex'.[107]) She decorated the room 'like the sea, in flowing purple'.[108] When Violet Dickinson objected to the seediness of the neighbourhood, Virginia defended its charms: 'All the lights in the Square are lighting, and it is turning silver grey, and there are beautiful young women still playing tennis on the grass.'[109] It was in this house that Lytton Strachey proposed to Virginia Stephen – an engagement that lasted a single day, since Virginia thought better of it by the next morning and Lytton had already decided to retract his offer.

Although the move to 29 Fitzroy Square ushered in a new sense of openness amongst the Bloomsbury friends – it was during this period that they began to address each other using first names, and that their talk frequently turned to matters of sex – Virginia often looked back at this period as an unhappy one. She did not particularly enjoy living with Adrian: he depressed her with his need for praise and his open preference for Vanessa. When Virginia and Adrian left Fitzroy Square for Brunswick Square in 1911, she felt that she was making an 'advance towards freedom'.[110]

The blue plaque at 29 Fitzroy Square reads: 'Virginia Stephen (Virginia Woolf), 1882-1941, novelist and critic, lived here 1907-1911'. The former tenants on the second and third floors of 29 Fitzroy Square had been George Bernard Shaw and his mother. A brown plaque commemorates their residence: 'George Bernard Shaw lived in this house from 1887-98. "From the coffers of his genius he enriched the world." '

21 Fitzroy Square

From 1909, Duncan Grant rented two rooms on the second floor of 21 Fitzroy Square to use as his studio. Maynard Keynes (who was having an affair with Duncan Grant at the time) paid the rent and used one of the rooms as his London *pied-à-terre*. During this period, Grant began to wander in and out of Virginia and Adrian's lives and residences. He turned up at 10 p.m. on Thursday evenings for whisky, buns and cocoa; he socialised with Clive and Vanessa Bell, and pronounced Vanessa 'radiant'.[111] But by 1910, Grant was in love with Adrian Stephen and confessed his affection for Adrian to Maynard Keynes. When Keynes came from Cambridge to stay at 21 Fitzroy Square, Grant wasn't always there: he might be staying with Adrian at 29 Fitzroy Square instead. As Keynes put it to Grant in a letter at this time: 'I don't know what to do about staying in London. You're married to Adrian now, which you weren't before.'[112] Nevertheless, both Grant and Keynes moved to Brunswick Square with Virginia and Adrian Stephen in 1911. (The blue plaque at 21 Fitzroy Square commemorates the residence here of Robert Cecil, third Marquis of Salisbury and Prime Minister.)

33 Fitzroy Square

In 1913, Roger Fry opened the Omega Workshops at 33 Fitzroy Square. Its purpose, as he told George Bernard Shaw, was to provide an outlet for the great number of young artists working in London whose work 'shows strong decorative feeling', and who would appreciate the opportunity 'to use their talents on applied art both as a means of livelihood and as an advantage to their work as painters and sculptors'.[113] Vanessa Bell and Duncan Grant were both heavily involved with the Omega

Workshops. They closed in 1919; the location is now occupied by the London Foot Hospital.

Leave Fitzroy Square by the **south-east** corner, walking south along **Fitzroy Street**. **8 Fitzroy Street** was the site of a house (now replaced by an office building) in which Vanessa Bell and Duncan Grant had adjacent studios.

Turn *left* at **Howland Street** and walk east, crossing **Tottenham Court Road**. Turn *right* (south) a short distance along Tottenham Court Road to **Torrington Place**. Turn *left* (east) into Torrington Place. Cross **Gower Street** and continue along Torrington Place to **Gordon Square**.

Detour: Alternatively, you can make a short detour here to walk by the two homes of the literary hostess Lady Ottoline Morrell, at **10 Gower Street** and at **44 Bedford Square**.

To reach **10 Gower Street**, turn *right* (south) down Gower Street from Torrington Place. 10 Gower Street has a blue plaque indicating that the house was once the Morrells' home. They moved back to London, to this address, from Garsington Manor in 1927.

Continue south along Gower Street to **Bedford Square**, which is almost immediately on the right. **44 Bedford Square** was the Morrells' London address twenty years earlier, when Ottoline held her 'Thursday evenings', a practice she began in 1907. Many years later, Woolf concluded that any history of the Bloomsbury group would have to have a chapter devoted to Ottoline Morrell at this period, 'even if it is only the appendix'.[114] In 1908 or 1909, Ottoline swooped down on one of Virginia Stephen's own Thursday evenings in Fitzroy Square, inviting Virginia to bring all her 'wonderful friends' to the grander surroundings of 44 Bedford Square. The following Thursday, Virginia accepted her invitation and took Rupert Brooke. Virginia and her friends were soon swept into 'that extraordinary whirlpool' of Ottoline's society, which included Augustus John, Winston Churchill, and Bertrand Russell.[115] In 1914, Ottoline and her husband, Philip, moved to Garsington Manor, and made it into a haven for artists, writers, and conscientious objectors. Ottoline's Garsington weekends were populated by leading names in the worlds of literature and art: Katherine Mansfield, Henry Lamb, Mark Gertler, T.S. Eliot, W.B. Yeats, Dorothy Brett, D.H. Lawrence, and all the members of the Bloomsbury group. Lawrence eventually caricatured Ottoline as Hermione Roddice in *Women in Love*.

After this detour, walk back up **Gower Street** to **Torrington Place**. Turn *right* (east) into Torrington Place and follow Torrington Place, turning *left* at **Byng Place**, into **Gordon Square**.

Gordon Square

Gordon Square is the 'heart of Bloomsbury' – nearly everyone in the Bloomsbury group lived or worked in Gordon Square at some point. As Lytton Strachey wrote to Virginia Woolf in 1919, when Virginia and Leonard were living in Richmond: 'Very soon I foresee that the whole Square will become a sort of College. And the rencontres in the garden I shudder to think of.'[116]

46 Gordon Square

46 Gordon Square was the house to which the Stephen siblings escaped from the darkness and gloom of 22 Hyde Park Gate. Virginia Stephen's room was at the top of the house, with windows looking out over the huge plane trees in the middle of the square. Virginia evoked the clutter of her room in a letter to Madge Vaughan:

> I wish you could see my room at this moment, on a dark winter's evening – all my beloved leather backed books standing up so handsome in their shelves, and a nice fire, and the electric light burning, and a huge mass of manuscripts and letters and proof-sheets and pens and inks over the floor everywhere. Tomorrow week they will be bad enough for a general clearance; then I start tidy and gradually work myself up into a happy frenzy of litter.[117]

It was from the drawing-room windows of 46 Gordon Square that Virginia Stephen's heart leapt at the sight of London trees, which she associated with the expansive possibilities of Bloomsbury's freedoms – a welcome antidote to the constrictions of 22 Hyde Park Gate, with old Mrs Redgrave washing herself across the way.

Virginia Stephen began to publish reviews while she lived at 46 Gordon Square; it was also at 46 Gordon Square that Thoby Stephen decided to be 'at home' on Thursday nights, thus laying the foundations for the Bloomsbury group.

Virginia and Adrian moved to Fitzroy Square in 1907; Vanessa and Clive Bell continued to live at 46 Gordon Square until 1916. Maynard Keynes took over the lease in 1916, but Clive and Vanessa maintained a set of rooms in the house. Keynes acquired the lease of the neighbouring building, 47 Gordon Square, in 1938. He connected the adjoining first floor rooms of the two houses to create a vast parlour where he often entertained with his wife, the ballerina Lydia Lopokova. The blue plaque on the front of 46 Gordon Square indicates that Keynes lived in the house from 1916 to 1946; the building is now owned by the University of London (Birkbeck College).

37 Gordon Square
Vanessa Bell and Duncan Grant rented rooms at this address.

41 Gordon Square
Leased by James and Alix Strachey, parts of this residence were sublet at various times to Lydia Lopokova, Lytton Strachey, Ralph Partridge and Dora Carrington.[118]

50 Gordon Square
Adrian Stephen and his wife Karin lived in this house, and let rooms to various friends and family members: Vanessa Bell and her children; Clive Bell; Arthur Waley. The brown plaque (London Borough of Camden) at 50 Gordon Square indicates that 'Here and in neighbouring houses during the first half of the 20th century there lived several members of the Bloomsbury group, including Virginia Woolf, Clive Bell, and the Stracheys'.

51 Gordon Square
Lytton Strachey's mother and sisters moved to this address in 1919. The blue plaque on the front of the building reads: 'Lytton Strachey, 1882-1932, biographer and critic, lived here.'
    Leave Gordon Square at the southern end, walking *left* (east) one block to **Tavistock Square.**

Tavistock Square

52 Tavistock Square
Tavistock Square was damaged extensively during World War II; only

one side of the Square still has its original houses. Virginia and Leonard Woolf moved to 52 Tavistock Square in 1924 and lived there for more than fifteen years. Their house was destroyed by German bombs in October 1940; the Tavistock Hotel now stands on the site.

It was at 52 Tavistock Square – and in her garden writing lodge at Monk's House – that Virginia Woolf completed most of her mature work: *Mrs Dalloway*; *To the Lighthouse*; *Orlando*; *The Waves*; *The Years*. One day in 1925, as Woolf walked around Tavistock Square,

> I made up, as I sometimes make up my books, *To the Lighthouse*; in a great, apparently involuntary, rush. One thing burst into another. Blowing bubbles out of a pipe gives the feeling of the rapid crowd of ideas and scenes which blew out of my mind, so that my lips seemed syllabling of their own accord as I walked. What blew the bubbles? When then? I have no notion. But I wrote the book very quickly; and when it was written, I ceased to be obsessed by my mother. I no longer hear her voice; I do not see her. I suppose that I did for myself what psychoanalysts do for their patients. I expressed some very long felt and deeply felt emotion. And in expressing it I explained it and then laid it to rest. But what is the meaning of 'explained' it? Why, because I described her and my feeling for her in that book, should my vision of her and my feeling for her become so much dimmer and weaker? Perhaps one of these I shall hit on the reason; and if so, I will give it.[119]

At 52 Tavistock Square, the Hogarth Press was housed in the basement, which also contained a converted billiard room at the back that became Virginia's study. The Woolfs lived on the top two floors of the house; the intervening two floors were occupied by a firm of solicitors, Dolman and Pritchard. Virginia often sat in the garden in the middle of the square to talk with Vanessa, whose London flat was a short distance away.

Leave Tavistock Square by the **south-east**, walking **south** along **Woburn Place**. Turn *left* (east) at **Bernard Street** and continue along Bernard Street to **Brunswick Square**, passing the Brunswick Shopping Centre, which will be on your left.

Brunswick Square

38 Brunswick Square

There is very little left of the original square. The west side of Brunswick

Square was cleared in the 1970s to make way for the Brunswick Shopping Centre. The School of Pharmacy of the University of London occupies much of the north side of Brunswick Square, and stands on the site of Virginia Stephen's third Bloomsbury house, 38 Brunswick Square. Virginia and Adrian moved there in 1911, taking some of their good friends from Fitzroy Square with them: Maynard Keynes and Duncan Grant occupied the ground floor, which Grant decorated with a large mural of London life. Adrian Stephen lived on the first floor, and Virginia took the second floor. Leonard Woolf was just back from Ceylon and in need of a place to live, so he was invited to take a bedroom and sitting room on the top floor.[120] Though the lease on 38 Brunswick Square was taken in Maynard Keynes' name, the Stephen siblings effectively ran the establishment – a task Virginia handled in an extremely businesslike manner. Each of the tenants purchased daily meals at a fixed rate, and all contributed to the wages for the cook and maid. Virginia collected the rents. While they lived together at 38 Brunswick Square, Leonard Woolf fell in love with Virginia Stephen and proposed marriage.

It was when Virginia decided to move to 38 Brunswick Square that George Duckworth feared for Virginia's virtue, and Vanessa consoled George with the reminder that the Foundling Hospital was just next door to Virginia's new home, in case Virginia needed help with any mistakes she might make. The Foundling Hospital – founded by Thomas Coram in the eighteenth century to provide a haven for children abandoned on London's streets – was demolished in the 1920s and its contents (including paintings by Hogarth) moved to 40 Brunswick Square. 40 Brunswick Square is still occupied by the Coram Family, previously known as the Thomas Coram Foundation for Children.

Virginia Woolf described the atmosphere at 38 Brunswick Square – the last days of what she called 'Old Bloomsbury' – in a talk to the Memoir Club:

> Indeed lustre and illusion tinged Bloomsbury during those last years before the war. We were not so austere; we were not so exalted. There were quarrels and intrigues. Ottoline may have been a Medusa; but she was not a passive Medusa. She had a great gift for drawing people under. Even Middleton Murry, it is said, was pulled down by her among the

vegetables at Garsington. And by this time we were far from drab. Thursday evenings with their silences and their arguments were a thing of the past. Their place was taken by parties of a very different sort. The Post-Impressionist movement had cast – not its shadow – but its bunch of variegated lights upon us. We bought poinsettias made of scarlet plush; we made dresses of the printed cotton that is specially loved by negroes; we dressed ourselves up as Gauguin pictures and careered round Crosby Hall. Mrs Whitehead was scandalized. She said that Vanessa and I were practically naked. My mother's ghost was invoked once more – by Violet Dickinson – to deplore the fact that I had taken a house in Brunswick Square and had asked young men to share it. George Duckworth came all the way from Charles Street to beg Vanessa to make me give up the idea and was not comforted perhaps when she replied that after all the Foundling Hospital was handy. Stories began to circulate about parties at which we all undressed in public. Logan Pearsall Smith told Ethel Sands that he knew for a fact that Maynard had copulated with Vanessa on a sofa in the middle of the drawing room. It was a heartless, immoral, cynical society it was said; we were abandoned women and our friends were the most worthless of young men.

Yet in spite of Logan, in spite of Mrs Whitehead, in spite of Vanessa and Maynard and what they did on the sofa at Brunswick Square, Old Bloomsbury still survives. If you seek a proof – look around.[121]

Virginia and Leonard Woolf left 38 Brunswick Square after their marriage in 1912.

Leave Brunswick Square by its **south-east** corner walking south-east along **Lansdowne Terrace**. Turn *left* (east) on **Guilford Street** and walk to **Mecklenburgh Place**. Turn *left* (north) into Mecklenburgh Place and follow it a few steps into **Mecklenburgh Square**.

Mecklenburgh Square

37 Mecklenburgh Square

Mecklenburgh Square was also badly damaged during the Blitz. The William Goodenough House is now situated on the north side of the square, on the former site of 37 Mecklenburgh Square, the house Virginia and Leonard leased from 1939. During this period, because London was under frequent attack by the Luftwaffe, Leonard and Virginia spent much of their time at Monk's House. During one attack in September 1940, a German time bomb sat unexploded in Mecklenburgh Square for several days, and the area was cordoned off and evacuated. Woolf described the devastation of 37 Mecklenburgh Square in her diary:

> We went to London on Friday. Bomb still unexploded. Not allowed in. Off it went next day. Blew out all windows, all ceilings, and smashed all my china – just as we'd got the flat ready! – oh damn. Uninhabitable now apparently – Press has been moved to Letchworth – What remains of it.[122]

Leave Mecklenburgh Square to the **south**, by way of **Guilford Street**. Proceed *right* (west) along **Guilford Street** to **Russell Square**. It was while she was walking through Russell Square in 1926 that Woolf had one of her experiences of a mystical connection to some abstract and powerfully moving reality, something which, for lack of a better word, she called 'it'.

There is an underground station in Russell Square to return to other parts of London. For one of the sillier dining experiences available in London, you might stop in the Russell Hotel to have a meal at Virginia Woolf's Brasserie. (You will even be given Virginia Woolf's Wine List, which tilts heavily towards American and Chilean vintages.) But if you have any energy left – and prefer more atmospheric surroundings for a meal – continue through Russell Square and follow the signs to the **British Museum**, one of Woolf's favourite destinations when she lived in Bloomsbury.

British Museum Reading Room
Woolf used the Reading Room at the British Museum frequently. In fact, one of the things she disliked most intensely about living in suburban Richmond was the fact that she couldn't dash from her house into the British Museum (or the London Library in St James's Square) to look up a book. Woolf was impressed by the famous writers whose names then circled the great dome of the Reading Room. She was equally impressed by the chill dignity and impersonality of the place, a haven for industrious scribblers who believed in the necessity of making books:

> ... I to the Brit[ish] Mus[eum]; where all was chill serenity, dignity and severity. Written up are the names of great men; and we all cower like mice nibbling crumbs in our most official discreet impersonal mood beneath. I like this dusty bookish atmosphere. Most of the readers seemed to have rubbed their noses off and written their eyes out. Yet they

have a life they like – believe in the necessity of making books, I suppose; verify, collate, make up other books, forever.[123]

When Woolf described the Reading Room and its vast dome, she usually pictured it as a great, impersonal mind. In *A Room of One's Own*, for example, the narrator enters the Reading Room and feels she has become a thought in a huge mind: 'The swing-doors swung open; and there one stood under the vast dome, as if one were a thought in the huge bald forehead which is so splendidly encircled by a band of famous names.'[124] The narrator in *Jacob's Room* also describes the Reading Room as an enormous mind, but sees it as a repository hoarding more knowledge than any single mind could hope to encompass:

> There is in the British Museum an enormous mind. Consider that Plato is there cheek by jowl with Aristotle; and Shakespeare with Marlowe. This great mind is hoarded beyond the power of any single mind to possess it. Nevertheless (as they take so long finding one's walking-stick) one can't help thinking how one might come with a notebook, sit at a desk, and read it all through.[125]

The names of famous writers and thinkers no longer encircle the dome of the British Museum's Reading Room. It was recently restored and is now located in the newly opened Queen Elizabeth II Great Court. (The Great Court is a lovely covered square at the heart of the British Museum; this space was inaccessible to visitors for a hundred and fifty years, until it was opened to the public in December 2000.) The gilt names that Woolf so often described were not re-inscribed at the bottom of the dome during the renovation. Those names had been added to the dome during a twentieth-century renovation, in 1907.[126] In fact, Miss Julia Hedge, a female reader who visits the Reading Room in *Jacob's Room*, wonders why the great dome lists no women writers:

> Not so very long ago the workmen had gilt the final 'y' in Lord Macaulay's name, and the names stretched in unbroken file round the dome of the British Museum ... Miss Julia Hedge, the feminist, waited for her books. They did not come. She wetted her pen. She looked about her. Her eye was caught by the final letters in Lord Macaulay's name. And she read them all round the dome – the names of great men which remind us – 'Oh damn,' said Julia Hedge. 'why didn't they leave room for an Eliot or a Brontë?'[127]

When the Reading Room was restored, this same question vexed the committee guiding the restoration: why were there no women writers? Why had no room been left for an Eliot or a Brontë?[128] But since the decision had already been taken to restore the Reading Room to its original 1857 decorative design, the gilt names of all writers had to be removed anyway. The Reading Room is now a public access reference room and has been renamed the Walter and Leonore Annenberg Centre. The Reading Room houses a small display detailing its history, along with a collection of books written by eminent authors who read and researched there – including material on Virginia Woolf.

Refreshments are available in two spots: at a self-service restaurant in the Great Court, and in an elegant but affordable restaurant (The Court Restaurant) located up a flight of stairs.

The Bloomsbury Workshop

The Bloomsbury Workshop is a small art gallery and bookshop specialising in Bloomsbury books and pictures. It is located just a few steps from the British Museum, at 12 Galen Place (off Bury Place). (The Bloomsbury Workshop will move in March 2002 to 5 Pied Bull Court, just across the courtyard; from that date, it will be open by appointment only.) Phone 020 7405 0632 for details, or check the website at www.bloomsburyworkshop.com.

FARTHER AFIELD

Richmond Upon Thames

Virginia and Leonard Woolf lived in Richmond upon Thames, in suburban London, from October 1914 to March 1924. They left central London because Virginia's doctors (and Leonard) thought a quieter place would aid Virginia's recovery from the mental collapse that began in 1913. Leonard chose Richmond for its beauty, and probably also for the fact that it was not too distant from his widowed mother, who lived in Putney.

How to get there

Richmond is the last stop – just after Kew Gardens – on the Richmond branch of the District line underground. The District Line stops at various central locations – South Kensington, Sloane Square, Embankment – but the traveller should be careful to change at Earl's Court, if necessary, to get the correct train to Richmond.

17 The Green

From October 1914 to March 1915, Leonard and Virginia lodged at 17 The Green with a Belgian landlady called Mrs le Grys. They had a large first-floor drawing room that overlooked the Green itself. Both Leonard and Virginia were amused by Mrs le Grys, whom Leonard described as 'an extremely nice, plump, excitable flibbertigibbet, about 35 to 40 years old'.[129] Virginia seemed to be recovering well from her mental collapse and had begun to write again. But then, as Leonard describes it, 'one morning she was having breakfast in bed and I was talking to her when without warning she became violently excited and distressed. She thought her mother was in the room and began to talk to her. It was the beginning of the terrifying second stage of her mental break-down.'[130] Leonard had already negotiated a lease for Hogarth House and they moved the next month.

17 The Green is little changed from the days when Virginia and Leonard Woolf lodged there, except for the tradesman's entrance that now occupies one of the ground-floor windows.

How to get there

Leave the Richmond station and walk *left* (south-west) along **Kew Road**, whose name changes first to the **Quadrant**, and then to **George Street**. At the **Square**, turn *right* into **Duke Street**, and then *left* along **The Green**. (If you miss the Duke Street turning and walk all the way to King Street, simply follow the signs along King Street to The Green. Coming from this direction, 17 The Green will be on your right.)

Hogarth House

The Woolfs lived in Hogarth House from 1 April 1915 to 13 March 1924. At the beginning of this period, Virginia was acutely ill, and had to be watched around the clock by a team of four nurses. As Leonard described it, the first fortnight was terrifying. Virginia was at first violent with the nurses; then the violence subsided but she began to talk incessantly, sometimes not stopping for two or three days at a time. At first the grammar of her sentences made sense, although what she said had little relation to reality. But then she became completely incoherent, uttering a stream of dissociated words, until she slipped into a coma.[131]

If Leonard remembered the mania of Virginia's language during this period of her illness, Virginia herself remembered the hallucinations. Like Septimus Warren Smith in *Mrs Dalloway*, Woolf heard the voices of the dead. Just before they moved from Richmond back to London, Virginia recalled the terrifying visions that visited her at Hogarth House:

> I've had some very curious visions in this room too, lying in bed, mad, & seeing the sunlight quivering like gold water, on the wall. I've heard the voices of the dead here.[132]

But Woolf also wrote that she felt 'exquisitely happy' at Hogarth House, and realised that the place suited them perfectly for the years she and Leonard lived there. She knew that 'nowhere else could we have started the Hogarth Press, whose very awkward beginning had rise in this very room, on this very green carpet'. She also knew that Richmond had provided her with a refuge from the violence of the war years in London, when 'aeroplanes were over London at night, & the streets were dark, & no penny buns in the window'.[133]

While she lived at Hogarth House, Woolf wrote her second novel, *Night and Day*, and her first experimental short fictions: *Kew Gardens*, *The Mark on the Wall*, *Monday or Tuesday*. She also 'made up *Jacob's Room* looking at the fire at Hogarth House'[134] and began to write *Mrs Dalloway*.

Hogarth House was built in 1720 by Lord Suffield. In the nineteenth century, the property was sold and divided. One half retained the name Suffield House, while the right-hand half was renamed Hogarth House. Leonard and Virginia fell in love with Hogarth House as soon as they saw it: as Leonard remembered, every room of the house (save one) was perfectly proportioned and panelled; the house had a lovely garden. When the clouds didn't veil the horizon, Woolf could look through the rear windows of Hogarth House to see the trees at Kew and Sir William Chambers' ten-storey pagoda.[135]

Hogarth House now contains offices on the basement, ground and upper floors, but it is still possible to imagine how lovely the Georgian building was when the Woolfs lived there. There is a blue plaque on the house with this inscription: 'In this house Leonard and Virginia Woolf lived 1915-24 and founded the Hogarth Press 1917.'

How to get there
From 17 The Green, return a few steps to **Brewer's Lane**. Turn *right* into Brewer's Lane; cross **George Street** into **Victoria Place**, a few steps to the *right* along George Street. At the end of Victoria Place, turn *left* into **Paradise Road**. Hogarth House is a short walk along Paradise Road, at number 34.

Kew Gardens
If you plan a full day's excursion into Richmond, you might alight at **Kew Gardens** on the way back into central London. Woolf often visited Kew while she lived in Richmond and after she moved back to central London. On at least one occasion, she spent a long afternoon with Vita Sackville-West at Kew Gardens – on the same day Vita gave Virginia driving lessons in Richmond Park. While at Kew, take a closer look at Sir William Chambers' pagoda (interior not open to the public) and visit the Marianne North Gallery, which contains North's beautiful flower paintings. Marianne North visited Woolf's great-aunt Julia Cameron in Sri Lanka, and Woolf wrote a humorous account of their encounter for her introduction to *Victorian Photographs of Famous Men and Fair Women*. (In Woolf's account, North complains because Mrs Cameron, having decided to photograph her, 'made me stand with spiky coconut branches running into my head ... and told me to look perfectly natural'.[136]) Visit the Duke's Garden, perhaps pausing there for an atmospheric reading of *Kew Gardens*, which Woolf wrote while living in Hogarth House.

OTHER SITES OF INTEREST

The British Library at St Pancras
Those interested in Virginia Woolf might want to make a fast visit to the British Library at its new St Pancras location. The John Ritblat Gallery

is open to the public and displays some of the treasures collected by the British Library since its founding. The visitor can view the *Magna Carta* (1215), the *Gutenberg Bible* (1455), Shakespeare's *First Folio* (1623), and other documents in the handwriting of Leonardo da Vinci, Jane Austen, Lewis Carroll and others. Two items are of particular interest. The exhibit includes a short extract from the only recording of Virginia Woolf's voice – a selection from a talk on 'Craftsmanship' she gave for the BBC on 29 April 1937. Nearby is a page from Woolf's corrected typescript of *Moments of Being*, highlighting a section in which she describes her father, Sir Leslie Stephen.

How to get there
The British Library is next to St Pancras railway station, and within walking distance of King's Cross and Euston railway stations. The nearest underground stops are King's Cross St Pancras, Euston and Euston Square. Bus routes 10, 30, 73 and 91 also pass the building. The public access areas are open on Monday, Wednesday, Thursday and Friday from 9.30 a.m. to 6 p.m.; Tuesday from 9.30 a.m. to 8 p.m.; Saturday from 9.30 a.m. to 5 p.m.; Sunday and Bank Holidays from 11 a.m. to 5 p.m. More information is available at the British Library's website at www.bl.uk, and at the website of the Virginia Woolf Society of Great Britain at www.orlando.jp.org/vwsgb/dat/material. The Virginia Woolf Society's website also contains Stuart Clarke's excellent overview of Virginia Woolf's broadcasts with the BBC.

National Portrait Gallery
The National Portrait Gallery houses a rich collection of portraits encapsulating the nation's history. Those interested in Virginia Woolf and the Bloomsbury group should be sure to visit the two rooms devoted to the early twentieth century (located on the Gallery's first floor). The National Portrait Gallery owns a wide array of Bloomsbury portraits, most of which were painted by Bloomsbury artists: Saxon Sydney-Turner painted by Vanessa Bell; Virginia Woolf painted by Vanessa Bell; Lytton Strachey painted by Dora Carrington; Desmond MacCarthy painted by Duncan Grant; Leonard Woolf painted by Vanessa Bell; Vanessa Bell painted by Duncan Grant; Clive Bell painted by Roger Fry, and so on.

There are also portraits of James Joyce, D.H. Lawrence and T.S. Eliot hanging nearby. The portraits offer an intimate glimpse into the faces of the Bloomsbury group, and open a window onto the artistic innovations of the artists in the group – artistic innovations in some cases similar to Lily Briscoe's idiosyncratic style in *To the Lighthouse*.

How to get there

The National Portrait Gallery is in St Martin's Place, just north of Trafalgar Square, opposite the church of St Martin-in-the-Fields. The nearest railway station is Charing Cross; the nearest underground stations are Leicester Square and Charing Cross. The Gallery is open on Monday, Tuesday, Wednesday, Saturday and Sunday from 10 a.m. to 6 p.m.; and on Thursday and Friday from 10 a.m. to 9 p.m. It is closed on New Year's Day, Good Friday, and 24-26 December. More information is available at the National Portrait Gallery's website at www.npg.org.uk.

Elizabeth Dalloway's Bus Ride

After leaving the National Portrait Gallery, one can walk south across Trafalgar Square to the Strand. In the Strand, board a bus heading east to Chancery Lane.

This path is the second half of Elizabeth Dalloway's ride on the top of a London omnibus. Elizabeth begins her morning by visiting the Army and Navy Stores with Doris Kilman. Elizabeth and Miss Kilman have tea; then Elizabeth boards a bus in Victoria Street – the number 11 bus – and rides on the top deck up Whitehall, along the Strand, past Somerset House and to the bottom of Chancery Lane, where she gets off. As Elizabeth rides the bus, freed from the oppressive weight of Miss Kilman's presence, her spirits soar and the bus becomes an impetuous pirate:

> Suddenly Elizabeth stepped forward and most competently boarded the omnibus, in front of everybody. She took a seat on top. The impetuous creature – a pirate – started forward, sprang away; she had to hold the rail to steady herself, for a pirate it was, reckless, unscrupulous, bearing down ruthlessly, circumventing dangerously, boldly snatching a passenger, or ignoring a passenger, squeezing eel-like and arrogant in between, and then rushing insolently all sails spread up Whitehall ... She was delighted to be free. The fresh air was so delicious.[137]

123

When Elizabeth gets off the bus in Chancery Lane, she thinks how different the City is from Westminster, and the surroundings – 'so serious ... so busy' – make her decide to take up a profession: 'She would become a doctor, a farmer, possibly go into Parliament, if she found it necessary, all because of the Strand.'[138] Then Elizabeth walks in the Temple, looks at the river, walks part of the way to St Paul's along Fleet Street (feeling like a pioneer), and eventually boards the Westminster bus heading towards home.

This part of the City – the area of Chancery Lane and Fleet Street – was the spot where Virginia and Leonard Woolf settled immediately after their marriage. Their first lodgings were at 13 Clifford's Inn, between Chancery Lane and Fetter Lane. (The building was demolished in 1934 and has been replaced by offices and flats also called Clifford's Inn.) Leonard Woolf remembered how they loved the bustle of City life in their first home together, and the sense of antiquity and continuity the location afforded them. They dined every night in the Cock Tavern:

> Every night we crossed Fleet Street and dined at the Cock Tavern. The Cock still remembered Tennyson; it had in its furniture and its food an air and flavour of considerable antiquity. It was a real old city eating house. One sat in wooden partitions and at night it was always pretty empty, only journalists from the dailies and lawyers from the Temple dropping in until quite late. Henry was a vintage head waiter, belonging to an era and tradition which, even in 1912, one felt was passing. Large, white faced, redheaded, he was incredibly solemn, slow, unruffled. It was a great day when at last he recognized one as a 'regular'. He would greet one with the ghost of the shadow of a smile, and, as one sat down, he would whisper confidentially: 'I can recommend the devilled bone tonight, Sir,' or: 'I am afraid I can't recommend the steak and kidney pudding tonight, Sir; it's not *quite* as good as usual.'[139]

The Cock Tavern – now called Ye Olde Cock Tavern – is located at 22 Fleet Street (phone: 020 7353 8570). Although interior renovations have been done, it is still a convenient spot for refreshments after this excursion. The Cock Tavern is open Monday to Friday, but closed at the weekends.

Highgate Cemetery
The Stephen family graves, including those of Julia Stephen, Leslie Stephen, Thoby Stephen and Stella Duckworth Hills, are located in the

eastern part of Highgate Cemetery, in north London. Highgate Cemetery also contains the grave of Karl Marx – a place of pilgrimage for visitors from around the world – and the graves of Herbert Spencer, George Eliot (as Mary Ann Cross), and a number of other important literary figures.

The Stephen family graves are located fairly close to the gates of the cemetery, and have recently been restored by the Virginia Woolf Society of Great Britain. Julia Stephen was buried here in 1895, at a brief ceremony that none of her children attended. Stella Duckworth Hills was buried next to her mother two years later. When Sir Leslie Stephen died in 1904, his children buried his ashes in his wife's grave. And when Thoby Stephen died in 1906, at the tragically young age of twenty-six, his ashes were buried here next to his parents too.[140]

How to get there
The East Cemetery at Highgate Cemetery is located in Swain's Lane, Highgate. The nearest underground station is Archway; the visitor can also take bus number 143, 210, or 271 to Lauderdale House, and then walk through Waterlow Park.

The cemetery opens weekdays at 10 a.m. (weekends at 11 a.m.), and closes at 5 p.m. (4 p.m. in winter) There is an admission charge of £1, and an additional £1 fee to take photographs. Maps are usually available at the cemetery's entrance. More information about Highgate Cemetery is available on 020 8340 1834. More information about the Stephen family gravesite is available in Vanessa Curtis's essay on the website of the Virginia Woolf Society of Great Britain at www.jp.org/vwsgb/dat/material.

CHAPTER THREE

Vita, Virginia, Knole and *Orlando*

'But what I was going to say was to beg for more illusions. I can assure
you, if you'll make me up, I'll make you.'
Virginia Woolf to Vita Sackville-West, 23 September 1925

'If I saw you would you kiss me? If I were in bed would you … '
Virginia Woolf to Vita Sackville-West, 5 December 1927

I

Virginia Woolf and Vita Sackville-West met at a dinner party given by
Clive Bell on 14 December 1922. It was not an auspicious beginning.
Vita neglected to mention the event in her diary; Virginia described Vita
in hers as 'florid, moustached, parakeet coloured'[1] – and even lacking
in artistic wit. Virginia instantly admired Vita's aristocratic bearing and
self-possession, but also noted that Vita was 'inclined to double chin'.
Little about their first meeting indicated how pivotal Virginia and Vita
would become to each other over the next ten years and, indeed, for the
rest of their lives. They soon became friends and publishing partners.
Then, smitten by curiosity and mutual affection, they rapidly developed
into confidantes. By December 1925, three years after their first

encounter, they had become lovers. The relationship changed both their lives, inspired two novels, and turned Knole – the largest country house in England – into a symbol of historical continuity and the androgynous literary imagination.

When Virginia and Vita first met, Vita was already a best-selling author. Her first novel had been published in 1919 to ecstatic reviews – one critic gushed 'we wish that all first novels were like Miss Sackville-West's'. In 1921, Vita's *The Dragon in Shallow Waters* appeared in first place – above D.H. Lawrence's *Women in Love* – in the 'Best-Sellers' column of *John O'London's Weekly*. Then Vita's *The Heir* appeared in 1922 and sold fourteen hundred copies in its first two weeks of publication. Virginia's *Jacob's Room* was published in the same year; it sold fourteen hundred copies in eighteen months.[2]

Because of Vita's wide popularity with readers, Leonard and Virginia Woolf were both eager to engage her talents. Leonard enlisted Vita first, asking her to write reviews for the *Nation & Athenaeum*, whose literary pages Leonard edited. Virginia then invited Vita to contribute a book to the Hogarth Press. Vita responded by writing *Seducers in Ecuador* in two weeks while on a walking tour with her husband in the Dolomites. When *Seducers in Ecuador* was reviewed by the *New York Evening Post* in 1925, the notice appeared on the same page as the paper's review of *Mrs Dalloway*. *Seducers in Ecuador* got top billing, with a languorous line drawing of its author and fulsome praise. At the bottom of the page, *Mrs Dalloway* was received more coolly, condemned for its 'dull and drear' fog of words and its 'sensitively realised redundancies'.[3]

But Virginia and Vita both regarded their respective literary talents very differently from either the book-buying audience or the *New York Evening Post*'s critics. Vita was awed by Virginia's prodigious creativity and her ability to write shimmering, lyrical prose; she admired Virginia's wicked wit and sharp intellect – she once said that, when Virginia talked, she could feel her intellectual 'muscles hardening'.[4] For her part, Virginia thought that Vita wrote with 'complete competency, and a pen of brass'.[5] Virginia said that Vita had a 'heart of gold, and a mind which, if slow, works doggedly; and has its moments of lucidity'.[6] (Leonard Woolf agreed with Virginia about

Vita's literary powers. Describing contemporary bestsellers, he said they were written by 'second-class writers whose psychological brew contains a touch of naivety, a touch of sentimentality, the story-telling gift, and a mysterious sympathy with the day-dreams of ordinary people. Vita was very nearly a best-seller of this kind'.)[7] But when Vita dedicated *Seducers in Ecuador* to her, Virginia was seduced by the gesture and responded with 'childlike dazzled affection'.[8] The two women exchanged books, letters, visits, secrets. By the summer of 1925, they had become intimate friends, intimate enough for Virginia to write flirtatiously to Vita: 'I have a perfectly romantic and no doubt untrue vision of you in my mind – stamping out the hops in a great vat in Kent – stark naked, brown as a satyr, and very beautiful. Don't tell me this is all illusion.'[9]

Vita and Virginia were utterly different creatures, and in that difference lay the heart of their mutual attraction. Virginia loved Vita's competence and self-assurance, her ability to drive cars, organise servants, make speeches, take control. She was also enchanted by the glamour of Vita's ancestry and social rank. Vita had 'her hand on all the ropes';[10] she was bold and unselfconscious; she spoke with 'a note in her voice that the Sackvilles ... were using to serfs in Kent 600 years ago, or even Normandy 300 years before that'.[11] Vita grew up at Knole, the largest country house in England; her ancestor Sir Thomas Sackville was the treasurer to Queen Elizabeth and delivered the death sentence to Mary, Queen of Scots. Vita's ancestors had been great literary patrons – Charles, the sixth Earl of Dorset, once left a hundred-pound note for Dryden under a plate at Knole; Vita might casually fish a letter from Boswell from an ancient desk. Vita was convinced that Shakespeare had connections with Knole, and that Thackeray based the character of Lord Steyne in *Vanity Fair* on her ancestor, the Duke of Dorset.

There was also, of course, Vita's sultry beauty. Virginia adored her legs: 'Oh they are exquisite – running like slender pillars up into her trunk, which is that of a breastless cuirassier ... all about her is ... savage, patrician.'[12] Vita was large-lipped and handsome; she had 'the body and brain of a Greek God'.[13] She was dusky, sensual, volcanically passionate. And she was known for her love affairs with women.

For her part, Vita was first interested in Virginia for her distinguished literary reputation, but she quickly found herself entranced in every other way. There was Virginia's eccentricity and extravagant humour. Virginia was hilarious; her jokes made Vita roar with laughter. Vita's conversations with Virginia were always stimulating, sometimes intimidating: when Virginia spoke, Vita felt as though 'the edge of my mind were being held against a grindstone'.[14] But more than anything, Vita was drawn by Virginia's vulnerability – her fragility and her fear of madness. Virginia inspired in Vita 'a feeling of tenderness which I suppose is because of her funny mixture of hardness and softness – the hardness of her mind, and her terror of going mad again.'[15] Even though Virginia was ten years older than Vita, Virginia excited all Vita's maternal instincts. Vita told her husband that Virginia was 'very, very sweet, and I feel extraordinarily protective towards her. The combination of that brilliant brain and that fragile body is very lovable – so independent in all mental ways, so dependent in all practical ways.'[16]

Their friendship might have remained a mere flirtation. But during the summer and autumn of 1925, two events occurred. Virginia became ill, suffering from recurrent bouts of headache and exhaustion. Then in September, Harold Nicolson, Vita's husband, was assigned to the British Legation in Tehran, and Vita agreed to leave England to be with him. Virginia's vulnerability combined with Vita's imminent departure to draw them yet closer together, and Virginia saw that 'if I do not see her now, I shall not – ever: for the moment for intimacy will be gone, next summer'.[17] At Leonard's urging, Virginia wrote to Vita and invited herself down to Long Barn, Vita's house in the country. As Virginia left, Leonard gave her a note to carry to Vita: 'I enclose Virginia & hope she will behave.'[18] She arrived on 17 December for a three-day stay. The second day Vita and Virginia shopped in Sevenoaks. The second night they saw the new moon from the garden and talked until three in the morning – intimately and amorously. That night their affair began in Vita's sitting-room, as Virginia lay on the couch in front of the fire.

Vita was elated and claimed credit for their mutual seduction: 'How right I was ... to force myself on you at Richmond and so lay the train for the explosion which happened on the sofa in my room here where you behaved so disgracefully and acquired me for ever.'[19] Virginia felt both exhilaration and fear, a premonition of the pain their relationship might bring them both. She later reminded Vita of 'that night you were snared, that winter, at Long Barn, you slipped out Lord Steyne's paper knife, and I had then to make the terms plain: with this knife you will gash our hearts I said.'[20]

But Virginia recorded a different set of feelings in her diary as soon as she returned home from Long Barn, feelings that dominated in her love for Vita:

> But Vita for 3 days at Long Barn, from which L[eonard] & I returned yesterday. These Sapphists *love* women; friendship is never untinged with amorosity ... I like her & being with her, & the splendour – she shines in the grocers shop in Sevenoaks with a candle lit radiance, stalking on legs like beech trees, pink glowing, grape clustered, pearl hung. That is the secret of her glamour, I suppose ... What is the effect of all this on me? Very mixed. There is her maturity & full breastedness: her being so much in full sail on the high tides, where I am coasting down backwaters; her capacity I mean to take the floor in any company, to represent her country, to visit Chatsworth, to control silver, servants, chow dogs; her motherhood ... her being in short (what I have never been) a real woman. Then there is some voluptuousness about her; the grapes are ripe; & not reflective. No. In brain & insight she is not as highly organised as I am. But then she is aware of this, & so lavishes on me the maternal protection which, for some reason, is what I have always most wished from everyone. What L. gives me, & Nessa gives me, & Vita, in her more clumsy external way, tries to give me. For of course, mingled with all this glamour, grape clusters & pearl necklaces, there is something loose fitting. How much, for example, shall I really miss her when she is motoring across the desert?[21]

Virginia's rumination records an image of Vita that, three years later, finds full expression in *Orlando*: Vita's passion, her voluptuousness, her self-assurance, her gorgeous legs and pearls. And Virginia's rumination also records why, next to Vanessa and Leonard, Vita occupied such a central place in Virginia's life – because she answered Virginia's desire for 'maternal protection'. Over the next two and a half years, Vita and Virginia maintained a passionate friendship, sleeping together perhaps a dozen times, discussing literature, corresponding teasingly when they

131

were apart, conjuring up in their letters romantic and tender versions of each other.

Vita departed for Persia on 20 January 1926. She went to Tavistock Square to say good-bye, and left Virginia 'standing on her doorstep in the misty London evening'.[22] Vita wrote to Virginia a few hours later, in the train on the way to Dover. Then, the next day, she wrote from Milan and Trieste that 'I am reduced to a thing that wants Virginia. I composed a beautiful letter to you in the sleepless nightmare hours of the night, and it has all gone: I just miss you, in a quite simple desperate human way.'[23] Virginia wrote back, portraying herself in the animal imagery she characteristically used with Leonard and Vanessa, the most beloved people in her life: 'Open the top button of your jersey and you will see, nestling inside, a lively squirrel, with the most inquisitive habits, but a dear creature all the same.'[24] Virginia turned Vita into affectionate and charming creatures, too: she became Virginia's 'dearest shaggy creature', her 'Towser', her 'Emperor moth'.[25] But Virginia also wanted Vita to 'make her up'. When Vita complained that Virginia masked her feelings in 'lovely phrases', Virginia protested and pleaded: 'I'm not cold; not a humbug; not weakly; not sentimental. What I am; I want you to tell me.'[26]

Vita responded that she wanted to steal Virginia away – 'steal her, take her away, and put her in the sun' of Luxor.[27] She wrote that she suffered from a 'terrible and chronic homesickness' for Virginia, and 'I miss you oh so much. How much, you'll never believe or know. At every moment of the day.'[28] In the meantime, when Virginia saw a crocus in the square, she thought 'May: Vita',[29] and laid plans for Vita's return: 'I want to take you over the water meadows in the summer on foot, I have thought of many million things to tell you … Yes, dearest Vita: I do miss you; I think of you: I have a million things, not so much to say, as to sink into you.'[30]

While Vita was in Persia, Virginia wrote at full gallop on *To the Lighthouse*, pouring some of the eroticism she felt towards Vita into her portrait of Lily Briscoe's daughterly, passionate attachment to Mrs Ramsay. Vita reworked her poem *The Land*, incorporating some of Virginia's suggestions. When Vita returned from Persia, their affair entered its most intense phase. On Vita's first overnight visit to Monk's

House, Virginia insisted, 'You have written enough, let us now talk about copulation'.[31] By November, Vita had begun to enclose her private notes to Virginia inside less revealing letters, so that Virginia could show them to Leonard. They met often at Tavistock Square, in Virginia's basement writing room, where Vita sat on the floor in the twilight as Virginia rumpled her hair. On one occasion, when Virginia was close to finishing *To the Lighthouse*, she talked to Vita about death:

> 'The one experience I shall never describe' I said to Vita yesterday. She was sitting on the floor in her velvet jacket & red striped silk shirt, I knotting her pearls into heaps of great lustrous eggs. She had come up to see me – so we go on – a spirited, creditable affair, I think, innocent (spiritually) & all gain, I think.[32]

Then, just before Vita was scheduled to return to Persia with Harold a second time, she insisted that Virginia spend the night with her at Knole, 'my last treat before going away'.[33] Virginia had visited Knole once before and had been completely unimpressed: the extremities and inward parts of the house had gone dead, she said; the chairs and pictures looked preserved – 'life has left them'. It seemed immoral that a solitary lord should sit alone at the centre of that vast building, since Knole was 'capable of housing all the desperate poor of Judd Street'.[34] And the architecture of the house wasn't even very attractive: 'too little conscious beauty for my taste: smallish rooms looking onto buildings: no views.'[35] Virginia made excuses to avoid a second visit, preferring to meet Vita at Long Barn or Tavistock Square. But she finally capitulated when it became clear that this was one of Vita's 'moonlight, romantic, stags barking, old man feeding them from a bucket in the snow, ideas'.[36] To secure just the right room for Virginia, Vita 'lied shamelessly ... bribed the housekeeper, suborned the housemaids'.[37] And Vita promised Virginia that they could be alone together practically the entire day.

When Vita departed for Persia the second time, on 28 January 1927, the letters she exchanged with Virginia were even more passionate. Vita begged Virginia to 'put "honey" when you write.'[38] Virginia immediately wrote back 'Dearest honey, are you well and happy ... and do you ever think of the basement'[39] and 'dearest honey ... Yes yes yes I do like you. I am afraid to write the stronger word'.[40] Vita implored Virginia to meet her in Greece as she journeyed home from Tehran, to make their absence from each other shorter; Virginia hatched plans for them to holiday together in Italy in October, and pleaded for facts she could use to keep 'making up stories about you': 'Do send me a heap of facts: you know how I love a fact: ... upon which I can build pinnacles and pagodas.'[41] Virginia said that she was 'settling down to wanting you, doggedly, dismally, faithfully'[42] and promised 'You shall ruffle my hair in May, Honey'.[43] Vita longed for their reunion at Long Barn in May, too, 'when the nightingales sing outside in the thorn bush and the irises come into flower in the night between sunset and sunrise'.[44]

Vita returned to England for good on 5 May 1927, the day *To the Lighthouse* was published. When she got to Long Barn, she found a copy of the novel, which Virginia had inscribed, 'In my opinion the best novel I have ever written'. When Vita opened it, all the pages were blank. They went up to Oxford together where Virginia was scheduled to give a lecture on 18 May. Virginia lovingly pictured Vita as 'a willow tree; so dashing, on her long white legs' and hoped for 'nightingales, moons, and love'.[45] In June, Virginia went to see Vita awarded the Hawthornden Prize, for the best literary production of 1926; she also wrote to Vita that 'I'd like 3 days doing nothing but eat and sleep at Long Barn more than anything. An occasional kiss on waking and between meals.'[46] Writing from a friend's house party a few days later, Vita threatened to drive to Sussex to wake Virginia in the middle of the night:

Do you know what I should do, if you were not a person to be rather strict with? I should steal my own motor out of the garage at 10 p.m. tomorrow night, be at Rodmell by 11.5 (yes, darling: I did a record on Friday, getting from Lewes to Long Barn in an hour and 7 minutes,) throw gravel at your window, then you'd come down and let me in; I'd stay with you till 5. and be home by half past six. But, you being you, I can't; more's the pity. Have you read my book? Challenge, I mean? Perhaps I sowed all my wild oats then. Yet I don't feel that the impulse has left me; no, by God; and for a different Virginia I'd fly to Sussex in the night.[47]

Virginia's reply was a pointed telegram: 'Come then.'[48]

But Vita did not come. In the summer of 1927, Vita's attentions began to wander. Vita had admitted to Harold much earlier that she was 'scared to death of arousing physical feelings in [Virginia], because of the madness. I don't know what effect it would have, you see.'[49] Harold saw the danger too, saying that Vita's affair with Virginia was '*such a powder magazine*':[50] 'It's not merely playing with fire; it's playing with gelignite.'[51] For all their intimacy, Vita had intermittently accused Virginia of being a 'cold fish': Virginia looked on their relationship as copy, she said, and kept 'so much of yourself up your sleeve'.[52] Though Virginia resented being told she had 'the cold heart of a fish',[53] she admitted that she sometimes maintained a protective distance: 'But you dont see, donkey West, that you'll be tired of me one of these days (I'm so much older) and so I have to take my little precautions. Thats why I put the emphasis on "recording" rather than feeling.'[54]

More than anything, Vita had come back from Persia charged with sexual vitality, longing for an escapade. Virginia was not immediately available. Vita found her unwell, 'incredibly lovely and fragile on two chairs under a gold cloak'.[55] Vita had a one-night fling with Mary Hutchinson, Clive Bell's estranged lover. When Vita confessed, Virginia wrote a jealous note of warning: 'Bad, wicked beast! To think of sporting with oysters – lethargic glucous lipped oysters, lewd lascivious oysters, stationary cold oysters … You only be a careful dolphin in your gambolling, or you'll find Virginia's soft crevices lined with hooks.'[56] In September, Mary Campbell, the wife of poet Roy Campbell, confessed her passion for Vita. Vita responded instantly, and within a few days they launched an affair, meeting almost every day to walk in the lanes and woods. When Vita's children returned to school, Mary and Roy Campbell moved into a cottage in the grounds of Long Barn. Vita made love to Mary Campbell on the sofa in her sitting room in the main house – the same place she and Virginia had begun their affair two years earlier.

When Virginia discovered Vita's attachment to Campbell, she responded even more jealously. 'Never do I leave you without thinking, its for the last time,' she told Vita, 'since I am always certain you'll be off and on with another next Thursday week.'[57] Vita's unfaithfulness had cast a pall over their relationship, she said – and at the same time had made it oddly more exciting: 'the truth is, we gain as much as we lose by this ... since all our intercourse is tinged with this melancholy on my part and desire to be white nosed and so keep you half an instant longer, perhaps, as I say we gain in intensity what we lack in the sober comfortable virtues of a prolonged and safe ... friendship.'[58] If she cared to, Virginia said, she could fill her letters to Vita 'to the brim with lovemaking unbelievable: indiscretions incredible'. But she refused to write letters of that sort to Vita now: 'Here occurs a terrific gulf. Millions of things I want to say can't be said. You know why. You know for what a price – walking the lanes with Campbell, you sold my love letters.'[59]

In this same jealous letter, Virginia described her intention to write about Vita in an entirely different way. Instead of love letters, she would write – indeed, she had already begun to write – a book called *Orlando*. And writing about Vita filled Virginia with physical rapture:

> I ... dropped my head in my hands: dipped my pen in the ink, and wrote these words, as if automatically, on a clean sheet: Orlando: A Biography. No sooner had I done this than my body was flooded with rapture and my brain with ideas ... But listen; suppose Orlando turns out to be Vita; and its all about you and the lusts of your flesh and the lure of your mind (heart you have none, who go gallivanting down the lanes with Campbell) – suppose there's the kind of shimmer of reality which some-times attaches to my people, as the lustre on an oyster shell (and that recalls another Mary) suppose, I say, that Sibyl next October says 'Theres Virginia gone and written a book about Vita' ... Also, I admit, I should like to untwine and twist again some very odd, incongruous strands in you: going at length into the question of Campbell; and also, as I told you, it sprung upon me how I could revolutionize biography in a night.'[60]

Vita was 'thrilled and terrified at the prospect of being projected into the shape of Orlando', and saw that 'any vengeance you ever want to take' lay completely in Virginia's huge imaginative powers. She gave Virginia her full permission.[61]

When Virginia conceived of *Orlando*, it was yet one more way to make Vita up, as Virginia had made Vita up so many times in her letters and her imagination already. But this time she might change the terms of her drifting relationship with Vita, dictate its direction, try to win Vita back. Writing *Orlando* was also an act of possession. In the pages of her novel, Virginia could define and immortalise Vita, and thus possess her fully and forever, whatever happened to their relationship in the realm of the real, off the page. Writing *Orlando* might be an act of revenge – Virginia could 'twist' the odd strands of Vita's incongruities and lay bare her many cruelties and infidelities. But writing *Orlando* was certainly an act of self-protection for Virginia: once she snared Vita in her web of words, her vision of Vita would remain beyond change, safe in the world of art, untainted by the incursions of other lovers.

From a practical standpoint, Virginia also saw that writing *Orlando* meant that she and Vita would have to spend time together. Over the next year, the novel became a game between them. Virginia reread Vita's book *Knole and the Sackvilles*, which chronicles the history of the house and its relation to the Sackville family. Then she peppered Vita with questions about her past – for what quality did Violet Trefusis first fall in love with Vita? What did Vita and Violet quarrel about? What did Vita and Lord Lascelles discuss? Did Vita grind her teeth at night? They visited Knole to choose family portraits as possible illustrations for the book; one day, walking down Bond Street together, Virginia saw a painting in a dealer's window and said, 'That's Shelmerdine.' Vita bought it. Virginia arranged for Vita to be photographed as a Lely portrait; Vanessa Bell and Duncan Grant also photographed her in nineteenth-century costume. Vita translated into French the phrases Virginia wanted and signed her translations 'Orlando'. Six weeks before *Orlando* appeared in print, Vita's imagination took fire in a different way and she decided to write *The Edwardians*, her own novel about Knole and the Sackvilles. The Hogarth Press published *The Edwardians* in 1930.

Meanwhile, Vita continued her affair with Mary Campbell. She was deeply stirred, physically and imaginatively, by the idea of Virginia's book about her sexual adventures: in her secret life with Mary Campbell, she began to call herself 'Orlando'. Vita wrote a series of passionate sonnets about their relationship. When she submitted them to the Woolfs at the Hogarth Press for publication, Virginia was gripped by another spasm of jealousy. In the spring of 1928, Vita also embarked on a short affair with an American woman, Margaret Voigt. Virginia chastised Vita for being a 'promiscuous brute' and launched into a tirade about Voigt's detestable American mannerisms: 'This is one of the effects of jealousy. I can't say how I detest hearing some one call you "Vita" in American on the telephone at 8 in the morning.'[62]

Yet writing *Orlando* was a frolic for Virginia. She finished the first full draft on 17 March 1928; it was published on 11 October 1928.[63] Vita had not seen any of the book before it appeared in print. When she received a specially bound copy from Virginia on publication day, Vita was 'dazzled, bewitched, enchanted, under a spell'. 'You have invented a new form of narcissism,' she wrote. 'I confess, – I am in love with Orlando – this is a complication I had not foreseen ... You made me cry with your passages about Knole, you wretch.'[64]

Orlando received rave reviews in the press and sold much more briskly than any of Virginia's previous novels: in three months it sold thirteen thousand copies in the United States alone. The *Daily Chronicle* observed that 'the book in Bloomsbury is a joke, in Mayfair a necessity, and in America a classic'. From a financial standpoint, the novel marked a turning point in Virginia's career: with her appeal to a more popular audience confirmed, she and Leonard no longer had to worry about money. And, in a fitting expression of one of *Orlando's* own central themes about women, places and writing, the novel provided Virginia with a room of her own. The Woolfs used the proceeds from *Orlando* to add an extension to Monk's House, a sitting/writing-room upstairs and a bedroom for Virginia downstairs. For the rest of her life, Virginia used this room to write when she visited Rodmell in the winter and her unheated garden hut ('the lodge') became too cold.

The composition of Orlando did little immediately to defuse Virginia's jealous affection for Vita. Virginia and Vita took their first trip abroad together just a few weeks before *Orlando's* publication. They booked separate rooms, but Vita came down the corridor to Virginia's room during a thunderstorm, and they talked in the dark about death. Then Harold was sent to Berlin, and the Woolfs visited them there in January 1929. When Virginia and Vita dined alone at the

Funkturm, Virginia declared her passion for Vita again. After Vita accused Virginia of being beset by 'suppressed randiness',[65] Virginia wondered to her plaintively: 'Have you any of those feelings left that the nightingales and the splash of frogs on water sometimes call out in me, on hot May nights, at Long Barn, as I told you when we ate duck on the Funkel tower?'[66] Later that summer, Virginia complained jealously when Vita went on a walking tour with Hilda Matheson, talks director at the BBC – so much so that Vita had to calm Virginia's nerves by insisting the trip had been an entirely impromptu affair.

But even if writing *Orlando* did not immediately diminish Virginia's attachment to Vita, it did move their relationship into a new key and, ultimately, mark the beginning of the end of Virginia's jealous passion. After a visit to Long Barn in July 1928, and after she finished correcting the proofs of *Orlando*, Virginia observed in her diary: 'I'm interested by the gnawing down of strata in friendship; how one passes unconsciously to different terms.'[67] By 1935, Virginia could write in her diary that 'My friendship with Vita is over ... Well, its like cutting off a picture: there she hangs, in the fishmongers at Sevenoaks, all pink jersey & pearls; & that's an end of it.'[68] For her part, Vita had moved on to other lovers, a progress that *Orlando* could not finally stop. Vita had also purchased Sissinghurst Castle, a sixteenth-century ruin, and was immersed in planning its restoration. When she finished writing the first draft of *Orlando*, Virginia had written to Vita:

> Did you feel a sort of tug, as if your neck was being broken on Saturday last at 5 minutes to one? That was when he died – or rather stopped talking, with three little dots ... Now every word will have to be rewritten ... The question now is, will my feelings for you be changed? I've lived in you all these months – coming out, what are you really like? Do you exist? Have I made you up?[69]

Virginia had, indeed, made Vita up anew – in a way that would assure Vita's fame and identify her forever with Knole. In the process, Virginia's feelings for Vita began a slow shift. Having used *Orlando* to express and explore her passion for Vita, Virginia could eventually let that passion cool. Having used *Orlando* to possess Vita fully in her imagination – and to enshrine her vision of Vita in the world of art,

139

away from the encroachments of other lovers – Virginia could begin to let Vita go. And having used *Orlando* to snare Vita in a web of words, Virginia could begin to free her to other lovers.

II

In January 1928, while Virginia was writing the first draft of *Orlando*, Vita's father Lionel Sackville-West, the third Lord Sackville, died at Knole. Vita was devastated. She loved her father dearly and his loss meant the end of a cherished relationship. Virginia became Vita's main source of consolation in the weeks that followed, sending her loving notes to lift her spirits and assure her of one continuing source of affection: 'If being loved by Virginia is any good, she does do that; and always will, and please believe it.'[70]

But Lord Sackville's death also meant that Vita lost Knole. Knole was entailed on the nearest male heir – in this case Vita's uncle, Charles Sackville. Virginia described Vita's misery to Vanessa Bell: 'The passion of her life is Knole, I think, and now this will belong to an uncle with a detestable American wife, and I suppose Vita will feel outcast.'[71] Vita did, indeed, feel cast out, and even joked weakly to Harold about retaking the house by storm: 'I want Knole ... I've got an idea about it: shall we take it some day? ... I've taken Dada's revolver. And the bullets.'[72] Vita went to Knole to handle the funeral arrangements. While she was there, she was sunk in melancholy, but also curiously at peace: it was the first and last time that Knole was wholly hers. For three days, she administered the household and gave orders, exercising a command she later described as marking a 'turning-point in my life'.[73] Then she left down the long curving driveway, never to return except as a guest.

Virginia saw immediately that *Orlando* might return Knole to Vita symbolically, by identifying Vita with the house forever. Virginia had thought she might 'revolutionize biography in a night' with *Orlando*, but she now saw she could perform a second revolutionary act at the same time: using her book to restore Knole to its rightful spiritual owner, even though that owner was a woman. It was an affectionate, consoling, and rebellious gesture: biographical fantasy as a form of literary restitution. As Virginia wrote, she transformed both Knole and Vita. In the pages of *Orlando*, Vita and her life were becoming emblems for every possible sort of feminine potential and expansion: sexual, social, literary. And Knole was being transmuted too, from a house that 'had gone dead' and had 'too little conscious beauty for my taste' to a work of art that made the past live in the present, and that provided the female artist with the ground for her work. Knole was becoming the place where Vita would become immortal – the spot where her 'soul would come and go for ever with the reds on the panels and the greens on the sofa'.[74]

Orlando is Vita's biography, told through the lens of fantasy. Virginia transforms aspects of Vita's life and personality into the story of Orlando, a stunningly beautiful boy who lives for three hundred years, from the reign of Queen Elizabeth I to the twentieth century. About the end of the seventeenth century, Orlando changes sex, waking up one morning to find himself female. Orlando associates with all the best-known authors of English literary history – Shakespeare, Dryden, Pope; he/she makes a happy marriage to a man (who may be a woman), has a child, and finally completes the poem he/she has been writing for several hundred years – just in time to win the Burdett Coutts Memorial Prize – and then returns to settle forever on her enormous country estate.

Virginia's passion for Vita is evident in her descriptions of Orlando's physical allure. The male Orlando has Vita's 'eyes like drenched violets, so large that the water seemed to have brimmed in them and widened them';[75] the male Orlando has, like Vita, 'a pair of the finest legs that a young nobleman has ever stood upright upon'[76] and 'teeth of an exquisite and almond whiteness'.[77] Once Orlando wakes up a woman, her beauty becomes even more ravishing. Orlando arranges her pearls around her neck – like Vita, Orlando is never without her pearls – and looks into her silver mirror:

> What woman would not have kindled to see what Orlando saw then burning in the snow – for all about the looking glass were snowy lawns, and she was like a fire, a burning bush, and the candle flames about her head were silver leaves; or again, the glass was green water, and she a mermaid, slung with pearls, a siren in a cave, singing so that oarsmen

leant from their boats and fell down, down to embrace her; so dark, so bright, so hard, so soft, was she, so astonishingly seductive that it was a thousand pities that there was no one there to put it in plain English, and say outright 'Damn it Madam, you are loveliness incarnate,' which was the truth.[78]

Such passionate evocations of Vita's physical charm fill the pages of *Orlando*: whenever Virginia describes Orlando, her prose is as seductive as Orlando's physical beauty. Such seductive language is an expression of Virginia's devotion and passion, certainly, but it is also a device calculated to entice Vita and woo her back. And it is also a device calculated toward possession: when Virginia describes and celebrates Vita's physical beauty in prose, that version of Vita becomes irrevocably hers.

Orlando's adventures turn on three plots: the search for love, the search for a poetic voice, and, intertwined with both these stories, the search to make her ancestral home more fully her own. The young Orlando first falls passionately in love with Sasha, a tempestuous Russian princess who betrays Orlando with another man. Orlando's affair with Sasha is broadly modelled on Vita's affair with Violet Trefusis, a liaison that nearly wrecked the Nicolson marriage. Vita and Violet eloped together to France in 1920, and again in 1921. (Vita had married Harold Nicolson in 1913; by this time they had two young sons.) Vita and Violet lived as husband and wife, with Vita dressing in men's clothes and Violet playing the role of the cherished female. Their husbands followed them to the continent to bring them back and the whole affair threatened to become a scandal. Public disgrace was only averted when Violet's mother, who was very rich, agreed to underwrite the Trefusis marriage financially if Violet's husband took her away from England permanently.

Orlando is next courted by the transvestite Archduchess/Archduke Harriet/Harry. This relationship is based loosely on Vita's courtship by Henry, Viscount Lascelles, a very tall, very shy man afflicted with a silly laugh, who, like the Archduke Harry, owned 'half Yorkshire'. The Archduchess Harriet begins to pursue Orlando during the reign of King Charles II (1660-85); to escape Harriet's unwanted attentions, Orlando asks to be sent to Constantinople as England's Ambassador. While Orlando is stationed in Constantinople during the seventeenth century – performing precisely the sort of pointless diplomatic tasks that Vita described to Virginia in her letters home from Tehran – a most astonishing transformation takes place: Orlando falls asleep for seven days and wakes up a woman. Though Orlando has a different body and begins to wear different clothing, he/she is still precisely the same person underneath. The transformation is a metaphor for Vita's bisexuality. And since Orlando possesses one hundred and fifty years of male memories, the transformation also gives Orlando – a male spirit newly confined to a female body – the opportunity to experience the limiting nature of conventional expectations for womanly behaviour.

This truth first comes home to Orlando on the ship returning to England. She realises that, as a woman, she can never again curse aloud; she realises that, though she is a strong swimmer, she will have to let a sailor save her if she falls overboard. She also realises with a start that she can never again fight with a sword, walk in a military procession, or sentence a man to death. When Orlando accidentally reveals an inch or two of leg – she is still unaccustomed to wearing skirts and hasn't learned to sit modestly – a blue-coated seaman sees her ankles and nearly falls from a mast. Orlando reflects on the foolishness that conventional behaviour requires of both sexes:

> 'To fall from a mast-head,' she thought, 'because you see a woman's ankles; to dress up like a Guy Fawkes and parade the streets, so that women may praise you; to deny a woman teaching lest she may laugh at you … Heavens!' she thought, 'what fools they make of us – what fools we are!' And here it would seem from some ambiguity in her terms that she was censuring both sexes equally, as if she belonged to neither; and indeed, for the time being she seemed to vacillate; she was man; she was woman; she knew the secrets, shared the weaknesses of each.[79]

Orlando's special vantage point – a male past joined to a female future – allows her to vacillate between the sexes and understand the experiences of both. From this perspective, she grasps sharply the extent to which conventional sexual expectations limit women. Equally importantly, she sees how those same conventional expectations cripple and constrain men.

The most important of Orlando's love affairs occurs shortly thereafter, when she meets Marmaduke Bonthrop Shelmerdine. Orlando's marriage to Shelmerdine is based on Vita's marriage to Harold Nicolson. Shelmerdine is always absent on voyages of exploration, journeys that parallel Harold's diplomatic missions to exotic countries such as Persia. Orlando and Shelmerdine use the pet name 'Mar', one of Vita's childhood nicknames, which she and Harold adopted after their marriage. Orlando and Shelmerdine are so attuned to each other emotionally that both initially suspect the other of cross-dressing – Orlando insists that Shelmerdine must be a woman, and Shelmerdine worries anxiously that Orlando might be a man. This hilarious confusion of genders on the eve of their wedding is a reference not only to the emotional compatibility of Vita and Harold, but also to the fact that, after their marriage, both remained practising bisexuals. In short, Orlando's marriage to Shelmerdine is an utterly unconventional affair, and in its unconventionality lies its perfection. During their wedding ceremony, the word 'obey' is drowned out by a clap of thunder. As Orlando puts it just after their wedding:

> She was married, true; but if one's husband was always sailing round Cape Horn, was it marriage? If one liked him, was it marriage? If one liked other people, was it marriage? And finally, if one still wished, more than anything in the whole world, to write poetry, was it marriage? She had her doubts.[80]

Just as Orlando's shipboard experience reflects on the damaging effects of conventional sexual expectations, so Orlando's unconventional marriage comments on the limiting effects of customary marriage arrangements. The marriage between Orlando and Shelmerdine works so perfectly precisely because it is so completely untraditional – the partners don't live together, yet they love each other deeply; they are genuine friends and allow other relationships; they are both committed to work. The marriage allows both partners complete freedom to live independently, to work privately, and to express themselves fully. And when they express their natures fully, both Orlando and Shelmerdine reveal their androgyny: the confusion of gender in their relationship is also a device for suggesting the essential androgyny of the human spirit.

Woolf had been pondering the idea of androgyny for some time but the notion first surfaces explicitly in the pages of *Orlando*. As Orlando knows, every woman is partly male and every male partly female:

> Different though the sexes are, they intermix. In every human being a vacillation from one sex to the other takes place, and often it is only the clothes that keep the male or female likeness, while underneath the sex is the very opposite of what is above.[81]

Woolf threads the theme of androgyny throughout *Orlando*: in Orlando's relationship to Sasha; in her relationship to the Archduchess/ Archduke Harriet/Harry. Orlando's unconventional marriage is important because it preserves her androgynous spirit – it allows her to lay claim to her past as a man and her future as a woman, and thereby remain most fully herself. In the world of *Orlando* – and increasingly in Woolf's thinking about gender relations – the only way to remain fully human is to recognise one's androgynous qualities and to live outside social convention, as naturally as possible. And the theme of androgyny is important to Orlando the poet too, since, as Woolf concluded when she wrote *A Room of One's Own* a year later, the only fully successful poet is the androgynous poet.

Parallel to the story of Orlando's search for love lies the story of her search for her distinctive poetic voice. As a boy of sixteen in the sixteenth century, he writes flamboyant tragedies; he also begins *The Oak Tree*, a poem inspired by his passion for nature and love for a magnificent oak tree on the grounds of his ancestral home. The manuscript of *The Oak Tree* accompanies Orlando through the centuries – it is the only work he saves when he burns all his manuscripts after a vicious attack by Nick Greene, the critic. *The Oak Tree* travels with Orlando to Constantinople and is finally completed in the nineteenth century, just in time for Orlando to bear a son and win the Burdett Coutts Memorial Prize. Not surprisingly, Orlando's poetic career echoes Vita's poetic career: as an adolescent, Vita wrote three plays in French and several full-length novels; she won the Hawthornden Prize for her poem *The Land* in 1927; the lines from *The Oak Tree* quoted in *Orlando* are actually lines from *The Land*.

At the very end of the novel, Orlando discovers her true 'self' and simultaneously discovers the true nature of her calling as an artist. Orlando has by this time finished *The Oak Tree* and brought it back to her ancestral home, where she thinks of burying the book under the oak tree itself, to give the poem back to the land that inspired it. But the chime of a clock recalls Orlando to her house; there, the house's past history merges with the present moment as Queen Elizabeth steps from a carriage and Marmaduke Bonthrop Shelmerdine simultaneously lands in an aeroplane. (Harold had once flown from Paris and landed in the cricket field at Knole.) A wild goose springs up over Shelmerdine's head and gives Orlando her image for the artist's calling: art is a wild-goose chase, she thinks, in which the writer struggles over and over again to net the present moment in words. And the present moment is precisely where *Orlando* ends: at the instant of its own publication, 'midnight, Thursday, the eleventh of October, Nineteen Hundred and Twenty-eight'.

The path of Orlando's career as a poet makes several points. Firstly, it expresses one of Woolf's characteristic ideas: that in the realm of art, the creative process is more important than the artistic product. Just as Lily Briscoe knows her painting will hang in an attic, but finishes it anyway, so Orlando learns that writing poems is tantamount to going on a wild-goose chase. Yet Orlando remains committed to the pursuit. Secondly, Orlando's career as a poet suggests an important truth about female authors: that the imaginative past of the woman writer is a male past. Orlando's male past is a metaphor for a female writer's experience of much of the great literature that has gone before her – as something moving and human, but something whose future might be remade when seen through the eyes of a different sex. Finally, and perhaps most importantly, Orlando's career as a poet suggests the importance of place to the development and maturation of any creative voice, but especially the female creative voice. Orlando is able to finish *The Oak Tree* only after she has made her house fully her own. In *Orlando*, Woolf permeates Knole with Vita, and portrays Vita as the very culmination of Knole's long history.

In this context, *Orlando* transforms Knole. Woolf first of all transmutes Knole's actual history into Orlando/Vita's personal history; she thus makes Vita the imaginative climax of Knole and its glorious past.

Woolf peoples Orlando's life with dramatic stories taken from the lives of the past owners of Knole. Like Thomas Sackville – author of 'Gorboduc' and treasurer to Queen Elizabeth – the early Orlando writes violent tragedies, receives the Order of the Garter, and delivers the death sentence to Mary, Queen of Scots. Like Charles Sackville, the sixth Earl, Orlando becomes a generous literary patron who supports Dryden and is praised by Pope. Orlando's gypsy wife, Rosina Pepita, is modelled on Vita's grandmother, Pepita, a gypsy dancer who bore Vita's grandfather five illegitimate children. This illegitimacy resulted in a notorious lawsuit in 1910 – a lawsuit in which Vita's uncles sued her mother and father over the right to succeed to Knole, its title and lands. Virginia adapts this lawsuit in *Orlando* to a court proceeding that challenges Orlando's claim to his property once he becomes that most illegitimate of social personages, a woman:

> No sooner had she returned to her home in Blackfriars than she was made aware of a succession of Bow Street runners and other grave emissaries from the Law Courts that she was a party to three major suits which had been preferred against her during her absence, as well as innumerable minor litigations, some arising out of, others depending on them. The chief charges against her were 1) that she was dead, and therefore could not hold any property whatsoever; 2) that she was a woman, which amounts to much the same thing; 3) that she was an English Duke who had married one Rosina Pepita, a dancer; and had had by her three sons, which sons now declaring that their father was deceased, claimed that all his property descended to them.[82]

Even the servants who appear in *Orlando* figure in the Sackville-West family annals. Mrs Grimsditch (the housekeeper), Mr Dupper (the chaplain), Mrs Stewkley, Mrs Field, old Nurse Carpenter, and the blackamoor Grace Robinson all work for Orlando – and also worked at Knole for Richard Sackville, third Earl of Dorset, during the early seventeenth century.

Virginia's description of Orlando's house is in many ways an accurate – or only slightly exaggerated – rendering of Knole itself. Orlando's great house has 365 bedrooms and 52 staircases; Vita tells the story in *Knole and the Sackvilles* that Knole has seven courtyards, 52 staircases and 365 rooms, making it a perfect emblem for the rhythmic passage of days, weeks, and years. Orlando's home covers first five acres of ground, then nine; the real Knole covers four acres and, like Orlando's house, has heraldic leopards worked into its stained glass windows. Both houses have a room furnished in silver, prepared for the visit of a king; both houses have a long gallery whose floors are made of ancient oaks sawn in two, so that the underside is rough timber; both houses have rooms reserved for Lady Betty, whose old recipe is still used to make the pot pourri that scents the air.

But Woolf selects and transforms two objects at Knole as especially important symbols for *Orlando*: an oak tree and a tapestry. Orlando's tapestry is inspired by tapestries that currently hang in two rooms at Knole – in the Spangle Bedroom and the Venetian Ambassador's bedroom. Woolf transforms the tapestry into the most beautiful and significant symbolic object inside the house, an anonymous work of art that lives and moves, and tells a classic tale of the relations between the sexes. It is Ovid's story of Daphne and Apollo, in which the beautiful nymph Daphne prefers her free life as a huntress to life as the lover of Apollo. Apollo and his huntsmen chase Daphne through the woods; just as they are about to catch her, she turns into a laurel tree, and is thus saved from Apollo's mastery.

This tapestry first comes to life after Orlando finishes furnishing his house: 'All was now ready; and ... it was evening and the innumerable silver sconces were lit and the light airs which for ever moved about the galleries stirred the blue and green arras, so that it looked as if the huntsmen were riding and Daphne were flying ... when all this and much more than all this was complete and to his liking, Orlando walked through the house with his elkhounds following and felt content.'[83] Near the close of the novel, Orlando takes one last tour of her house, and reverently revisits her tapestry, making sure that 'still the hunter rode; still Daphne flew'.[84]

Though Knole displays several tapestries depicting stories out of Ovid, none specifically tells the tale of Daphne and the hunters. But in her poem *The Land*, Vita had retold the Daphne/Apollo myth, linking it to an ancestral female memory that transcends the individual personality. As Vita put it, just before describing how Daphne slipped from Apollo's grasp to become a tree, 'Women still have memories of woods

/ Older than any personal memories.'[85] It is likely that Woolf had this section of *The Land* in mind when she pictured Daphne and Apollo on Orlando's tapestry. In Vita's poem, the tale of Daphne and Apollo is a story about the constraints of traditional relationships between the sexes, about the ways in which ancestral memory finds its culmination in individual memory, and about the importance of being rooted in the earth. All these themes are crucial to *Orlando*, too, and come together in the portrayal of Daphne and Apollo on the swaying tapestry that adorns Orlando's wall, and that gives Orlando such a sense of being at the centre of the life of her house.[86]

The second object that Woolf transforms into a central symbol for *Orlando* is an oak tree. Vita often wrote under an oak tree in Knole's park, on a hill known as the Masthead. At one time, the Masthead afforded a lovely view of the countryside around Knole. But Woolf exaggerates and expands the view from Orlando's oak tree, making it include all of Britain and Britain's history. Orlando strides out to sit under his oak tree early in the novel, during the reign of Queen Elizabeth; he sees galleons sailing off to explore, and armadas setting off to battle:

> [Orlando] had walked very quickly uphill through ferns and hawthorn bushes, startling deer and wild birds, to a place crowned by a single oak tree. It was very high, so high indeed that nineteen English counties could be seen beneath, and on clear days thirty, or forty perhaps, if the weather was very fine. Sometimes one could see the English Channel, wave reiterating upon wave. Rivers could be seen and pleasure boats gliding on them; and galleons setting out to sea; and armadas with puffs of smoke from which came the dull thud of cannon firing; and forts on the coast; and castles among the meadows; and here a watch tower; and there a fortress; and again some vast mansion like that of Orlando's father, massed like a town in the valley circled by walls. To the east there were the spires of London and the smoke of the city; and perhaps on the very sky line, when the wind was in the right quarter, the craggy top and serrated edges of Snowden herself showed mountainous among the clouds. For a moment Orlando stood counting, gazing, recognising. That was his father's house; that his uncle's. His aunt owned those three great turrets among the trees there. The heath was theirs and the forest; the pheasant and the deer, the fox, the badger, and the butterfly.[87]

This exaggerated view from the oak tree encompasses all of Britain and captures Britain's history as it unfolds. It thus transforms Knole, putting the house at the very centre of the British landscape, and at the heart of the story of Britain's development. And since Orlando is the owner of Knole, Virginia thus places Orlando/Vita at the centre of British space and British history, too.

But Woolf's symbolic transformation of the oak tree itself is just as suggestive. In Woolf's hands, the oak tree becomes Orlando's first connection to place, the source of his tie to the land that inspires his poetry. Orlando ties his 'floating heart' to the oak tree; this tie results in a poetic 'vision', and in the first drafts of his poem:

> He sighed profoundly, and flung himself – there was a passion in his movements which deserves the word – on the earth at the foot of the oak tree. He loved, beneath all this summer transiency, to feel the earth's spine beneath him; for such he took the hard root of the oak tree to be; or, for image followed image, it was the back of a great horse that he was riding; or the deck of a tumbling ship – it was anything indeed, so long as it was hard, for he felt the need of something which he could attach his floating heart to; the heart that tugged at his side; the heart that seemed filled with spiced and amorous gales every evening about this time when he walked out. To the oak tree he tied it and as he lay there, gradually the flutter in and about him stilled itself; the little leaves hung; the deer stopped; the pale summer clouds stayed; his limbs grew heavy on the ground; and he lay so still that by degrees the deer stepped nearer and the rooks wheeled round him and the swallows dipped and circled and the dragon-flies shot past, as if all the fertility and amorous activity of a summer's evening were woven web-like about his body.[88]

The hard root of the oak tree provides Orlando's connection to the earth's spine, to something hard and real that anchors Orlando in the present moment, and draws all the summer's transiency and amorous activity into fleeting artistic suspension. The oak tree is at the centre of Orlando's connection to place, and as such is crucial to his poetic art.

But most important is Woolf's symbolic transformation of the buildings that comprise Knole. Woolf's description of the exterior of the house is visually accurate, and made Vita cry when she first read it:

> There it lay in the early sunshine of spring. It looked a town rather than a house, but a town built, not hither and thither, as this man wished or

that, but circumspectly, by a single architect with one idea in his head. Courts and buildings, grey, red, plum colour, lay orderly and symmetrical; the courts were some of them oblong and some square; in this was a fountain; in that a statue; the buildings were some of them low, some pointed; here was a chapel, there a belfry; spaces of the greenest grass lay in between and clumps of cedar trees and beds of bright flowers; all were clasped – yet so well set out was it that it seemed that every part had room to spread itself fittingly – by the roll of a massive wall; while smoke from innumerable chimneys curled perpetually into the air.[89]

But as Orlando contemplates what this loveliness means, Knole becomes something far greater than a beautiful and harmonious piece of architecture: it becomes a living symbol of art itself. Woolf transforms Knole into an artistic masterpiece, and into an emblem of the perfect relationship between an artist and her work. Far from being a house that has 'gone dead' – as Woolf thought of Knole when she first visited – Orlando sees his home as a living monument to lost generations:

This vast, yet ordered building, which could house a thousand men and perhaps two thousand horses was built, Orlando thought, by workmen whose names are unknown. Here, have lived for more centuries than I can count, the obscure generations of my own obscure family. Not one of these Richards, Johns, Annes, Elizabeths has left a token of himself behind him, yet all, working together with their spades and their needles, their love-making and their child-bearing, have left this.

Never had the house looked more noble and humane. Why, then, had he wished to raise himself above them? For it seemed vain and arrogant in the extreme to try to better that anonymous work of creation; the labours of those vanished hands. Better was it to go unknown and leave behind you an arch, a potting shed, a wall where peaches ripen, than to burn like a meteor and leave no dust.[90]

In this loving description, Knole has become a living work of art, a place where generations of people, working together, have created a masterpiece that perfectly expresses the human spirit. People have worked and died there, but live on in the mortar and the bricks, in the arches and the potting sheds they left behind. This image looks forward to Woolf's last novel, *Between the Acts*, in which the communal labour of villagers building a wall keeps civilisation alive in the darkest days of

World War II. It also looks forward to *A Room of One's Own*, where Woolf describes literary masterpieces in the same way she describes Knole in *Orlando*: 'For masterpieces are not single and solitary births; they are the outcome of many years of thinking in common, of thinking by the body of the people.'[91] Woolf has transformed Knole into an architectural masterpiece that expresses the communal spirit of the people who built it; at the same time, thinking about Knole has given Woolf a place to articulate new ideas about the importance of community to the artistic act.

The labour that has built Orlando's house is communal; it is equally important that the labour that has produced his house is anonymous. The idea of artistic anonymity was becoming increasingly important to Woolf. She was growing contemptuous of the expression of too much 'personality' in literature; she was becoming impatient with the insistent 'I' – usually a male mannerism – that characterised modern writing. Woolf was beginning to think that the perfect relationship between artists and their work was an impersonal and anonymous one: that the best writers submerged their personalities when they wrote and that the most successful artistic labour was performed in complete obscurity. In *A Room of One's Own*, Woolf predicts that an ideal female poet will arise to rewrite the world; her work will be characterised by impersonality and anonymity. This is precisely the posture that Woolf has Orlando adopt when he looks at his house, built by so many vanished hands: 'Why, then, had he wished to raise himself above them? For it seemed vain and arrogant in the extreme to try to better that anonymous work of creation ... Better was it to go unknown.'

On the strength of this vision, Orlando vows to add his own anonymous touches to the house, and thereby both possess his house more fully and bequeath something of himself to posterity. Since the house is already so enormous that adding even a single stone seems superfluous, Orlando decides to provide furniture. And furnish it he does, buying crimson damask cushions by the hundred and Venetian crystal glasses in dozens. In a wonderful conceit that draws on the idea of the close connection between describing something and laying claim to it, Woolf furnishes Orlando's house in Vita's own language: she transcribes and exaggerates Vita's own lists of the furnishings at Knole, lists that appear in Vita's book *Knole and the Sackvilles*. In this way, Orlando – and Vita – furnish Knole, and by furnishing Knole make it their own.

By the end of the novel, Woolf has transformed Knole into the living embodiment of an artistic masterpiece – a communal and anonymous expression of the human urge to create, and the human connection to place that fosters it. At the same time, Woolf transforms Vita/Orlando into the living personification of the consummate artist, vitally connected to the place in which she is rooted. Once Orlando has furnished his house and made it fully his own, he is ready to take up *The Oak Tree* again. His efforts to finish his poem are interrupted by a journey to Constantinople, a sex change, and an utterly unconventional wedding ceremony. But when the female Orlando writes the last words of *The Oak Tree* several centuries later, she has become the perfect female author. She draws fully on all the male and female aspects of her personality – she is androgynous. She does not seek to elevate herself above the poets and artisans who have gone before her – she is impersonal and anonymous. And the fact that she possesses a place of her own – a vast house whose corridors whisper of the past and the present – is the central secret of her success as a writer.

Orlando is an important book in Woolf's career. In it she worked out in fictive form many of the key ideas about women, places and writing that animated her thinking for the rest of her life. But *Orlando* is also a remarkable testament to Woolf's affection for Vita. In the pages of *Orlando*, Woolf made Vita up in a way that expressed and captured her love for her, and thus allowed Woolf to possess her fully and forever in imagination. Woolf transformed Vita in the pages of *Orlando*, too, making her into a stirring vision of bisexual loveliness, into a figure who summed up all of history in the present moment, into the living personification of the female artist who will shape the future. And then Virginia began to let Vita go. But she released Vita with a parting gift: she transformed Knole into a living work of art and connected Vita to Knole irrevocably. In the pages of *Orlando*, Vita stalks the galleries of Knole in Turkish dress forever.

III

Knole today: Sights, views, excursions

KNOLE HOUSE

Knole was given to the National Trust in 1946 by Vita's uncle, the fourth Lord Sackville; its current tenant is Vita's first cousin, the sixth Lord Sackville. Knole is open from April to October; its hours are Wednesday to Saturday, 12 noon to 4 p.m., and Sundays and Bank Holidays, 11 a.m. to 5 p.m. Knole Park is open daily for pedestrians only, courtesy of Lord Sackville. (Lord Sackville's private garden is open to the public from May to September on the first Wednesday of each month, from 11 a.m. to 4 p.m., with the last admission at 3 p.m. This private garden opening is courtesy of Lord Sackville.)

Knole was built between 1456 and 1486 by Thomas Bourchier, Archbishop of Canterbury. On Bourchier's death, he willed the house to the See of Canterbury, and the house was used by several archbishops, including Archbishop Cranmer. Henry VIII was so impressed by Knole that he confiscated it for his own use, much discomfiting the reluctant Cranmer, who tried to argue that Knole was too small to accommodate Henry and his large retinue. Henry VIII enlarged Knole considerably, spending great sums of money on its renovation, but there is no record of his having spent much time there.

Upon Henry VIII's death, the house passed to his daughter, Queen Elizabeth I, who bestowed it in 1561 on her favourite, Robert Dudley, Earl of Leicester. When Leicester abandoned claim to Knole, Elizabeth presented it in 1566 to her cousin, Thomas Sackville, who eventually became Lord Buckhurst and first Earl of Dorset. Thomas Sackville remodelled the buildings extensively between 1603 and 1608. His descendants have lived at Knole ever since.

The buildings at Knole are woven into the fabric of English history by virtue of their use as both a royal and an archiepiscopal palace; its collection of furnishings is especially rare and important. Charles Sackville, the sixth Earl of Dorset, served as Lord Chamberlain under William III between 1689 and 1697. In this position, Sackville had the right to take for himself any pieces of furniture cast off from the royal palaces – furniture that might be worn, or that might bear the monogram or coat of arms of the previous monarch. As a result, Knole possesses an extraordinary collection of seventeenth-century furniture and textiles, ranging from chairs of state made at the time of James I and Charles I, to later works by the artisans Thomas Roberts, Gerreit Jensen, and Francis Lapière. Later tenants of Knole added other masterpieces, such as a large number of important paintings by Reynolds.

This same Charles, the sixth Earl of Dorset, is the Sackville ancestor who provides the inspiration for many of the details of Orlando's life: Nell Gwyn's affection for him; the decision to furnish Knole with silver; his relationships with major literary figures. Vita describes him in this way in *Knole and the Sackvilles*:

> One of the most jovial and debonair figures in the Knole portrait-gallery [is] Charles, the sixth Earl – let us call him the Restoration Earl – the jolly, loose-living, magnificent Maecenas, 'during the whole of his life the patron of men of genius and dupe of women, and bountiful beyond measure to both'. He furnished Knole with silver, and peopled it with poets and courtesans; he left us the Poets' Parlour, rich with memories of Pope and Dryden, Prior and Shadwell, D'Urfey and Killigrew; he left us the silver and ebony stands on which he was in the habit in hours of relaxation of placing his cumbersome periwig ... he left us his gay and artificial stanzas to Chloris and Dorinda ... He disturbed London by a rowdy youth; he was reported to have passed on his mistresses to the King ... Last but not least, Charles Sackville is connected with that most attractive figure of the English stage – Nell Gwyn.[92]

How to get there

By car: Knole is located in the town of Sevenoaks. From London, go to the M25 London Orbital. At junction 5, go south on the A21, and from there exit very soon, following signs to Sevenoaks. Knole is at the southern end of Sevenoaks on the A225. (Parking is available for cars visiting the house during opening hours. Parking is also available whenever the National Trust Shop and Brewhouse Restaurant are open: Wednesday to Saturday 11 a.m. to 4.30 p.m.; Sundays and Bank Holiday Mondays, 11 a.m. to 5 p.m.; and during the Christmas season for gift shopping.)

CHAPTER THREE

By train: There is a frequent train service from Charing Cross to
Sevenoaks. From Sevenoaks station, taxis are available for the short (1¾
mile) trip to Knole. There is also a connecting bus service: Chartwell
Explorer from Sevenoaks station, with combined transport/admission
ticket available. Also from London on weekends and certain other days,
May to September.

For additional information, phone 01732 450 608, or check the
National Trust website at www.nationaltrust.org.

The Approach

As she neared the end of the first draft of *Orlando*, Woolf told Vita what
Orlando was doing at the novel's close: 'You are driving down to Knole,
and as you go, you exhibit the most profound and secret side of your
character.'[93] Once Orlando reaches Knole, she steers her car up the
curving drive through Knole Park. The drive today looks just as Woolf
described it in *Orlando*:

> Masterfully, swiftly, she drove up the curving drive between the elms and
> oaks through the falling turf of the park whose fall was so gentle that had it
> been water it would have spread the beach with a smooth green tide. Planted
> here and in solemn groups were beech trees and oak trees. The deer stepped
> among them, one white as snow, another with its head on one side, for some
> wire netting had caught in its horns. All this, the trees, deer, and turf, she
> observed with the greatest satisfaction as if her mind had become a fluid that
> flowed round things and enclosed them separately. Next minute she drew
> up in the courtyard, where, for so many hundred years she had come, on
> horseback or in coach and six, with men riding before or coming after;
> where plumes had tossed, torches flashed, and the same flowering trees that
> let their leaves drop now had shaken their blossoms. Now she was alone.
> The autumn leaves were falling. The porter opened the great gates.[94]

Herds of fallow and Japanese deer still live in Knole Park. They feed on
the park's grasses – but also congregate around visitors who lunch under
trees close to the house's main entrance. The visitor is advised to be wary
– the deer will nuzzle for a taste of your sandwich, but they will also bite.

The House

The following discussion focuses on features of Knole that relate to
Vita, and that Woolf adopted or transformed in *Orlando*. The National

156

Trust shop at Knole sells an excellent comprehensive guide, written by Robert Sackville-West. This guide provides a history of the house and its furnishings.[95]

The Green Court

The Green Court is the largest of the seven courtyards at Knole. Three sides of the courtyard – the ones that are two storeys in height – were tacked on by Henry VIII, probably to house the many attendants who travelled with him. The higher, three-storeyed range, directly opposite the entry gate, is one of the oldest parts of Knole. It was the original west façade of Archbishop Bourchier's mid-fifteenth-century building.

The Great Hall

This room is part of Archbishop Bourchier's house, built around 1460. The room was thoroughly renovated between 1605 and 1608 by Thomas Sackville, first Earl of Dorset; he installed the plasterwork ceiling, the oak panelling, and the ornamented oak screen.

The upper portion of the screen hides the Musicians' Gallery, where Thomas Sackville's private orchestra probably performed. Sackville-West family legend has it that the young Vita played in the gallery during formal dinners, concealing herself behind the screen and peering down on the adults dining below.

The pedestal at the far end of the room holds a copy of the manuscript of *Orlando*. Virginia gave Vita the manuscript shortly after the novel appeared in print – Virginia came down to Long Barn for the night on 6 December 1928, bringing the bound manuscript as a gift to its subject. Vita eventually bequeathed the manuscript to Knole, where it became the property of the National Trust. The manuscript is usually kept open at the pages on which Woolf describes Knole.

The Great Staircase

This staircase was also remodelled by Thomas Sackville, first Earl of Dorset, between 1605 and 1608. The nude reclining on a couch is a plaster figure representing Giannetta Baccelli, a renowned dancer and the mistress of the third Duke of Dorset.

The heraldic leopards adorning the staircase hold the Sackville coat of arms. The Sackville leopards also appear in the stained glass on the stairway; light filters through them and forms yellow pools on the floor. In *Orlando*, the reader first meets Orlando in the attic of his huge home, which is decorated with these same windows:

> Were not the bars of darkness in the room, and the yellow pools which chequered the floor, made by the sun falling through the stained glass of a vast coat of arms in the window? Orlando stood now in the midst of the yellow body of an heraldic leopard.[96]

The heraldic leopard appears close to the end of *Orlando* too, where it becomes a symbol for the immortality of Knole, since the house will live on after Orlando and contain her spirit: 'Though she could hardly fancy it, the body of the heraldic leopard would be making yellow pools on the floor the day they lowered her to lie among her ancestors. She, who believed in no immortality, could not help feeling that her soul would come and go forever with the reds on the panels and the greens on the sofa.'[97] (Vita had also written a poem describing these leopards. Called 'Leopards at Knole', it was published in 1921 as part of *Orchard and Vineyard*.)

To the left, near the door, stands a brown doorstop – a figure of William Shakespeare. (This doorstop came from Vita Sackville-West's bedroom. Her mother – who had a passion for fresh air – always insisted that doors be kept open.) In *Orlando*, Woolf places Shakespeare in Orlando's house during the reign of Queen Elizabeth, when Orlando sees Shakespeare sitting at the servants' dinner table, writing. This vision of the poet as an obscure and anonymous figure recurs to Orlando throughout the novel, and at novel's end she realises she has been 'haunted! Ever since I was a child'[98] by the image of the man in the dirty ruff who sat quietly and namelessly at Twitchett's table, lost in visions of 'ogres, satyrs, perhaps the depths of the sea'.[99]

The doorstop in the shape of Shakespeare was certainly at Knole when Woolf visited the house with Vita.[100] But whether Shakespeare actually had any connection to Knole or the Sackville family is a more doubtful matter – and a question that leads to a suggestive digression on the mutual influences of literary texts. Woolf read Vita's *Knole and the Sackvilles* before writing *Orlando*; in the early edition of the book that

Woolf would have seen, Vita makes no mention of Shakespeare's possible connection to the Sackville family. But then Woolf wrote *Orlando*, and associated Shakespeare with Knole's ancient lineage and artistic magnificence. The connection seems to have fired Vita's imagination: in her 1948 revision of *Knole and the Sackvilles*, she adds a section in which she recounts her wild dreams as a child of finding Shakespeare's manuscripts hidden beneath the floorboards in the attic at Knole. Vita goes on to speculate that her dreams of finding a connection between Knole and Shakespeare might not have been so far-fetched after all: that recent commentators suggested that Thomas Sackville might be the model for Sir Toby Belch in *Twelfth Night*; that the manor of Stratford-on-Avon came into the possession of the Sackville family in 1674; that Thomas Sackville and Shakespeare certainly came face to face at least once in their lives, at the conference of English and Spanish plenipotentiaries, at Somerset House in 1604.[101] Thus, though Vita's affection for Knole is one of the inspirations for *Orlando*, Woolf's vision of Knole in turn colours and romanticises Vita's response to the house and its history.

The Brown Gallery

The Brown Gallery is the first of a series of rooms that have been known since the eighteenth century as the Show Rooms. Its walls are decorated with a series of historical portraits, many of which were commissioned by the fourth Earl of Dorset in the seventeenth century. But the most important feature of this room is its furniture, most of which was collected by the sixth Earl of Dorset during his tenure from 1689 to 1697 as Lord Chamberlain to William III. This furniture – some of it dating to the early seventeenth century, to the reigns of James I and Charles I – came to Knole, where it was stored under dustsheets and left unused. As a result, much of the fabric is in a remarkable state of preservation.

In *Knole and the Sackvilles*, Vita captures the melancholy feel of this room with its abandoned furniture: 'Some of the best pieces of the English furniture are ranged down each side of this gallery: portentously important chairs ... and all have their attendant stool squatting beside them. They are lovely, silent rows, for ever holding out their arms, and for ever disappointed.'[102] Near the end of *Orlando*, Woolf evokes the room in the same elegiac tone, using the same image of arms held out expectantly: 'Rows of chairs with all their velvets faded stood ranged against the wall holding their arms out for Elizabeth, for James, for Shakespeare it might be, for Cecil, who never came. The sight made her gloomy. She unhooked the rope that fenced them off. She sat on the Queen's chair.'[103]

Lady Betty Germain's Bedroom and Dressing Room

Lady Elizabeth Germain lived at Knole as a guest in the eighteenth century, during the reigns of George I and George II. Lady Betty was a distant relation of the Sackvilles; she was the widow of Sir John Germain, from whom she inherited the great house of Drayton in Northamptonshire. She developed a close friendship with the Duke and Duchess of Dorset and, since she had no heirs, left Drayton to their younger son, Lord George Sackville.

Lady Betty corresponded with Jonathan Swift; she sewed in her rooms as she looked out over the garden; she made pot pourri – her old recipe is still used at Knole. Vita found these two rooms – Lady Betty's bedroom and dressing room – to be lovely, precisely because they were so small: they maintained a reassuring sense of human scale after the pomp and size of the great rooms at Knole. Lady Betty's portrait hangs in her dressing room.

Orlando furnishes this room with pot pourri in the seventeeth century; after her return from Constantinople, she is so happy to be home that she buries 'her face in the pot pourri, which was made as the Conqueror had taught them many hundred years ago and from the same roses'.[104] Near the close of the novel, after Orlando has returned to her house for good, she 'opened a manuscript book lying on Lady Betty's table; she stirred her fingers in the aged rose leaves'.[105]

The Spangle Bedroom

The Spangle Bedroom takes its name from the magnificent hangings on the bed. They are made in a very rare appliqué pattern, and were originally sewn with small metallic sequins, or spangles, many of which can still be seen. When the hangings were new, they must have shimmered in the light as the breeze from the open window moved them.

The Spangle Bedroom also contains Brussels tapestries that Lord Dorset took from Queen Mary's apartments at Whitehall Palace a few months after she died in 1694. The tapestries depict scenes out of Ovid's *Metamorphoses*: the stories of Mercury and Argus, and of Cephalus and Procris. These tapestries, combined with Vita's use of Ovid's story of Daphne and the hunters in *The Land*, probably inspired the swaying tapestry that figures so prominently in *Orlando*. But Woolf places Orlando's Daphne tapestry in a different room: in a room that seems very like the Venetian Ambassador's room.

The Billiard Room

The Billiard Room is really a large recess off the Leicester Gallery, containing a seventeenth-century billiard table. But note the portrait (number 167) of Thomas D'Urfey (1653-1723), a poet and composer who was given a home at Knole for many years by Charles Sackville, the sixth Earl of Dorset. Vita notes in *Knole and the Sackvilles* that Charles Sackville probably treated D'Urfey with contempt, but there is no suggestion that D'Urfey behaved as badly as Orlando's pensioner, Nick Greene.[106]

The Leicester Gallery

In 1561, Queen Elizabeth gave Knole to her great favourite, Robert Dudley, Earl of Leicester. This room is named after him; he may have remodelled it during the short period he possessed it, from 1561 to 1566, before the Queen granted the house to her cousin, Thomas Sackville.

The Leicester Gallery contains many important paintings and pieces of furniture: paintings by Mytens; 'Armada' chests dating back to the seventeenth century. When Vita was growing up, the Leicester Gallery contained a haunting portrait of Catherine Fitzgerald, the Countess of Desmond hanging on one of its doors. The eyes of this portrait seemed to follow Vita in the dark as she walked through the gallery with a candle.[107]

The Venetian Ambassador's Room

This room is named after the Venetian ambassador to the court of James I, Nicolo Molino, who visited Knole and is said to have slept in this room. (His portrait hangs in the Leicester Gallery – see number 174, by Daniel Mytens: Nicolo Molino, Venetian Ambassador to the Court of James I.) The room was redecorated in around 1730 by Lionel, first Duke of Dorset. In her 1922 edition of *Knole and the Sackvilles*, Vita described the tapestries hanging on the walls as being Burgundian, with 'medieval figures walking in a garden'. C.J. Philips, who published a *History of the Sackville Family* in 1929, described the tapestries as being classical in theme. But in her guidebook to Knole written for the National Trust in 1948, Vita says that the tapestries depict scenes from *Orlando Furioso*, Ariosto's sixteenth-century epic in which the hero fights Moors and is driven mad by love. This alteration may be another instance of Vita's re-visualising Knole in the context of Woolf's *Orlando*.[108]

The Venetian Ambassador's Room was one of Vita's favourite rooms at Knole. Harold kissed her for the first time here.[109] The room seemed to have a life of its own; it seemed to 'miss its inhabitants more than do any of the other rooms'.[110] Vita describes the Venetian Ambassador's Room in *Knole and the Sackvilles*:

> It is almost a relief to go from here (the King's Bedroom) to the Venetian Ambassador's Bedroom. Green and gold; Burgundian tapestry, medieval figures walking in a garden; a rosy Persian rug – of all rooms I never saw a room that so had over it a bloom like the bloom on a bowl of grapes and figs. I cannot keep the simile, which may convey nothing to those who have not seen the room, out of my mind. Greens and pinks originally bright, now dusted and tarnished over. It is a very grave, stately room, rather melancholy in spite of its stateliness. It seems to miss its inhabitants more than do any of the other rooms. Perhaps this is because the bed appears to be designed for three: it is of enormous breadth, and there are three pillows in row. Presumably this is what the Italians call a *letto matrimoniale*.[111]

Woolf's evocation of this room in *Orlando* has the same flavour – and the same colours. It is the 'heart of the house';[112] she places Orlando's tapestry of Daphne and the hunters in the Ambassador's bedroom:

For the room – she had strolled into the Ambassador's bedroom – shone like a shell that has lain at the bottom of the sea for centuries and has been crusted over and painted a million tints by the water; it was rose and yellow, green and sand-coloured. It was frail as a shell, as iridescent and as empty. No Ambassador would ever sleep here again. Ah, but she knew where the heart of the house still beat. Gently opening a door, she stood on the threshold so that (as she fancied) the room could not see her and watched the tapestry rising and falling on the eternal faint breeze which never failed to move it. Still the hunter rode; still Daphne flew. The heart still beat, she thought, however faint, however far withdrawn; the frail indomitable heart of the immense building.[113]

Woolf's Daphne tapestry moves and comes to life in the faint breeze; this detail is also inspired by one of Vita's descriptions in *Knole and the Sackvilles*. As a child, Vita walked with a candle through the darkened staterooms at Knole: 'There were no electric torches in those days. The light gleamed on the dull gilding of furniture and into the misty depths of mirrors, and started up a sudden face out of the gloom; something creaked and sighed; the tapestry swayed, and the figures on it undulated and seemed to come alive.'[114]

Lady Betty Germain's China Closet
The window of this room overlooks the Water Court, one of the seven courtyards at Knole. Its name derived from the well which once stood in the middle; this well served the fifteenth-century kitchens along the right hand range of buildings.

The Ballroom
This room dates to the days of Archbishop Bourchier when it would have been used as the main living room of the house, the place to which the archbishop and his retinue retired after meals in the Great Hall. Thomas Sackville, the first Earl, probably used it as his dining room; in subsequent years it became the ballroom.

The chimneypiece and overmantel – one of the finest pieces of Renaissance sculpture in England – constitute the central feature of the ballroom. The walls are covered with portraits of Sackville ancestors, but Vita's favourite part of the room was the frieze that appears close to the ceiling:

163

Fortunately, the frieze in the ball-room cannot be hidden [by Sackville family portraits]. It used to delight me as a child, with its carved intricacies of mermaids and dolphins, mermen and mermaids with scaly, twisting tails and salient anatomy, and I was invariably contemptuous of those visitors to whom I pointed out the frieze but who were more interested in the pictures. It always fell to my lot to 'show the house' to visitors when I was there alone with my grandfather, for he shared the family failing of unsociability, and whenever a telegram arrived threatening invasion he used to take the next train to London for the day, returning in the evening when the coast was clear. It mattered nothing that I was every whit as bored by the invasion as he could have been; in a divergence between the wishes of eighty and the wishes of eight, the wishes of eight went to the wall.[115]

This frieze captured Woolf's imagination, too. She had already described Clarissa Dalloway as a mermaid lolloping on the waves; 'Dolphin' was Woolf's affectionate nickname for her sister, Vanessa, and, intermittently, for Vita. In *Orlando*, this frieze comes to life and glows, as in this passage when Orlando surveys his house after furnishing it: 'the carved chairs held their arms out and dolphins swam upon the walls with mermaids on their backs'.[116] The ballroom frieze is described in evocative terms throughout *Orlando*.

A portrait of Richard Sackville, fifth Earl of Dorset, by Robert Walker (number 226) hangs on the wall in the ballroom, opposite the great chimneypiece. This same portrait appears in *Orlando*, captioned 'Orlando as Ambassador'.

A portrait of Cicely Baker (number 231) hangs to the right of the window. Cicely Baker was the daughter of John Baker of Sissinghurst, and married Thomas Sackville, the first Earl of Dorset, who received Knole from Queen Elizabeth in 1566. When Vita and Harold discovered this connection between Knole and Sissinghurst, they decided that it made Sissinghurst a 'family' property – and therefore very attractive as a place that might begin to console Vita for the loss of Knole.

The Cartoon Gallery

The Cartoon Gallery takes its name from the copies of Raphael's Cartoons that hang on its walls. This set of six cartoons was a gift from Charles I to Lionel Cranfield, first Earl of Middlesex; they were prob-

ably painted in the workshop of Franz Cleyn. The Cartoons were
brought to Knole by Cranfield's grandson, the sixth Earl of Dorset, very
early in the eighteenth century.

Raphael's Cartoons were not Vita's favourite part of this room; she
most liked its light and its floors:

> The colour of the Cartoon Gallery, when I have come into it in the
> evening, with the sunset flaming through the west window, has often
> taken my breath away. I have stood, stock still and astonished, in the
> doorway. The gallery is ninety feet in length, the floor formed of black
> oaks planks irregularly laid, the charm of which is that they are not
> planks at all, but solid tree-trunks, split in half, with the rounded half
> downwards; so is the tradition, and I like to believe it; and on this oak
> flooring lie the blue and scarlet patches from the stained west window,
> more subduedly echoed in the velvets of the chair coverings, the coloured
> marbles of the great Renaissance fireplace, and the fruits and garlands of
> the carved woodwork surrounding the windows. There is nothing garish:
> all the colours have melted into an old harmony that is one of the prin-
> cipal beauties of these rooms. The walls here in the Cartoon gallery are
> hung with rose-red Genoa velvet, so lovely that I almost regret Mytens'
> copies of the Raphael cartoons hiding most of it ...[117]

These rough-hewn floors – which Woolf has Orlando install when he
furnishes his house – appear repeatedly in *Orlando*. Orlando slides
along them when she returns home after Constantinople; at the end of
the novel, Orlando, 'calling her troop of dogs to her ... passed down
the gallery whose floor was laid with oak trees sawn across'.[118]

The guides on duty in this room correct the Sackville family tradition: the floors are *not* solid tree trunks split in half.

The King's Room

The King's Room is probably the most famous room at Knole. Millais
used it as the setting for his *Eve of St Agnes* in 1863; Horace Walpole,
Fanny Burney and Maria Edgeworth all visited the room and
wondered at its contents. Sackville family legend – and the version
that Vita described in *Knole and the Sackvilles* in 1922 – had it that
the gold and silver fabrics on the great bed, and the matching silver
furniture in the room, were prepared for a visit to Knole by James I.
Vita later attributed the beginning of this legend to a muddle by Fanny

Burney, who reported the facts incorrectly in a letter to her sister in 1779. Vita always meekly repeated the legend as a child, but eventually concluded that the story was false: a contemporary account of the journeys of James I did not mention a visit to Knole; and the style of the carving and upholstery suggests a much later date. The bed and its upholstered furniture were most likely brought to Knole from Whitehall Palace by the sixth Earl of Dorset after the death of Queen Mary in 1694.

The other silver furniture in the room is equally famous and was made for various members of the Sackville family during the seventeenth century. Vita found the room terribly vulgar. In her 1922 edition of *Knole and the Sackvilles*, she writes:

> The King's bedroom is the only vulgar room in the house. Not that the furniture put there for the reception of James the First is vulgar: it is excessively magnificent, the canopy of the immense bed reaching almost to the ceiling, decked with ostrich feathers, the hangings stiff with gold and silver thread, the coverlet and the interior of the curtains heavily embroidered with a design of pomegranates and tiger-lilies worked in silver on a coral satin ground, the royal cipher embossed over the pillows – all this is very magnificent, but not vulgar. What is vulgar is the set of furniture made entirely in silver: table, hanging mirror, and tripods – the florid and ostentatious product of the florid Restoration. There is a surprising amount of silver in the room: sconces, ginger-jars, mirrors, fire-dogs, toilet-set, rose-water sprinklers, even to a little eye-bath, all of silver, but these smaller objects have not the blatancy of the set of furniture. Charles Sackville ... cannot have known when he had too much of a good thing.[119]

After the publication of *Orlando*, Vita published a new detail she might have told Virginia:

> I often longed to brush my hair with what I wrongly supposed to be King James' brushes, but having been strictly brought up not to touch anything in the show rooms I didn't dare.[120]

Accordingly, Woolf gives Orlando an 'inordinate passion' for silver, and has him use the last of his money to 'provide mirrors of solid silver and chairs of the same metal ... for the furnishing of the royal bed chambers'.[121] Best of all, Woolf gives the female Orlando prerogatives that Vita did not have in real life: Orlando 'brushed her short hair with King James' silver brushes'[122] – not once, but twice in the novel. She also 'bounced up and down upon his bed (but no King would ever sleep there again, for all Louise's new sheets) and pressed her cheek against the worn silver counterpane that lay upon it.'[123] (Louise was Vita's French maid.)

Knole Park

Knole Park is open to the public free of charge every day of the year. It encompasses about a thousand acres; its varied terrain makes it an excellent spot for strolling and picnicking. *Orlando* enthusiasts should visit three spots in particular. (The National Trust's free leaflet contains a map of Knole Park – an excellent tool for this walk.)

The Cricket Pitch

A tour of the interior of Knole will return the visitor to the main gates, which are on the west side of the house. From the front of the house, follow the signs to the tearoom, which is located on the house's north side. Just opposite the tearoom, walk up the hill to the Cricket Pitch.

Harold once landed on the Cricket Pitch when he flew in a private plane from Paris to Knole. Vita watched him approach and called 'Here Hadji, here!' This scene is commemorated in the closing pages of *Orlando*.

From the Cricket Pitch, the vantage affords a striking impression of Knole's size. When Woolf described this same view in *Orlando*, she adopted Vita's image of Knole as a medieval town. Vita describes the view in *Knole and the Sackvilles*:

There are two sides from which you may first profitably look at the house. One is from the park, the north side. From here the pile shows best the vastness of its size; it looks like a medieval village. It is heaped with no attempt at symmetry; it is sombre and frowning; the grey towers rise; the battlements cut out their square regularity against the sky; the buttresses of the old twelfth-century tithe-barn give a rough impression of fortifications. There is a line of trees in one of the inner courtyards, and their green heads show above the roofs of the old breweries; but although they are actually trees of a considerable size, they are dwarfed and unnoticeable against the mass of the buildings blocked behind them. The whole pile

167

soars to a peak which is the clock-tower with its pointed roof: it might be the spire of the church on the summit of the hill crowning the medieval village. At sunset I have seen the silhouette of the great building stand dead black on a red sky; on moonlight nights it stands black and silent, with glinting windows, like an enchanted castle. On misty autumn nights I have seen it emerging partially from the trails of vapour, and heard the lonely roar of the red deer roaming under the walls.[124]

(Woolf's description of this same view can be found on page 151.)

The Masthead

Leave the Cricket Pitch and continue to walk in the same direction (east) along the north wall of Knole. The kitchen gardens lie just to the east of the house. Pass the kitchen gardens to the Broad Walk; turn *right* and follow the Broad Walk to the Masthead, the hill at the southeast end of Knole Park.

The Masthead formerly afforded an easy and sweeping view of the surrounding countryside: when deer hunting was a popular sport amongst the nobility in the early days of Knole, people would gather on the Masthead for a panoramic view of the hunt on the lands below. When Vita lived at Knole, there was a wooden tower built on this hill – the tower was also known by the name 'The Masthead' – and from the top of this tower one could view the entire park. (The structure called 'The Masthead' has been destroyed, probably when troops camped in Knole Park at the end of World War II.)[125] Vita Sackville-West enjoyed the view from the Masthead enormously: she often came to this hill, where she sat beneath an oak tree to write. This fact – and this location – is the inspiration for Orlando's poem *The Oak Tree*.

Though Knole Park has long been known for its great beech and oak trees, seventy per cent of the Park's trees were lost during the great storm of 1987. Many of these trees were vulnerable because of their great age; many have since been replaced by the Sackville family.

The Chapel

From the Masthead, return to the south side of the house. The Chapel is not open to the public, but it figures importantly in *Orlando*, and is therefore worth a quick look from the exterior of the house if the visitor happens to be at Knole on the right day. Since the Chapel is located along the south wall of Knole, it can only be seen when the private gardens are open: May to September, on the first Wednesday of each month. The Chapel is located at the extreme eastern end of the south side of Knole, and is distinguishable both by its tall east-facing windows and the cross on the peak of its roof.

As a child, Vita Sackville-West slept in a bedroom that connected to the Chapel. In *Knole and the Sackvilles*, Vita recalls that she often hid in the chapel when she had been naughty, withdrawing to the pulpit to sulk. In Vita's 1948 revision of *Knole and the Sackvilles*, she adds a memory that may have been stimulated by Woolf's intense re-imagining of the literary events connected to Knole: Vita remembers that, as she hid in the pulpit, she thought of John Donne preaching at Knole when he was rector at Sevenoaks, and reducing Lady Anne Clifford to tears.[126]

The chapel still houses the gifts sent to Thomas Sackville by Mary, Queen of Scots. One of these gifts was a triptych of the Procession to Calvary. In *Orlando*, Woolf re-imagines this gift as a small prayer book: when Orlando sits down in the Chapel, he picks up 'a little book bound in velvet, stitched with gold, which had been held by Mary Queen of Scots on the scaffold, and the eye of faith could detect a brownish stain, said to be made of a drop of the Royal blood'.[127]

Vita and Harold Nicolson were married in the Chapel at Knole; in *Knole and the Sackvilles*, Vita gives a striking description of the appearance of the Chapel during a thunderstorm. Woolf probably had Vita's description in mind for her account of Orlando's wedding, which Woolf sets it in the Chapel, during a thunderstorm: 'and now a bird was dashed against the pane, and now there was a clap of thunder, so that no one heard the word Obey spoken or saw, except as a golden flash, the ring pass from hand to hand.'[128]

LONG BARN AND WITHYHAM

Long Barn

Vita and Harold purchased Long Barn in 1915 and lived there for the next fifteen years. (They also always maintained a London residence: a house at 182 Ebury Street; a house in Neville Terrace; a flat for Harold in King's Bench Walk; eventually, a set of rooms that Harold shared with Nigel in Albany, off Piccadilly.) Long Barn is a very old house. Tradition has it that William Caxton was born there and when the Nicolsons were remodelling, they found a coin behind the plaster that dated to 1360.[129]

When the Nicolsons bought Long Barn, their first son, Ben, was seven months old; their second son, Nigel, was born in 1917. The Nicolsons set about an ambitious renovation scheme. They tore down an ancient barn on the property and reassembled its timbers as the basis of a new wing, built at right angles to the old house. This new wing had a fifty-foot-long drawing room on the ground floor which they called 'the Big Room'; when renovations were complete, Long Barn contained a total of seven main bedrooms and four bathrooms. Once their second son arrived, both children lived outside the main house, with their nanny in a cottage just up the hill. Over the next few years, the Nicolsons acquired property adjoining Long Barn: Harold bought Vita the adjacent field as a gift for her twenty-fourth birthday in 1916; then Vita's mother bought them Brook Farm, another neighbouring property.

Maintaining two homes – one in the country and one in the city – was an expensive proposition, and Vita worried about their finances. But she vowed 'to make £300 a year by writing. I've got three or four stories written, which could begin a book, and Harold who has a sense of humour could do a sort of "Xmas Garland" book quite easily.'[130] The Nicolsons eventually built a study for Harold off 'the Big Room', but Vita's sitting room – where she also wrote – was the best room in the house apart from the Big Room. It had windows on two sides and a fine fireplace. It was in her sitting-room that Vita began her affairs with Violet Trefusis (the model for Sasha in *Orlando*), with Virginia Woolf, and with Mary Campbell.

The Nicolsons also planted a garden. Harold laid out a formal plan shortly after they bought the house, and over the years they added lawns, walled terraces, beds of flowers. When Vita won the Hawthornden Prize, they planted the 'Hawthornden wood'. By the spring of 1926, Vita could tell Harold that 'Your new poplar walk is alive. The wood is a blaze of primulas, anemones, tulips, azaleas, irises, polyanthus ... The apple garden is a mass of lupins and irises. The turf is perfect ... The roses are beautifully pruned; the lilac is smothered in blossom. Your honeysuckle by the big room door also.'[131]

In the fifteen years she lived at Long Barn, Vita wrote the books that established her reputation as a poet and novelist: *Heritage, The Dragon in Shallow Waters, The Heir, Challenge, Grey Wethers, Seducers in Ecuador, The Land, The Edwardians.* As her son Nigel Nicolson has remarked, Vita had wanderlust and hated being yoked to routine – whether in marriage, or family life, or conventional relationships between the sexes.[132] Long Barn provided her with an anchor for her wanderings. As she wrote in 'Night: For Harold Nicolson' (1921), invoking Long Barn's interior and exterior spaces:[133]

> Moonlight through lattice throws a chequered square;
> Night! And I wake in my low-ceilinged room
> To cherished silence deep with harmony ...
> My Saxon Weald! My cool and candid Weald!
> Dear God: the heart, the very heart, of me
> That plays and strays a truant in strange lands,
> Always returns and finds its inward peace,
> Its swing of truth, its measure of restraint,
> Here among meadows, orchards, lanes and shaws.

After Vita and Harold moved to Sissinghurst Castle, they let Long Barn – most notably in 1936 to Charles and Anne Lindbergh whom they had met a few years earlier on a lecture tour of the United States. (Harold wrote a biography of Anne Lindbergh's father, Dwight Morrow, which was published in 1935.) Long Barn was bombed during World War II, and Vita sold the house in 1944.

Long Barn is privately owned; the house is not open to the public. But the Long Barn gardens are usually open twice a year as part of the National Garden Scheme Charitable Trust. For more information, see the National Garden Scheme's web site at www.ngs.org.uk.

How to get there
Long Barn lies at the western end of the village of Sevenoaks Weald, not too far from Sevenoaks and Knole. (For Vita, Long Barn's proximity to Knole was one of its attractions.)

By car: From London, go to the M25 London Orbital. At junction 5, go 4½ miles south on the A21 (signposted Sevenoaks/Hastings) to the junction with the B245 where there is also a sign to Weald. Take the fourth exit off the roundabout, to Sevenoaks Weald. At the Windmill Pub, the name changes to Long Barn Road. After about half a mile, there is a church on the left; Long Barn is a few yards further along on the same side, on a sharp right-hand bend.

By train: There is frequent train service from Charing Cross to Sevenoaks. From the Sevenoaks station, hire a taxi for Sevenoaks Weald.

Withyham

Vita Sackville-West's ashes lie with her ancestors in the Sackville Chapel at the Church of St Michael and All Angels, Withyham, East Sussex.

In her account of Lady Anne Clifford's visit to Withyham, Vita described the underground vault containing the Sackville coffins:

> I have been down into that vault myself, and it is not a cheerful expedition. In a small, dark cave underground, beneath the church, among grey veils of cobwebs, the coffins of the Sackvilles are stacked on shelves; they go back to the fourteenth century, and are of all sizes, from full-gown men down to the tiny ones lapped in lead. But, of course, when Anne Clifford went there there were not so many as there are now; the pompous ones were not yet in their places, with their rusty coronets, save those of the old Treasurer and his son; and their blood did not run in the veins of Lady Anne so on the whole she had less reason to be impressed than I.[134]

Though there has been a church on this spot since the thirteenth century, the Church of St Michael and All Angels was rebuilt in the seventeenth century after parts of it were destroyed by lightning. The reconstruction was completed in 1672; the Sackville family chapel was finished eight years later; other parts of the Church's interior were reordered in the nineteenth century. The most arresting feature of the Sackville Chapel is the monument to Thomas Sackville, the youngest son of the fifth Earl and Countess of Dorset, who died in 1675 at the age of thirteen. The monument portrays the grieving parents on both sides of the boy; the figures of his twelve siblings are carved on the sides of the tomb, with the six sons on the north side and the six daughters on the south side.

Young Thomas Sackville's oldest brother, Charles, became the sixth Earl of Dorset when his father died in 1677. It was this Charles, the sixth Earl, who provided the model for many of Orlando's actions in *Orlando*, including furnishing Knole with silver furniture for the King's Bedroom and writing poetry to Chloris and Dorinda. A final tribute was paid to Charles by another eminent poet: Alexander Pope wrote the epitaph on his monument in the Sackville Chapel.[135]

There is a tablet in memory of Vita Sackville-West on the wall of the Sackville Chapel at Withyham. Her ashes lie in the crypt below, placed in a small pink marble sarcophagus that formerly held the ink-wells she used for writing at both Long Barn and Sissinghurst.

Other sites in or near Withyham

There are three other sites in or near Withyham – Old Buckhurst, Buckhurst Park, and Penns in the Rocks – that, while not directly related to Virginia Woolf, might be attractive to those interested in the Sackville family. The gardens of Buckhurst Park and Penns in the Rocks may be open on occasion as part of the National Gardens Scheme Charitable Trust. For more information, see the National Gardens Scheme's web site at www.ngs.org.uk.

Old Buckhurst

The original seat of the Sackville family. This was once one of the largest country houses in England. The stone gatehouse is all that remains today of the original building. (Private home; not open to the public.)

Buckhurst Park, Withyham

The oldest ancestral seat of the Sackville family. The present house was first built by Sir Thomas Sackville, the first Earl of Dorset, at the end of the sixteenth century. It was completed by his son Richard. The Sackville family continued to spend time here even after Sir Thomas Sackville was given Knole by Queen Elizabeth I.

Penns in the Rocks
(Off the A26, seven miles southwest of Tunbridge Wells.) From 1672, the present house belonged to William Penn, the Quaker and founder of the State of Pennsylvania. Penn seems not to have spent much time here, since he owned large tracts of land in both North America and other parts of England. After Penn's death, the house passed to his son, grandson, and great-grandson, and then through various hands until it was purchased in 1925 by Lady Dorothy Wellesley, a close friend of Vita Sackville-West. Dorothy Wellesley entertained many writers there, including Leonard and Virginia Woolf. The Woolfs entered into a publishing venture with Dorothy Wellesley, in which she helped to subsidise the Hogarth Press's Living Poets series. Over a five-year period from 1928 to 1932, Wellesley and the Woolfs published twenty-four volumes in the series.[136]

How to get there
By car: Withyham lies on the B2110 southwest of Tunbridge Wells, near Groombridge. From London, go to the M25 London Orbital. At junction 5, go south on the A21, and from there south on the A26. (Follow these same directions from Knole: turn *left* out of the Park onto the A225, then join the A21 south; at the junction with the A26, take the A26 south.) At Tunbridge Wells, pick up the A264 travelling west (follow the signs for East Grinstead). Go through Langton Green and then straight on to the B2110 towards Groombridge. In Groombridge, fork *right* at the mini-roundabout, remaining on the B2110 (Withyham Road). Once in Withyham, the **Dorset Arms** pub is on the left; a few yards beyond is a signpost for the **Withyham Parish Church**.

By bus: There is an occasional bus from Tunbridge Wells Station to Withyham (Dorset Arms). For more information, check the Metrobus website at www.metrobus.co.uk.

SISSINGHURST CASTLE

In 1930, a neighbour threatened to build a poultry farm next to Long Barn. Fearing that the view from the terrace would be spoiled, Vita and

Harold began to look for a new house. Dorothy Wellesley's estate agent told Vita about an old property up for sale just outside the village of Sissinghurst. Vita and Dorothy drove over to see it; Vita instantly fell in love.

When Harold did some research at the London Library, he discovered that during the reign of Henry VIII, the dilapidated castle at Sissinghurst had been the property of Sir John Baker. Baker's daughter Cicely had married Thomas Sackville in 1554; Queen Elizabeth turned Knole over to Sackville and his wife twelve years later. This connection meant that Sissinghurst could be considered a 'family' property – a consideration that, since Vita had lost Knole at her father's death, meant a great deal to her. They took Harold's mother to see the property in the rain. Though both she and the two Nicolson sons were completely unimpressed – their younger son exclaimed 'But we haven't got to live *here*?' – Harold and Vita decided to buy. They completed the purchase of Sissinghurst in April 1930.[137]

Sissinghurst was a wreck. It had been used as a prison during the Seven Years' War and later as a parish workhouse. Not a single room was habitable; it had no running water or electricity; the garden consisted largely of mud and brambles. But Vita and Harold saw the potential in both buildings and gardens, and they set to work. Appropriately, a good deal of the money used to renovate Sissinghurst came from Vita's writing, and especially from *The Edwardians*, the best-selling novel about Knole that *Orlando* had inspired her to write. As she worked to rebuild and replant Sissinghurst, the property eventually became something like Vita's own private version of Knole.[138]

Over the years, Vita and Harold restored Sissinghurst's structures and shaped them into an unconventional plan that suited their style of living entirely – a style that allowed for members of the family to remain apart during the day and come together in the evening. The Priest's House was remodelled to contain a bedroom for their two sons, Nigel and Ben. The South Cottage housed a bedroom for Vita, a bedroom for Harold, and Harold's sitting room. The north wing of the old stables was converted into a fifty-foot-long parlour, which was to be used as the family's common sitting room and library. Vita's sitting-room/study was on the first floor of the Elizabethan tower. The Nicolsons deliberately made no provisions for guest rooms, so as to be able to avoid guests. (More recently, the south wing – which was once divided into two labourers' cottages – was converted into a private residence, where Nigel Nicolson now lives.)

Then Vita and Harold set about creating the garden, which is now one of the most celebrated gardens in England. Their garden was an extravagance; they created it when their work afforded them the time and the money to create it. Nigel Nicolson describes it best in his *Portrait of a Marriage*:

> Harold made the design; Vita did the planting. In the firm perspectives of the vistas, the careful siting of an urn or statue, the division of the garden by hedges and walls and buildings into a series of separate gardens, the calculated alternation between straight lines and curved, one can trace his classical hand. In the overflowing clematis, figs, vines and wistaria, in the rejection of violent colour or anything too tame or orderly, one discovers her romanticism. Wild flowers must be allowed to invade the garden; if plants stray over a path, they must not be cut back, the visitor must duck; rhododendrons must be banished in favour of their tenderer cousin, the azalea; roses must not electrify, but seduce; and when a season had produced its best, that part of the garden must be allowed to lie fallow for another year, since there is a cycle in nature that must not be disguised.[139]

Shortly after Vita bought Sissinghurst, Virginia introduced her to an antiques dealer in Warren Street, from whom Vita bought a Spanish table and an oak cupboard. She also acquired the Woolfs' old Minerva printing press – the press on which T.S. Eliot's *The Waste Land* had been hand-printed. (The press is still on display at Sissinghurst.) Flooded with the feeling that she had, finally, come home to stay, Vita sat down to write a new poem. She called it *Sissinghurst* and dedicated it to 'V.W.' (Some have seen the poem as a withdrawal, and as a farewell to Virginia.[140]) Vita's mother was enraged at the dedication and tried, unsuccessfully, to suppress the poem by buying up the entire edition from the Hogarth Press. (Vita's mother had been even more enraged by *Orlando*. Lady Sackville glued a newspaper photograph of Virginia inside the flyleaf of her own copy, and wrote beside it: 'The awful face of a mad woman whose successful mad desire is to separate people who care for each other. I loathe this woman for having changed my Vita and taken her away from me.'[141])

Virginia first visited Sissinghurst on 23 May 1930, when it was still a ruin. She stayed at Sissinghurst only one night, in Harold's bedroom in the South Cottage when he was away. Virginia first climbed Vita's tower in March of 1932, when she and Leonard came to lunch. Sissinghurst reminded Virginia of Knole: 'So we ate cold salmon & raspberries & cream & little variegated chocolates given by Lady Sackville, now at their feet, & drank oh lots of drinks; & then climbed Vita's tower; lovely pink brick; but like Knole, not much view, save of stables.'[142] From Vita's point of view, too, Sissinghurst was like Knole, but with a difference – it was a place to which Vita felt connected by history and emotion, but it was a place that was entirely hers, and could never be taken away from her. Twenty years later, when her son Nigel broached the question of giving Sissinghurst over to the National Trust – it was clear that the cost of maintaining Sissinghurst was becoming impossible, especially as more and more visitors discovered the delights of the garden – Vita replied that he could do so after her death. But not while she was alive: 'I said Never never never. *Au grand jamais, jamais.* Never, never, never … no Nat. Trust or any other foreign body shall have my darling … It is bad enough to have lost my Knole, but they shan't take S/hurst from me.'[143]

Over the years, Vita grew increasingly solitary and retreated into her tower and her garden. The retreat into Sissinghurst, and into religion, marked the end of Virginia's vision of Vita in the grocer's shop at Sevenoaks, 'pink glowing, grape clustered, pearl hung' – the vision that inspired *Orlando*. It was a visit to Sissinghurst in 1935 that convinced Virginia that at least one aspect of their friendship was over:

Then on Sunday we went to Sissinghurst: in the bitter wind with the country all lying in its June green & blue outside the window. Now thats an odd observation I have to make. My friendship with Vita is over. Not with a quarrel, not with a bang, but as ripe fruit falls. No I shant be coming to London before I go to Greece, she said. And then I got into the car. But her voice saying 'Virginia?' outside the tower room was as enchanting as ever. Only then nothing happened. And she has grown very much the indolent county lady, run to seed, incurious now about books; has written no poetry; only kindles about dogs, flowers, & new buildings. S[issinghurst] is to have a new wing; a new garden; a new wall. Well, its like cutting off a picture: there she hangs, in the fishmongers at Sevenoaks, all pink jersey & pearls; & thats an end of it. And there is no bitterness, & no disillusion, only a certain emptiness.[144]

Even with the passion spent, Vita and Virginia remained friends for the rest of their days. They saw each other in the country, either at Monk's House or at Sissinghurst. When the war began, Vita kept the Woolfs supplied with butter, since Sissinghurst made its own. Vita once phoned Virginia from Sissinghurst in the middle of an air raid; riveted by the idea that she had just talked to someone who might be killed at any minute, Virginia summed up their relationship: 'You have given me such happiness.'[145]

Vita died at Sissinghurst in 1962.

A Walk around Sissinghurst
The National Trust sells an excellent guide to Sissinghurst and its gardens, written by Nigel Nicolson. Mr Nicolson's guide is an indispensable companion to the visitor's tour of Sissinghurst. The following section provides some additional information about some of the structures on the grounds.

The Tower
Though the Nicolsons bought Sissinghurst in 1930, they didn't move out of Long Barn until 1932. They divided their time in the country between the two houses while Sissinghurst was under renovation.

Of course the centre of Vita's life at Sissinghurst was her Tower writing room. The Nicolson family camped out in the Tower at weekends while the other buildings were being renovated; one morning over breakfast, Harold used his butter knife to pry loose one of the bricks that walled up the adjoining turret-room. Vita peered into the room and declared that it would be her library. And, she added, waving a teaspoon around the room in which they sat, 'This will be my sitting room.' The

Tower remained her sitting and writing room for the rest of her life, the place to which she retired to work for long stretches of each day, and into which few other people dared venture. Even her sons were loath to disturb her there – they stood at the foot of the stairs and shouted up if Vita was wanted on the telephone, or if lunch was ready.[146] Vita wrote some twenty books in this room, including *All Passion Spent*, *Pepita* and her long poem *The Garden*.

Vita's writing room is on the first floor of the Tower. It can be viewed through the gate; it remains very much as she left it. Her desk has a picture of the Brontë sisters and a photo of Virginia Woolf; all her library is still ranged around the walls. One shelf is dedicated to her own works; another to novels by Woolf. On this last shelf sit two copies of *To the Lighthouse*. One is the dummy copy that Vita received from Virginia the day she returned home from Persia, which also happened to be the day *To the Lighthouse* was published. The book is entirely blank and is inscribed on the flyleaf in Virginia's hand, 'In my opinion the best novel I have ever written'.

The South Cottage and Priest's House

The South Cottage and Priest's House became the Nicolson family's private living quarters. The buildings are still used as private residences and are not open to the public.

The South Cottage was the building in which Harold and Vita lived. It contains Harold's sitting-room, and bedrooms for both Vita and Harold. The South Cottage provided some nice surprises while it was being renovated: as Vita tells it, the workmen uncovered '*the* most lovely, huge, stone Tudor fireplace in my bedroom'.[147] The Nicolsons planted a white rose against the cottage wall on the day they bought Sissinghurst; it still grows there, and flowers profusely every summer.[148]

The Priest's House was reserved for the Nicolsons' two sons. It contained their bedroom, the kitchen, and the family dining-room. This arrangement meant that Vita and Harold had to walk from the South Cottage to the Priest's House for meals, a fact that initially disturbed Harold: 'when we are old we shall die if we have to go a long country walk from meal to meal. And at night.'[149] But Vita liked their plan, and they adhered to it, eventually adding a loggia (for outdoor summertime dining) made from fragments of the old house found in the orchard.[150]

It was in the Priest's House that Vita died in 1962.

The Long Library

The major Sissinghurst project for 1935 was the completion of the Long Library. The room had formerly been a stable; the Nicolsons added a window and made a fireplace from fragments of an Elizabethan fireplace found on the grounds. They had hoped to recreate the feeling of their fifty-foot-long Big Room at Long Barn, but Harold never much liked the proportions of the room, and Vita herself called it 'A FAILURE. Try as I may, I cannot get it to come together.'[151] Today's visitor is likely to have a very different reaction: the Long Library is filled with thousands of the books Vita and Harold collected in forty years of reviewing, and with the furniture Vita eventually inherited from her mother, Lady Sackville. But the Nicolsons soon abandoned the Long Library as a family sitting-room and returned for this purpose to the Priest's House.

How to get there

Sissinghurst Castle Garden is open from April to mid-October daily, except Mondays. (Sissinghurst is also closed on Bank Holiday Mondays.) On Tuesdays through Fridays, the garden is open from 1 p.m. to 6.30 p.m.; on Saturdays and Sundays, the garden is open from 10 a.m. to 6.30 p.m. Note: the ticket office and exhibition open at noon on Tuesdays through Fridays, though garden admission doesn't begin until an hour later. Owing to the garden's limited capacity, a timed ticket system is used, with tickets available for purchase on the day of the visit. For more details of opening hours, restrictions, and shop times, call 01580 710 701, or visit the National Trust website at www.nationaltrust.org.uk.

By car: Sissinghurst is located two miles north-east of Cranbrook and one mile east of Sissinghurst village on the A262. From London, take the M20 to Maidstone, and leave the motorway at junction 6 onto the A229 travelling south. Take the A229 to the A262; travel east on the A262 a short distance to Sissinghurst.

By train: Trains leave Charing Cross regularly for Staplehurst station; Sissinghurst is over five miles from Staplehurst. A bus meets certain trains at Staplehurst on Thursdays and Sundays; otherwise, taxis may be hired at Staplehurst. For more information, phone the Sissinghurst information line at 01580 710 701.

CHAPTER FOUR

Cambridge and *A Room of One's Own*

'Only Cambridge will never be to him what it was, even to me ... Oh the
sound of Grace coming through Adrian's windows in Nevilles court in
the summer when we were young!'
Virginia Woolf to Quentin Bell, 1 November 1928

'But when I think of Cambridge, I vomit – that's all – a green vomit,
which gets into the ink and blisters the paper.'
Virginia Woolf to Lytton Strachey, 21 May 1912

I

Cambridge was a part of the fabric of Virginia Woolf's life from the day
she was born. Her grandfather, Sir James Stephen, was Regius Professor
of Modern History at Cambridge in the mid-nineteenth century; her
father, Sir Leslie Stephen, was a Fellow at Trinity Hall, and a beloved
figure in sports and intellectual circles around the University. Her aunt
Caroline Emelia lived a writer's life at Cambridge, where she produced
learned treatises on the history of the Quaker movement; her cousin
Katherine Stephen was the Principal of Newnham. All her brothers
went to Cambridge; so did her male cousins. She married a Trinity man.

In the next generation, her nieces and nephews were students at King's and Newnham. Cambridge education was a family affair for Woolf – something she described with affection and viewed with suspicion. That education had, after all, been withheld from her – a fact that left her feeling at a disadvantage for her entire life.

Woolf's first introduction to Cambridge came through her father. Sir Leslie Stephen had gone up to Trinity Hall as an undergraduate in 1850 and was elected Fellow of the College in 1854. During his fourteen years at Trinity Hall, Stephen was known for two things: for his fanatical devotion to athletics and for his radical ideas about education. Stephen thought nothing of walking from Cambridge to London and back to attend a dinner party; he challenged friends to races that pitted his speed at walking cross-country against their speed at running along clear towpaths by the Cam. Stephen invented the athletic match between Oxford and Cambridge, and achieved fame as Trinity Hall's rowing coach when he led the college's boats to victory in 1859 and 1862. (He even wrote a college boating song.) As a teacher and reader of examinations, Stephen was equally enthusiastic about educational reform. He argued for enriching the educational experience of the average undergraduate by providing a more general course of instruction in history, geology and the spirit of the classics. Stephen argued that practical courses – even accountancy – should be part of a university education, since these subjects would both prepare students for meaningful work, and encourage parents from a wider mix of social classes to send their sons to Cambridge. His proposed reforms were not enacted during his years at Cambridge, but laid the groundwork for changes in the next decades.[1]

Stephen's career at Cambridge was cut short by a matter of principle. In Stephen's day, almost all college fellowships required the holder to be ordained as a clergyman in the Church of England, and Stephen accordingly took Holy Orders shortly after his appointment to Trinity Hall. But he was a rationalist at heart and, as time passed, he realised that he did not really believe many of the things his position obliged him to preach. As Stephen put it, he became convinced that Noah's flood was a fiction, and that it was wrong for him to read or teach the story as the sacred truth. Later, Stephen would write a book entitled *An Agnostic's Apology*, in which he argued that there was simply no way of knowing the truth or falsity of most theological propositions. Torn between his desire to retain his comfortable position at the Hall, and his inveterate need for complete intellectual honesty, Stephen informed the Master of Trinity Hall that he could no longer take part in chapel services. Shortly thereafter, he resigned his tutorship at the College. He decided to make his living as a writer and literary critic, and left Cambridge for London in 1864.

When his daughter Virginia was born nearly twenty years later, Stephen's Cambridge legacy of athleticism and wide-ranging, honest intellectual inquiry shaped her daily life. She trudged the banks of the Thames with her father from Hammersmith to Putney, and remembered 'being walked off my legs round the Serpentine'.[2] Stephen routinely took his daughters to the Hammersmith Bridge to watch the Cambridge and Oxford crews practise for their annual race; many years later, Virginia was still laying bets with Leonard on the race's outcome. Most of Virginia's education was supervised by her parents at home. She attended some classes in history and Greek at King's College, Kensington, which was within walking distance of Hyde Park Gate, and her father later engaged Clara Pater to teach her Latin, and Janet Case (a Girton graduate) to teach her Greek. But Stephen himself took charge of her wide reading in history and biography, usually by recommending books to her from his large library and then discussing them with her as she returned them. The reading schedule was rigorous enough that Virginia, who was fifteen in 1897, saw it as preparation for Cambridge. That spring, Cambridge debated a proposal to admit the women of Newnham and Girton Colleges to titular degrees – that is, to allow the women who passed the University's rigorous examinations to use the letters 'B.A.' after their names just as men did. As a Cambridge household, the Stephen family was immersed in the debate and a cousin – F. W. Maitland, who was Downing Professor of the Laws of England and later Leslie Stephen's biographer – emerged as the most forceful public voice in favour of the proposal. At home in London, Virginia followed the vote avidly and dreamed that her reading would prepare her for the University: 'Already I am an expert upon William [of Orange] ... & when I have mastered C[arlyle]'s 2 vols. I shall be eligible for the first B.A. degree – if the ladies succeed.'[3]

185

Sadly, the ladies did not succeed. Passions ran high against the proposal – both because it seemed improper for women to share lectures with men, and because granting women degrees admitted them to voting rights in the governance of the University. The Great Northern Line scheduled special trains out of King's Cross to accommodate all the male graduates expected to return for the vote. Since the Cambridge railway station lay on the outskirts of town, crowds of undergraduates met the trains with horses and carriages to carry the voters to the Senate House, where the vote took place. An effigy of a woman student – dressed in bloomers, riding a bicycle – was hung from the windows of the building across the street; the crush was so great at the Senate House that the voters couldn't fit through the doors, and temporary exits were fixed through the windows. The final tally was 1,707 against admitting women to degrees and 661 in favour. When the result was announced, an undergraduate crowd surged down Silver Street to Newnham, where the senior members had gathered under an archway to appeal to the crowd's 'gentlemanly instincts' to turn back. The crowd did turn back – to Market Square, where the undergraduates ripped doors and shutters from shops for a huge victory bonfire that burned through the night.[4]

So Virginia did not 'go up' to Cambridge. She continued to study Greek, history and literature at home in Hyde Park Gate. Her older brother, Thoby, went up to Trinity College in 1899. Leslie Stephen continued to hope that Virginia would follow in his footsteps as a writer, and Virginia continued to have the run of his large and unexpurgated library. In later years, she would remember her hours in her father's study with great warmth and even argue that her education was in some respects better than what she might have been given at Cambridge. But Virginia was also keenly aware that Thoby's life at Cambridge with his new friends – Clive Bell, Leonard Woolf, Lytton Strachey – was much more expansive than hers. She complained to him in 1903: 'I have to delve from books, painfully and all alone, what you get every evening sitting over your fire and smoking your pipe with Strachey etc. No wonder my knowledge is but scant. Theres nothing like talk as an educator I'm sure.'[5]

During Thoby's years at Cambridge, Virginia experienced her

brother's university education vicariously. Thoby corresponded with Virginia about Shakespeare and gave her advice on translating Sophocles. He also introduced her to his friends – an important moment in the intellectual history of the new century, since Thoby's two sisters and his Cambridge friends eventually made up the nucleus of the Bloomsbury group. Virginia and Vanessa went up to Cambridge to visit Thoby during May week in 1900 and attended their first Trinity Ball. They met Clive Bell, who later became Vanessa's husband. When they visited Thoby in his rooms – chaperoned by their cousin Katherine Stephen, Principal of Newnham and formidable intellectual presence – they also met Leonard Woolf. He never forgot the startling impression the two sisters made:

> I also met Thoby's two sisters, Vanessa and Virginia Stephen, when they came up to see him. The young ladies – Vanessa was twenty-one or twenty-two, Virginia was eighteen or nineteen – were just as formidable and alarming as their father, perhaps even more so. I first saw them one summer afternoon in Thoby's rooms; in white dresses and large hats, with parasols in their hands, their beauty literally took one's breath away, for suddenly seeing them one stopped astonished and everything including one's breathing for one second also stopped as it does when in a picture gallery you suddenly come face to face with a great Rembrandt or Velasquez ... Sitting with them in their brother's room was their cousin, Miss Katherine Stephen, Principal of Newnham, with whom they were staying. But Miss Stephen was in her cousin's room for a tea-party, not in her capacity of cousin, but in her capacity of chaperone, for in 1901 a respectable female sister was not allowed to see her male brother in his rooms in a male college except in the presence of a chaperone. I liked Miss Stephen very much, but it could not be denied that she was a distinguished, formidable, and rather alarming chaperone ... Vanessa and Virginia were also very silent and to any superficial observer they might have seemed demure ... [But] the observant observer would have noticed at the back of the two Miss Stephens' eyes a look which would have warned him to be cautious, a look which belied the demureness, a look of great intelligence, hypercritical, sarcastic, satirical.[6]

Adrian Stephen came up to Trinity in 1902; Virginia and Vanessa travelled to Cambridge to help him buy furniture for his new rooms. Meanwhile, Thoby's friends Lytton Strachey and Leonard Woolf were elected to the Apostles – an elite Cambridge discussion society founded in the nineteenth century that had also elected the likes of Arthur Hallam, Alfred Tennyson, Alfred North Whitehead, and Bertrand Russell. Thoby and Clive Bell were never elected to the Apostles – a matter of irritation to both men – but they were still drawn into the orbit of the other members, who included Roger Fry, E.M. Forster, John Maynard Keynes, Desmond MacCarthy, Saxon Sydney-Turner and, most important, the philosopher G.E. Moore. Moore was a Fellow of Trinity, an influential thinker, and one of the senior members of the Apostles. He dominated the group's discussions, demanding that his undergraduates question every concept and strive for precision in expression. Moore valued the subjectivity of states of consciousness above all, and insisted that: 'By far the most valuable things, which we know or can imagine, are certain states of consciousness which may be roughly described as the pleasures of human intercourse and the enjoyment of beautiful objects.'[7] A few years later, the supremacy of these two things – loving friendships and aesthetic experience – became a central Bloomsbury belief.

Thoby left Cambridge in 1903 and returned to 22 Hyde Park Gate, where Virginia was still reading constantly, writing literary exercises, and studying Greek. She was also tending to her father in his last illness, and when Leslie Stephen died in 1904, Virginia was beset by her second serious attack of mental illness. She went first to Burnham Wood and then to Cambridge to recuperate: she stayed for several weeks late that year with Leslie Stephen's sister, her aunt Caroline Emelia Stephen, who had settled at the Porch, on Grantchester Street. At the Porch, Caroline Emelia lived a quiet writer's life, producing books about Quaker theology and her own family history. Virginia could sit at a window that overlooked trees of 'pure gold and orange', and be comforted by the silence of Cambridge, in which she could 'hear only birds songs, and the rustle of leaves'.[8]

While she stayed at the Porch, Virginia also had the opportunity to understand her aunt's way of thinking, which was very different from the dominant rationalism on which Cambridge prided itself. Caroline Emelia Stephen contributed political and religious essays to contemporary magazines; her niece, Katherine Stephen, invited her to lecture to the women students at Newnham. Caroline Emelia had written a book about better ways of serving the poor; as a devout Quaker, she wrote about the importance of pacifism and about the importance of setting oneself apart from the dominant culture. Caroline Emelia's home became a gathering place for the Quaker students attending Cambridge, and through her writing and advocacy, she almost single-handedly revived the English Society of Friends at the turn of the century. In short, Caroline Emelia's way of thinking provided an antidote to the insistence on reason – and to the competition, jealousy and exclusivity – that seemed sometimes to dominate university life.[9]

Virginia's feelings for her aunt Caroline Emelia were ambivalent. Virginia insisted that she disagreed 'entirely with her whole system of toleration and resignation, and general benignity, which does seem to me so woolly'.[10] Caroline Emelia was so 'soporific' that Virginia yearned to 'blow her up with gunpowder'.[11] Yet Virginia also saw that her aunt was 'a very wise and witty old lady',[12] and over the years, her attitude towards her softened. Unlike many of the less intellectual women of Leslie Stephen's generation, Caroline Emelia was durable and tough: 'The Quaker is like some glossy evergreen; I feel she will rustle her leaves over all our graves ... she is about as tough an old heathen as they make; we shant develop such thews and sinews not if we live 80 years.'[13] While staying with Caroline Emelia, Virginia assisted F.W. Maitland with her father's biography – she read and sorted her parents' love letters – and began to generate ideas for her first published essays. Caroline Emelia Stephen became intensely interested in her niece's literary career and, like her brother Leslie, hoped that Virginia would carry on the Stephen family tradition of writing. When Caroline Emelia died a few years later, she left £100 to Vanessa, but £2,500 to Virginia. This generous bequest allowed Virginia to try her hand as a writer from the outset. Because of the emotional and financial independence that it gave her, the bequest also came to assume an important symbolic weight many years later in *A Room of One's Own*.

After Thoby left Cambridge, he and his friends took pains to keep the stimulating atmosphere of their undergraduate days alive. Some of them collaborated on a book of poetry called *Euphrosyne*; Thoby decided to be 'at home' to friends who called on Thursday evenings at the Stephen siblings' new house in Gordon Square, Bloomsbury. Virginia eagerly recorded the meetings in her diary, happy finally to have direct access to the kind of intellectual exchange she had missed by not being a student at Cambridge: 'Sydney-Turner and Strachey came after dinner and we talked till twelve';[14] 'Home and found Bell, and we talked about the nature of good till almost one!'[15] In true Cambridge style – and under the inspiration of G.E. Moore's *Principia Ethica*, which they had all recently read – Thoby's friends and sisters busily dissected the great abstractions. Someone might use the word 'truth' or 'beauty', and it was as if a bull had been let into a bull ring. As Woolf remembered many years later,

> The bull might be 'beauty', might be 'good', might be 'reality'. Whatever it was, it was some abstract question that now drew out all our forces. Never have I listened so intently to each step and half-step in an argument. Never have I been at such pains to sharpen and launch my own little dart ... It filled me with wonder to watch those who were finally left in the argument piling stone upon stone, cautiously, accurately, long after it had completely soared above my sight ... One had glimpses of something miraculous happening high up in the air. Often we would still be sitting in a circle at two or three in the morning ... The marvellous edifice was complete, one could stumble off to bed feeling that something very important had happened. It had been proved that beauty was – or beauty was not – for I have never been quite sure which – part of a picture.[16]

From Woolf's point of view, 'these Thursday evening parties were, as far as I am concerned, the germ from which sprang all that has since come to be called ... by the name of Bloomsbury'.[17] The young people had a giddy sense of widened horizons, of new worlds opening up, of being in the vanguard of unimaginably new ways of thinking and behaving. Virginia was publishing literary essays and had started work on a novel; Vanessa began exhibiting her paintings around London regularly; Lytton Strachey was offered (and refused) the editorship of *The Spectator*.

Over the next few years, Virginia continued to make day trips to Cambridge to see friends and relatives. Just as Cambridge's intellectual passions produced the heady beginnings of the Bloomsbury group, so Cambridge naturally produced Virginia Stephen's suitors. Once Vanessa married Clive Bell – she accepted his proposal two days after Thoby's death from typhoid in 1906 – Virginia was increasingly interested in the idea of marriage herself. All her suitors were, inevitably, Cambridge men, and five of them proposed marriage before Virginia settled on Leonard Woolf. The first was Walter Headlam, a Fellow of King's and a great classical scholar – and a man almost old enough to be Virginia's father, who had also pursued both Virginia's mother and her half-sister, Stella Duckworth.[18] Headlam wanted to dedicate his translation of *Agamemnon* to Virginia, who was flattered, but not smitten. Then there was Hilton Young, one of Thoby's contemporaries at Trinity. Young was handsome and genial; he proposed to Virginia in a punt on the Cam; he was gently rejected. In 1911, Walter Lamb – another of Thoby's friends at Trinity who had become a lecturer at Newnham – proposed to Virginia in Richmond Park. But Virginia told Vanessa that 'there is something pathetic in him'.[19] In the same year, Virginia also got a proposal from Sydney Waterlow, a brilliant classicist-turned-diplomat who knew the entire circle from his days at Trinity College. Waterlow was perhaps the only suitor who recognised Virginia's potential sensuality: he thought that Vanessa was the icy and artistic sister, while Virginia was the emotional one, interested in life instead of beauty.[20] But Virginia did not return the compliment, and told Waterlow in no uncertain terms to 'stop thinking of me as the person you want to marry'.[21]

The most tempting proposal of marriage Virginia received from Thoby's Cambridge circle at this period came from a man who remained an intimate for the rest of her life: Lytton Strachey. Lytton had stayed at Cambridge longer than most of his friends, writing a dissertation on Warren Hastings and hoping to be awarded a Fellowship at Trinity. But he was rejected for the position twice and was finally forced to vacate his rooms on K staircase in the Great Court. Strachey moved back to his family's home in London; from there, he wrote reviews for *The Spectator* and the *New Quarterly*, and pursued affairs of the heart with Maynard Keynes and Duncan Grant. In February 1909, feeling that his affairs with Keynes and Grant had collapsed, anxious to escape from his parents' house, and drawn by Virginia's wit and intelligence, he proposed to her. She immediately accepted; they both immediately realised their folly. Before the conversation ended,

Lytton managed to extricate himself from the situation. The next day Virginia and Lytton had what he called an 'eclaircissement': 'She declared she was not in love with me, and I observed finally that I would not marry her.' Lytton relayed the entire adventure in letters to Leonard Woolf, who was in Ceylon, and insisted that Leonard should propose to Virginia in his stead – 'If you came and proposed she'ld accept. She really would'. Lytton was right, though Leonard's proposal wouldn't come for another three years.[22]

In the meantime, Virginia had another flirtation with a Cambridge man who did not propose: Rupert Brooke. Brooke came up to King's College on a classics scholarship in 1906, shortly after Thoby had gone back to London. He was active in the University theatre and wrote poetry; he was elected to the Apostles in 1908, and became President of the University's Fabian Society; he was breathtakingly handsome. (Henry James met Brooke on a visit to Cambridge and asked his host if Brooke's poetry was any good. When the host said that it wasn't, James replied: 'Thank goodness. If he looked like that and was a good poet too, I do not know what I should do.') Brooke moved outside King's to Grantchester to write his dissertation during his fourth year at the University, first taking rooms in the Orchard, and then settling at the Old Vicarage. The lovely countryside around Grantchester transformed Brooke overnight into a prophet of nature: he wrote 'Arcady' at the top of his letters, and promised that friends who visited him would find a paradise 'of Laughter and Bodies and Flowers and Love and People and Sun and Wind'.[23] This was a very different world from sceptical, satirical Bloomsbury, which christened Brooke and his entourage 'Neo-Pagans'. In a daring mood, Virginia (who had first met Brooke at Talland House and became reacquainted with him through Cambridge) went to stay with Brooke for a week at Grantchester in 1911. It was August, and she was working on her first novel, *The Voyage Out*; the proofs of Brooke's first book of poetry were lying about, scattered on the grass. Suddenly he asked, 'Virginia, what is the brightest thing you can think of?' When she replied, 'A leaf with the light on it', her line was immediately incorporated into his poem 'Town and Country'.[24] They took off their clothes and had a nude moonlight swim in Byron's pool. Later that month, Virginia went on a camping trip with Brooke,

Maynard Keynes, and several others. She was careful to keep everyone informed of her adventures, and Adrian was happy to spread the news. He wrote to Clive Bell that, 'I shall see the Goat today and hear how her Rupert romance is going on. She told me that he said he did not want to marry for several years at any rate but did want to copulate occasionally and promiscuously. I am afraid that her bathe has not been taken quite seriously enough for her taste but perhaps she will now have gone a step further.'[25]

After Brooke died of blood poisoning on his way to Gallipoli during World War I, Woolf responded to his canonisation as a patriot with some irony. He was a barefoot Pied Piper, she said, who enchanted happy disciples into following him:

> He was living at Grantchester; his feet were permanently bare; he disdained tobacco and butcher's meat; and he lived all day, and perhaps slept all night, in the open air ... Under his influence the country near Cambridge was full of young men and women walking barefoot, sharing his passion for bathing and fish diet, disdaining book learning, and proclaiming that there was something deep and wonderful in the man who brought the milk and in the woman who watched the cows.[26]

But, irony or not, Brooke always occupied a special place in Woolf's Cambridge memories.

When Woolf later looked back on this period of her life, Cambridge figured as a source of pleasure, of excitement, of belonging. When she was nearly forty, she went to a party and found a large semi-circle of Cambridge youths: 'I was amused at the repetition of certain old scenes from my own past – the obvious excitement, & sense of being the latest & best ... of God's works, of having things to say for the first time in history.'[27] People associated with Cambridge made her feel reverent and religious: 'Then we had Norton to dinner, and I felt a kind of reverence for him, as the representative of old Cambridge, as we knew it, in the days of "personal emotions"; I must say I think it probably the highest type in the world, and it solves all my religious feelings.'[28] Cambridge was a lovely place that reminded her of her past; when Woolf retraced her steps along old paths, it evoked 'that growing maternal affection which now comes to me, of myself there; of Rupert'.[29] She looked wistfully back at the University as it had been 'in my day',[30] and she once lamented, when she saw her nephew Julian bored at King's, 'Only Cambridge will never be to him what it was, even to me. Oh the sound of Grace coming through Adrian's windows in Nevilles court in the summer when we were young!'[31]

But there were always darker feelings running counter to Woolf's fond sense of attachment to Cambridge. Ethel Smyth described Woolf as being 'most calm & cool & Cambridge',[32] and Woolf agreed that Cambridge had a tendency to turn people emotionally cold: 'I grant that having been born within the Polar region of Cambridge I tend by education not instinct to frigidify.'[33] Cambridge also squashed imagination and fostered egotism: 'This is a judgment upon Cambridge generally .... You lose all generosity and all power of imagination. Moreover, you inevitably become a complete egoist.'[34] Cambridge bred 'unalloyed melancholy';[35] Woolf deplored the 'Cambridge infection'[36] that trapped people into a conviction of the superiority of the life there. Woolf told her nephew Julian that the worst culprits were exclusive societies, like the Apostles, which fostered envy and conceit: 'As for your Apostles, much though I respect them singly, I begin to think that these Societies do more harm than good, merely by rousing jealousies and vanities. What d'you think? it seems to me the wrong way to live, drawing chalk marks round ones feet, and saying to the Clives etc you can't come in.'[37]

Of course, much of Woolf's mistrust of Cambridge and all of its associated institutions sprang from the fact that, as enmeshed in Cambridge culture as Woolf was, she had also been systematically excluded from it. She had not been eligible to sit for 'the first B.A. degree', a fact for which she blamed both her father and the University. Leslie Stephen, after all, 'spent perhaps £100 on my education',[38] while he spent thousands on his sons. Many years later, Woolf complained to Desmond MacCarthy about the inferiority of 'my wretched little £150 education', which paled in comparison to MacCarthy's Cambridge education, which cost 'about four thousand five hundred and fifty pounds'.[39] Woolf always felt that the informality of her home schooling put her at a disadvantage: she was ashamed of the fact that she did sums by counting on her fingers; she bemoaned her intermittent lack of confidence – 'my inadequacy; what shifts and squeaks I'm put to every time I dip my pen';[40] she described herself (only half) jokingly as 'an illiter-trate (who can't spell)'.[41] Even at the height of her public acclaim, when Goldsworthy Lowes Dickinson (Fellow of King's College) wrote to her to say how much he liked *A Room of One's Own*, Woolf thanked him warmly, but insisted that she was 'a complete outsider' when it came to the question of education.[42]

Woolf's resentment about her education and Cambridge was intensi-fied by the events surrounding the second attempt to admit women to the University. By 1921, the women's colleges at both Oxford and Cambridge were continuing to grow in size, and their members were performing impressively as women were admitted to more and more university examinations. But neither University allowed women full membership, or allowed women to receive an actual university degree. Just after World War I, when women won the right to vote, their posi-tion at Oxford and Cambridge seemed scandalous, especially since the University of London and all the provincial universities had been granting women degrees for nearly thirty years.[43] Both universities reopened the question of admitting women to full membership, and Oxford voted in favour of the proposition in 1921.

Cambridge was not so progressive. The University Senate debated and voted on two different proposals in 1920: to admit women to full membership in Cambridge, or to create a separate women's university. Both propositions were roundly rejected. An embarrassed administra-tion formulated two more propositions for the following year. The first recommended that women be admitted to full membership in the University, but that their numbers be restricted to five hundred. The second recommended, as an alternative, that women be admitted to titular degrees – that is, that they be allowed to use the letters 'B.A.' after their names, even though they did not technically possess Cambridge degrees. (This second proposal was the same proposition that had been offered and rejected in 1897.) When the vote was taken in October 1921, the University Senate again rejected the proposal for full membership in the University. But it voted in favour of granting titular degrees to women. It was a vote that furthered the women's cause significantly, since they could now say they had earned the equivalent of a Cambridge degree when they applied for jobs. But it was a vote that still excluded women as members of the University, and thereby denied them any meaningful participation in University governance or decision-making.

When the results were announced, one elderly M.A. from Corpus Christi – the Reverend Pussy Hart, vicar of Ixworth – shouted to a mob of undergraduate men milling outside the Senate House, 'Now go and tell Newnham and Girton!' The mob surged, screaming, up Newnham Walk. When it reached the entrance to the college, someone found a coal cart, and the mob used it as a battering ram to smash down the Clough Memorial Gates. The principal of Newnham blocked the undergraduate men from entering the college and wreaking more havoc, but the damage had been done, and apologies began to pour in from around the University the next day.[44] Describing this scene in 1937, Woolf concluded that it provided a lesson in the effects of an elitist education: 'The finest education in the world does not teach people to hate force, but to use it ... education, far from teaching the educated generosity and magnanimity, makes them on the contrary so anxious to keep their possessions'[45] that they will use force to retain them. Cambridge did finally grant women full membership in the University, but it was not until 1948, seven years after Woolf's death.

Notwithstanding Woolf's discomfort with many aspects of Cambridge's culture, she and Leonard continued to be firmly rooted in it. By the 1920s, most of their friends were still connected to Cambridge in some way: Maynard Keynes was a Fellow of King's, a lecturer in economics, and eventually became the Bursar of King's; G.E. Moore was still at Trinity; Lytton Strachey often came to Cambridge to stay with George ('Dadie') Rylands, who worked at the Woolfs' Hogarth Press and then settled in as a Fellow of King's; Strachey's sister Pernel was Principal of Newnham; E.M. Forster gave the Clark Lectures at Trinity in 1927, and was afterwards elected a Supernumerary Fellow of King's. Leonard regularly came up to Cambridge to attend dinner meetings of the Apostles and Virginia usually accompanied him. On one of these occasions, Virginia walked over to Newnham to dine with Pernel Strachey and recorded the walk along the Backs towards Silver Street in her diary: 'A lovely place full, like all places, now, of this wave of the past. Walking past the Darwins I noticed the willows.' This description later reappears as part of the introduction to the women's college in *A Room of One's Own*. As Leonard and Virginia began to make names for themselves as writers, they were both invited to lecture to various Cambridge groups. By 1924, Woolf had published three novels, a collection of experimental short stories, and a stream of journalism and criticism. She lectured to a Cambridge undergraduate society called the Heretics that year on the subject of modern fiction. She then reworked her lecture into the famous essay 'Mr Bennett and Mrs Brown', an essay that has been read as Woolf's experimental manifesto.

In October 1928, Woolf was invited to lecture to the women at Newnham and Girton on the topic of women and fiction. She drove up to Cambridge on 20 October with Vanessa, Angelica and Leonard; they dined at Newnham and stayed with Pernel Strachey, Newnham's Principal. That night, Woolf read her lecture to the Newnham Arts Society, whose secretary was Elsie Phare. The following afternoon they lunched in George 'Dadie' Rylands' rooms at King's – a lunch that Woolf describes extravagantly in *A Room of One's Own*. The following week, on 26 October, Woolf returned to Cambridge, this time with Vita Sackville-West, to repeat her lecture for the ODTAA Society at Girton. She saw her nephew Julian before the lecture and dined afterwards with Margaret Thomas, one of the students responsible for inviting her to Girton. When she returned home, she recorded her impressions in her diary, and laid the groundwork for the dramatic contrast of men's and women's colleges that begins *A Room of One's Own*:

> I am back from speaking at Girton, in floods of rain … Starved but valiant young women – that's my impression. Intelligent eager, poor; & destined to become schoolmistresses in shoals. I blandly told them to drink wine & have a room of their own. Why should all the splendour, all the luxury of life be lavished on the Julians & the Francises, & and none on the Phares & the Thomases?[46]

As we shall see, Woolf's ruminations about women and fiction, combined with her two trips to Cambridge to present her lectures, culminated a year later in *A Room of One's Own*, which appeared in print in October 1929. In *A Room of One's Own*, Woolf concludes that a woman needs two things if she hopes to write successfully: a room of her own and an income of £500 a year.

As time passed, and Woolf became more assured of her public reputation – *Orlando* had moved her into the ranks of best-selling novelists – she increasingly felt it her duty to take a public stand against institutions that did not treat women equally. Woolf's feminism sharpened with age; when she passed her fiftieth birthday in 1932, she consciously took up a position as a cultural 'outsider'. She decided that the writer's best weapon was refusal – refusal to accommodate institutions that excluded anyone. Accordingly, she made it a principle to refuse academic honours when they were offered to her. She turned down the offer of an honorary doctorate from the University of Manchester in 1933; in 1939, she declined an honorary degree from the University of Liverpool. In 1932, Trinity College honoured Woolf by inviting her to give the Clark Lectures the following year. She was the first woman writer ever offered the lectures; her distinguished predecessors included her friends E.M Forster and T.S. Eliot. But Woolf declined the honour anyway, a refusal made poignant by the fact that Leslie Stephen had delivered the very first Clark Lectures in 1883, a year after she was born. She recorded her pride – and her decision for principled refusal – in her diary:

> And this morning I opened a letter; & it was from 'yours very sincerely J.J. Thompson' – the Master of Trinity; & it was to say that the council have decided to ask me to deliver the Clark Lectures next year. Six of them. This, I suppose, is the first time a woman has been asked; & so it is a great honour – think of me, the uneducated child reading books in my room at 22 H.P.G. – now advanced to this glory. But I shall refuse: because how could I write 6 lectures, to be delivered in full term, without giving up a year to criticism; without becoming a functionary; without sealing my lips when it comes to tilting at Universities; without putting off my Knock at the Door ... But I am rather inclined to smile ... Yes; all that reading, I say, has borne this odd fruit. And I am pleased; & still more pleased that I wont do it; & like to think that father would have blushed with pleasure could I have told him 30 years ago, that his daughter – my poor little Ginny – was to be asked to succeed him: the sort of compliment he would have liked.[47]

A year later, Woolf also decided 'not to accept the Leslie Stephen lectureship' at Trinity Hall which, as it turned out, was not offered to her.[48]

In the 1930s, Woolf's strategy of refusal – a strategy that was coloured by Caroline Emelia Stephen's Quaker ideas about pacifism and non-cooperation – crystallised into a second feminist book about women and education. Woolf had been mulling over her ideas for a long time, but they were galvanised, as if by a bolt of lightning, in April 1935, after an encounter with E.M. Forster at the London Library. As they waited together for their books, Forster told Woolf that the Library's Executive Committee had discussed allowing women to return as members of the Library Committee – they had been banned from membership by Sir Leslie Stephen when he was President of the London Library at the end of the nineteenth century. Woolf thought that Forster had probably offered her name as a prospective Committee member; Forster went on to say that the Committee had insisted that ladies were 'quite impossible' and couldn't serve. Woolf was enraged that Forster wanted an 'exception' to be made in her case, since he clearly thought she was more reasonable than most women. She went home and, trembling with anger, recorded both the encounter and the germ of *Three Guineas* in her diary:

> And so I quieted down & said nothing & this morning in my bath I made up a phrase in my book on Being Despised which is to run – a friend of mine, who was offered … one of those prizes – for her sake the great exception was to be made – who was in short to be given an honour – I forget what – … She said, And they actually thought I would take it. They were, on my honour, surprised, even at my very modified & humble rejection. You didnt tell them what you thought of them for daring to suggest that you should rub your nose in that pail of offal? I remarked. Not for a hundred years, she observed … God damn Morgan for thinking I'd have taken that … The veil of the temple – which, whether university or cathedral, was academic or ecclesiastical I forget – was to be raised, & as an exception she was to be allowed to enter in. But what about my civilisation? For 2,000 years we have done things without being paid for doing them. You cant bribe me now.[49]

Three Guineas was published in 1938, just after Hitler invaded Austria. It is an angry, resentful book that argues that women have been belittled and excluded by a male culture intent on maintaining its dominance, and that war is an inevitable outcome in a society that denigrates half its population. Much of *Three Guineas* focuses on the question of women's exclusion from formal education, especially in places like Cambridge. Woolf concludes that women's only reasonable option is to withdraw entirely from the dominant culture; in her discussion of the inequities in women's education, she advocates at one point that all women's colleges should be burnt to the ground.

Three Guineas was the least favourably received of all of Woolf's works. Many of her friends disliked the book so much they were embarrassed to talk to her about it at all. Keynes, for example, had also written a book on the causes of war, and Woolf was eager to hear his response to *Three Guineas* – but he simply failed to write or mention anything about the book after it was published. Woolf was relieved to learn that she had not infuriated Pernel Strachey, who was still Principal of Newnham, and who had written her a fund-raising letter very much like the one Woolf replies to in *Three Guineas*.[50] Woolf was viciously attacked in the press by a number of Cambridge figures, including Queenie Leavis, who had been in the audience when Woolf gave her women and fiction lecture ten years earlier and who had gone on to become an influential literary critic.[51] With *Three Guineas*, Woolf finally expressed the full force of her anger at having been denied a university education. It was an anger that was intensified by the familial nature of her many ties to Cambridge and complicated even more by her fond memories of idyllic times spent there in her youth.

II

A Room of One's Own is probably Virginia Woolf's most famous work, and the Cambridge visits that produced it have been much mythologised. But in actuality, Woolf's lectures to Newnham and Girton on 'Women and Fiction' were not terrifically successful performances. When Woolf appeared at Newnham, she was an hour late and hadn't told anyone she was bringing Leonard. The students scrambled to rearrange the seating plan and one of them complained that the college's food – certainly never gourmet fare – was ruined beyond eating by the delay. The room was dark; the sound was bad; Woolf sat at a table and read her talk verbatim – a very dull means of presentation. One student confessed she slept through the entire lecture: 'If only I had known it was to become *A Room of One's Own*!' Although the women of Newnham and Girton didn't view their position at Cambridge in the same light that Woolf did, they sensed her compassion and were delighted when she encouraged them to write novels and submit their manuscripts to the Hogarth Press.[52] In her lectures at both colleges, Woolf stressed the importance of private rooms and financial security to the woman writer's success; she also noted that, historically, the novels of many women had been marred by their anger at confining circumstances.

After Woolf's lectures (which she gave just after *Orlando* had been published), Woolf continued to be intrigued by the question of women and fiction, and by the vein of fantasy and humour she had mined in *Orlando*. She decided to write 'a history, say of Newnham or the womans movement, in the same vein'.[53] The result was *A Room of One's Own*, a funny, fanciful, fictionalised recreation of her talks, drawing on the events that surrounded them. For *A Room of One's Own*, Woolf adopts the persona of Mary Beton, and tells the story of women and fiction at Oxbridge (the predominantly male university) and at Fernham College (the struggling women's college), neither of which, she is careful to point out, actually exists. Woolf considers the effects of exclusion, poverty, discouragement, and anger on women's minds and writing; thinly disguised places at Cambridge become symbols for the very different circumstances of men and women at the university, and in society at large.

A Room of One's Own begins with the narrator sitting on the banks of a river – with its willows and punts, clearly the Cam – lost in thought about women and fiction. A particularly engrossing thought occurs to her and, in her excitement, she stands up and begins to stride across the grass. Suddenly, the gesticulating figure of a man blocks her way; she has, in her reverie, walked on the turf reserved for college fellows: 'His face expressed horror and indignation. Instinct rather than reason came to my help; he was a Beadle; I was a woman. This was the turf; there was the path. Only the Fellows and Scholars are allowed here; the gravel is the place for me.'[54] As the narrator remarks, no very great harm is done by being evicted from the grass though, as she walks on, she realises she has forgotten her 'little fish' of an idea.

Still absorbed in thought, the narrator decides to visit the college library – though it is not named, it is Trinity College's Wren Library – to take a look at the manuscripts of Milton's *Lycidas* and Thackeray's *Henry Esmond*. The great authors' revisions might reveal something about style, she thinks, and style certainly has some bearing on the question of women and fiction. But as she opens the library door, she is excluded a second time:

> instantly there issued, like a guardian angel barring the way with a flutter of black gown instead of white wings, a deprecating, silvery, kindly gentleman, who regretted in a low voice as he waved me back that ladies are only admitted to the library if accompanied by a Fellow of the College or furnished with a letter of introduction.[55]

This time the narrator becomes angry. She curses the great library as she leaves, vowing never to return: 'Never will I wake those echoes, never will I ask for that hospitality again, I vowed as I descended the steps in anger.'[56] She walks by the Chapel of King's College and hears the organ inside; she realises that she has no right to enter that building either, even if she wanted to, and thinks that the verger might demand her baptismal certificate before he let her in, or a letter from the Dean.

As the narrator makes her way along gravel paths towards her luncheon engagement, these three exclusions – from the lawn, from the library, and from the chapel – coalesce into a reverie about money: how *did* these ancient colleges become so magnificent, so civilised, so exclusive? She thinks of the 'unending stream of gold and silver' that must have flowed into the colleges' courts 'perpetually to keep the stones coming and the masons working; to level, to ditch, to dig and to drain'.[57] First it came from kings; then it came from merchants, but the money always flowed back to the university from its thankful graduates, and with that the narrator arrives at the door of her host for lunch.

This luncheon party at a men's college – an embellished account of Woolf's lunch in Rylands' rooms at King's College the day after her Newnham lecture – gives the narrator an opportunity to meditate on the connection between comfortable living and rational, unhurried discourse. The actual lunch party included Leonard, Maynard Keynes, and Lytton Strachey; Rylands remembered E.M. Forster being there too, so that the gathering was a thoroughly Cambridge, thoroughly Bloomsbury affair. Rylands' rooms were beautiful: they had been decorated by Dora Carrington, another Bloomsbury friend; they overlooked the lovely Backs along the Cam.[58] In retrospect, Rylands was certain that King's kitchens couldn't have produced the meal described in *A Room of One's Own*, but then Woolf's purpose was to evoke the splendid extravagance of life in a men's college, and its capacity to free the human mind from distraction and anger. The lunch in *A Room of One's Own* begins with soles, 'sunk in a deep dish, over which the college cook had spread a counterpane of the whitest cream'; it continues with 'partridges, many and various ... with all their retinue of sauces and salads'; it ends with pudding, 'wreathed in napkins, a confection which rose all sugar from the waves'. There is yellow wine followed by red wine, which 'lit, halfway down the spine ... the more profound, subtle and subterranean glow, which is the rich yellow flame of rational discourse'. In this atmosphere, the human mind is set free; anger vanishes: 'No need to hurry. No need to sparkle. No need to be anybody but oneself ... how good life seemed, how sweet its rewards, how trivial this grudge or that grievance, how admirable friendship and the society of one's kind.'[59]

After lingering through the afternoon at the sumptuous King's lunch, the narrator walks to her next engagement, at Fernham College. Again lost in thought, she takes a wrong turn while she muses over the red houses and 'the willows and the river and the gardens that run down to the river'[60] – the same houses and willows that Woolf noticed on her 1925 visit to Cambridge when she walked to visit Pernel Strachey at Newnham.[61] As the narrator pushes open the gates of Fernham – no beadle to block her entry here – she fancies she sees the bent figure of the great classical scholar Jane Harrison. Then her dinner arrives: 'Here was the soup. It was a plain gravy soup. There was nothing to stir the fancy in that.' Beef came next, with greens and potatoes – 'a homely trinity, suggesting the rumps of cattle in a muddy market, and sprouts curled and yellowed at the edge, and bargaining and cheapening, and women with string bags on Monday morning'. Prunes and custard followed; finally, the college kitchen produced biscuits and cheese, alongside which a jug of water was passed, 'for it is the nature of biscuits to be dry, and these were biscuits to the core'. Compared to the civilised extravagance of lunch at a men's college, the meal at Fernham was awful. But the narrator refrains from saying so, because 'if I said anything of the kind I should have been prying and searching into the secret economies of a house which to the stranger wears so fine a front of gaiety and courage'.[62] If the effect of an excellent meal at an Oxbridge men's college is to free the mind and light the soul, the effect of a terrible dinner at Fernham is just the opposite:

> The human frame being what it is, heart, body and brain all mixed together, and not contained in separate compartments as they will be no doubt in another million years, a good dinner is of great importance to good talk. One cannot think well, love well, sleep well, if one has not dined well. The lamp in the spine does not light on beef and prunes.[63]

And, the narrator might add, one cannot write well if one has dined on beef and prunes: poverty generates anger just as exclusion does, and an angry writer is not a successful writer.

When the narrator retires to talk privately with her friend, who lectures on science at Fernham, she can't stop herself from bringing up the question of money: remembering the 'unending stream of gold and silver' that must have flowed into the men's colleges, she wonders what lies beneath the 'gallant red brick' of the women's colleges? Her friend tells the story of Fernham's founding: of committees formed about the year 1860; of contributions sought; of rejections received; of the utmost difficulty raising the thirty thousand pounds needed to open the college. And, sixty years later, money is still very tight. With so little money available to spend on the real necessities of education, 'we cannot have wine and partridges and servants carrying tin dishes on their heads, she said. We cannot have sofas and separate rooms. "The amenities," she said, quoting from some book or other, "will have to wait."'[64]

When Newnham students read Woolf's description of dinner at their college, some of them were embarrassed. She had arrived so late, after all, that 'dinner in Clough Hall ... suffered considerably': 'Her purpose was, of course, to evoke pity for the poverty of the women's colleges: but at the time it made us, her hosts, decidedly uncomfortable.'[65] A

Girton woman – M.C. Bradbrook, who eventually became Professor of English at Cambridge as well as Mistress of Girton – declared defensively that 'we undergraduates enjoyed Mrs Woolf, but felt that her Cambridge was not ours'.[66] Woolf had clearly hit a nerve. The students at Newnham and Girton saw themselves as pioneers, pushing into the new territory of higher education for women and clearing the path for others to follow. They were pleased to have been accepted into the selective, intellectually demanding society of Newnham and Girton. Yet they were also keenly aware of their unequal status at the University, and it rankled. They had, after all, only recently been allowed to compete for University prizes, and to borrow books from the University library under their own names.[67]

The remainder of *A Room of One's Own* moves away from specific Cambridge places, but the ethos of Cambridge is very much on the narrator's mind as she continues to explore the questions of women and fiction, poverty and anger. Curious about the money that has *not* flowed into Fernham for fine dinners and private rooms, the narrator goes to the British Museum in London to try to discover the clue to women's poverty. She discovers shelves and shelves of books written about every aspect of women's character and history – all written by men: 'Have you any notion how many books are written about women in the course of one year? Have you any notion how many are written by men? Are you aware that you are, perhaps, the most discussed animal in the universe?'[68] She is especially struck by the work of Professor von X, who is engaged in completing his monumental treatise on 'The Mental, Moral, and Physical Inferiority of the Female Sex'. The narrator realises that the Professor's title makes her very angry; she notes that, oddly, the Professor himself seems very angry. But why should he be angry? 'His was the power and the money and the influence. He was the proprietor of the paper and its editor and sub-editor. He was the Foreign Secretary and the Judge.' Yet 'the professors – I lumped them together thus – were angry'. The narrator suspects the professor might be angry because he fears something will be taken away from him – just as rich people are sometimes angry because 'they suspect that the poor want to seize their wealth'. But perhaps Professor von X's angry insistence on the inferiority of women is also a way of protecting his superiority – 'That was what he was protecting rather hot-headedly and with too much emphasis, because it was a jewel to him of the rarest price'.[69] The narrator doesn't have to look far to find real-life versions of Professor von X at Cambridge:

> I will quote, however, Mr Oscar Browning, because Mr Oscar Browning was a great figure in Cambridge at one time, and used to examine the students at Girton and Newnham. Mr Oscar Browning was wont to declare 'that the impression left on his mind, after looking over any set of examination papers, was that, irrespective of the marks he might give, the best woman was intellectually the inferior of the worst man'.[70]

Oscar Wilde had described Browning (Fellow of King's) as 'everything that is kind and pleasant';[71] Browning had also been mentor to Woolf's cousin J.K. Stephen (Katherine Stephen's younger brother), and had charmed E.M. Forster by insisting that Forster read history with him.[72] Browning was no longer at King's when Woolf wrote *A Room of One's Own*, but his attitudes still lingered in Senior Combination Rooms around the University.

The narrator's exploration of the question of 'women and poverty' eventually brings her to the real heart of her argument about women and fiction. Towards the close of *A Room of One's Own*, she argues that, to write a masterpiece, the human mind must be both androgynous and 'incandescent' – it must be able to express itself freely, fully, and without impediment. And anger is the chief impediment to incandescence: the narrator mentions a string of woman writers (Charlotte Brontë among them) whose work is brilliant, but marred by the sharp stain of rage. Realising that she is herself not a victim of 'the poison of fear and bitterness',[73] the narrator considers what it is that has freed her from anger. The answer: a gift of money. In an acknowledgement of the liberating effects of her aunt Caroline Emelia Stephen's legacy of £2,500, Woolf's narrator explains that her inheritance from her aunt Mary Beton calmed her soul much more than getting the right to vote:

> However, as I say, my aunt died; and whenever I change a ten-shilling note a little of that rust and corrosion is rubbed off; fear and bitterness go. Indeed, I thought … remembering the bitterness of those days, what a change of temper a fixed income will bring about. No force in the

world can take from me my five hundred pounds. Food, house, and clothing are mine for ever. Therefore not merely do effort and labour cease, but also hatred and bitterness. I need not hate any man; he cannot hurt me. I need not flatter any man; he has nothing to give me. So imperceptibly I found myself adopting a new attitude towards the other half of the human race. It was absurd to blame any class or any sex as a whole. Great bodies of people are never responsible for what they do.[74]

Her inheritance has made her free; her inheritance has eliminated her anger and made her more tolerant of other people's foibles and habits. So, the narrator concludes, if a woman is to write successfully, she needs an independent income of at least £500 a year.

But successful writing requires a second matter: a private room. As the narrator surveys the kinds of writing women have produced from the sixteenth century to the present, she notes that, once women began to earn money by their pens, their characteristic genre was the novel. Why should women write novels rather than poetry? The narrator concludes that the novel fits women's circumstances because of its subject matter: women are trained in the observation of character and the analysis of emotion; both these skills express themselves naturally in the genre conventions of the novel. And there is a second reason why women in the nineteenth century wrote novels rather than poetry:

Had it something to do with being born of the middle class, I asked; and with the fact, which Miss Emily Davies a little later was so strikingly to demonstrate, that the middle-class family in the early nineteenth century was possessed only of a single sitting-room between them? If a woman wrote, she would have to write in the common sitting room. And, as Miss Nightingale was so vehemently to complain, – 'women never have an half hour ... that they can call their own' – she was always interrupted. Still it would be easier to write prose and fiction there than to write poetry or a play. Less concentration is required.[75]

Citing the work of Emily Davies (the founder of Girton College) Woolf concludes that nineteenth-century women wrote novels because novels suit themselves to public rooms. The novel comes naturally to women because of the looseness of its shape: it is a flexible, indeterminate form that does not require the intense concentration of poetry; it can be written in a parlour overrun with children and guests, by a woman whose attention is constantly demanded elsewhere. But if women are to succeed as writers in the future, they must reshape the genre of fiction, and for that task they must concentrate. They need privacy; they need quiet; they need rooms of their own with locks on the doors.

The narrator concludes that these two possessions – an independent income and a room of one's own – are the key to the question of women and fiction. Interestingly, Woolf came to both of these ideas through iconoclastic Cambridge women – that is, through a Cambridge tradition running counter to the dominant Cambridge culture that worked relentlessly to exclude women. It was, after all, Woolf's Quaker aunt Caroline Emelia Stephen who left her a large enough inheritance that she could begin her writing career without worry. And, though Woolf didn't mention it, the women of Newnham and Girton – unlike the women of Woolf's fictional Fernham – already had rooms of their own. (Girton women, in fact, had two rooms apiece.) Emily Davies, Girton's founder, had insisted that 'each student will have a small sitting room to herself, where she will be free to study undisturbed ... probably the opportunity for a certain amount of solitude ... will be the one most welcomed by the real student'.[76] And as one of the Newnham students present at Woolf's lecture on *Women and Fiction* noted later, the chief joy of being a female student at Cambridge was having this private room to think and write:

> But even more precious than anything outside the room was the room itself; to have a room of one's own – that was the supreme pleasure, the unspoilable joy of being at Newnham.[77]

Woolf's experience of Cambridge and its many exclusions is just as central to Woolf's other feminist works as it is to *A Room of One's Own*. The main difference between the feminism of *A Room of One's Own* and the feminism of Woolf's later career is her shifting attitude towards women's anger. On the pages of *A Room of One's Own*, Woolf insists that anger is a damaging emotion, one that mars a woman's ability to write a perfectly expressive piece of fiction. But in Woolf's feminist works of the 1930s – *The Years* and *Three Guineas* – Woolf views women's anger as an inescapable cultural fact, and more openly expresses her own mounting rage at what she sees as corrupt institutions that put women at a disadvantage. Again, Cambridge and the question of a woman's education lie at the heart of the matter.

The Years was published in 1937. Woolf had laboured over it for nearly five years, first beginning it as an 'essay-novel' and then revising away long discursive sections that discussed adverse social conditions shaping young women's lives and education. (These deleted 'essays' were subsequently printed under the title *The Pargiters*.) *The Years* begins with a scene in which three Pargiter sisters – Milly, Delia and Eleanor – sit in the family drawing room, looking out of the window, bored. Woolf describes the scene in a way that accentuates their plight: they have nothing to do but attend to the needs of the household and fantasise about the attractive young man who runs up the steps next door. Woolf's 'essay' blames the Pargiter sisters' bored helplessness on the fact that they have no access to education. The women's colleges were only just in existence in 1880 and 'there was a great prejudice ... against them'.[78] But even if it had been respectable to send a young woman to college in 1880, the Pargiter daughters wouldn't have gone: as Woolf noted in *A Room of One's Own*, money was generally not available for the education of Victorian girls. Colonel Pargiter won't send his daughters to school because to do so would take money away from his sons; the three Pargiter boys must attend Eton, and then Oxford or Cambridge, an education that costs nearly £3,000 for each son. Given Colonel Pargiter's social prejudices – paternal prejudices that were widespread in 1880 – the sisters each receive an education that costs a few hundred pounds, so that the family's money can be lavished on the boys. All the Pargiter daughters find their horizons limited by what Woolf in *Three Guineas* calls 'Arthur's Education Fund'.

The education of their cousin, Kitty Malone, the daughter of an Oxford don, should in all logic be better. But it is not, and Kitty's situation gives Woolf the opportunity to paint a particularly shocking picture of the position of a young woman of intelligence at Oxbridge in 1880. Kitty's father is Master of St Katharine's and is writing a monumental history of the college. Kitty sometimes helps him with his work, but her real family function is social: she is expected to assist at teas for undergraduates and to show visiting Americans the sights of Oxford. We first meet Kitty at the end of one of her obligatory dinner party appearances, where the guests of honour have been Dr 'Chuffy' Andrews, the renowned author of *The Constitutional History of England*, and the Professor Howard Fripps, Americans from Harvard. Kitty has a very original mind, but her father has opted not to give her a formal education. Instead, she takes history lessons from Miss Lucy Craddock, a middle-aged woman from Scarborough, who would have 'given my eyes to have the opportunities you have'.[79] Kitty perpetually comes to her lessons unprepared, since her mother insists that her social responsibilities must come first. And her position as the daughter of a don gives her an insider's look at the realities of Oxbridge professors. When Mrs Fripp, the visiting American, says that Dr 'Chuffy' Andrews has been charming at dinner, Kitty remembers his 'hyena' laugh and thinks angrily to herself, 'Did you really like the way he spits when he talks?'[80] And when Lucy Craddock calls Dr Andrews the 'greatest historian of his age', the reason for Kitty's anger becomes clear: Kitty replies that 'he doesn't talk history to me', and remembers 'the damp feel of a heavy hand on her knee' at dinner.[81]

Woolf's lingering anger at Cambridge is most forcefully expressed in *Three Guineas*, a work about education, feminism and pacifism that appeared in June 1938, just two months after Hitler invaded Austria. In *Three Guineas*, Woolf writes an extended letter to a man who has asked her to contribute money to his society, a society that seeks to prevent war by promoting culture and intellectual liberty. As *Three Guineas* unfolds, Woolf argues that she can best prevent war by spending her three available guineas very differently: by contributing her first guinea to rebuild a women's college at Cambridge, her second guinea to support the entry of women into the professions, and only her third guinea to the gentleman's society promoting culture and intellectual liberty.

In a long opening chapter, Woolf discusses the way in which the current educational system, dominated by Oxford and Cambridge, fosters war. The powerful men of England, she says, have all become powerful by virtue of their expensive University educations. A University degree is not only a recognition of subjects mastered, she argues, but, more importantly, a ticket to an exclusive society of insiders. Above all, Oxford and Cambridge have taught these insiders the art of domination. A University education shows a man how to be superior; it shows him how to exclude others from his ranks. Far from teaching a hatred for violence, a University education – at least as it is traditionally shaped – incites a man to commit violence, since he likes what he possesses and wants to keep other people from having it. This, Woolf argues, is the message of the riot that damaged the gates of Newnham when women were admitted to titular degrees in 1921. It is also the message of ceremonial university clothing: caps, gowns, and ermine trim are symbols of rank and exclusion; they assert the wearer's superiority; by doing so, they incite people to jealousy and competition. They thus create war:

> For there, in courts and universities, we find the same love of dress. There, too, are velvet and silk, fur and ermine. We can say that for educated men to emphasize their superiority over other people, either in birth or intellect, by dressing differently, or by adding titles before, or letters after their names are acts that rouse competition and jealousy – emotions which, as we need scarcely draw upon biography to prove, nor ask psychology to show, have their share in encouraging a disposition towards war.[82]

From this perspective, if the exclusivity of the universities fosters war, the exclusivity of competitive societies at universities is even worse. This was Woolf's position when she lectured her nephew Julian against the evils of the Apostles. And she uses a photo of a Cambridge ceremony to stress her point: one of the illustrations in *Three Guineas* portrays Lord Baldwin, Chancellor of Cambridge, in his ceremonial robes. As Woolf remarked in her diary, on the occasion of T.S. Eliot accepting an honorary degree from the University just one week after *Three Guineas* was published: 'And it hits the crest of the wave. Tom being given his degree at Cambridge: walking in procession with the other bigwigs: Trinity feast; Tattoo; honours List – if anyone reads it, the illustration is pat to hand.'[83]

But it is not only the exclusivity of places like Cambridge that fosters war. There is a second factor: the custom of educating daughters in the private home. Woolf begins *Three Guineas* by drawing a distinction between herself and her male correspondent. They both belong to the educated classes; they both earn their livings. And there the resemblance ends, creating a chasm between them so large that Woolf doubts they can speak across it. The difference lies in the amount of money spent on their education. In an angry indictment of the practice of spending all the family education money on sons – and an angry evocation of her own home education, while her brothers went to Cambridge – Woolf argues that 'Arthur's Education Fund' deprives women of more than just book learning. She begins by quoting Mary Kingsley, niece of Charles Kingsley, the famous Professor of Modern History at Cambridge:

> Let us then ask someone else – it is Mary Kingsley – to speak for us. 'I don't know if I ever revealed to you the fact that being allowed to learn German was *all* the paid-for education I ever had. Two thousand pounds was spent on my brother's, I still hope not in vain.' Mary Kingsley is not speaking for herself alone; she is speaking, still, for many of the daughters of educated men. And she is not merely speaking for them; she is also pointing to a very important fact about them, a fact that must profoundly influence all that follows: the fact of Arthur's Education Fund. You, who have read *Pendennis*, will remember how the mysterious letters A.E.F. figured in the household ledgers. Ever since the thirteenth century English families have been paying money into that account. From the Pastons to the Pendennises, all educated families from the thirteenth century to the present moment have paid money into that account. It is a voracious receptacle. Where there were many sons to educate it required a great effort on the part of the family to keep it full. For your education was not merely in book-learning; games educated your body; friends taught you more than books or games. Talk with them broadened your outlook and enriched your mind ... And to this your sisters, as Mary Kingsley indicates, made their contribution. Not only did their own education, save for such small sums as paid the German teacher, go into it; but many of those luxuries and trimmings which are, after all, an essential part of education – travel, society, solitude, a lodging apart from the family house – they were paid into it too.[84]

Woolf goes on to say that the fact of Arthur's Education Fund infuriates women, and makes them see educational institutions through very different eyes than men: to women 'the noble courts and quadrangles of Oxford and Cambridge' look like 'the boat train starting for abroad while the guard slams the door in their faces'.[85] Thirty-five years earlier, Woolf had complained to her brother Thoby that she had to 'delve from books, painfully and all alone'[86] while he discussed great ideas over his pipe with Lytton Strachey and other friends at Trinity. In *Three Guineas*, all Woolf's private anger at being excluded from her brother's Cambridge education finally surfaces publicly, and drives her thinking about the causes of violence in the modern world.

Woolf argues, then, that the daughter's exclusion from University education – and her restriction to the education of the private home – is one of the chief causes of war. Without any means of earning her own income, Woolf says, and with marriage as the only profession open to her, a woman must behave in a way that is 'consciously and unconsciously in favour of war':[87] she must 'bolster up the system which provided her with maids; with carriages; with fine clothes; with fine parties – it was by these means that she achieved marriage'.[88] She must accept the views of the dominant culture – views that are predicated on the arts of dominance and killing – because it is only by doing so that she can wheedle men 'into giving her the means to marry or marriage itself'.[89]

Woolf argues that the only way to prevent war is to provide women with an alternative to the education of the private home, and for this reason, she will contribute her guinea to rebuilding the women's college at Cambridge. But the contribution comes with a stipulation: the women's college must be organised along entirely different lines to men's colleges:

> Obviously, then, it must be an experimental college, an adventurous college. Let it be built on lines of its own. It must be built not of carved stone and stained glass, but of some cheap, easily combustible material which does not hoard dust and perpetrate traditions. Do not have chapels. Do not have museums and libraries with chained books and first editions under glass cases. Let the pictures and the books be new and always changing. Let it be decorated afresh by each generation with their own hands cheaply ... Next, what should be taught in the new college, the poor college? Not the arts of dominating other people; not the arts of ruling, of killing, of acquiring land and capital. They require too many overhead expenses; salaries and uniforms and ceremonies. The poor college must teach only the arts that can be taught cheaply and practised by poor people; such as medicine, mathematics, music, painting and liter-

ature. It should teach the arts of human intercourse; the art of under-standing other people's lives and minds ... The aim of the new college, the cheap college, should be not to segregate and specialize, but to combine.[90]

But when informed by the treasurer of the building fund that her building plan and curriculum are impractical, Woolf at first vows that no guinea of her earned money shall be spent to support a college along the old lines. Rather than doing that, the college should be burned to the ground:

No guinea of earned money should go to rebuilding the college on the old plan; just as certainly none could be spent upon building a college upon a new plan; therefore the guinea should be earmarked 'Rags. Petrol. Matches.' And this note should be attached to it. 'Take this guinea and with it burn the college to the ground. Set fire to the old hypocrisies. Let the light of the burning building scare the nightingales and incarnadine the willows. And let the daughters of educated men dance round the fire and heap armful upon armful of dead leaves upon the flames. And let their mothers lean from the upper windows and cry, "Let it blaze! Let it blaze! For we have done with this 'education'!" '[91]

But the reality, of course, is that though education at the women's colleges of Cambridge is imperfect, women need it to get jobs and earn money. And only if they earn money can they prevent war. So Woolf finally decides she will give her guinea to rebuild the women's college after all. But she prescribes a way of acting and living within the University system that is resistant to the system's evils. Woolf draws on Caroline Emelia Stephen's example of Quaker pacifism to suggest a way of living apart from the dominant culture, of refusing to co-operate with it or bolster its incipient violence. It is, of course, precisely the model of refusal that Woolf practised in her own life during the 1930s:

If we are asked to teach, we can examine very carefully into the aim of such teaching, and refuse to teach any art or science that encourages war. Further, we can pour mild scorn upon chapels, upon degrees, and upon the value of examinations. We can intimate that a prize poem can still have merit in spite of the fact that it has won a prize; and maintain that

a book may still be worth reading in spite of the fact that its author took
a first class with honours in the English tripos. If we are asked to lecture
we can refuse to bolster up the vain and vicious system of lecturing by
refusing to lecture. And, of course, if we are offered honours and degrees
for ourselves we can refuse them – how, indeed, in view of the facts,
could we possibly do otherwise? But there is no blinking the fact that in
the present state of things the most effective way in which we can help
you through education to prevent war is to subscribe as generously as
possible to the colleges for the daughters of educated men. For, to repeat,
if those daughters are not going to be educated they are not going to earn
their livings; if they are not going to earn their livings, they are going
once more to be restricted to the education of the private house; and if
they are going to be restricted to the education of the private house they
are going, once more, to exert all their influence both consciously and
unconsciously in favour of war.[92]

Towards the end of *Three Guineas*, Woolf proposes the creation of an
'Outsiders' Society' – a community of women like herself who refuse to
belong to any group, fearing that societies in and of themselves 'sink the
private brother, whom many of us have reason to respect, and inflate in
his stead a monstrous male, loud of voice, hard of fist, childishly intent
upon scoring the floor of the earth with chalk marks, within whose
mystic boundaries human beings are penned, rigidly, separately, artifi-
cially'.[93] This Outsiders' Society will work in its own way for equality
and peace. Members will swear not to take up arms; they will refuse to
make munitions or nurse the wounded; they will neither incite nor
dissuade their brothers from fighting – they will instead remain
completely indifferent to war, since the very act of fighting is a man's
'sex characteristic'. Most important, members of the Outsiders' Society
will cast aside all emotions associated with patriotism, since a close
examination of English history reveals that women have little to thank
England for:

'Our country,' she will say, 'throughout the greater part of its history has
treated me as a slave; it has denied me education or any share in its
possessions. "Our" country still ceases to be mine if I marry a foreigner.
"Our" country denies me the means of protecting myself, forces me to
pay others a very large sum annually to protect me … Therefore if you
insist upon fighting to protect me, or "our" country, let it be understood,
soberly and rationally between us, that you are fighting to gratify a sex
instinct which I cannot share; to procure benefits which I have not shared

and probably will not share; but not to gratify my instincts, or to protect myself or my country. For,' the outsider will say, 'in fact, as a woman, I have no country. As a woman I want no country. As a woman my country is the whole world.'[94]

Since *Three Guineas* appeared in the charged atmosphere of a country confronting the possibility of war – not only had Hitler invaded Austria, but his designs on Czechoslovakia were becoming clear, and Mussolini had moved definitively into Hitler's camp – its arguments against patriotism seemed deliberately provocative. The book generated a good deal of controversy. Woolf's nephew Quentin Bell wrote that: 'What really seemed wrong with the book – and I am speaking of my own reactions at the time – was the attempt to involve a discussion of women's rights with the far more agonising and immediate question of what we were to do in order to meet the ever-growing menace of Fascism and war.'[95] Queenie Leavis, who had attended Woolf's 'Women and Fiction' lectures at Girton ten years earlier, and had remained at Cambridge to collaborate with F.R. Leavis on the influential literary magazine *Scrutiny*, was more vituperative. *Three Guineas* 'affects me like Nazi dialect without Nazi convictions,' she wrote. 'It seems to me the art of living as conceived by a social parasite.'[96]

Three Guineas is still the most controversial of Woolf's books. Many readers find its arguments muddled and historically inaccurate; just as many readers see *Three Guineas* as a radical, deliberately non-linear, convincing investigation into the history of women's rights and the causes of war. *Three Guineas* certainly remains the most provocative of Woolf's works, if only because its withering anger makes it so different from everything else she wrote. For all Woolf's lingering nostalgia for the beauty of Cambridge – and for the happy peace of the youthful days she associated with the University – Woolf finally concluded that Cambridge and institutions like it brought civilisation to the brink of disaster. And her anger – at the threat of war, at being deprived of a University education, at the many exclusions that Cambridge repre-sented – expressed itself in all its fury in *Three Guineas*. As she had told Lytton Strachey as early as 1912, Cambridge got into her ink 'and blister[ed] the paper'.[97]

III

Cambridge today: walks, views, excursions

How to get there

By train: There is frequent train service between London (King's Cross Station) and Cambridge. Depending on the time of day, the trip takes from forty-five minutes to just over an hour. For schedules and fares, consult www.railtrack.co.uk. Since parking is very limited in Cambridge, the train is the recommended route.

By bus: National Express runs frequent buses between London and Cambridge, most of which leave from the Victoria coach station. For information on schedules and fares, phone National Express at 08705 808 080 or consult the website at www.GoByCoach.com. The bus trip to Cambridge usually takes about two hours.

By car: From London, go to the M25 orbital and then take the M11 to Cambridge.

A WALK THROUGH *A ROOM OF ONE'S OWN*

This walk follows the narrator's steps through *A Room of One's Own*. The walk is given in the sequence it appears in the book. Since the opening times of various colleges change during the year, it may not be practical to visit all the sites in this order. But be sure to remember that the Wren library is open only a few hours a day, generally Monday to Friday from 12 p.m. to 2 p.m., and, during full-term, also on Saturdays from 10.30 a.m. to 12.30 p.m.

The best place to begin this walk is behind Trinity College, inside the College grounds. Sit on a bench overlooking the Cam, and take in the same view Mary Beton did. (The colours may be different when you visit: Mary Beton's excursion around Cambridge begins in the month of October):

Here then was I (call me Mary Beton, Mary Seton, Mary Carmichael or by any name you please – it is not a matter of any importance) sitting on the banks of a river a week or two ago in fine October weather, lost in thought. That collar I have spoken of, women and fiction, the need of coming to some conclusion on a subject that raises all sorts of prejudices and passions, bowed my head to the ground. To the right and left bushes of some sort, golden and crimson, glowed with the colour, even it seemed burnt with the heat, of fire. On the further bank the willows wept in perpetual lamentation, their hair about their shoulders. The river reflected whatever it chose of sky and bridge and burning tree, and when the undergraduate had oared his boat through the reflections they closed again, completely, as if he had never been. There one might have sat the clock round lost in thought. Thought – to call it by a prouder name than it deserved – had let its line down into the stream.[98]

How to get there

To find this view of the Cam, you must walk to the back of **Trinity College** and enter through the **Brewhouse Gate**. Begin at Trinity's main gate. With the main gate to your back, walk *right* along **Trinity Street** to **Trinity Lane**; turn *right* into Trinity Lane and follow it to **Garret Hostel Lane**, where you make another *right* turn. (If you reach the main gate of Trinity Hall, you have walked too far.) Follow Garret Hostel Lane toward the river, and enter the back gates (Brewhouse Gate) of the Trinity College grounds; the gate will again be to your *right*. (If you cross the Cam, you have walked too far.) There are benches just past the gate entrance.

The Wren Library

Walk a little further along the path, to the entrance to the Wren Library (but be careful to keep to the path, as Mary Beton failed to do). It was as she opened this door that Mary Beton was turned away by a kindly old gentleman who reminded her, in sorrowful tones, that ladies were not admitted to the library. These days, the black-gowned beadles will just as likely be women as men.

Woolf says in the opening pages of *A Room of One's Own* that much of her argument is fictional, and her narrator's visit to the Wren Library provides an interesting example of the way Woolf transforms fact for her narrative purposes. The Wren Library houses Trinity College's rare and extensive collection of books; because of its architectural beauty, the library has also always been a destination for visitors to Cambridge. As a result, Trinity College controls (rather strictly) the number of people allowed inside. The standard visitors' guide to Cambridge written during

Woolf's day (whose ninth edition was revised in 1928 for republication in 1929 – at just about the same time Woolf was preparing *A Room of One's Own*) indicates that the Wren Library was open to the general public in October 1928 from 2 p.m. to 4 p.m. (If accompanied by a Fellow of the College, members of the general public could enter the library between 9 a.m. and 4 p.m.) In short – Mary Beton would have been allowed to enter the Wren Library if she appeared at the door during public visiting hours, rather than in the morning. The current Trinity College librarian concurs with this point, indicating that women were never barred from the Wren Library simply because they were women.[99]

So Woolf has transformed the details of what might have been an actual encounter. But her purpose, of course, is to make a more fundamental point. Women were never barred from the Wren Library because they were women; they were barred from the Wren Library because they were not members of Trinity College. But if women were admitted as members of Trinity – as Woolf thought they should have been – they would then have the right to enter the library whenever they chose.

Mary Beton wants to visit the Wren Library to examine the manuscripts of Milton's *Lycidas* and Thackeray's *Henry Esmond*, both of which she knows are on display there – she wants to investigate what the authors' revisions reveal about the naturalness of their style. Today's visitor can still see the *Lycidas* manuscript on display in a glass case (along with other treasures such as Shakespearean folios, and letters written by Isaac Newton and Lord Byron). *Henry Esmond* is gone, but A.A. Milne's manuscript of *Winnie-the-Pooh* is now on display.

For current public opening times of the Wren Library, consult the Trinity College website at www.trin.cam.ac.uk. (The opening times generally do not vary much: Monday to Friday from 12 p.m. to 2 p.m., and, during full term, on Saturdays from 10.30 a.m. to 12.30 p.m.)

King's College

Exit Trinity College by the same path you entered; proceed back along **Garret Hostel Lane**. When you reach **Trinity Lane**, turn *right* and walk just past the entrance to **Trinity Hall**; then take the first *left* turn into **Senate House Passage**. As you walk past Trinity Hall and into Senate

House Passage, notice, as Mary Beton did, the magnificence of the **King's College** chapel, where people will perhaps be gathering for services. As you leave Senate House Passage, turn *right* into **King's Parade** and proceed to the main gates of **King's College**. (King's is open to the public during term time Monday to Friday from 9.30 a.m. to 3.30 p.m., on Saturdays from 9.30 a.m. to 3.15 p.m., and on Sundays from 1.15 p.m. to 2.15 p.m. Out of term time, the hours are Monday to Saturday from 9.30 a.m. to 4.30 p.m., and Sundays from 10 a.m. to 5 p.m. Check the King's College website for details and changes: www.kings.cam.ac.uk.)

Woolf's lunch with Dadie Rylands took place in his rooms at King's College. As Mary Beton enters the college on her way to lunch, she muses on the fact that this noble courtyard was once a swamp, and that it took an enormous amount of money to build the college and its magnificent chapel:

> The outside of the chapel remained. As you know, its high domes and pinnacles can be seen, like a sailing-ship always voyaging never arriving, lit up at night and visible for miles, far away across the hills. Once, presumably, this quadrangle with its smooth lawns, its massive buildings, and the chapel itself was marsh too, where the grasses waved and the swine rootled. Teams of horses and oxen, I thought, must have hauled the stone in wagons from far countries, and then with infinite labour the grey blocks in whose shade I was now standing were poised in order one on top of another, and then the painters brought their glass for the windows, and the masons were busy for centuries up on that roof with putty and cement, spade and trowel. Every Saturday somebody must have poured gold and silver out of a leathern purse into their ancient fists, for they had their beer and skittles presumably of an evening. An unending stream of gold and silver, I thought, must have flowed into this court perpetually to keep the stones coming and the masons working; to level, to ditch, to dig and to drain … Certainly, as I strolled round the court, the foundation of gold and silver seemed deep enough; the pavement laid solidly over the wild grasses. Men with trays on their heads went busily from staircase to staircase. Gaudy blossoms flowered in window-boxes. The strains of the gramophone blared out from the rooms within. It was impossible not to reflect – the reflection whatever it may have been was cut short. The clock struck. It was time to find one's way to luncheon.[100]

Rylands' rooms were in the Old Lodge, which is located on the south side of the Back Lawn.

George ('Dadie') Rylands was a member of the second generation of Bloomsbury. He was born in 1902 and died in 1999; when he came up to Cambridge he was elected a member of the Apostles, and came to know Maynard Keynes, Lytton Strachey and the other members of the group. Rylands was a poet and Shakespearean scholar; he helped Maynard Keynes found the Cambridge Arts Theatre. From July to December of 1924, he worked as an assistant at the Hogarth Press, where he came to know Leonard and Virginia quite well. When Rylands was appointed Fellow of King's College, he returned to Cambridge to take up his position as a don, and lived there for the rest of his life. Virginia Woolf felt a good deal of affection for Rylands and described him as 'a sensitive vain youth, with considerable grit in him'.[101] The Hogarth Press published several of Rylands' books of poetry, including *Russett and Taffeta* (1925), which he dedicated to Virginia.

When Rylands returned to King's as a Junior Fellow, he was given a grand set of rooms of the sort normally reserved for Senior Fellows – but it was a temporary measure, since the Old Lodge was scheduled to be demolished shortly. The rooms faced north and were rather bleak; Rylands engaged Dora Carrington to brighten them up. She chose colours inspired by Rylands' collection of Crown Derby china, and completed the painting project in forty-eight hours. Jane Hill describes Carrington's work on Rylands' rooms:

> Sponges and brushes (both ends) were used for applying paint, on top of which she intagliated an erratic spiral pattern in the wet paint. The walls were painted pale green. The door jambs were burnt orange flanked on the outside with charcoal blue and dove grey and on the inside with dove grey and willow green. The intersections of the doors were painted stone; the panels were bordered with charcoal and dull red and the designs were punched through the stencils in charcoal and orange. As well as four doors, Carrington painted the wooden fireplace surround, and the existing tiles with drapes and bows, Dadie's initials, a compass and rule, feather and open book, trumpets and horns.[102]

Ryland's rooms are not open to the public. As of this writing, King's College is still in the process of deciding what use to make of them in the future.

While at King's, walk by the buildings where E.M. Forster, John

Maynard Keynes, and Roger Fry lived. These sites do not relate to *A Room of One's Own*, but are interesting for their historical connections to members of the Bloomsbury group.

As an undergraduate, **E.M. Forster** (1879-1970) had the set of rooms W7, located on the top floor of the Bodley Building. Forster came up to King's College in 1897 and went down in 1901; while at King's he studied with both Goldsworthy Lowes Dickinson and Oscar Browning. Browning – who, as Woolf noted in *A Room of One's Own*, believed emphatically that 'the best woman was intellectually the inferior of the worst man'[103] – made himself charming to the undergraduates at King's. He called from his open window to any passing undergraduate to come and share his lobsters or play duets; when Forster planned to read history with Goldie Dickinson, Browning came to Forster and disarmingly insisted otherwise: 'You're not coming to me at all, you *must* come to me.' And so Forster read his history essays to Oscar Browning.[104]

Forster was elected to the Apostles in 1901. He opens his second novel, *The Longest Journey*, with a scene loosely based on a meeting of the Apostles, in rooms loosely based on Forster's own rooms in King's W7. Like Rickie Elliot, Forster sometimes felt at sea during the unrelentingly abstract discussions of philosophical issues – in this case, whether the cow in the meadow was still there when no one was looking at it. Rickie's attention wanders from the abstractions of ontology to the details of the Cambridge college around him:

Rickie, on whose carpet the matches were being dropped, did not like to join in the discussion. It was too difficult for him. He could not even quibble. If he spoke, he should simply make himself a fool. He preferred to listen, and to watch the tobacco-smoke stealing out past the window-seat into the tranquil October air. He could see the court too, and the college cat teasing the college tortoise, and the kitchen-men with supper-trays upon their heads. Hot food for one – that must be for the geographical don, who never came in for Hall; cold food for three, apparently at half-a-crown a head, for some one he did not know; hot food, *a la carte* – obviously for the ladies haunting the next staircase; cold food for two, at two shillings – going to Ansell's rooms for himself and Ansell, and as it passed under the lamp he saw that it was meringues again. Then the bedmakers began to arrive, chatting to each other pleasantly, and he could hear Ansell's bedmaker say, 'Oh dang!' when she found she had to lay Ansell's tablecloth; for there was not a breath stirring. The great elms were motionless, and seemed still in the glory of midsummer, for the darkness hid the yellow blotches on their leaves, and their outlines were still rounded against the tender sky.[105]

After he left King's in 1901, Forster published five novels and then returned to Cambridge in 1927, to give the Clark Lectures. These lectures were so well-received that Forster was elected a Supernumerary Fellow at King's, a position he held until 1933. As a Supernumerary Fellow, Forster gave a few lectures a year, but didn't live in Cambridge for more than one or two weeks at a time – he lived with his mother in Abinger Hammer in Surrey. After his mother died, Forster was named an Honorary Fellow of King's in 1945 and was invited to take up residence at the college – an unusual event that recognised Forster's literary eminence. At first, Forster had a study on A staircase and actually lived with friends at 3 Trumpington Street. But when the friends moved in 1953, he again took up residence inside King's, and remained there until his death in 1970.

John Maynard Keynes (1883-1946) lived in Cambridge all his life. His father was a Fellow of Pembroke College who eventually took a position in University administration; his mother was an early graduate of Newnham. Keynes attended Eton and then returned as an undergraduate to King's College in 1902, where, like most of the undergraduates of his day, he came under the influence of Oscar Browning. (Keynes and Browning were never particularly close, but once Browning had retired and Keynes had become a Fellow himself, he helped Browning with tax advice and other financial matters.) At the urging of Lytton Strachey and Leonard Woolf, the Apostles elected Keynes to their membership in 1903. Keynes's undergraduate rooms were located in A Staircase of the Wilkins Building.[106]

Keynes was elected to a Fellowship at King's in the spring of 1909 and that summer moved into a suite of rooms over the gatehouse leading from King's Lane to Webb's Court. He occupied these rooms until he died. During World War I, Keynes edited the *Economic Journal* and worked for the Treasury in Whitehall, a position that involved him in the intricacies of inter-Allied war credits, the system that made it possible for Russia and France to buy munitions.

It was during this period that Bertrand Russell brought D.H. Lawrence to Cambridge to meet Keynes – one of the formative occasions that created Lawrence's famous antipathy towards Bloomsbury, and thus engendered one set of lingering, negative public attitudes towards the Bloomsbury group and its members. Lawrence was convinced of the madness of World War I. He wanted to organise a community of thinkers ('Rananim') who would live on an island far from the corruptions of modern culture, and create there a new, spiritually vibrant civilisation, based largely on the organic rhythms of heterosexual intercourse. (Lawrence had just finished writing *The Rainbow* before his Cambridge visit.) Lawrence wanted to meet Keynes, because Keynes could direct the economic side of Lawrence's social revolution. Lawrence felt 'frightfully important coming to Cambridge – quite momentous the occasion is to me'.[107] But when he entered Keynes's rooms at King's, Lawrence's feelings about Keynes and Cambridge quickly shifted:

> We went into his rooms at midday and it was very sunny. He was not there, so Russell was writing a note. Then suddenly the door opened and K was there, blinking from sleep, standing in his pyjamas. As he stood there gradually a knowledge passed into me, which has been like a little madness to me ever since. And it was carried along with the most dreadful sense of repulsiveness – something like carrion – a vulture gives me the same feeling.[108]

Lawrence was very much the outsider at Cambridge, and was utterly repelled by the homo-erotic atmosphere at King's. As Lawrence said later, 'Truly I didn't know it [homosexuality] was wrong, till I saw K that morning in Cambridge. It was one of the crises of my life. It sent me mad with misery and hostility and rage.'[109] Lawrence afterwards got in the habit of comparing Keynes and Keynes's Bloomsbury homosexual friends to black beetles, rats and scorpions, and said: 'It is this horror of little swarming selves I can't stand.'[110]

After World War I, Keynes left the Treasury. He was devoted to teaching – between 1919 and 1937, he took only one term off – and his lectures on economics were wildly popular with students. (His students heard his most famous book before anyone else: in 1919, he lectured to undergraduates from the proofs of *Economic Consequences of the*

Peace.) Keynes became the greatest economist of the twentieth century. His book *The General Theory of Employment, Interest and Money* (1936) created Keynesian economics, the theory whose patterns still dominate thinking about modern economic systems.

As bursar of King's, Keynes also put the college on a solid financial footing by selling off many of its agricultural holdings and investing the money in securities. Keynes even left his mark on Cambridge architecturally: his monument is the Cambridge Arts Theatre, which he had built in 1935.

Keynes's rooms in Webb's Court were decorated by Duncan Grant and Vanessa Bell. After a visit in 1923, Virginia Woolf described his drawing room as 'the pleasantest sitting room I have ever been in'.[111] Duncan Grant's biographer describes the decorations:

> [Duncan] and Vanessa designed eight allegorical figures for Maynard's sitting-room in Webb's Court, King's College, Cambridge. These covered Duncan's earlier decoration and extended further down the room, the eight panels filling most of one side wall. The figures represent Science, Political Economy, Music, Classics, Law, Mathematics, Philosophy and History. Draped female figures alternate with male nudes, each holding an object associated with one of the eight subjects. The figures, like statuary in a niche, fill the entire panel, their heads touching the upper border. The ground behind each is mottled and the border framed with a band of gold paint. But the artists' decorative concern did not stop there: in order to make this line of figures merge with the room as a whole, Duncan and Vanessa advised on its colour scheme and on the choice of curtains.[112]

Roger Fry (1866-1934) was also an undergraduate at King's College. Fry was one of the oldest members of the Bloomsbury group: he came up to Cambridge in 1885, almost fifteen years before Thoby Stephen and Leonard Woolf arrived at Trinity. While at King's, Fry circulated for awhile in the orbit of Oscar Browning, but eventually declared Browning a fraud – and a man afflicted with a serious 'want of good taste'.[113] Fry was elected to the Apostles; he graduated from King's with a first class degree in Natural Science in 1888. Though he wrote a fellowship dissertation on phenomenology and Greek painting in the hope of obtaining a Fellowship at King's, he was elected to one. Once back in London, Fry abandoned science to train as a painter and subsequently made his reputation in the world of art, both as an artist and as a theoretician. Fry is perhaps best known for being the chief organiser of two exhibitions of Post-Impressionist paintings, one in 1910 and another in 1912. These shows exhibited Dègas, Manet, Cèzanne, Gauguin, and other important continental painters to the British public for the first time, and quickly remade the world of British art. The impact of the two shows was so far-reaching that Virginia Woolf credited them – only half-jokingly – with changing human nature itself. Writing of the first Post-Impressionist exhibition, Woolf declared that 'in or about December 1910, human character changed'.[114]

Roger Fry lived at 67 Trumpington Street and at 16 King's Parade.

From King's College to Newnham

In *A Room of One's Own*, Mary Beton left the sumptuous lunch at the men's college in the fading hours of a late October day. As she walked across the courtyard, 'gate after gate seemed to close with gentle finality behind me. Innumerable beadles were fitting innumerable keys into well-oiled locks.'[115] If Mary Beton heard gate after gate shutting behind her, she left King's College by the main entrance. But the walk from King's to Newnham is better made along the Backs, which are most easily reached through King's rear entrance. This entrance can be found by walking along the south side of the **Back Lawn**, crossing the King's bridge, and walking along the side of **Scholar's Piece** to the rear gate. (Roger Fry described an autumnal view from King's bridge like this: 'Life does not seem to flow with the same dull round of increasing commonplace within a quarter of a mile of King's bridge, from where one can now watch the golden chestnut and lime leaves flutter down through the rising purple haze on to the river.'[116])

After exiting the rear gate of King's, walk first to the *right* along the **Backs**, for another view of King's Chapel, with its 'high domes and pinnacles … like a sailing-ship always voyaging never arriving'.[117] Then follow the path back to the *left* (south), towards **Silver Street**, noting the same things that Mary Beton saw as she walked towards Fernham:

> What was the truth about these houses, for example, dim and festive now with their red windows in the dusk, but raw and red and squalid, with

their sweets and their boot-laces, at nine o'clock in the morning? And the willows and the river and the gardens that run down to the river, vague now with the mist stealing over them, but gold and red in the sunlight – which was the truth, which was the illusion about them? I spare you the twists and turns of my cogitations, for no conclusion was found on the road to Headingley, and I ask you to suppose that I soon found out my mistake about the turning and retraced my steps to Fernham.[118]

When Woolf made this same walk on the way to dine at Newnham with Pernel Strachey in 1925, she thought of Cambridge's beauty, and of Rupert Brooke: 'A lovely place full, like all places, now, of this wave of the past. Walking past the Darwins I noticed the willows; I thought with that growing maternal affection which now comes to me, of myself there; of Rupert; then I went to Newnham.'[119] The Darwin family home, Newnham Grange, is located halfway down Silver Street. Gwen Darwin, the granddaughter of Charles Darwin, grew up at Newnham Grange and eventually married Jacques Raverat, a friend of both Brooke and Woolf at Cambridge. Newnham Grange is now part of Darwin College.

Upon reaching Silver Street, turn *right* (west), and follow Silver Street past its intersection with **Queens Road/Newnham Road**. Past the intersection, Silver Street becomes **Sidgwick Avenue**. Follow Sidgwick Avenue to the main gate of **Newnham College**, which will be on the *left*. Go to the Porter's window and ask to enter the college. Then exit through the vestibule to the *right*, and out into the main courtyard. Follow the signs to the **Old Labs** for a good look at **Clough Hall**, with its windows 'curved like ships' windows among generous waves of red brick'.[120]

As Mary Beton enters Fernham, the lovely freedom of the place moves her to fantasy. The season switches from autumn to spring. The Fernham courtyard is a riot of flowers and flowing grass. There is no rolled turf here – and no beadle to bar Mary Beton's entry. Jane Harrison walks by:

A wind blew, from what quarter I know not, but it lifted the half-grown leaves so that there was a flash of silver grey in the air. It was the time between the lights when colours undergo their intensification and purples and golds burn in window-panes like the beat of an excitable heart; when for some reason the beauty of the world revealed and yet soon to perish (here I pushed into the garden, for, unwisely, the door was left open and no beadles seemed about), the beauty of the world which is so soon to perish, has two edges, one of laughter, one of anguish, cutting the heart asunder. The gardens of Fernham lay before me in the spring twilight, wild and open, and in the long grass, sprinkled and carelessly flung, were daffodils and bluebells, not orderly perhaps at the best of times, and now wind-blown and waving as they tugged at their roots. The windows of the building, curved like ships' windows among generous waves of red brick, changed from lemon to silver under the flight of the quick spring clouds. Somebody was in a hammock, somebody, but in this light they were phantoms only, half guessed, half seen, raced across the grass – would no one stop her? – and then on the terrace, as if popping out to breathe the air, to glance at the garden, came a bent figure, formidable yet humble, with her great forehead and her shabby dress – could it be the famous scholar, could it be J— H— herself? All was dim, yet intense too, as if the scarf which the dusk had flung over the garden were torn asunder by star or sword – the flash of some terrible reality leaping, as its way is, out of the heart of the spring. For youth –[121]

And then Mary's dinner of thin soup and homely beef arrives: 'Here was my soup. Dinner was being served in the great dining-hall. Far from being spring it was in fact an evening in October ... There was nothing to stir the fancy in that.'[122]

Jane Harrison was an early graduate of Newnham who, after a successful career giving lectures that popularised the study of the Greek classics, returned to Newnham as a lecturer in classical archeology. She remained at Newnham in this capacity from 1898 to 1922, when she moved to Paris with her student Hope Mirrlees. Harrison's work on the classics influenced Woolf's novels in a number of ways. Harrison died in the spring of 1928; Woolf attended her funeral.[123] Harrison's appearance in A Room of One's Own is Woolf's tribute both to her place in women's education, and to the power of her ideas about Greek culture.

Woolf's lecture on 'Women and Fiction' was given in the College Dining Hall, located in Clough Hall. About two hundred students attended the lecture, which took place after their dinner was cleared away. Woolf sat on a dais at one end of the room, opposite the gallery. A look into the dining hall reveals another aspect of Woolf's fictive transformation in A Room of One's Own: far from being plain and severe, as Woolf presents it in her book, the Newnham dining hall is spacious, beautifully ornamented, and quite elegant.

After her dessert of prunes and custard, Mary Beton shares a drink and some talk with the friend who invited her to Fernham, Mary Seton. Mary Seton is loosely modelled on Pernel Strachey, Lytton Strachey's sister, who served as Principal of Newnham from 1923 to 1941. Woolf's cousin Katherine Stephen served as Principal of Newnham from 1911 to 1920.

Though Woolf focused on the privations of Fernham College in *A Room of One's Own*, she also saw the women's colleges of Cambridge as oases of serenity and beauty, where women could exist together in an easy, unforced camaraderie that united them like a 'vapour'. In 'A Woman's College from Outside', which Woolf first intended to include as a chapter in *Jacob's Room*, and then contributed instead to a book prepared by the Edinburgh University Women's Union, Woolf evokes the peace and lyrical beauty of Newnham at night, when its women are united by sleep and by laughter.

The feathery-white moon never let the sky grow dark; all night the chestnut blossoms were white in the green, and dim was the cow-parsley in the meadows. Neither to Tartary nor to Arabia went the wind of the Cambridge courts, but lapsed dreamily in the midst of grey-blue clouds over the roofs of Newnham. There, in the garden, if she needed space to wander, she might find it among the trees; and as none but women's faces could meet her face, she might unveil it blank, featureless, and gaze into rooms where at that hour, blank, featureless, eyelids white over eyes, ringless hands extended upon sheets, slept innumerable women. But here and there a light still burned ...

The cards were spread, falling with their red and yellow faces on the table, and hands were dabbled in the cards. Good Bertha, leaning with her head against the chair, sighed profoundly. For she would willingly have slept, but since night is free pasturage, a limitless field, since night is unmoulded richness, one must tunnel into its darkness. One must hang it with jewels. Night was shared in secret, day browsed on by the whole flock. The blinds were up. A mist was on the garden. Sitting on the floor by the window (while the others played), body, mind, both together, seemed blown through the air, to trail across the bushes. Ah, but she desired to stretch out in bed and to sleep! She believed that no one felt her desire for sleep; she believed humbly – sleepily – with sudden nods and lurchings, that other people were wide awake. When they laughed all together a bird chirped in its sleep out in the garden, as if the laughter –

Yes, as if the laughter (for she dozed now) floated out much like mist and attached itself by soft elastic shreds to plants and bushes, so that the garden was vaporous and clouded. And then, swept by the wind, the bushes would bow themselves and the white vapour blow off across the world.

From all the rooms where women slept this vapour issued, attaching itself to shrubs, like mist, and then blew freely out into the open. Elderly women slept, who would on waking immediately clasp the ivory rod of office. Now smooth and colourless, reposing deeply, they lay surrounded, lay supported, by the bodies of youth recumbent or grouped at the window; pouring forth into the garden this bubbling laughter, this irresponsible laughter: this laughter of mind and body floating away rules, hours, discipline: immensely fertilising, yet formless, chaotic, trailing and straying and tufting the rose-bushes with shreds of vapour.[124]

A WALK AROUND OTHER SITES IN CENTRAL CAMBRIDGE

This walk passes other sites associated with Virginia Woolf and Cambridge. The walk is best begun in front of the Senate House, on the Old Schools Site, where Trinity Street changes to King's Parade.

The Senate House
The Senate House is the ceremonial centre of the University. It is the place where degrees are conferred, examination results posted and important lectures delivered. It is also the spot where votes on issues concerning the whole University are taken, such as the votes seeking to admit women to Cambridge degrees in 1897, 1921 and 1947.

On the corner opposite the Senate House is the Cambridge University Press Bookshop. This spot is the oldest bookshop site in England, where books have been sold continuously since 1581. Beginning in 1845, it operated as the Macmillan bookshop, before the Macmillan brothers moved their business to London to make their fortune as publishers. It was from this building that an effigy of a woman student, dressed in bloomers and riding a bicycle, was hung during the contentious vote on admitting women to the titles of degrees in 1897.

Trinity Hall
Walk down **Senate House Passage** to **Trinity Hall**, the college where Leslie Stephen lived as a don.

Leslie Stephen read mathematics as an undergraduate at Trinity Hall and accepted a clerical fellowship there in 1854. In 1862, he stopped conducting college worship services and resigned as a tutor. He left Cambridge for London in 1864, and formally resigned his Trinity Hall fellowship in 1868, almost fifteen years before Virginia Stephen was born.

Virginia Woolf's grandfather was a Trinity Hall man, too. Sir James Stephen took the LL.B. from Trinity Hall in 1812, and later became under-secretary for the colonies. An ardent abolitionist, Stephen drafted an important bill for the abolition of slavery in 1833. Later, he served as Regius Professor of Modern History at Cambridge from 1849 to 1859.

In his *Sketches from Cambridge* (1865), Leslie Stephen describes the charms of Trinity Hall:

> It is enough to say that our college has all that is essential to the ideal of a college. There is the ancient corner of building, half merged in more modern structures, which our founder acquired or did not acquire, together with an adjacent field, from certain monks. There is the less venerable court, which affords a perfect example of Elizabethan architecture. There is the atrocious pile of obtrusive ugliness which some sixty years ago repaired the ravages of a fire. We have of course a hall, which has been restored to show the old oak roof, and a chapel, which causes me to live in daily fear of another restoration and another liberal subscription. Of course, too, we are 'bosomed deep in tufted trees', though, in spite of University commissioners, no beauty lies as yet beneath our towers and battlements. We have a lawn of velvet turf, hitherto devoted to the orthodox game of bowls, but threatened by an invasion of croquet, for female influence is slowly but surely invading our cloisters. Whether, like the ivy that gathers upon our ancient walls, it may ultimately be fatal to their stability remains yet to be seen.[125]

Henry James was more rhapsodic about Trinity Hall's charms. Writing in 1878, James said: 'If I were called upon to mention the prettiest part of the world, I should draw a thoughtful sigh and point the way to the garden of Trinity Hall.'

Trinity Hall owns several well-known drawings of Leslie Stephen and a bust of his father, Sir James; there is a Leslie Stephen Room for meetings. After Stephen's death in 1904, the Leslie Stephen lectureship was endowed in his memory. The lecture is given in alternate years on a literary topic; one of the electors is always the Master of Trinity Hall.

(Trinity Hall is usually open to visitors from 9 a.m. to 12 p.m., and again from 2 p.m. to 5.30 p.m. For current opening times, check the Trinity Hall website at www.trinhall.cam.ac.uk.)

Trinity College

Leaving Trinity Hall, proceed *left* (north) along **Trinity Lane**, following the bend back to **Trinity Street**. At Trinity Street, turn *left* (north) and proceed to the main gates of Trinity College.

Seven members of the Bloomsbury group were undergraduates at Trinity College: Clive Bell, Leonard Woolf, Lytton Strachey, Desmond MacCarthy, Saxon Sydney-Turner, Thoby Stephen and Adrian Stephen. As Leonard Woolf tells the story, he became very intimate with Lytton Strachey and Thoby Stephen at Trinity, 'and so the foundations of what became known as Bloomsbury were laid'.[126] Thoby had rooms in Trinity Great Court; Leonard Woolf tells a wonderful story of an encounter there between two very different generations of Cambridge men:

> When [Thoby's] father, Sir Leslie Stephen, came up to stay a weekend with him, Lytton and I were had in to meet him ... I found myself, a nervous undergraduate, sitting opposite to this very tall and distinguished old gentleman in Thoby's rooms in Trinity Great Court and expected to make conversation with him – not helped in any way by Thoby – it seemed to me ... What added enormously to the alarm was that he was stone deaf and that one had to sit quite near to him and shout everything one said to him down an ear-trumpet. It is remarkable and humiliating to discover how imbecile a not very imaginative, or even an imaginative, remark, can sound when one shouts it down an ear-trumpet into the ear of a bearded old gentleman, six foot three inches tall, sitting very upright in a chair and looking as if every word you said only added to his already unendurable sorrows. However it must be said that this awkwardness and terror were gradually dissipated by him. He had immense charm and he obviously liked to meet the young and Thoby's friends. Unlike Henry James, he could see through our awkwardness and even grubbiness to our intelligence, and was pleased by our respect and appreciation. In the end we were all talking and laughing naturally (so far as this is possible down an ear-trumpet) and enjoying one another's company.[127]

It was in this same set of rooms that Leonard Woolf first met Virginia Stephen.

In the course of his years at Cambridge, Leonard Woolf had rooms in Great Court and New Court, as did both Saxon Sydney-Turner and Lytton Strachey (Strachey's Great Court rooms were in K Staircase). Desmond MacCarthy had rooms in Whewell's Court; Clive Bell had rooms in New Court. Adrian Stephen had rooms in Nevile's Court, not far from the dining hall, and it was this spot that Virginia Woolf remembered many years later when she lamented her nephew Julian's boredom at King's and fondly recalled the sound of grace coming through Adrian's windows before the undergraduates sat down to dine. Nevile's Court is also where Woolf houses Jacob in *Jacob's Room*. Close to the beginning of the novel, the narrator moves through the Great Court and into Nevile's Court, where Jacob is not to be found in his rooms. The narrator then describes the view through the white pillars of the Wren Library. (This view is best seen from one of the benches set into the wall of the dining hall along the east side of Nevile's Court, looking towards the Wren Library):

> The waiters at Trinity must have been shuffling china plates like cards, from the clatter that could be heard in the Great Court. Jacob's rooms, however, were in Neville's Court; at the top; so that reaching his door one went in a little out of breath; but he wasn't there. Dining in Hall, presumably. It will be quite dark in Neville's Court long before midnight, only the pillars opposite will always be white, and the fountains. A curious effect the gate has, like lace upon pale green. Even in the window you hear the plates; a hum of talk, too, from the diners; the Hall lit up, and the swing-doors opening and shutting with a soft thud. Some are late.[128]

A few pages later, Woolf evokes the late evening atmosphere of Trinity College in a lyrical passage that is reminiscent of her portrait of Newnham by night:

> The laughter died in the air. The sound of it could scarcely have reached any one standing by the Chapel, which stretched along the opposite side of the court. The laughter died out, and only gestures of arms, movements of bodies, could be seen shaping something in the room. Was it an argument? A bet on the boat races? Was it nothing of the sort? What was shaped by the arms and bodies moving in the twilight room?

A step or two beyond the window there was nothing at all, except the enclosing buildings – chimneys upright, roofs horizontal; too much brick and building for a May night, perhaps. And then before one's eyes would come the bare hills of Turkey – sharp lines, dry earth, coloured flowers, and colour on the shoulders of the women, standing naked-legged in the stream to beat linen on the stones. The stream made loops of water round their ankles. But none of that could show clearly through the swaddlings and blanketings of the Cambridge night. The stroke of the clock even was muffled; as if intoned by somebody reverent from a pulpit; as if generations of learned men heard the last hour go rolling through their ranks and issued it, already smooth and time-worn, with their blessing, for the use of the living.

Was it to receive this gift from the past that the young man came to the window and stood there, looking out across the court? It was Jacob. He stood smoking his pipe while the last stroke of the clock purred softly round him. Perhaps there had been an argument. He looked satisfied; indeed masterly; which expression changed slightly as he stood there, the sound of the clock conveying to him (it may be) a sense of old buildings and time; and himself the inheritor; and then to-morrow; and friends; at the thought of whom, in sheer confidence and pleasure, it seemed, he yawned and stretched himself.[129]

(Trinity College is generally open to visitors during the day. For current opening times, check the Trinity College website at www.trin.cam.ac.uk.)

Four other sites of interest

Leave Trinity College by the front gate. Turn *right* (south) along **Trinity Street** and return to the front gates of King's College. Opposite King's, turn *left* (east) into **St Edward's Passage**.

There are three sites of interest inside St Edward's Passage. The **Cambridge Arts Theatre** is on the south side. When John Maynard Keynes was the bursar of King's College, he acquired this land and had the Cambridge Arts Theatre built in 1935. His wife, Lydia Lopokova, performed there as Nora in Ibsen's *A Doll's House* during the theatre's first season.

When Julian Bell was an undergraduate at King's College, he lived for a time at **Number 12 St Edward's Passage**.

Virginia Woolf often ordered her books from G. David, Booksellers, now located at **Number 16 St Edward's Passage**.

Leave St Edward's Passage and return to **King's Parade**; on reaching

King's Parade turn *left*. Just past the turning into **King's Lane** on the right is the facade of what was formerly the **Bull Hotel**, Trumpington Street. The façade now conceals a new building, part of St Catharine's College. Virginia and Leonard often stayed at the Bull during their visits to Cambridge, and on one occasion Woolf used the hotel to paint an unflattering portrait of the English middle classes:

> Among external things, we were at Cambridge for the week end; kept warm at the Bull – & there's a good subject – The Hotel. Many people from Macclesfield talking about motor cars. Mothers, to me pathetic, looking half shyly at their sons, as if deprecating their age. A whole life opened to me: father, mother, son, daughter. Father alone has wine. An enormous man, like an advertisement of Power: sits in chair. Daddy you'll be miserable in it says girl, herself bovine. Mother a mere wisp; sits with eyes shut; had spent hours driving up writing characters of maids. Shall I remember any of this?[130]

A TRIP TO GRANTCHESTER

> I only know that you may lie
> Day long and watch the Cambridge sky,
> And, flower-lulled in sleepy grass,
> Hear the cool lapse of hours pass,
> Until the centuries blend and blur
> In Grantchester, in Grantchester ...
> 'The Old Vicarage, Grantchester'
Rupert Brooke

Every visitor to Cambridge should make the short detour to Grantchester, to have tea at the Orchard Tea Gardens and walk past Byron's Pool. One can drive or walk to Grantchester (a distance of about two miles), but the most atmospheric way of travelling there is by punt.

Rupert Brooke moved to Grantchester to escape the distractions of college life and work uninterrupted on his fellowship dissertation. He lived first at the Orchard, where he rented rooms from June 1909 to December 1910.[131] When some 'horrible people' appeared as fellow tenants at the Orchard, Brooke arranged to rent rooms at the Old Vicarage, just down the road. He moved there in May 1911, renting three rooms on the ground and first floors. The next year, Brooke wrote his celebrated poem, 'The Old Vicarage, Grantchester', while on an extended visit to Germany: he became homesick for Grantchester, took to his usual table at the Café des Westens in Berlin, and penned his famous plaint for 'Grantchester! Ah, Grantchester! There's peace and holy quiet there'.[132]

During the period Brooke lived in Grantchester, he entertained a steady stream of guests. Lytton Strachey stayed for a night; E.M. Forster – an 'old King's man of 27 or 29', as Brooke put it – stayed several days. Augustus John came to Cambridge to paint Jane Harrison's portrait at Newnham, and camped in a field near Grantchester with his lover, six children, and various grooms and servants. Brooke ferried the party around the river. Brooke camped and went on outings with his 'Neo-Pagan' friends: Ka Cox, Gwen Darwin, Jacques Raverat. In August 1911, young Virginia Stephen stayed for a week with Brooke at the Old Vicarage and they took their naked moonlight swim in Byron's Pool.

Many years later, after Gwen Darwin's husband Jacques Raverat died, Woolf wrote to her about Rupert Brooke, his poetry, Cambridge and Grantchester:

> I feel that Jacques was thinking a great deal of Rupert at the end. Rupert was a little mythical to me when he died. He was very rude to 'Nessa once, and Leonard, I think, rather disliked him; in fact Bloomsbury was against him, and he against them. Meanwhile, I had a private version of him which I stuck to when they all cried him down, and shall preserve somewhere infinitely far away – but how these feelings last, how they come over one, oddly, at unexpected moments – based on my week at Grantchester [in 1911], when he was all that could be kind and inter-esting and substantial and goodhearted (I choose these words without thinking whether they correspond to what he was to you or anybody). He was, I thought, the ablest of all the young men; I did not then think much of his poetry, which he read aloud on the lawn; but I thought he would be Prime Minister, because he had such a gift with people, and such sanity, and force; I remember a weakly pair of lovers meandering in one day, just engaged, very floppy (A.Y. Campbell and his bride who now writes on Shelley). You know how intense and silly or offhand in a self-conscious kind of way the Cambridge young then were about their loves – Rupert simplified them, and broadened them – humanised them – and then he rode off on a bicycle about a railway strike. Jacques says he thinks Rupert's poetry was poetry. I must read it again. I had come to think it mere barrel organ music, but this refers to the patriotic poems, and

perhaps is unfair: but the early ones were all adjectives and contortions –
weren't they? My idea was that he was to be Member of Parliament and
edit the Classics, a very powerful, ambitious man, but not a poet. Still all
this is no doubt wholly and completely wrong.[133]

How to get there

By car: From the centre of Cambridge, take **King's Parade** to **Silver
Street**; turn *right* (west) into Silver Street and follow it a short distance
to **Newnham Road** (A1134). Turn *left* into Newnham Road and pass
straight through the first roundabout onto **Barton Road** (A603). Follow
the A603 around a curve to the *right* to **Grantchester Road**; turn *left*
into Grantchester Road; follow Grantchester Road into the village of
Grantchester.

By foot: The first part of the walk is identical to the drive: take
King's Parade to **Silver Street**; turn *right* (west) into Silver Street and
follow it a short distance to **Newnham Road** (A1134). Turn *left* into
Newnham Road and pass straight through the first roundabout onto the
A603. The A603 (**Barton Road**) will turn to the *right*; instead, continue
straight into **Grantchester Street**. Follow Grantchester Street to **Eltisley
Avenue**; take Eltisley Avenue to **Grantchester Meadows** (always bearing
right). The macadam road will end in a footpath across the meadows to
Grantchester.

By punt: This is by far the most atmospheric way to get to
Grantchester. Scudamore's Punting Company is located in the centre of
Cambridge, at the end of **Mill Lane**. One can hire a punt to travel north
along the Cam, behind the colleges, or south towards Grantchester; one
can either punt oneself, or hire a guide to do the hard work.
Recommendation: hire a guide to punt you to Grantchester; have a meal
at the Orchard; walk by the Old Vicarage, Byron's Pool, and around the
village of Grantchester. Then walk back to Cambridge along the
meadows. (Scudamore's Punting Company, Cambridge: 01223 359 750.)

The Orchard

The Orchard is a short walk up the hill from the punt landing at
Grantchester. Brooke described Grantchester and his life at the Orchard
in a letter written in July 1909:

It is a lovely village on the river above Cambridge. I'm in a small house, a sort of cottage, with a dear plump weather-beaten kindly old lady in control. I have a perfectly glorious time, seeing nobody I know day after day. The room I have opens straight out onto a stone verandah covered with creepers, and a little old garden full of old-fashioned flowers and *crammed* with roses. I work at Shakespeare, read, write all day, and now and then wander in the woods or by the river. I bathe every morning and sometimes by moonlight, have all my meals (chiefly fruit) brought to me out of doors, and am as happy as the day's long. I am chiefly sorry for all you people in the world. Every now and then dull bald spectacled people from Cambridge come out and take tea here.[134]

The Orchard is open for meals (morning coffee, light luncheon, afternoon tea) seven days a week from 11 a.m. to 7 p.m. Meals may be taken either inside or outside under the trees; there is also a small museum devoted to Brooke. (Phone: 01223 845 788; Fax: 01223 845 862.)

The Old Vicarage

Exit the Orchard's car park and turn **left**. Walk about two hundred yards along the road to the Old Vicarage.

Lytton Strachey at one point contemplated taking rooms in the Old Vicarage, too. Brooke described the house's lovely garden to him in a letter:

> The garden is the great glory. There is a soft lawn with a sundial and tangled, antique flowers abundantly; and a sham ruin, quite in a corner; built fifty years ago by Mr Shuckburgh, historian and rector of Grantchester; and *most* attractive ... In the autumn it will be very Ussher-like.[135]

The Old Vicarage is now a private home; it is not open to the public. But the clock in the entryway is permanently stopped at 'ten to three', as is the Church's clock in Brooke's poem.

Byron's Pool

Continue along the road in the same direction, past the Old Vicarage. After half a mile, there is a sign-posted path on the **right** leading to Byron's Pool. The path will take you through a wooded area, and then along the river. Byron's Pool is the wide section of water just at the weir; it was formerly the mill pond for the Trumpington Mill.

Byron's Pool has a long history of literary associations. Trumpington Mill, which serves as the setting for Chaucer's *The Reeve's Tale*, once stood beside it. It became known as Byron's Pool after Lord Byron, then an undergraduate at Trinity College, came to swim in the pool. (In Byron's day, the pool was fourteen feet deep in spots; Byron and his friends threw plates, eggs and shillings into the pool – and then dived to the bottom to retrieve them.) Byron's Pool is also said to be the setting for Tennyson's early poem 'The Miller's Daughter'.[136] Brooke describes the pool in 'The Old Vicarage, Grantchester':

> Still in the dawnlit waters cool
> His ghostly Lordship swims his pool,
> And tries the strokes, essays the tricks,
> Long learnt on Hellespont, or Styx.
> Dan Chaucer hears his river still
> Chatter beneath a phantom mill.
> Tennyson notes with studious eye,
> How Cambridge waters hurry by.[137]

Walk back along the same route through the village of Grantchester and past the Orchard, noting the village church – whose clock some people remember having been stopped in Brooke's time. (It is no longer.) Just past the Rupert Brooke Public House, pick up the footpath back to Cambridge. (The footpath will be on your **right**.) The footpath runs across Grantchester meadows, with some lovely views of King's College chapel in the distance. (When Sylvia Plath lived in Eltisley Avenue as a Fulbright Scholar at Newnham, she concluded that, viewed from Grantchester meadows, 'the spires of King's Chapel looked like glistening pink sugar spikes on a little cake'.) The footpath ends in a street called **Grantchester Meadows.** Follow Grantchester Meadows to **Eltisley Avenue,** and Eltisley Avenue to **Newnham Road** and **Silver Street.** This walk takes you past the Porch, the home of Caroline Emelia Stephen, which is located at 33 Grantchester Street (at the corner where Eltisley Avenue meets **Merton Street** and **Grantchester Street**).

The Porch

The Porch (33 Grantchester Street) was the home of Virginia Woolf's aunt Caroline Emelia Stephen from 1897 until her death in 1909. 'The Nun', as Woolf called her, had visited Cambridge to lecture to the women of Newnham and Girton as early as 1888. She settled in Cambridge permanently in 1895, choosing the town as her final residence to be close to sympathetic family members: her niece Katherine Stephen was Vice-Principal of Newnham College at the time, and another niece, Helen, was teaching in Newnham Croft. Her widowed sister-in-law, Mary Stephen, moved to Godmanchester, which was also nearby. Caroline Emelia first lived in rented rooms and then bought Berrington Villa, a house located at 33 Grantchester Street, with views across the meadows.[138] She renamed the house 'The Porch', after George Herbert's poem 'The Church Porch', and after a cottage in Freshwater, on the Isle of Wight, where she had spent a happy holiday with Anny and Minny Thackeray many years earlier.[139]

Virginia Stephen visited her aunt at The Porch fairly often, especially after Thoby went up to Trinity in 1899. Her longest stay occurred in the autumn of 1904, when she went to The Porch to recuperate after Leslie Stephen's death. She rested, wrote, and absorbed the quiet of the Cambridge setting. She described the view into the garden from the window of The Porch and praised the beauty of her Cambridge surroundings:

> This is an ideal retreat for me. I feel as though I were living in a Cathedral Close, with the big bell of the Quakers voice tolling at intervals ... I can sit alone by an open window for hours if I like, and hear only birds songs, and the rustle of leaves. The trees are pure gold and orange, and no place in the world can be lovelier than Cambridge. It is a very small world, I expect, as far as society goes, but what there is is amazing, and all well known to me.[140]

While Virginia stayed with her aunt, she learned about Caroline Emelia's Quaker ideas about pacifism and non-cooperation, and even made plans to attend a Quaker meeting when Violet Dickinson came to visit. (Virginia asked Violet Dickinson to offer a description of this Quaker meeting to Mrs Lyttelton, editor of Women's Supplement of the *Guardian*. It was her first, tentative bid for publication.) In her writings about the Society of Friends, Caroline Emelia Stephen often discussed the importance of moments of illumination, which she typically described as being like 'flash[es] of light'. For Caroline Emelia, these insights were literal manifestations of a Divine voice; for her niece Virginia, these momentary insights meant something very different. But in her essay on 'Divine Guidance', Caroline Emelia Stephen compared these intermittent flashes of insight to the beacon of a lighthouse. It is a description reminiscent of Godrevy lighthouse, which Caroline Emelia had seen while visiting her brother and his family in St Ives:

> And let us remember that the intermittent character of all vivid religious experience lies in our varying degrees of consciousness of the divine presence and control, not in that control itself. That of which we catch occasional glimpses is the unchanging eternal nature of divinely ordered life.
>
> Have you even seen a revolving lighthouse at night from across the sea, with its steadfast light alternately hidden and displayed? Have you watched the faint spark as it glows into splendour for a few seconds and then fades away again into darkness? And have you considered how the very fact of its intermittency is the means by which it is recognised and its message is conveyed? It is a light given not to read by, but to steer our course by. Its appearances and disappearances are a language by which the human care that devised it can speak to the watchers and strugglers at sea. That care does not wax and wane with the light; but in its unchanging vigilance it provides a means of communication which no unaltering beam could afford.[141]

By 1905, new houses were beginning to constrict Caroline Emelia's views from the Porch, so she bought a neighbouring public house – the Royston Arms – to preserve her space. When she died four years later, her will indicated which nieces and nephews she most wished to support. Vanessa and Adrian Stephen were each left £100; Virginia was left £2,500. And Katherine Stephen was left £3,000, The Porch, and the Royston Arms, with the provision that the Society of Friends should get right of first refusal if Katherine Stephen decided to sell the pub.[142]

How to get there
One passes The Porch on the walk back from Grantchester. To walk to The Porch from the centre of Cambridge, take **King's Parade** to **Silver**

Street; turn *right* (west) into Silver Street and follow it a short distance to **Newnham Road** (A1134). Turn *left* into Newnham Road and pass straight through the first roundabout onto the A603. The A603 (**Barton Road**) will turn to the *right* after a short distance; instead, continue straight into **Grantchester Street.** Follow Grantchester Street to **Eltisley Avenue.** The Porch is located at 33 Grantchester Street, at the corner where Eltisley Avenue meets **Grantchester Street** and **Merton Street.** It is a private home and is not open to visitors.

CHAPTER FIVE

Monk's House and *Between the Acts*

'We are at Rodmell on the loveliest spring day: soft: a blue veil in the air
torn by birds voices. I am glad to be alive & sorry for the dead ... '
Virginia Woolf's *Diary*, 24 March 1932

'So complete & holy [is] the old habitual beauty of England: the silver
sheep clustering; & and the downs soaring, like birds wings sweeping up
& up ... This has a holiness. This will go on after I'm dead.'
Virginia Woolf's *Diary*, 16 September 1932

I

Virginia Woolf took her houses in the country seriously. Having
grown up spending summers away from London, by the sea, she never
lost her taste for the pleasant alternation of city and country life: she
loved the excitement of haunting London streets during the grey
winter months, followed by the respite of weekends and late summers
in the open rural air, striding through fields, or sitting in her well-
tended garden. For Woolf, the English countryside was an escape, a
sanctuary, a source of inspiration. It was a place where she gloried in
her solitude and her writing. Virginia Woolf owned Monk's House, in

243

Rodmell, East Sussex, for twenty-three years, from 1919 until the day she died in March 1941. During that time, the house and the land-scapes surrounding it became an emblem for her of peace, continuity, and replenishment.

Virginia's first forays into the Sussex countryside began after Leslie Stephen's death, when she took possession of a house in Firle, near Lewes, in 1911. Virginia Stephen had fallen in love with the soft beauty of the South Downs on weekend visits with friends who lived in the area. When she rented a home of her own – the house at Firle was the first extended lease she took independently of her siblings – she named it 'Little Talland House', and thereby linked her adult love of the Sussex countryside to the magic of her childhood summers in Cornwall. Later, Virginia and Leonard took the lease of Asheham House, a much more elegant and secluded home just a few miles away. They spent weekends and holidays at Asheham from 1912 until 1919. But in 1919, their landlord decided to move his farm-bailiff into Asheham, and Woolf began to scour the countryside for other suitable houses in the vicinity.

She settled first on the Round House, an eccentric, circular, truncated windmill built in the centre of Lewes. On a whim, Woolf contracted for the Round House at the price of £300. She quickly realised that she had made a mistake: its rooms were very small; it was in the centre of town; its garden was not large enough. When Virginia brought Leonard down to Lewes for an inspection tour a few weeks later, they saw a placard in an auctioneer's office offering something better: 'Lot 1. Monks House, Rodmell. An old fashioned house standing in three quarters of an acre of land to be sold with possessions.' Leonard muttered 'That would have suited us exactly'. Virginia bicycled over to see it the next day, pedalling against a stiff, cold wind.[1]

She was instantly charmed. Monk's House offered quiet, seclusion, the delightful thought of an eccentric monastic connection, and a very promising garden. Though Virginia was determined to keep her enthu-siasm for Monk's House in check – after all, she and Leonard already owned the Round House – she couldn't help describing Monk's House with rising eagerness, and ending her description with a possessive evocation of the street at Rodmell:

'These rooms are small, I said to myself; you must discount the value of that old chimney piece & the niches for holy water. Monks are nothing out of the way. The kitchen is distinctly bad. Theres an oil stove, & no grate. Nor is there hot water, nor a bath, & as for the E.C. [earth closet] I was never shown it.' These prudent objections kept excitement at bay; yet even they were forced to yield place to a profound pleasure at the size & shape & fertility & wildness of the garden. There seemed an infinity of fruitbearing trees; the plums crowded so as to weigh the tip of the branch down; unexpected flowers sprouted among cabbages. There were well kept rows of peas, artichokes, potatoes; raspberry bushes had pale little pyramids of fruit; & I could fancy a very pleasant walk in the orchard under the apple trees, with the grey extinguisher of the church steeple pointing my boundary ... It is an unpretending house, long & low, a house of many doors; on one side fronting the street of Rodmell, & wood boarded on that side, though the street of Rodmell is at our end little more than a cart track running out on to the flat of the water meadows.[2]

Virginia and Leonard bought Monk's House for £700 and sold the Round House at a small profit two weeks later. When Virginia Woolf moved into Monk's House in the summer of 1919, she knew 'that will be our address for ever and ever; Indeed I've already marked out our graves in the yard which joins our meadow'.[3]

As it turned out, Monk's House failed to provide the inspiration of an ancient ecclesiastical history. When Leonard Woolf researched the matter many years later, he discovered that the house had probably not been used for 'retreats' by the monks of the Lewes Priory, but had passed instead from one secular family to another since 1707.[4] But Monk's House provided many other sorts of inspiration for its new owners. To begin with, they bought furnishings for their house at a sale of the prior owner's possessions: a few pieces of furniture, some cutlery, garden tools. Best of all, they treated themselves to three nineteenth-century paintings of the Glazebrook family, which had owned Monk's House from 1796 until 1877. Virginia loved the paintings' palpable link to their house's long history; she also admired their primitive style. When they acquired these paintings, Virginia and Leonard acquired a piece of Monk's House's past. Virginia had always been moved by the idea of a house's previous owners remaining to 'haunt' it lovingly – in her story 'A Haunted House', a ghostly couple return to their former home to watch its current owners live and love there. With her three

Glazebrook family portraits, Virginia repopulated Monk's House with the spirits of its earlier inhabitants, and immersed herself firmly in the continuity of the house's history.

The Woolfs also laboured to make their old house fit for the twentieth century. When they bought it, Monk's House had a wretched kitchen, no hot water, no bath, and an earth closet in the garden instead of indoor toilet facilities. In winter, they trekked across frozen ground to the 'romantic chamber'[5] in the garden. The Woolfs immediately renovated the kitchen, adding a solid fuel oven. Six years later, in 1926, they added a bathroom and a lavatory with the proceeds of *Mrs Dalloway*. Vita Sackville-West tells the story of their glee at their new indoor plumbing: 'They both run upstairs every now and then and pull the plug just for the sheer fun of it, and come down and say, "It worked very well that time – did you hear?"'[6] Virginia and Leonard knocked down the wall between the dining room and the drawing room to make one large, comfortable 'combined drawing eating room', with five windows, beams down the middle, and 'flowers & leaves nodding in all round us'.[7] They commissioned Duncan Grant and Vanessa Bell to design tables and other furnishings for them in the Omega Workshop style. Then they began to plan for an extension to the house, the extra rooms that were eventually added with the profits from *Orlando*.

Virginia gloried in reclaiming the garden as much as renovating the house. Back from one of their first spring weekends in Rodmell, she looked forward to the joy of many subsequent days spent in the open air, bent over the dark earth of flower beds:

> Back from Monk's House an hour ago, after the first week end – the most perfect, I was going to say, but how can I tell what week ends we mayn't spend there? The first pure joy of the garden I mean. Wind enough outside; within sunny & sheltered; & weeding all day to finish the beds in a queer sort of enthusiasm which made me say this is happiness. Gladioli standing in troops: the mock orange out. Kitchen wall battered down. We were out till 9 at night, though the evening was cold. Both stiff & scratched all over today; with chocolate earth in our nails.[8]

As it turned out, the garden became more Leonard's passion than Virginia's. Virginia predicted that Leonard had 'the making of a fanat-

ical lover of that garden',[9] and her prediction was accurate. He had two
fish ponds in the garden – one large round pond and a second rectan-
gular pond, reserved especially for the convalescence of ailing fish.
Leonard planted exotic flower species; he ran three heated greenhouses
at one point and employed a full-time gardener. In 1928, Leonard
persuaded Virginia that they should purchase an adjoining field, which
assured their unspoiled view of the Downs.

Though they sometimes quarrelled over the time and money Leonard
devoted to the garden – Virginia wanted to travel away from Rodmell
more; then they agreed to schedule long walks together on Wednesdays
and Sundays to 'counteract the tremendous draw of the garden'[10] –
Virginia took affectionate satisfaction in the simple outdoor delights
Monk's House offered. She liked their two elm trees, which they named
Leonard and Virginia. She laughed at Leonard, who couldn't stop going
outside to look at his pears and weigh his potatoes. She liked the swallows skimming over the terrace, and the thought of taking honey from
the hives at dusk. When World War II threatened their very existence at
Monk's House, the trees and birds in the garden became emblems of the
endurance of natural life in the face of human destruction:

> All the birds are sitting up in L[eonard] & V[irginia]. The twig carrying
> has begun, & this goes on while all the guns are pointed & charged & no
> one dares pull the trigger. Not a sound this evening to bring in the human
> tears. I remember the sudden profuse shower one night just before war
> wh. made me think of all men & women weeping.[11]

All these natural phenomena – trees, birds carrying twigs for nests,
rain resembling human tears – are taken into the pages of *Between the
Acts*, where they reappear as symbols of continuity and endurance.

When the Woolfs went to Monk's House for their summer stays, they
sometimes had guests. T.S. Eliot came to visit with his wife Vivien; E.M.
Forster was invited to stay, and was very annoyed at being left to fend
entirely for himself. But Virginia and Leonard were more often alone,
and Virginia gloried in their shared solitude:

> Back from a good week end at Rodmell – a week end of no talking,
> sinking at once into deep safe book reading; & then sleep: clear trans-

parent; with the may tree like a breaking wave outside; & all the garden
green tunnels, mounds of green: & then to wake into the hot still day, &
never a person to be seen, never an interruption: the place to ourselves:
the long hours.[12]

Virginia looked forward to this uninterrupted, solitary time for
writing. She worked on all her major novels at Monk's House, either in
her garden writing hut during the warm months or, after the house's
extension was built, in her bedroom during the winter. Virginia's work-
room, whether in Rodmell or London, always contained a large, plain,
wooden table, covered with an untidy mix of manuscripts, letters, and
what Lytton Strachey called 'filth packets' (odds and ends of string,
broken cigarette holders, used matches, rusty paper clips – Leonard
insisted that Virginia was an untidy writer, 'indeed an untidy liver, an
accumulator').[13] Virginia never wrote at this table – at least not when
she was composing the initial drafts of her novels. Instead, she sat in a
very low armchair, with a large plywood board across her knees, and
wrote in pen and ink into a notebook she had bound for herself in a
gaily coloured paper. She wrote regularly every morning; later in the
day, she typed and revised.

Virginia's afternoon routine usually also involved a long walk – over
the fields, across the river, along the downs. She might pass traces of
Sussex's earlier civilisations – Iron Age barrows, the supposed line of
the Roman road along the highway. There were also local reminders of
the prehistory that antedated human beings in the area. In the nineteenth century, Dr Gideon Mantell discovered fossilised bones of the
prehistoric iguanodon in Sussex; he is commemorated by a plaque in
the Lewes High Street. As Virginia walked, she soaked in every detail,
made up phrases, and then recorded the luscious raw description in her
diary:

> This is the last day of August, & like almost all of them of extraordinary
> beauty. Each day is fine enough & hot enough for sitting out; but also full
> of wandering clouds; & that fading & rising of the light which so enrap-
> tures me in the downs: which I am always comparing to the light beneath
> an alabaster bowl, &c. The corn is now stood about in rows of three four
> or five solid shaped yellow cakes – rich, it seems, with eggs & spice: good
> to eat. Sometimes I see the cattle galloping 'like mad' as Dostoevsky

would say, in the brooks. The clouds – if I could describe them I would: one yesterday had flowing hair on it like the very fine white hair of an old man. At this moment they are white in a leaden sky; but the sun, behind the house, is making the grass green. I walked to the racecourse today & saw a weasel.[14]

As time went by, Monk's House and the landscapes surrounding it became associated with two crucial themes for Virginia: experiences of startling – almost mystical – insight; experiences of the power and pathos of the continuity of human history. She described one of her fertile moods at Rodmell as 'something mystic, spiritual; the thing that exists when we aren't there'.[15] On another occasion, she described her moods at Rodmell as terrifying, yet full of insight into whatever it is that is most 'real':

> Often down here I have entered into a sanctuary; a nunnery; had a religious retreat; of great agony once; & always some terror: so afraid one is of loneliness: of seeing to the bottom of the vessel. That is one of the experiences I have had here in some Augusts; & got then to a consciousness of what I call 'reality': a thing I see before me; something abstract; but residing in the downs or sky; beside which nothing matters; in which I shall rest & continue to exist. Reality I call it. And I fancy sometimes this is the most necessary thing to me: that which I seek. But who knows? – once one takes a pen & writes? How difficult not to go making 'reality' this & that, whereas it is one thing.[16]

Woolf later thought that one of these mystical moods at Rodmell was the first impulse toward her masterpiece *The Waves* (1931), an abstract, poetic novel in which she dramatised a world refracted through the eyes of multiple, impersonal selves. But moments of intense, timeless insight into 'reality' pervade all of Woolf's best work: the dinner scene in *To the Lighthouse*; Clarissa's vicarious reenactment of Septimus's death; Orlando's vision of the wild goose springing up above Shelmerdine's head.

As time went by, Woolf also associated Monk's House, its landscapes, and Rodmell's villagers with the idea of human continuity – the idea that human history is a procession of the lives of obscure people, and that the life of any individual plays a part in that pageant. Leonard Woolf expressed this idea in terms of the quiet spiritual continuum he

249

felt at both Monk's House and Hogarth House, the Woolfs' London home from 1915 to 1924:

> In the atmosphere of both houses, Monks House in Rodmell and Hogarth House in Richmond, there was something similar. In both one felt a quiet continuity of people living. Unconsciously one was absorbed into this procession of men, women, and children who since 1600 or 1700 sat in the panelled rooms, clattered up and down stairs, and had planted the great Blenheim apple-tree or the ancient fig-tree. One became a part of history and of a civilization by continuing in the line of all their lives. And there was something curiously stable and peaceful in the civilization of these two houses.[17]

Virginia expressed the same idea in slightly different terms, with a novelist's eye, by mythologising their sometime servant Mabel Mockford as the 'unconscious breathing of England'. Virginia's writing hut was within sight of St Peter's, the village church where Mabel went for her wedding:

> & theres Mabel the Bride in her white dress at the pump. The bridegroom, a carter out of work, wears white socks. Are they pure? I doubt it. They are going to spend their honeymoon near Pevensey. He was 15 minutes late & we saw her come in wearing a wreath. And I felt this is the heart of England – this wedding in the country: history I felt; Cromwell; The Osbornes; Dorothy's shepherdesses singing: of all of whom Mr & Mrs Jarrad seem more the descendants than I am: as if they represented the unconscious breathing of England.[18]

Monk's House and the villagers of Rodmell represented the continuity of human history – the idea that human history endured in the lives of the obscure, and that any single life gained significance by connecting itself to that unconscious pageant. Monk's House and the villagers of Rodmell represented the continuity of English history – for Woolf, as for E.M. Forster in *Howard's End*, the real heart of England beat in its houses and its ordinary people. Above all, Monk's House and Rodmell represented the continuity of personal history – with their peace and stability, they provided the place where an imaginative soul could find and quiet itself, and set about the serious business of capturing reality in a net of words.

But the peace of Virginia's beloved Sussex countryside was shattered in the 1930s by the increasing power of the Fascists in Italy and the Nazis in Germany. While she was struggling with the composition of *The Years* – her most bitingly anti-patriarchal, anti-Fascist, anti-war novel – Mussolini was threatening to invade Ethiopia and Hitler was preparing to reoccupy the Rhineland. (Mussolini invaded Ethiopia in October 1935; Hitler marched into the Rhineland in March 1936.) England and France embarked on a policy of appeasement; a walk through the countryside in September 1935 provided Virginia with an image of inaction, futility, and violence:

Cant write today ... We saw a snake eating a toad: it had half the toad in, half out; gave a suck now & then. The toad slowly disappearing. L. poked its tail; the snake was sick of the crushed toad, & I dreamt of men committing suicide & cd. see the body shooting through the water.[19]

This image of monstrous futility – which Virginia associated with suicide by drowning – reappears as a central symbol in *Between the Acts* six years later.

Over the next four years, Hitler invaded Austria, reclaimed the Sudetenland, and threatened to destroy Prague by air. Then Germany invaded Poland in September 1939, and England and France declared war. Holland and Belgium quickly fell to Germany in the Blitzkrieg; Paris fell to the Germans in June 1940. The British Expeditionary Forces were routed from the beaches of Dunkirk, and abandoned most of their equipment in France. A local village man, who had been plucked from Dunkirk and landed at Ramsgate in a rowing boat, was said to be the only survivor of his regiment. He was the brother of Louie Everest, the Woolfs' cook; when Louie looked out of her window early one morning after the evacuation of Dunkirk she saw him, 'a soldier whom she did not recognise at first, hatless, his tunic bloody and full of holes, his boots in rags, lying exhausted outside the front door'.[20]

Invasion seemed certain, and invasion would come along the south coast of England, through the Sussex and Kent countryside. Harold Nicolson warned Vita that there might be a complete civilian evacuation of Sussex and Kent. The Woolfs were issued gas-masks. Virginia attended fire drills and lectures on first aid. They knew that the Gestapo had prepared an arrest list for Great Britain. Though no one could know with any certainty who appeared on it, the Woolfs' leftist leanings and publishing connections made them likely candidates. As it turned out, both 'Leonard Woolf, Schriftsteller' and 'Virginia Woolf, Schriftstellerin' were named on the Gestapo list, along with Harold Nicolson, Lytton Strachey, Sigmund Freud, and a host of other acquaintances and friends.[21]

There was also, of course, the matter of Leonard's Jewishness. Leonard and Virginia had always known that Hitler's anti-Semitic threats were aimed at people exactly like them. Virginia was very clear on this issue: 'I reflect: capitulation will mean all Jews to be given up. Concentration camps.'[22] Like many people in their position, they formulated suicide plans: 'This morning we discussed suicide if Hitler lands. Jews beaten up. What point in waiting? Better shut the garage doors. This a sensible, rather matter of fact talk.'[23] Leonard kept gas in the garage so they could asphyxiate themselves if Hitler won; later, Leonard and Virginia acquired a prescription for morphia from Virginia's brother, Adrian, who had become an army doctor. Discussions of the rationality of suicide were in the air during 1940 and 1941: Vita and Harold discussed how to procure something 'painless & private' from their doctor; the Woolfs debated the question with Rose Macaulay and Kingsley Martin.[24]

Against this backdrop, Virginia kept to a normal routine as much as possible. She finished her biography of Roger Fry and corrected the proofs; it was published in July 1940. She worked at her memoirs, which she called A Sketch of the Past, and used them to reconnect herself to happy memories of the Cornish countryside – a coast not threatened by invasion. She wrote at a novel called Poyntz Hall, which eventually became Between the Acts. In it, she balanced the long history of an English country village against 'The Present Day': a time of violence, fragmentation, and imminent destruction.

Virginia also took part in local village life, though she was always wary about being drawn too much into it. She talked to the Brighton Workers' Education Association on the subject of modern poetry; she gave a hilarious lecture to the Rodmell Women's Institute on the Dreadnought Hoax, an earlier escapade in which she and her brother had disguised themselves as Abyssinian dignitaries and talked their way onto the flagship of the British Royal Navy. She was elected Treasurer of the Rodmell Women's Institute. She even worked with the Women's Institute on a village play – a performance of Coleridge's blank verse tragedy *Remorse*. Though Virginia was appalled by the 'readymade commonplaceness'[25] of the project, she simultaneously wrote about a village pageant in *Between the Acts*, and used it as an emblem for the history and survival of England.

But it was difficult to maintain the fiction of normality while the Battle of Britain was being fought in the skies over her head. To prepare the way for invasion, Hitler's Luftwaffe launched a concentrated attack on targets in southeast England in August, 1940, using about five hundred (but sometimes up to a thousand) aircraft a day. The Royal Air Force fought back heroically and shot down 496 German planes in the week ending 17 August alone. Many air battles were fought over Rodmell; at this point, Leonard and Virginia would probably have been safer in their London home than at Monk's House. On one occasion, as they were playing bowls on the terrace, a German bomber came in low and close enough for them to see the German black cross on its side:

> We went out on to the terrace, began playing. A large two decker plane came heavily & slowly – L. said a Wellesley something. A training plane said Leslie. Suddenly there was pop pop from behind the Church. Practising we said. The plane circled slowly out over the marsh & back, very close to the ground & to us. Then a whole volley of pops (like bags burst) came together. The plane swung off, slow & heavy & circling toward Lewes. We looked. Leslie saw the German black cross. All the workmen were looking. Its a German; that dawned. It was the enemy. It dipped among the fir trees over Lewes & did not rise. Then we heard the drone. Looked up & saw 2 planes very high. They made for us. We started to shelter in the Lodge. But they wheeled & Leslie saw the English sign. So we watched – they side slipped glided swooped & roared for about 5 minutes round the fallen plane as if identifying & making sure – then made off towards London ... It wd have been a peaceful matter of fact death to be popped off on the terrace playing bowls this very fine cool sunny August evening.[26]

On another occasion, the planes were more menacing:

> They came very close. We lay down under the tree. The sound was like someone sawing in the air just above us. We lay flat on our faces, hands

behind head. Dont close yr teeth said L. They seemed to be sawing at something stationary. Bombs shook the windows of my lodge. Will it drop I asked? If so, we shall be broken together. I thought, I think, of nothingness – flatness, my mood being flat. Some fear I suppose. Shd we take Mabel to garage. Too risky to cross the garden L. said. Then another came from Newhaven. Hum & saw & buzz all round us. A horse neighed on the marsh. Very sultry. Is it thunder? I said. No guns, said L. from Ringmer, from Charleston way. Then slowly the sound lessened. Mabel in kitchen said the windows shook. Air raid still on, distant planes.[27]

Gun emplacements were built on the banks of the River Ouse; a passenger train was bombed at Newhaven; a British fighter crashed at Southease – all within walking distance of Monk's House: 'So, the Germans are nibbling at my afternoon walks.'[28] Vita called up from Sissinghurst in the middle of an air raid, to say that she couldn't make the drive over to Rodmell. Riveted by the thought that she had just talked 'to someone who might be killed any moment',[29] Virginia wrote Vita an elegiac letter that carried the hint of a farewell: 'What can one say – except that I love you and I've got to live through this strange quiet evening thinking of you sitting there alone ... You have given me such happiness.'[30]

In September 1940 the fighter battles over Rodmell were succeeded by bombing raids over London. The Woolfs' new house in Mecklenburgh Square was heavily damaged in September; Virginia managed to salvage her diaries and many of Leslie Stephen's books, but other papers and possessions were lost. In October, 52 Tavistock Square, where the Woolfs had lived for almost twenty years, was gutted. They had their remaining possessions carted down for storage in a Rodmell farmhouse. The German bombers on their way to London were still intercepted over the English Channel and the Sussex country-side; one day, Virginia saw a squadron of British aircraft returning to base: '12 planes in perfect order, back from the fight, pass overhead.'[31] As Virginia sat in her writing lodge finishing *Between the Acts*, she was struck by the beauty and quiet of the scene before her – a natural still-ness summed up in the image of cows feeding and a pear tree hung with fruit. The scene was made eerie by its fragility – the likelihood of its imminent destruction, the expectation of the 'cadaverous twanging' of the German planes passing overhead on their way to bomb London:

Ought I not to look at the sunset rather than write this? A flush of red in the blue; the haystack in the marsh catches the glow; behind me, the apples are red in the trees. L. is gathering them. Now a plume of smoke goes from the train under [Mount] Caburn. And all the air a solemn stillness holds. Till 8:30 when the cadaverous twanging in the sky begins; the planes going to London. Well its an hour still to that. Cows feeding. The elm tree sprinkling its little leaves against the sky. Our pear tree swagged with pears; & the weathercock above the triangular church tower above it ... Last night a great heavy plunge of bomb under the window. So near we both started. A plane had passed dropping this fruit. We went onto the terrace. Trinkets of stars sprinkled & glittering. All quiet ... Caburn was crowned with what looked like a settled moth, wings extended – a Messerschmitt it was, shot down on Sunday.[32]

As autumn gave way to winter, the bombing runs over London continued, though the threat of invasion slackened for a few months, until the return of good weather over the Channel. As she worked revising the manuscript of *Between the Acts* in January, Virginia sank into a 'trough of despair'.[33] By February 1941, invasion was in the air again: Virginia noted in her diary that 'the 3rd week in March is fixed for invasion';[34] Harold Nicolson wrote in his 'We know that the Great Attack is impending'.[35] Virginia finished *Between the Acts* on 26 February, but took little satisfaction in it. After a first blush of enthusiasm, she reread her novel and concluded that it was 'silly and trivial'.[36] Besides, with the world at war, there was no literate world left, no printer to consider, no reading public. There was no 'echo' out there – no one to read her books and respond. And there was certainly no echo at Rodmell: 'only waste air'.[37] The problem, as Virginia clearly saw, was that 'we live without a future'.[38]

Then, sometime in early March 1941, Virginia began to hear voices again. Her hands shook; her head became 'stupid'; she could no longer rely on being able to write intelligibly. Leonard thought she was on the verge of complete nervous collapse, brought on by the stress of the war raging around her. On 18 March, she may have tried to commit suicide and failed: she came back from a walk to the river drenched and told Leonard that she had slipped and fallen into a dike. Vanessa came to tea at Monk's House two days later and was shocked by Virginia's appearance. Vanessa wrote her sister a blunt letter, in which she told her how

255

much she relied on Virginia, and reminded Virginia of the danger of their position: 'What shall we do when we're invaded if you are a helpless invalid?'[39] On 'Tuesday', Virginia wrote Leonard a sane, determined, generous letter, in which she affirmed her love for him, but reasoned that she had no choice, since she was losing control and wouldn't recover:

> Dearest,
> I feel certain that I am going mad again: I feel we cant go through another of those terrible times. And I shant recover this time. I begin to hear voices, and cant concentrate. So I am doing what seems the best thing to do. You have given me the greatest possible happiness. You have been in every way all that anyone could be. I dont think two people could have been happier till this terrible disease came. I cant fight it any longer, I know that I am spoiling your life, that without me you could work. And you will I know. You see I cant even write this properly. I cant read. What I want to say is that I owe all the happiness of my life to you. You have been entirely patient with me and incredibly good. I want to say that – everybody knows it. If anybody could have saved me it would have been you. Everything has gone from me but the certainty of your goodness. I cant go on spoiling your life any longer.
> I dont think two people could have been happier than we have been.[40]

V.

On Friday, 28 March, just before lunch, Virginia put on her fur coat and picked up her walking stick. She walked down to the River Ouse, along the bank toward Southease, and put a large rock in her pocket. Then she waded into the water and, though she could swim, allowed herself to be pulled under.

Virginia's body was found three weeks later by some teenagers, not far from where Leonard found her walking stick, close to the Southease swing bridge. Leonard had her body cremated and buried her ashes in the garden at Monk's House, under the elm trees Leonard and Virginia, in a spot that looked out over the field and water-meadows. A plaque sits close to the spot now, inscribed with the closing words of *The Waves*:

> Death is the enemy.
> Against you I will fling myself, unvanquished and unyielding, O Death!
> *The waves broke on the shore.*[41]

II

Between the Acts is the darkest and most violent of Virginia Woolf's novels. Yet even *Between the Acts* – written from 1938 to 1941, first when war threatened England and then when invasion seemed certain – struggles towards and achieves an affirmative vision. *Between the Acts* is not set at Monk's House. Its story unfolds on a June day in 1939, just before Britain's entry into the war, at Pointz Hall, an Elizabethan manor house threatened by events unfolding on the continent. But the land-scapes and details of Monk's House and the Rodmell countryside permeate *Between the Acts*, from the paintings on the walls of the sitting room to the garden pool inhabited by a mysterious carp, to the vestiges of prehistory suggested by ancient monuments and dinosaur bones. And English village life permeates *Between the Acts* just as much, a village life that symbolises continuity, and serves as a backdrop against which a middle-class couple prepares to fight for their marriage as the civilised world teeters on the brink of collapse.

In the world of *Between the Acts*, the literal location of Pointz Hall is indeterminate. The elderly dreamer Lucy Swithin says they live one hundred and fifty miles from the sea; her rationalist brother Bartholomew insists the correct number is thirty-five. The train from London takes over three hours to reach 'this remote village in the very heart of England',[42] yet the view from Pointz Hall encompasses Bolney Minster, a church north of Rodmell, on the way to London. The state-liness of Pointz Hall may have been inspired by the Elizabethan manor house at Glynde, near Glyndebourne, where Leonard and Virginia attended the opera in 1934 and 1935. It may also have been inspired by Legh Manor, near Bolney, or Firle Place, on the walk to Charleston. What is most important about Pointz Hall is the way it embodies a sense of continuous English history – from its pre-Reformation chapel (now converted to a pantry) to its great barn, built over seven hundred years ago from the same stone as the adjoining village church.

The past owners of Pointz Hall – 'the old families who had all inter-married, and lay in their deaths intertwisted, like the ivy roots, beneath the churchyard wall'[43] – have been supplanted by the Oliver family, the relative newcomers who have owned Pointz Hall for only a hundred and twenty years. Bartholomew Oliver and his widowed sister, Lucy Swithin, grew up in Pointz Hall; Bart's son Giles and Giles's wife Isa are the real protagonists of *Between the Acts*. Their marriage has reached a point of crisis. Wounded by social constrictions, frightened by the threat of war, scarred by marital infidelity, Isa and Giles circle each other in angry silence throughout the day on which the action of the novel is set. They finally confront each other at night, after the village pageant, to speak to each other for the first time and perhaps redeem their marriage.

Isa Oliver is a very unhappy wife. She is thirty-nine – 'the age of the century' – a mother with two children, thick at the waist, a would-be poet. Isa scribbles her poetry in account books to hide her literary aspirations from Giles. She sees herself as 'abortive' – she loathes domesticity and maternal possessiveness; she is consumed by intense love and equally intense hatred for her husband, the man she has come to see merely as 'the father of my children'; she knows her poetry is worthless. Isa shares an intense moment of communication with only one person in the novel, William Dodge, a homosexual visitor she befriends and takes for a tour of the greenhouse. Isa feels at ease with Dodge and talks to him as if they have known each other all their lives. Since both Dodge and Isa feel they are social outsiders – Dodge because he is homosexual and Isa because she is an unconventional wife – they respond to each other as like spirits, as 'conspirators' against the social expectations that force people's souls. In her anger at her husband, Isa's attentions have wandered to Rupert Haines, a gentleman farmer who lives nearby. But for much of *Between the Acts*, Isa sees relations between men and women in terms of violence. As the narrator puts it, Isa's generation lives by the newspaper rather than the book, and Isa thinks repeatedly of a newspaper report of British soldiers in Whitehall luring a girl to their barracks to rape her.[44] From Isa Oliver's point of view, English soldiers protecting the very heart of the British government in Whitehall are just as threatening as the German soldiers poised to attack across the English Channel. When Woolf portrays Isa's fear of the British soldiers in Whitehall, she makes a point that she elaborated at much greater length in *Three Guineas*, a political essay published in 1938: that violence is institutionalised in governmental structures run by men; that this generalised violence expresses itself in the sexual victimisation of women; that institutionalised violence leads to just the sort of armed stand-off England faced in June of 1939.

Giles Oliver is as desperately unhappy as his wife. Social exigencies have forced him into a livelihood he hates. Given his choice, he would have farmed. But he was not given his choice: he fell desperately in love with Isa, married, and became a stockbroker to support his family and Pointz Hall. Now Giles lives in the city, comes to the country for the weekend, and changes for dinner – a round of habit and convention he abhors. Giles is enraged. He is consumed with anger at his life. He is consumed with anger at the war threatening to destroy Europe and Pointz Hall. He focuses his anger on his aunt Lucy, whom he sees as an ineffectual old fogy:

> Only the ineffective word 'hedgehog' illustrated his vision of Europe, bristling with guns, poised with planes. At any moment guns would rake that land into furrows; planes splinter Bolney Minster into smithereens and blast the Folly. He, too, loved the view. And blamed Aunt Lucy, looking at the views, instead of – doing what? ... as for himself, one thing followed another; and so he sat, with old fogies, looking at views.[45]

Giles also vents his anger on William Dodge, whom he chooses to hate because Dodge has not become the conventional man Giles has. Dodge becomes a 'peg on which to hang his rage as one hangs a coat on a peg, conveniently'; Dodge is 'a toady; a lickspittle; not a downright plain man of his senses ... not a man to have straightforward love for a woman ... but simply a____'.[46] At this word which Giles can't say in public – probably the word 'bugger' – Giles purses his lips and grips the arms of his chair in a yet more violent rage.

Finally, Giles vents his anger with Isa by courting Mrs Manresa, the nouveau-riche, self-styled 'wild child of nature'[47] who appears at Pointz Hall on the day of the pageant. Giles follows Mrs Manresa around the grounds of Pointz Hall; he takes her for a visit to the greenhouse; as he approaches Isa with 'the Manresa in his wake', Isa reflects that 'It made no difference; his infidelity – but hers did'.[48] In the world of *Between the Acts*, Giles is an emblem of wounded, trapped, enraged masculinity in the middle years of the twentieth century. He is also an emblem of the frustration and futility that haunt modern life, and that threaten to erupt into violently expressive action. On his way across the fields of Pointz Hall, Giles sees the same snake and toad that Virginia saw on her walk near Rodmell in 1935:

> There, couched in the grass, curled in an olive green ring, was a snake. Dead? No, choked with a toad in its mouth. The snake was unable to swallow; the toad was unable to die. A spasm made the ribs contract; blood oozed. It was birth the wrong way round – a monstrous inversion. So, raising his foot, he stamped on them. The mass crushed and slithered. The white canvas on his tennis shoes was bloodstained and sticky. But it was action. Action relieved him. He strode to the Barn, with blood on his shoes.[49]

This image, and Giles's response, is also politically emblematic – of governments choked by their own aggression, an aggression which is bound to erupt into the violence and war confronting England in June 1939.

Against this backdrop of threatened violence, and a marriage torn asunder by frustration and disappointment, Woolf poses two symbols of continuity and affirmation, both connected to the Rodmell country-side: Lucy Swithin and Miss La Trobe's village pageant. Lucy Swithin, Bartholomew Oliver's sister, is an elderly woman of compassion and imagination, a frail widow who is 'given to increasing the bounds of the moment by flights into past or future'.[50] The Pointz Hall servants have nicknamed her 'Batty'; the villagers call her 'Old Flimsy'. Though alert to the violence of modern life, Lucy is possessed of a sensibility that is almost mystical in its serenity. Her brother Bart is amazed that, in a skull shaped so like his own, there could exist 'a prayable being';[51] he places Lucy among the 'unifiers', while he is a 'separatist'. Lucy's hold on present reality sometimes seems tenuous: she habitually drifts off 'on a circular tour of the imagination – one-making. Sheep, cows, grass, trees, ourselves – all are one'.[52] Lucy is deeply religious and wears a gold cross around her neck; she is the only overtly religious character in Woolf's work who is treated without irony. Lucy is, in fact, the sort of heroine who emerges in Woolf's late fiction: like Eleanor Pargiter at the end of The Years, Lucy Swithin is an older woman who is freed by age from the necessity of respecting social conventions, and who uses her freedom from convention to behave in socially eccentric ways.

Like Isa, Lucy befriends William Dodge. She takes him on a tour of Pointz Hall, showing him the room where she was born, showing him the children's nursery, which she calls 'the cradle of our race'.[53] William is so touched by her compassion and honesty that he nearly confesses the story of his difficult life to her: how they held him under a bucket of dirty water at school; how he married to avoid being labelled a homosexual; how he sees himself as 'a half-man' and is afflicted with self-loathing.[54] Like William, Lucy is an outsider who lives on the fringes of social acceptability. When their eyes meet in a mirror, she smiles, and he feels that he has been healed.

Lucy's affirmative presence is linked to three things that Woolf associated with the Rodmell countryside: the visible remnants of prehistoric life; fish in ponds; swallows building nests. Lucy is mesmerised by the idea of the connection of the prehistoric past to the present day. Lucy's favourite reading is an Outline of History, in which she can trace the unbroken link between the distant past and the very real human present. Whenever she reads her Outline of History, Lucy imaginatively enters a vivid world of jungles, iguanodons, and mammoths – a world so real to her that she has difficulty separating it from the present moment. On one occasion, the servant Grace enters with the tea tray as Lucy reads, and it takes Lucy a long time to return from the prehistoric past to the present:

> Forced to listen, she had stretched for her favourite reading – an Outline of History – and had spent the hours between three and five thinking of rhododendron forests in Piccadilly; when the entire continent, not then, she understood, divided by a channel, was all one; populated, she understood, by elephant-bodied, seal-necked, heaving, surging, slowly writhing, and, she supposed, barking monsters; the iguanodon, the mammoth, and the mastodon; from whom presumably, she thought, jerking the window open, we descend.
>
> It took her five seconds in actual time, in mind time ever so much longer, to separate Grace herself, with blue china on a tray, from the leather-covered grunting monster who was about, as the door opened, to demolish a whole tree in the green steaming undergrowth of the primeval forest.[55]

Lucy's Outline of History makes her feel that the life of the past lives on in the present moment. The very vividness of her connection to the past makes her feel that life itself – both animal and human – is continuous. And if life is continuous, it is indestructible. In the face of war in Europe, Lucy's Outline of History gives her a broad perspective on human life: that human life is only a small part of 'life itself', and that 'life itself' will somehow survive even an unprecedented worldwide armed conflict.

Woolf links Lucy to a second emblem of natural continuity associated with the Rodmell countryside: the swallows who return from Africa every year to build their nests. In the spring of 1940, Woolf was moved by the fact that the birds in their elm trees had begun their 'twig carrying' though all the guns of Europe were 'pointed & charged';[56] in the same way, Lucy is moved by the swallows who fly into the Pointz Hall barn with straw in their beaks. For Lucy, the swallows mean hope: they continue to build nests for their young, not knowing that war threatens life. The swallows also mean continuity and natural endurance: Lucy insists that the same swallows return from Africa to England every year, and that their predecessors have done so for millennia, since 'before there was a channel, when the earth ... was a riot of rhododendrons'.[57]

Finally, Woolf links Lucy to the affirmative image of fish rising in a pool of water, an image drawn from Leonard's fish ponds at Monk's House. Woolf uses fish as symbols of mystery and insight throughout her work, from *To the Lighthouse* through *Orlando* and *The Waves*; she once wrote to Hugh Walpole of her 'passion' for observing the fish in the garden at Monk's House: 'There should be four, and one carp; but it is the rarest event to see them all together – and yet I can assure you that so to see them matters more to us both than all that is said at the Hague.'[58] In the same way, Lucy gazes into the Pointz Hall lily pond hopefully, and is rewarded and renewed by a glimpse of the elusive great carp:

> Lucy still gazed at the lily pool. 'All gone,' she murmured, 'under the leaves.' Scared by shadows passing, the fish had withdrawn. She gazed at the water. Perfunctorily she caressed her cross. But her eyes went water searching, looking for fish. The lilies were shutting; the red lily, the white lily, each on its plate of leaf ... Then something moved in the water; her

favourite fantail. The golden orfe followed. Then she had a glimpse of silver – the great carp himself, who came to the surface so very seldom. They slid on, in and out between the stalks, silver; pink; gold; splashed; streaked; pied.

'Ourselves,' she murmured. And retrieving some glint of faith from the grey waters, hopefully, without much help from reason, she followed the fish; the speckled, streaked and blotched; seeing in that vision beauty, power, and glory in ourselves.[59]

For Lucy, as for Woolf, a glimpse of the elusive silver fish matters more than anything: it represents an insight into the mystery of life, a moment of vision that is rare, beautiful, and moving. And it is a vision that renews Lucy's faith in the future, since it suggests that 'beauty, power and glory' reside in 'ourselves'.

The second affirmative symbol that Woolf balances against the backdrop of war is Miss La Trobe's village pageant. Miss La Trobe is an outsider in the village that surrounds Pointz Hall: no one knows where she comes from – it may be the Channel Islands; she is a lesbian; she smokes cigarettes and often carries a whip. The villagers dislike her and nickname her 'Bossy'. But Miss La Trobe is a dedicated playwright who is 'always all agog to get things up'. She is devoted to the idea of making her audience 'see': for Miss La Trobe, a vision imparted – even for an instant – is relief from her agony. Miss La Trobe strives to unite her audience, to bind them together for a moment in the common emotion generated by her play. Above all, Miss La Trobe tries to evoke and create moments of order: 'she was the one who seethes wandering bodies and floating voices in a cauldron, and makes rise up from its amorphous mass a re-created world. Her moment was on her – her glory.'[60]

To these ends, Miss La Trobe fashions a pageant that portrays the unfolding of British history from the time of Chaucer to the present day. The play's vignettes focus on the complexities of male-female relationships through the ages, re-enacting everything from a scene at the Globe Theatre to a Restoration farce. But the most important aspect of the pageant is its acting troupe, the village inhabitants who are descended from families living in the area for centuries. These actors are like Mitchell's boy, who delivers fish: 'He had to deliver right over the hill at Bickley; also go round by Waythorn, Roddam, and Pyeminster, whose names, like his own, were in Domesday Book.'[61] The village actors continue the lives of their ancestors into the present; had someone called roll, they might answer '*Adsum*; I'm here in place of my grandfather or great-grandfather, as the case might be'.[62] Miss La Trobe casts the villagers in her pageant in individual roles, but also as anonymous toiling souls, the backdrop of universal human life against which the individual life of the play is enacted. She has them pass in single file in and out between the trees at the back of the stage, singing a song about cyclic repetition and endurance. Like Mabel Mockford and the other Rodmell villagers Woolf came to see as 'the unconscious breathing of England',[63] the village acting troupe embodies the continuity of human life and of English history, even in the face of imminent destruction. What Miss La Trobe predicts, using actors who are rooted in the countryside around Pointz Hall, is the survival of England in the shape of a village pageant.[64]

But Miss La Trobe's artistic vision faces challenges. First of all, she must deal with the difficulty of sustaining the dramatic emotion in her audience. On one occasion, during a gap in the action of her play, her stage is empty and the dramatic illusion fails. Miss La Trobe is about to lose her audience; then the cows mooing in the field behind the stage take up the burden: 'From cow after cow came the same yearning bellow. The whole world was filled with dumb yearning ... It was the primeval voice sounding loud in the ear of the present moment.'[65] The audience is united in its response to the cows' cries; the cows carry the emotion of the play over the rocky passage and preserve Miss La Trobe's hold over her audience. On another occasion, when Miss La Trobe again has an empty stage that threatens her dramatic illusion, she is saved by a rain shower that seems to express the audience's collective sorrow: 'No one had seen the cloud coming. There it was, black, swollen, on top of them. Down it poured like all the people in the world weeping. Tears. Tears. Tears.'[66] In both instances, nature randomly supports Miss La Trobe's artistic vision; in both instances – cows lowing and rain falling like tears – Woolf uses images drawn from her daily experiences at Monk's House.

Miss La Trobe's biggest challenge is dramatising for her audience 'The Present Time. Ourselves' – an experience of chaos, self-consciousness, fragmentation and desperation. First, she exposes her audience to 'present-time reality' by doing nothing. She leaves her stage blank; as the interval with an empty stage grows longer and longer, her audience becomes restless and uncomfortable: they fail at first to realise that, as they sit in the audience, they themselves have become both the actors and the subject of the drama. Next, Miss La Trobe stages a dramatic symbol of affirmation and renewal: by means of a painted cloth and a man with a hod on his back, she conveys 'civilization (the wall) in ruins; rebuilt (witness man with hod) by human effort'.[67] Finally, in the novel's most striking image of a world on the verge of disintegration, Miss La Trobe has her actors dramatise the present moment by walking into the audience carrying scraps of reflective glass and metal – pieces of mirrors; tin cans; bits of scullery glass. As the shining surfaces reflect the audience in 'scraps, orts and fragments', they pose the crucial question of both Miss La Trobe's pageant and *Between the Acts*: '*Look at ourselves, ladies and gentlemen! Then at the wall; and ask how's this wall, the great wall, which we call, perhaps miscall, civilization, to be built by* (here the mirrors flicked and flashed) *orts, scraps and fragments like ourselves?*'[68] As the audience shares a moment of collective insight – the gramophone plays triumphant music; Mrs Manresa cries – their momentary shared understanding seems to predict hope for the human race: 'Dawn rose; and azure; from chaos and cacophony measure ... Compelled from the ends of the horizon; recalled from the edge of appalling crevasses; they crashed; solved; united.'[69]

Then the village rector, the Reverend G.W. Streatfield, mounts the stage to sum up the play's meaning. Hasn't the play taught us, he asks, that we are all connected to each other, that we are all part of one whole? Hasn't the play taught us, he asks, the supreme importance of 'effort renewed',[70] even when all seems dark? Just as Rev. Streatfield reaches the climax of his speech, 'The word was cut in two. A zoom severed it. Twelve aeroplanes in perfect formation like a flight of wild duck came overhead. *That* was the music. The audience gaped; the audience gazed. Then zoom became drone. The planes had passed.'[71] The British aircraft returning from a sortie along the English Channel – like the twelve aeroplanes Virginia watched fly in perfect formation over her head in September 1940 – drown out Rev. Streatfield's peroration and suggest a more ominous counterpoint to the village pageant's moment of affirmation: that perhaps the real music is violence after all; that perhaps the future holds only death, and the destruction of human civilisation as Woolf and her countrymen know it.

In the closing pages of *Between the Acts*, the action shifts to renewed confrontation and renewed effort on a different stage: the Oliver marriage. As Miss La Trobe leaves the grounds of Pointz Hall, she heads for the village pub. There, as she sits drinking and smoking, the setting of her next drama rises before her: she sees high ground at midnight; a rock; two scarcely perceptible figures. Simultaneously at Pointz Hall, Isa and Giles Oliver prepare to confront each other alone for the first time all day. As the curtain rises on their conflict, their struggle merges with Miss La Trobe's dramatic vision. Isa and Giles seem on the verge of acting out Miss La Trobe's next play; their confrontation will be violent, but there exists a possibility that it may result in new life. The closing words of *Between the Acts* evoke the terrifying world of prehistory; they also suggest, most tentatively, the possibility of continuity and renewal:

> Alone, enmity was bared; also love. Before they slept, they must fight; after they had fought, they would embrace. From that embrace another life might be born. But first they must fight, as the dog fox fights with the vixen, in the heart of darkness, in the fields of night ... The window was all sky without colour. The house had lost its shelter. It was night before roads were made, or houses. It was the night that dwellers in caves had watched from some high place among rocks.
> Then the curtain rose. They spoke.[72]

When Virginia Woolf wrote the last words of *Between the Acts* on 26 February 1941, she completed her portrait of a world in which confrontation and effort took centre stage and closed the play. It was a world threatened by destruction, a world in which individual battles against fear and desperation were fought against the backdrop of worldwide catastrophe. But it was also a world in which fragile moments of affirmation could still exist. In fact, the very composition of *Between the Acts* was itself a moment of affirmation: writing *Between the Acts* for a world that had no audience, no 'echo', was an act of faith. In writing *Between the*

Acts, Woolf confronted her world, expended all the effort at her command, and composed for herself a world in which affirmation was fleetingly possible. In composing that world, she composed, for one last time, herself. Then the drone of the airplanes returned and the voices threatened. She confronted them directly, too, and in one final act of defiance and control, walked to the river.

III

Rodmell today: sights, excursions, walks

RODMELL

Monk's House

After Virginia committed suicide, Leonard Woolf lived in Monk's House until his death in 1969. His companion, Trekkie Parsons, sold Monk's House to the University of Sussex; in 1980, the University of Sussex in turn donated the house to the National Trust. Monk's House is open to visitors from April to October, usually on Wednesday and Saturday afternoons from 2 p.m. to 5.30 p.m. For more information, visit the National Trust's website at www.nationaltrust.org.uk, or phone their regional office at 01892 890 651. The National Trust sells an excellent, inexpensive guidebook that describes the furnishings of Monk's House in great detail.

How to get there

By car: Monk's House is four miles south-east of Lewes, off the former A275 in Rodmell Village, near the Church. From London, go to the M25 London Orbital. At junction 7, take the M23 south towards Brighton. The M23 leads to the A23 south; then take the A27 east towards Lewes. The A27 bypasses Lewes; turn off towards Kingston at the western roundabout; go through Kingston and rejoin the former A275, turning *right* at the junction. (There is no access to the former A275 from the A26.) Approaching Rodmell, turn *left* at the Abergavenny Arms public house. Monk's House is on the *right* near the end of the main street. The National Trust maintains a small car park.

By train: Take the train to Lewes. There is a good taxi service at the Lewes train station; the ride to Monk's House from Lewes is not a long one.

By bus: Take the Metrobus 123 (Lewes to Newhaven), which stops at the Lewes train station (tel. 01273 474 747). Metrobus schedules are also posted on the Metrobus website at www.metrobus.co.uk.

The Sitting Room

When the Woolfs bought Monk's House, this large room had a wall down the middle, which they removed. Virginia was delighted when she first saw the effect: 'Yes, Rodmell is a perfect triumph, I consider – but L. advises me not to say so. In particular, our large combined drawing eating room, with its 5 windows, its beams down the middle, & flowers & leaves nodding in all round us.'[73] It was in this room that the Woolfs planned to 'sit, eat, play the gramophone, prop our feet up on the side of the fire and read endless books'.[74] It was also in this room that they did most of their entertaining.

The Woolfs commissioned Vanessa Bell and Duncan Grant to decorate the large painted table and chairs; the chairs bear Virginia's initials on their backs. Grant also designed the canvas-work fire-screen, which his mother worked in cross-stitch, and the tiles that top the second table in the room. Facing the fire is one of Virginia's favourite reading chairs – an upholstered armchair covered in a modern reprint of a fabric designed by Vanessa Bell. The walls of the sitting room are painted in a green that Virginia described this way: 'Would I be allowed some rather garish but vibrating and radiating green and red lustres on the mantelpiece?'[75] A similar colour is used on the walls of her bedroom.

The Dining Room and Kitchen

The Dining Room and Kitchen are filled with furniture, paintings, and ceramics decorated by Vanessa Bell and Duncan Grant. The six dining chairs and the music cabinet (left of the door to the kitchen) were designed by Bell and Grant for an exhibition at the Lefevre Gallery in 1932; the well-worn trays on the table under the kitchen window were painted by Vanessa. Vanessa's watercolour of Virginia in the sitting room at 52 Tavistock Square – a Christmas gift to Leonard in 1935 –

hangs facing the entry door. The bowling set the Woolfs used for their constant games sits under the stairway. (Leonard beat Virginia consistently in their Monk's House tournaments. He kept careful records of their matches: in the long series running from 1935 until 1940, they played over 1,200 games together, with Leonard winning about 1,000 of them.)[76]

But the most interesting features of the Dining Room and the Kitchen are the three primitive paintings Leonard and Virginia acquired from the sale of the prior owner's possessions. These paintings were related to the Glazebrook family, which owned Monk's House from 1796 until 1877. The painting hanging over the dining room mantel pictures three Glazebrook children and their parents in about 1850. Virginia's description of it to Margaret Llewelyn Davies captures the style of all three pictures:

> I wish I had your generous impulses. Then I might give you in return one of the three pictures which I bought at the sale of the Monk's House furniture the other day. They're the work of an early Victorian blacksmith, and sold for 4/-the-three. For myself, I dont ask anything more of pictures. They are family groups, and he began the heads very large, and hadn't got room for the hands and legs, so these dwindle off till they're about the size of sparrows claws, but the effect is superb – the character overwhelming.[77]

E.M. Forster admired this painting so much that the Woolfs loaned it to him for his rooms at Cambridge. It hung at King's College until the 1950s.

The other two Glazebrook paintings – one painting of two figures with a horse and dog; the other of a lady by a window – hang on opposite walls in the kitchen. Though Virginia altered many of the details of each painting, the idea of two paintings confronting each other in an empty room may have inspired a scene in *Between the Acts*. In that scene, Woolf imagines the vibrating life of an empty room, and the mute transactions that give a house life even in the absence of human beings:

> So, with one last look, he left the dining-room.
> Two pictures hung opposite the window. In real life they had never met, the long lady and the man holding his horse by the rein. The lady

was a picture, bought by Oliver because he liked the picture; the man was an ancestor. He had a name. He held the rein in his hand. He had said to the painter:

'If you want my likeness, dang it sir, take it when the leaves are on the trees.' There were leaves on the trees. He had said: 'Ain't there room for Colin as well as Buster?' Colin was his famous hound. But there was only room for Buster. It was, he seemed to say, addressing the company not the painter, a damned shame to leave out Colin whom he wished buried at his feet, in the same grave, about 1750; but that skunk the Reverend Whatshisname wouldn't allow it.

He was a talk producer, that ancestor. But the lady was a picture. In her yellow robe, leaning, with a pillar to support her, a silver arrow in her hand, and a feather in her hair, she led the eye up, down, from the curve to the straight, through glades of greenery and shades of silver, dun and rose into silence. The room was empty.

Empty, empty, empty; silent, silent, silent. The room was a shell, singing of what was before time was; a vase stood in the heart of the house, alabaster, smooth, cold, holding the still, distilled essence of emptiness, silence.[78]

Upper rooms

The upper portion of Monk's House is not open to the public. It contains two bedrooms, a bath and a sitting room (built over Virginia's bedroom), whose windows look into the garden. Vanessa Bell provided the tile for one of the upstairs fireplaces; Duncan Grant provided the tile for the second. Leonard's study – 'Hedgehog Hall' – was at the very top of the house, and features a balcony with views of the church and the orchard. The bath is situated directly over the kitchen, with the result that the cook often heard Virginia reciting her day's writing aloud to herself as she bathed.[79]

Bedroom

Virginia's bedroom is entered from the exterior of Monk's House: the Woolfs never cut a door to it from the house's interior, so when Virginia retired for the night, she trudged through the kitchen, out the back door, and then off into her bed. This room, and the sitting-room above it, was added to Monk's House in 1929, with the profits from *Orlando*. Virginia was extremely proud of the fact that her writing had finally earned them this much money: 'After all, I say, I made £1,000 from willing it early one morning … I am summoning Philcox [the builder] next week to plan a room – I have money to build it, money to furnish it.'[80] Once the room was built, Virginia relished the idea of watching the stars in the night sky as she fell asleep: 'I shall pull open my curtains & see the stars at night. Really a marvellous spectacle – all for nothing.'[81]

Virginia also used her bedroom as a writing room in the winter, when her unheated garden lodge became too cold. The most obvious and lovely feature of the room, aside from its light and openness, is the fireplace decoration. The tiles around the fireplace were decorated by Vanessa Bell; they are inscribed 'VW from VB 1930'. In the centre is an oval panel showing Godrevy lighthouse, with a red-sailed Cornish lugger moving towards it.

The Garden

The Fish Ponds

There are three ponds at Monk's House. The pond closest to the house, inside the walled area, was known as the 'clinique', and was used for the convalescence of ailing fish. In the farthest section of this same walled area are two busts: Stephen Tomlin's famous bust of Virginia Woolf (1931), and Charlotte Hewer's bust of Leonard Woolf (1968).

Beyond the walled area, in the large expanse of lawn that the Woolfs used for lawn bowls and archery, lies a larger round pond. The two elm trees, which the Woolfs named 'Leonard' and 'Virginia', formerly grew in the hedge that now separates the garden from the adjoining field. Both Virginia's and Leonard's ashes were scattered under these trees. One of the trees fell in a gale in 1943; the second died of Dutch elm disease in 1985.

Virginia associated the fish in the ponds at Monk's House – like the pilchards at St Ives – with mystery, with the elusive nature of insight, and with the difficulty of netting reality in words. Virginia had written to Hugh Walpole about the almost mystical importance of seeing the carp in Leonard's pool; in similar fashion, Lucy Swithin in *Between the Acts* sees the great carp in the pond at Pointz Hall and has a momentary vision that preserves her hope in the future. In 1929, Woolf wrote a short story entitled 'The Fascination of the Pool'. In that story, the giant carp again represents all that is most important and most elusive about human experience – those things that, like the elusive carp, can never quite be caught. The pond in which the carp swims also becomes the occasion for Woolf's extended meditation on the way a place can evoke the life of past generations. The narrator sits by the side of a fishpond while her 'liquid thoughts' seem 'to stick together and to form recognisable people':[82]

> And one saw a whiskered red face formed in the pool leaning low over it, drinking it. I came here in 1851 after the heat of the Great Exhibition. I saw the Queen open it. And the voice chuckled liquidly, easily, as if he had thrown off his elastic side boots and put his top hat on the edge of the pool. Lord, how hot it was! and now all gone, all crumbled, of course, the thoughts seemed to say, swaying among the reeds. But I was a lover, another thought began, sliding over the other silently and orderly as fish not impeding each other. A girl; we used to come down from the farm (the placard of its sale was reflected on the top of the water) that summer, 1662. The soldiers never saw us from the road. It was very hot. We lay here. She was lying hidden in the rushes with her lover, laughing into the pool and slipping into it, thoughts of eternal love, of fiery kisses and despair. And I was very happy, said another thought glancing briskly over the girl's despair (for she had drowned herself). I used to fish here. We never caught the giant carp but we saw him once – the day Nelson fought at Trafalgar. We saw him under the willow – my word! what a great brute he was! They say he was never caught.[83]

The Church and the Orchard

When Virginia saw Monk's House initially, one of the first things she thought was: 'I could fancy a very pleasant walk in the orchard under the apple trees, with the grey extinguisher of the church steeple pointing my boundary.'[84] As time went by, St Peter's Church became a symbol for Virginia of the continuity of village life. Though she sometimes hated the church's bells, and certainly abhorred the idea of organised religion, she told Hugh Walpole that 'I love the old women doddering along in their black bonnets, and the thought of all the years, and all the processions; and how buried there are their ancestors for centuries – I must explain that our garden abuts on the churchyard, and when we are looking at our beehives, they are often burying someone on the other side of the wall.'[85]

In her short story 'In the Orchard', written in 1922, Woolf connects the Church to the orchard in a visionary way. She weaves together the sights and sounds that might surround a sleeper under the apple trees at Monk's House: children's voices from the village school; hymns from St Peter's; birdsong; leaves 'flat like little fish' against the blue sky. She even includes the squeak of the 'golden feather on the Church tower' as it turns in the wind, and makes the entire scene into a vision that unites the vast sweep of the wind over the downs to the tiny details of bird life and slanting boughs under the apple trees:

Miranda slept in the orchard, lying in a long chair beneath the apple-tree. Her book had fallen into the grass ... Four feet in the air over her head the apples hung. Suddenly there was a shrill clamour as if they were gongs of cracked brass beaten violently, irregularly, and brutally. It was only the school-children saying the multiplication table in unison, stopped by the teacher, scolded, and beginning to say the multiplication table over again ... Then the very topmost leaves of the apple-tree, flat like little fish against the blue, thirty feet above the earth, chimed with a pensive and lugubrious note. It was the organ in the church playing one of Hymns Ancient and Modern. The sound floated out and was cut into atoms by a flock of fieldfares flying at an enormous speed – somewhere or other. Miranda lay asleep thirty feet beneath.

Then above the apple-tree and the pear-tree two hundred feet above Miranda lying asleep in the orchard bells thudded, intermittent, sullen, didactic, for six poor women of the parish were being churched and the Rector was returning thanks to heaven.

And above that with a sharp squeak the golden feather of the church tower turned from south to east. The wind changed. Above everything else it droned, above the woods, the meadows, the hills, miles above Miranda lying in the orchard asleep. It swept on, eyeless, brainless, meeting nothing that could stand against it, until, wheeling the other way, it turned south again ... Miranda slept in the orchard, or was she asleep or was she not asleep? Her purple dress stretched between the two apple-trees. There were twenty-four apple-trees in the orchard, some slanting slightly, others growing straight with a rush up the trunk which spread wide into branches and formed into round red or yellow drops. Each apple-tree had sufficient space. The sky exactly fitted the leaves. When the breeze blew, the line of the boughs against the wall slanted slightly and then returned. A wagtail flew diagonally from one corner to another. Cautiously hopping, a thrush advanced towards a fallen apple; from the other wall a sparrow fluttered just above the grass. The uprush of the trees was tied down by these movements; the whole was compacted by the orchard walls. For miles beneath the earth was clamped together; rippled on the surface with wavering air;

and across the corner of the orchard the blue-green was slit by a purple streak. The wind changing, one bunch of apples was tossed so high that it blotted out two cows in the meadow ('Oh, I shall be late for tea!' cried Miranda), and the apples hung straight across the wall again.[86]

The Writing Lodge

Virginia trekked out across the garden to her writing lodge every morning at around 10 a.m. – as Leonard put it, she had the 'daily regularity of a stockbroker who commutes every day'.[87] She stayed there until about 1 p.m., sitting in a low chair and writing on a board stretched across her knees. Virginia's writing rooms always contained a large, plain, solid wooden table, but she did not use the table for her main work of composing novels. Virginia stopped work for lunch; she invariably took an afternoon walk across the downs or along the river; after tea she might write letters, or read, or work at journalism until dinner and bedtime.

Virginia's writing lodge began as a toolhouse whose windows overlooked the downs. From the outset, she was enchanted by its views over the marshes: 'I don't think Cornwall beats this. I have a garden room which looks across the watermeadows to Mt Caburn.'[88] In 1934, the Woolfs moved the writing lodge to its present location at the bottom of the garden, in hopes of improving the views yet more. (Virginia worried about the cost, estimated by the builder at £157. But then she decided that 'an improved view is worth £157'.)[89] At the same time, they added a small brick patio where their guests could gather to watch bowls being played, or linger as the summer light faded over the East Sussex landscape. Virginia evokes the atmosphere of these long evenings in the Monk's House garden in her essay 'The Moment: Summer's Night'.

After Virginia's death, the writing lodge was enlarged yet again, and was used as a studio by Trekkie Parsons. This second extension now houses an exhibit of photographs detailing life at Monk's House. The visitor can view Virginia's original writing room through the glass partition. Despite increased foliage, there is still a lovely view out over the downs, encompassing Mount Caburn. It is the view that Virginia saw whenever she looked up from her writing.

A Walk to the River Ouse

Virginia left on her daily walks from Monk's House through gates at the top of her garden that have since been removed. (There is still a gap in the hedge.) Today's visitor should exit the property and walk down the lane to the National Trust car park. There is a path leading from the car park down to the River Ouse.

This path was the first leg of one of Virginia's habitual walks: from here, once she reached the river, she could walk in either direction. If she walked south, she could pick up the South Downs Way, and hike along it northwest towards Kingston, or east towards Charleston.

On the day of her death, once she reached the river she walked south, towards the Southease bridge (a *right* turn at the junction of path and river). Once Leonard found her suicide note, he ran down to the river and almost immediately found her walking stick on the bank near the bridge at Southease. Virginia's body was found three weeks later by some picnickers, just a short distance away, floating in the water near the Asheham side. The body had become wedged against some object in the meantime – perhaps against the piers of the swing bridge at Southease, or against one of the fences that keep cows out of the water at low tide. She still had her hat on, since it had been held in place by an elastic band. Leonard found a large stone in the pocket of her fur coat.

Other Rodmell Sites

The Abergavenny Arms

There has been a pub in this location since the seventeenth century. It was at first called the Old Bell (perhaps a name it acquired when St Peter's Church got its second bell in 1625), but in the early nineteenth century the pub was renamed the Abergavenny Arms to honour Lord Abergavenny, the lord of the manor. For a short time in the 1970s it was called the Holly, after the owner's daughter. But when the pub changed hands again more recently, local preference resulted in the name reverting to the Abergavenny Arms.

Shortly after they bought Monk's House, Virginia walked up to the crossroads one night and thought of the Abergavenny Arms as an emblem of the village's sociability. She also thought that she might like to visit the pub one night, to be inspired by the rhythms of the Rodmell men's talk:

> I had reason to observe nocturnal habits last night, for after my recuperative draught was over, Lottie was still not home; & when 10 struck L. determined to go in search. Bicycling alone along a road in ruts in the dark she might well have fallen – & so forth. I went on foot up to the cross roads; thus passing all the men coming back from the public house, & saying more 'Good nights' than in a week of daylight – proving what I've said of the sociability of nightfall. Then, too, they'd had their lamps lit for them by Mr Malthouse's beer. Presumably every man in the place spends his evenings in the public house of course; & I should like once in a way to hear their talk.[90]

At the end of *Between the Acts*, Miss La Trobe visits the local pub after the village pageant. As she sits and sips her beer, listening to the talk of the local men, their 'words of one syllable'[91] sink into her consciousness. Soon smoke fills the room and she can no longer see their earth-coloured jackets. But her vision of them 'upheld her', and the opening scene of her next play wells up in her mind.

The Abergavenny Arms is an excellent choice for lunch before touring Monk's House.

The Old Poor Cottages
As you exit Monk's House and walk to the **right** towards the National Trust car park, look for the Old Poor Cottages on the **left**. The bottom cottage was occupied in the Woolfs' time by Mrs Grey. Mrs Grey's predicament inspired Virginia's biting essay 'Old Mrs Grey', in which a sick, suffering old woman who wants only to die is kept alive like a rook 'with a nail through it'.[92]

Park Cottages
From the Old Poor Cottages, continue towards the car park; at the car park, turn **left** and continue along the street past the Briar Cottages and several new homes. The Park Cottages will be on your **right**.

The Woolfs purchased the Park Cottages in 1929, as part of a plan to live at Monk's House without resident servants. Their cooks Annie

Thompsett (who worked for the Woolfs from 1929 to 1934) and Louie Everest (who worked for them from 1934 to 1969) lived in the left cottage. Their gardener, Percy Bartholomew, lived in the right cottage.

An Old Flint Wall

Continue along the street in the same direction, passing Pear Tree Cottage, Thatched Cottage, and Rose Cottage. On the *left* is a wide driveway in front of a house called Momentai. The point of Woolfian interest here is the old flint wall in front of the driveway: it is the only thing remaining of the ruined house, burned down long before the Woolfs moved to Rodmell, which inspired Woolf's story 'The Widow and the Parrot: A True Story'.[93]

FARTHER AFIELD: OUTSIDE RODMELL

Virginia Stephen rented or owned three other residences in the Sussex countryside before she and Leonard bought Monk's House: Little Talland House in Firle (1911-1912); Asheham House, near Beddingham (1912-1919); the Round House in Lewes (1919). If you have a car, short visits to these spots can be combined with visits to Charleston Farmhouse, Berwick Church and Lewes.

Asheham House

Virginia Stephen's second house in the country was Asheham House (also spelled Asham), which she discovered on a rural walk with Leonard in October 1911, before they were married. They occupied Asheham from 1912 to 1919. Asheham was built around 1820 and was a large, elegant house in a beautiful setting, with a view across the Ouse valley towards Rodmell.[94] In fact, one of Asheham's chief glories was this view: in the Woolfs' time, the house looked across fields full of sheep, to the pastures of the Ouse Valley, and then past the villages of Rodmell and Iford to the Downs beyond. Asheham was so atmospheric that it seemed to have a personality of its own. As Leonard described it, 'I have never known a house which had such a strong character, personality of its own – romantic, gentle, melancholy, lovely'.[95]

Virginia initially asked Vanessa to share the lease of Asheham, but once Virginia and Leonard were married, Asheham quickly became their country retreat. Local legend had it that Asheham was haunted. Even Leonard Woolf admitted that the house seemed to emit extraordinary sounds: 'It is true that at night one often heard extraordinary noises both in the cellars and in the attic. It sounded as if two people were walking from room to room, opening and shutting doors, sighing, whispering. It was, no doubt, the wind sighing in the chimneys, and, when there was no wind, probably rats in the cellar or the attic.'[96]

Virginia and Leonard spent their wedding night at Asheham in August 1912. The legend that Asheham was haunted – and the rumour that treasure was buried somewhere on the site – may have partly inspired Woolf's short story 'A Haunted House', which was published as part of her collection *Monday or Tuesday* in 1921. In 'A Haunted House' a ghostly husband and wife return – hundreds of years after the death of each partner – to the house in which they spent the happiest years of their married life. They walk hand in hand through the house, being careful not to wake the current owners, who lie fast asleep, 'love upon their lips'. The ghostly couple finally find the 'buried treasure' they left behind when death separated them like a glass many years ago: their shared moments in the garden, in the drawing room, upstairs. At the end of the story, the current owners wake suddenly, and realise that the happiness they share with each other is part of a continuum of happy moments generated by the house. One of the current owners wakes and cries out: 'Oh, is this *your* – buried treasure? The light in the heart.'[97]

During the years that Virginia and Leonard rented Asheham, a steady stream of Bloomsbury guests came to visit. Roger Fry and Clive Bell came for the house warming party; Vanessa Bell painted some of her finest Post-Impressionist works at Asheham: *The Haystack*, *Portrait of Virginia Woolf*, *Portrait of Henry Doucet*. Lytton Strachey, Maynard Keynes, and E.M. Forster were frequent guests, as were G.E. Moore and Pernel Strachey, Principal of Newnham College, Cambridge. Then in 1918, the Woolfs were given a year's notice that their landlord required the house for his farm bailiff. They purchased Monk's House the following year.

Asheham House remained much as it had been in the Woolfs' time until 1932, when it was sold and became engulfed by a huge cement works, which quarried raw materials out of the hill behind the house. As Quentin Bell describes it, 'Asheham itself was blotted out of sight by vast corrugated iron sheds, the valley was coated with toxic white dust ... and the hill itself was hollowed out as though it had been a diseased tooth'.[98] The cement works also 'irretrievably ruined'[99] the Woolfs' view of the South Downs from Monk's House: the factory sat, with its lorries and scaffolding, right in the middle of the vista they saw from their grassy terrace. Woolf bemoaned the destruction of Asheham and the countryside; she railed against the developers as 'these damnable buggers'.[100] She told Vita Sackville-West that 'this kind of outrage is among the real sorrows of life'. Finally, Asheham House was razed in 1994 by the East Sussex County Council, to allow the enlargement of the Beddingham landfill.[101]

How to get there
The former site of Asheham House is southeast of Lewes, off the A26. From London, go to the M25 London Orbital. At junction 7, take the M23 south towards Brighton. The M23 leads to the A23 south; then take the A27 east, passing Lewes, to Beddingham. At the Beddingham roundabout, take the A26 south towards Newhaven and Seaford for about a mile and a quarter, to the sign reading 'Beddingham landfill' (on the *left*). Stop the car in the small lay-by (on the *left*) about a hundred yards after the sign. Asheham House formerly stood beyond the gate, down a long, quiet road. The site has been swallowed up by the landfill.

Little Talland House
Over Christmas of 1910, Virginia stayed in Lewes (at the Pelham Arms Hotel) with her brother Adrian. It was her first trip to this part of Sussex; she decided she liked the countryside almost as much as Cornwall; while she was there, she discovered a suitable house for rent and took possession of it in January 1911. She christened the house 'Little Talland House', in honour of her childhood summers in St Ives.

Little Talland House was a fairly new, semi-detached house in Firle, near Lewes. It was set on the main street of the village; it contrasted, perhaps to its disadvantage, with the older houses on the street. Virginia described it to Leonard – who had just returned from Ceylon and whom she still addressed as 'Mr Woolf' – as a 'hideous suburban villa'.[102] But Leonard came to stay at Little Talland House with Virginia (and Desmond MacCarthy and Marjorie Strachey) for a weekend in September 1911, anyway. While the house was unprepossessing on the outside, it was perfectly comfortable inside. As Virginia described it: 'I spent yesterday finishing off the cottage. Its right underneath the downs, and though itself an eyesore, still that dont matter when one's inside. I have one gooseberry bush; 3 mongrels, thought by some to grow currants ... There is a Bath, and a W.C.'[103]

How to get there
Though Little Talland House is privately occupied and not open to the public, it is worthwhile to drive by it and to visit other sites in the village. The house is located in Firle (called West Firle on Ordnance Survey 123). From the site of Asheham House, return north along the A26 to the A27; at the Beddingham roundabout, take the A27 east (*right*) for about a mile and a quarter. The turn into Firle village will be on your *right*, just past a sign for Glynde, Ringmer and Glyndebourne. After turning into this smaller road, pass the entrance to **Firle Place** (on your *left*); follow the road's sharp curve to the *left* and pass the **Ram Inn**. After the Ram Inn, the road turns sharply *right* and then curves back to the *left*. Little Talland House is just after the second curve, on the *left* side of the village street, across from the Village Reading Room (Memorial Hall). It is the *left* half of the two attached houses, each of which has a large gable, brick on the ground floor, and mock Tudor beams on the first and attic floors.

Firle Churchyard [Graves of Vanessa Bell, Duncan Grant and Quentin Bell]
The graves of Vanessa Bell, Duncan Grant and Quentin Bell are on the north side of the churchyard (to the *left* of the Church door), between the old yew tree and the wall.

How to get there
From Little Talland House, continue along the village street, past the

village shop and post office. The entrance to the churchyard is at the end of the street, through wrought iron gates on the *left*.

Church of St Michael and All Angels, Berwick

In 1940, Vanessa Bell and Duncan Grant were given the commission to execute a series of decorations at St Michael and All Angels Church, Berwick. Both artists were enthused by the idea: they had frequently drawn wall murals before, both at Charleston and in friends' homes; they were both interested in the notion of extending painting beyond the bounds of the picture frame; they both had a taste for the religious murals of Piero della Francesca and Giotto. When Grant met George Bell, bishop of Chichester, to discuss the scheme, he suggested that all the artists in his household – Vanessa, Quentin Bell, Angelica Bell – be part of the project. In the end, Angelica did not participate, but Quentin, Vanessa and Duncan each decorated various parts of the Church.

The decorations at Berwick Church are perhaps most interesting for the way they incorporate contemporary local material. In Vanessa's *Nativity*, the barn is a Sussex barn at Tilton, Mount Caburn stands in the background, and a shepherd on the Firle estate modelled for his ancient counterpart. Angelica Bell, daughter of Vanessa and Duncan Grant, is the Virgin in the *Annunciation*. Several other friends and family members are also represented in various places.

For more information on St Michael and All Angels – and a virtual tour of the Church, including colour photographs of Duncan Grant's and Vanessa Bell's work – visit this website: www.inn-quest.co.uk/berwick/berwick.htm.

After touring Berwick Church, one can find a pleasant lunch at the Cricketers Arms pub, or continue on to Charleston and Lewes.

How to get there

From Firle, return to the A27. Continue *right* (east) on the A27 for just over four miles, passing the turning to Charleston Farmhouse (on the *right*) and driving through Selmeston. Berwick lies south of the A27, two and a quarter miles east of the Charleston turning. Turn *right* into the village lane just past signs for the Cricketers' Arms (on the *right*). The village lane passes the Cricketers' Arms (on the *right*). Turn *left* at the T-junction; the Church's car park will be on your *left*.

Charleston Farmhouse

Charleston Farmhouse was the country home of Vanessa Bell, Duncan Grant and Clive Bell. Leonard Woolf discovered Charleston during World War I, when Vanessa was living with Duncan Grant and David Garnett on a farm at Wissett. Grant and Garnett were conscientious objectors and were therefore required to work on the land in lieu of military service; to that end, they took up poultry farming at Wissett Lodge in 1916. But when the local tribunal declared their farm work at Wissett wasn't of sufficient 'national importance', they had to find more serious agricultural labour in a different place. Virginia and Leonard suggested Charleston Farmhouse:

> I wish you'd leave Wissett, and take Charleston. Leonard went over it, and says its a most delightful house and strongly advises you to take it. It is about a mile from Firle, on that little path which leads under the downs. It has a charming garden, with a pond, and fruit trees, and vegetables, all now rather run wild, but you could make it lovely. The house is very nice, with large rooms, and one room with big windows fit for a studio. At present it is used apparently as a weekend place, by a couple who keep innumerable animals, and most of the rooms are used by animals only. They say it only takes half an hour to walk to Glynde Station, through the Park, and you have Firle, with its telephone, quite near, so you would be more accessible than we are. There is a w.c. and a bathroom, but the bath only has cold water. The house wants doing up – and the wallpapers are awful. But it sounds a most attractive place – and 4 miles from us, so you wouldn't be badgered by us.[104]

Vanessa Bell moved into Charleston with Grant, Garnett and her two children in October 1916. They lived there through the war years; when the war ended in 1918, Garnett went his own way and Vanessa and Duncan returned to London to live. But Charleston remained Bloomsbury's rural escape. Clive Bell, Vanessa Bell and Duncan Grant always kept rooms there, and the three lived at Charleston full time during World War II, when London was under attack by the Luftwaffe. In later years, Vanessa, Clive and Duncan spent much of their time at Charleston. After Vanessa and Clive died, Duncan Grant lived alone at Charleston until just before his death in 1978.

Virginia's attitude toward Vanessa's freewheeling life at Charleston –

three children; constant guests; lovers; servants; always painting in the garden – ranged from jealousy to sheer relief that she could escape it all. Virginia envied Vanessa's ability to create a place that could hold all that vibrant life in being – a place that, like Talland House, reverberated with the voices of children and the satisfaction of good work. At Charleston, as she told Violet Dickinson, Vanessa 'presides over the most astonishing menage; Belgian hares, governesses, children, gardeners, hens, ducks, and painting all the time, till every inch of the house is a different colour'.[105] But just as often, Virginia returned from tea at Charleston thankful for the quiet and seclusion of Monk's House.

Charleston was the Bloomsbury group's chief country retreat. Lytton Strachey and E.M. Forster were frequent visitors, as were Roger Fry and Desmond MacCarthy. Before he married Lydia Lopokova in 1925, Maynard Keynes kept a bedroom at Charleston, and in that room wrote his prophetic *Economic Consequences of the Peace*. In their fifty years of residence at Charleston, Vanessa Bell and Duncan Grant decorated the house in their distinctive style, with bright murals, tiles and a price-less collection of Post-Impressionist paintings.

Charleston Farmhouse has been restored, and is now maintained and operated by the Charleston Trust. Entry is by guided tour; visitors are shown all the major rooms, and given an excellent overview of the life and decorative style of the house. Those interested in the life and work of Virginia Woolf should ask the guide to point out several items of partic-ular interest. The first is the table around which the famous luncheon in *A Room of One's Own* took place. This table was in George Rylands' rooms at King's College, Cambridge, and was donated by Rylands to Charleston at his death. (The table is temporarily located in the library.) The second item is in the dining room: a glass-fronted cabinet from 22 Hyde Park Gate. The third item is Julia Stephen's dressing table, located in the spare room. This dressing table stood in Julia's bedroom at 22 Hyde Park Gate, and Virginia Woolf remembered it vividly from the day her mother died: 'Led by George with towels wrapped around us and given each a drop of brandy in warm milk to drink, we were taken into the bedroom … I remember the long looking-glass; with the drawers on either side … and the great bed on which my mother lay.'[106] The fourth item stands in the studio, to the right of the fireplace. This glass-fronted, early nineteenth century cabinet belonged to William Makepeace Thackeray, who was the father of Leslie Stephen's first wife, Minny Thackeray. Vanessa Bell inherited the cabinet when her father died.[107]

How to get there

From Berwick, return to the A27 and turn *left* (west). The turning to Charleston is just over two miles from the Berwick turning, on the *left*. Charleston Farmhouse lies near the end of the road, to the *right*. John Maynard Keynes's former country home – Tilton (private residence: not open to the public) – lies to the *left*. (For those without a car, buses from Lewes stop at the end of the lane; taxis from Lewes can also be hired.) It was along this small road, in a ditch, that Maynard Keynes once left a still life by Cezanne.[108]

Charleston is open from April to October, from 2 p.m. until 6 p.m., on Wednesdays, Thursdays, Fridays, Saturdays and Sundays. Summer opening hours are slightly longer; details can be obtained from the Charleston website at www.charleston.org.uk, or by phoning 01323 811 626. There is a tea shop at Charleston which serves tea and cakes from 2 p.m. to 5 p.m. Wednesday to Sunday. A tour of Charleston takes a little over an hour, but the visitor should leave additional time to walk in the garden.

LEWES – SOME ADDITIONAL SITES ASSOCIATED WITH VIRGINIA WOOLF

Since Lewes was the large town nearest Rodmell, the Woolfs often shopped and dined there. (Virginia usually rode her bicycle to Lewes from Rodmell.) They also owned a house in Lewes for a short period of time. Lewes is a convenient spot to end this tour, perhaps with dinner at the Pelham Arms.

How to get there

From Charleston, take the A27 west (*left*) back towards Lewes. At the junction with the A26, take the roundabout into Lewes, towards the town centre. Drive through the Cuifail Tunnel; at the junction leaving the tunnel, turn *left* towards the town centre. Follow the signs towards the public car parks and park at the bottom of the town and hill. (Parking further into Lewes is very difficult.) This walk begins at the bottom of the High Street and heads up the hill, passing various sites associated with the Woolfs.

The White Hart Hotel – 55 High Street

The auction at which Leonard and Virginia bought Monk's House took place at the White Hart Hotel, in the first floor room above the hotel entrance. Woolf described the auction in her diary:

> The sale was on Tuesday. I don't suppose many spaces of five minutes in the course of my life have been so close packed with sensation. Was I somehow waiting to hear the result, while I watched the process, of an operation? The room at the White Hart was crowded. I looked at every face, & in particular every coat & shirt, for signs of opulence, & was cheered to discover none. But then, I thought, getting L. into line, does *he* look as if he had £800 in his pocket? Some of the substantial farmers might well have their rolls of notes stuffed inside their stockings. Bidding began. Someone offered £300. 'Not an offer', said the auctioneer, who was immediately opposed to us as a smiling courteous antagonist, 'a beginning.' The next bid was £400. Then they rose by fifties. Wycherley standing by us, silent & unmoved, added his advance. Six hundred was reached too quick for me. Little hesitations interposed themselves, but went down rather dismally fast. The auctioneer egged us on. I daresay there were six voices speaking, though after £600, 4 of them dropped out, & left only a Mr Tattersall competing with Mr Wycherley. We were allowed to bid in twenties; then tens; then fives; & still short of £700, so that our eventual victory seemed certain. Seven hundred reached, there was a pause; the auctioneer raised his hammer, very slowly; held it up a considerable time; urged & exhorted all the while it slowly sank towards the table. 'Now Mr Tattershall, another bid from you – no more bidding once I've struck the table – ten pounds? five pounds? – no more? for the last time then – *dump!*' & down it came on the table, to our thanksgiving – I purple in the cheeks, & L. trembling like a reed – 'sold to Mr Wycherley.' We stayed no longer. Out we went into the High Street, & very nearly quarrelled over the address of Roger's House.[109]

The White Hart Hotel provides accommodation and meals. Information and reservations may be made by phoning 01273 476 694 or 01273 474 676.

Wycherleys – 56 High Street

Wycherleys were the estate agents who located Monk's House for the Woolfs and bid for them at the White Hart auction. In the Woolfs' day,

Wycherleys' office was located on the current site of the ladies' clothes shop Monsoon.[110]

Bow Windows Bookshop – 175 High Street

This bookshop deals in old, rare and fine books. It stocks several areas of special interest, including books dealing with the Bloomsbury group. The Bow Windows Bookshop bought the Woolfs' books after Leonard Woolf's death; from Bow Windows, the books went in a lot to Washington State University. Alan and Jennifer Shelley own the shop; they can also be reached by phone (01273 480 780), at their postal address (175 High Street, Lewes, East Sussex BN7 1YE), or at their email address (rarebooks@bowwindows.com).

The Round House

Virginia and Leonard Woolf owned the Round House in Lewes for June and July, 1919. As Virginia told Dora Carrington, 'It's the butt end of an old windmill, so that all the rooms are either completely round or semi-circular'.[111]

The Woolfs were given notice at Asheham in the spring of that year – the landlord needed the house for his farm-bailiff – and Virginia immediately began to house-hunt. It was at this point that she took the lease of Higher Tregerthen in Cornwall, but she and Leonard quickly realised that Cornwall was too far away to serve as a weekend retreat. Imminently houseless, and having just argued with Vanessa over the way in which her woodcuts for *Kew Gardens* had been printed. Virginia went into Lewes in a disconsolate mood, with three hours to spare. To pass the time, she asked an estate agent about houses, and was sent to the Round House, in Pipe Passage:

> Off I went, up Pipes Passage, under the clock, & saw rising at the top of the sloping path a singular shaped roof, rising into a point, & spreading out in a circular petticoat all round it. Then things began to go a little quicker. An elderly and humble cottage woman the owner, showed me over. How far my satisfaction with the small rooms, & the view, & the ancient walls, & the wide sitting room, & the general oddity & character of the whole place were the result of finding something that would do, that one could conceive living in, that was cheap (freehold £300) I don't know; but as I inspected the rooms I became conscious of a rising desire

286

to settle here; to have done with looking about; to take this place, & make it one's permanent lodging. Perhaps later it will amuse me to read how I went from one grade to another of desire; till I felt physically hot & ardent, ready to surmount all obstacles. I liked the way the town dropped from the garden leaving us on a triangular island, vegetables one side, grass the other; the path encircling the round house amused me; nor are we overlooked. In short I took it there & then, being egged on by Wycherley's hesitation, & hints of a purchaser who had already asked for the refusal. Lewes that afternoon, with its many trees & laburnums, & water meadows, & sunny bow windowed houses, & broad High Street looked very tempting & dignified. The end of the story, which I must curtail, is that we have bought the Round House, & are now secure of a lodging on earth so long as we need sleep or sit anywhere.[112]

The Round House was – and still is – a charming structure. It was built as a windmill in 1802 and stands on the western walls of Lewes Castle. (Its mill was relocated to Racehill around 1835.) But neither Virginia nor Leonard really wanted a house in the middle of a town, and Virginia quickly realised her mistake. She blamed Vanessa and their argument over *Kew Gardens* first: 'Did you realise that it was your severity that plunged me into the recklessness of buying a house that day?'[113] Then when she took Leonard to see the Round House for the first time, he was distinctly cool, and she declared that 'the Round House no longer seemed so radiant & unattainable when we examined it as owners'.[114] Luckily, it was on this same trip into Lewes that they saw the placard advertising the sale of Monk's House. They bought Monk's House at auction on 1 July 1919 and disposed of the Round House shortly thereafter.

How to get there
The Round House is in Pipe Passage, which opens off Lewes High Street opposite the Bull House Restaurant. (Turn *right* into Pipe Passage; the Bull House Restaurant is easily recognised by the large legend: '1768-1774 – Thomas Paine lived here.') The Round House is privately owned and is not open to the public.

The Pelham Arms
Virginia and Adrian Stephen spent a week at the Pelham Arms over the Christmas holiday of 1910. It was during this visit that Virginia discov-

ered Little Talland House, thus beginning her lifelong connection to the Sussex countryside. As she wrote to Ottoline Morrell from the Pelham Arms:

> Here I am sitting over an inn fire, and listening to the creaking of an enormous sign, painted with your family arms ... I am very much tempted to buy a house here. One has the most lovely downs at one's door, and there are beautiful 18th century houses, with Corinthian pillars inside, oak panels, and marble mantelpieces. Are country cottages very expensive? Do the roofs leak? One misses such a lot in London. Even now, when it is about to rain, there are wonderful colours.[115]

Although the Pelham Arms no longer has rooms to hire, it is a convenient place to dine at the end of the day. Although Virginia told Clive Bell that 'the charges at this Inn are so exorbitant that one couldn't come often' the prices for meals now seem quite reasonable.[116]

How to get there
The Pelham Arms is located at the west end of the High Street, a five-minute walk from the Round House.

Some Sources for Pointz Hall: Glynde Place and Firle Place

In *Between the Acts*, Woolf describes Pointz Hall in these terms:

> Pointz Hall was seen in the light of an early summer morning to be a middle-sized house. It did not rank among the houses that are mentioned in guide books. It was too homely. But this whitish house with the grey roof, and the wing thrown out at right angles, lying unfortunately low on the meadow with a fringe of trees on the bank above it so that smoke curled up to the nests of the rooks, was a desirable house to live in. Driving past, people said to each other: 'I wonder if that'll ever come into the market?' and to the chauffeur: 'Who lives there?'[117]

Both Glynde Place and Firle Place are much more magnificent that Pointz Hall: Glynde Place is an Elizabethan mansion; Firle Place is an extensive Tudor estate set in an ancient park. But Woolf's imagination was no doubt kindled by the historical continuity suggested by both houses: Glynde Place is built on land owned by the same family for eight hundred years; Firle Place has been home to the Gage family for more than five hundred years. Like Pointz Hall, both Glynde Place and Firle Place suggest the unfolding pageant of human history, and the many ways in which the past lives on in the present. (Charleston Farmhouse was part of the Firle Estate when Vanessa Bell, David Garnett and Duncan Grant settled there in 1916.)

How to get there
Glynde Place is located just north of the A27, three miles east of Lewes. From Lewes, take the A27 east; pass through the Beddington round-about; take the first turning north (*left*) after the roundabout. (There is a large sign for Glynde Place pointing the way.) Glynde Place is open during May on bank holiday and Sunday afternoons, and from June to September on Wednesday, Sunday and bank holiday afternoons. For more information, phone 01273 858 224, or consult the Tour UK website at www.touruk.co.uk/houseesuss-glynde.

Firle Place is located just a few miles south of Glynde Place. From Glynde Place, return to the A27 and turn *left* (east). After about half a mile, the turn into Firle will be on your *right*. The turning is marked with a sign for Firle Place.

Firle Place is open from June to September on Wednesday, Thursday and Sunday afternoons. For more information, phone 01273 858 335, or consult the Tour UK website at www.touruk.co.uk/houses/house-esuss_firle.htm

A DAY'S WALK IN VIRGINIA WOOLF'S FOOTSTEPS: MONK'S HOUSE TO CHARLESTON FARMHOUSE

Virginia Woolf's daily walks took her in all directions over the Downs – along the river, up Itford Hill towards Mount Caburn, 'over the cornfield & up onto the down'[118] for a view of the sea over Telscombe. Sometimes she walked alone; sometimes she walked with Leonard; in all cases she was 'extremely happy walking on the downs … I like to have space to spread my mind out in'.[119] One of Virginia's favourite walks was to Charleston Farmhouse to visit Vanessa. Along the high footpath from Rodmell to Firle, she passed Iron Age barrows and tumuli, and saw grand estates spreading themselves below her. All these sights gave her a vivid sense of the continuous pageant of human life in this part of Sussex. Virginia readily admitted that she could 'never say how much I adore and respect nature',[120] but one of her long walks along the Downs lit her mind with the idea of 'old habitual beauty of England'. 'This has a holiness,' she said. 'This will go on after I'm dead':

> Yet on my walk – too long – I was tired … on my walk I almost felt my mind glow like hot iron – so complete & holy was the old habitual beauty of England: the silver sheep clustering; & the downs soaring, like birds wings sweeping up & up – I said [to] myself that beauty had become almost entirely satisfactory (oh my legs in the snapshot). I mean, I can fasten on a beautiful day, as a bee fixes itself on a sunflower. It feeds me, rests me, satisfies me, as nothing else does … This has a holiness. This will go on after I'm dead.[121]

The walk from Monk's House to Charleston is about six miles long and involves steep climbing at Itford Hill. But the exertion is rewarded by the beautiful views. The walk also reveals an important fact about Virginia Woolf's health: she was a woman with a good deal of physical stamina who enjoyed hard exercise.

How to get there
The walk from Monk's House to Charleston is marked on Ordnance Survey maps 122 and 123; due to the length of the walk (2½ to 3 hours) it is a good idea to pack refreshments or to have lunch in Firle. Leave from the National Trust car park at Monk's House. Follow the farm track down to the **River Ouse**; turn *right* (south) at the river and follow the path to the swing bridge at **Southease**. Cross the bridge; then cross the railway line at **Southease Halt** and walk through **Itford Farmyard**. When you reach the main Newhaven Road (the A26), cross the road and turn *right* (south). After a short distance, look for the **South Downs Way** footpath sign to Itford Hill.

The steep climb up Itford Hill will give you a view of the former location of **Asheham House** to the north, now a landfill next to a cement works. Continue over the escarpment and along the South Downs Way for about two miles, watching for the Iron Age tumuli that dot the area. Climb to **Firle Beacon** (passing the radio towers) where, on a clear day, one can see **Glynde Place** and **Firle Place** to the north, and the sea between Newhaven and Seaford to the south. It was of a similar view of the sea (over Telscombe, to the west) that Woolf wrote to Janet Case: 'And then nature – no, I shall never say how much I adore and respect nature. We crept on to the Downs yesterday and saw the sea over Telscombe, and a Hawk kill a partridge, and a white owl.'[122]

At the Firle Beacon car park, you have two choices. You can continue along the South Downs Way, along the top of the Downs, towards Charleston. Or you can descend along the Firle Bostal (the road leading north, away from the sea) down Firle Beacon and into Firle village. This latter route is the recommended walk, since it passes **Little Talland House** and the graves of Vanessa Bell and Duncan Grant.

After descending along **Firle Bostal** (a distance of a little over a mile), turn *right* at the school at the bottom of the hill into **The Street**. You will pass the **Ram Inn** – a convenient spot for refreshments – in a few hundred yards on the *left*. Continue through the village of Firle. **Little Talland House** (Virginia Stephen's first house in the country) will be on the *left*, near the beginning of the village, across from the Village Reading Room. **Firle Churchyard** – with the graves of Vanessa Bell, Duncan Grant and Quentin Bell – is at the end of the village street, just past the village shop and post office. (The graves are on the north side of the Churchyard.) Inside the church, the Piper window in the Gage family chapel is worth a visit.

To continue the walk to Charleston, return from the Churchyard to the village shop and post office. At the post office, take the track (the **Dock**) signposted for Charleston (1½ miles). The path passes first through **Firle Park**. Cross the park with Firle Place on your *right*. As you exit the park you will see the **Dower House** directly in front of you. The Dower House was the home of Quentin Bell and his wife Olivier. Follow the path to the *left* of the Dower House; walk through the field and uphill towards the **Tower**. Continue through the next field, keeping the Tower on your *left*. Continue along the path, ignoring paths to the left and the right, until you reach **Charleston**. If you see a pink-painted cottage on your *left*, you have just missed your turning: this building is Maynard Keynes' cottage, **Tilton**.[123] (It is not open to the public.)

Guided tours are also available to many of these sites. Contact TALLAND TOURS by email: m.sherman@ukonline.co.uk.

NOTES

Introduction

1. 'Flumina Amem Silvasque', in *The Essays of Virginia Woolf*, ed. Andrew McNeillie (New York and London: Harcourt Brace Jovanovich) Vol. II, p. 161.

2. 'Haworth, November, 1904', in *The Essays of Virginia Woolf*, ed. Andrew McNeillie (New York and London: Harcourt Brace Jovanovich) Vol. I, p. 7. Virginia Stephen's first essay to appear in print in the *Guardian* was a review of *The Son of Royal Langbrith* by W.D. Howells, but Virginia actually wrote her Haworth essay first. See Virginia's letter to Violet Dickinson of 26 November 1904, *VW Letters*, I, p. 158.

3. 'Great Men's Houses', in *The London Scene* (New York: Random House, 1975) p. 23.

4. 'Great Men's Houses', p. 24.

5. 'Great Men's Houses', p. 25.

6. 'Street Haunting: A London Adventure', in *Collected Essays*, ed. Leonard Woolf (New York: Harcourt, Brace & World, 1967), Vol. IV, p. 155.

7. 'Street Haunting', p. 160.

8. 'Street Haunting', p. 160.

9. 'Street Haunting', p. 162.

10. 'Street Haunting', p. 165.

11. 'The Moment: Summer's Night', in *Collected Essays*, ed. Leonard Woolf (New York: Harcourt, Brace & World, 1966), Vol II, p. 293.

12. 'The Moment', p. 294.

13. 'The Moment', p. 296.

14. 'Literary Geography', *The Essays of Virginia Woolf*, ed. Andrew McNeillie (New York and London: Harcourt Brace Jovanovich) Vol. I, p. 35.

15. 'Haworth, November, 1904,' p. 5.

16. 'Flumina Amem Silvasque', p. 161.

17. *Mrs Dalloway*, p. 151-2.

Chapter One   *St Ives and* To the Lighthouse

1. Quentin Bell imagines the Stephen family's journey to St Ives along these lines in his *Virginia Woolf* (London: Hogarth Press, 1972; New York: Harcourt Brace Jovanovich, 1972) Vol. I, p. 31. Sometimes today's traveller has a few more minutes to make the change of trains – but the connection is always a very close one.

2. 'A Sketch of the Past', in *Moments of Being*, ed. Jeanne Schulkind (New York and London: Harcourt Brace Jovanovich, 1985), p. 127.

3. 'A Sketch of the Past', p. 64.
4. 'A Sketch of the Past', p. 71.
5. 'A Sketch of the Past', pp. 129-30.
6. 'A Sketch of the Past', p. 134.
7. Bell, *Virginia Woolf*, Vol. I, p. 32.
8. Marion Whybrow, *St. Ives, 1883-1993: Portrait of an Art Colony* (Woodbridge, Suffolk: The Antique Collectors' Club, 1994), pp. 69, 27, 46.
9. Whybrow, p. 44.
10. 'A Sketch of the Past', p. 131.
11. 'A Sketch of the Past', pp. 131-2.
12. *A Passionate Apprentice: The Early Journals*, 1987-1909, ed. Mitchell Leaska (New York: Harcourt Brace Jovanovich, 1990), p. 295.
13. *A Passionate Apprentice*, p. 293.
14. 'A Sketch of the Past', p. 133.
15. 'A Sketch of the Past', pp. 67-9.
16. 'A Sketch of the Past', pp. 127-8; 135.
17. *To the Lighthouse* (New York: Harcourt Brace Jovanovich, 1981), p. 182. (First published Hogarth Press, 1927.)
18. *To the Lighthouse*, p. 52.
19. *To the Lighthouse*, p. 86.
20. *To the Lighthouse*, p. 82.
21. *To the Lighthouse*, pp. 97, 105.
22. *To the Lighthouse*, pp. 37-8.
23. *To the Lighthouse*, p. 38.
24. *To the Lighthouse*, p. 45.
25. *To the Lighthouse*, p. 62-3.
26. *To the Lighthouse*, p. 19-20.
27. *To the Lighthouse*, p. 51.
28. *To the Lighthouse*, p. 49.
29. *To the Lighthouse*, p. 49.
30. *To the Lighthouse*, pp. 18-19; 48.
31. *To the Lighthouse*, p. 164.
32. *To the Lighthouse*, p. 165.
33. *To the Lighthouse*, pp. 166-7.
34. *To the Lighthouse*, pp. 186.
35. *To the Lighthouse*, p. 206.
36. *To the Lighthouse*, p. 207.
37. *To the Lighthouse*, p. 192.
38. *To the Lighthouse*, p. 202.
39. *To the Lighthouse*, p. 191.
40. *To the Lighthouse*, pp. 208-9.
41. *The Diary of Virginia Woolf*, ed. Anne Olivier Bell, assisted by Andrew McNeillie (London and New York: Harcourt Brace Jovanovich, 1977-1984), Vol. III, 208.
42. 'A Sketch of the Past', p. 128.
43. *A Passionate Apprentice*, pp. 284-5.
44. 'A Sketch of the Past', pp. 128-9.
45. 'A Sketch of the Past', p. 135.
46. 'A Sketch of the Past', pp. 65-6.
47. Whybrow, pp. 22, 43.
48. *To the Lighthouse*, p. 13.

49. *To the Lighthouse*, p. 19.

50. *To the Lighthouse*, p. 171.

51. *To the Lighthouse*, p. 32.

52. *To the Lighthouse*, pp. 163-5.

53. *To the Lighthouse*, pp. 164-5.

54. *A Passionate Apprentice*, p. 286.

55. 'A Sketch of the Past', p. 132.

56. I am grateful to Sheila Wilkinson and David Wilkinson, who mapped out this walk and its distances on one of their visits to St Ives.

57. 'A Sketch of the Past', pp. 130-1.

58. *The Letters of Virginia Woolf*, ed. Nigel Nicolson and Joanne Trautmann (London: Hogarth Press; New York: Harcourt Brace Jovanovich, 1975-1980) Vol. I, p. 416.

59. *A Passionate Apprentice*, pp. 282-3.

60. 'A Sketch of the Past', p. 134.

61. I am grateful to Sheila and David Wilkinson, who suggested this route from the Badger Inn to Trencrom, and who marked out its distances for me during one of their stays in St Ives.

62. Antony Charles Thomas, *'To the Lighthouse': The Story of Godrevy Light* (Redruth, Cornwall: Penwith Books, 1973), pp. 2-7.

63. *To the Lighthouse*, p. 188.

64. *To the Lighthouse*, p. 204.

65. *To the Lighthouse*, pp. 206-7.

66. *To the Lighthouse*, pp. 202-3.

67. *To the Lighthouse*, p. 186.

68. I am grateful to Sheila and David Wilkinson for providing this route to Godrevy Point for me.

69. *VW Letters*, I, p. 414.

70. *VW Letters*, I, p. 415.

71. *VW Letters*, I, p. 416.

72. Sheila Wilkinson's careful research uncovered the fact that the former Lelant Hotel is now known as the Badger Inn.

73. *VW Diaries*, II, p. 105.

74. *VW Letters*, II, p. 462.

75. Paul Delany, *D.H. Lawrence's Nightmare: The Writer and His Circle in the Years of the Great War* (New York: Basic Books, 1978), p. 209.

76. *VW Letters*, II, p. 340.

77. *VW Letters*, II, p. 382.

78. Delany, p. 216.

79. Claire Tomalin, *Katherine Mansfield: A Secret Life* (New York: Alfred A. Knopf, 1988) p. 146.

80. Delany, pp. 316-17.

81. *VW Diaries*, II, p. 53.

82. *VW Letters*, II, p. 460.

83. *VW Letters*, III, p. 309.

84. *VW Letters*, III, p. 311.

85. Martin Gayford, 'Still Winding and Wonderful: Zennor's Literary and Artistic Connections' in *The Charleston Magazine*, Issue 19, Spring/ Summer 1999, p. 11.

86. *A Passionate Apprentice*, p. 297. I am grateful to Rosemary Sumner, who has made this walk many times and in all weathers, for helping me confirm its details.

87. *A Passionate Apprentice*, p. 297.

Chapter Two   Mrs Dalloway *and the streets of London*

1. Leslie Stephen, *Sir Leslie Stephen's Mausoleum Book*, ed. and with an introduction by Alan Bell (Oxford: Clarendon Press, 1977, pp. 42-3; Virginia Woolf, 'Old Bloomsbury', in *Moments of Being*, ed. Jeanne Schulkind (New York and London: Harcourt Brace Jovanovich, 1985) pp. 182-3.

2. Virginia Woolf, 'A Sketch of the Past', in *Moments of Being*, ed. Jeanne Schulkind (New York and London: Harcourt Brace Jovanovich, 1985), pp. 75-7.

3. 'A Sketch of the Past', p. 78.

4. 'A Sketch of the Past', p. 78.

5. 'A Sketch of the Past', p. 72

6. Virginia Woolf, '22 Hyde Park Gate', in *Moments of Being*, ed. Jeanne Schulkind (New York and London: Harcourt Brace Jovanovich, 1985), p. 177.

7. 'Old Bloomsbury', p. 183; 'A Sketch of the Past', p. 92.

8. 'Old Bloomsbury', p. 184.

9. 'Old Bloomsbury', pp. 184-5

10. For an interesting discussion of frames, windows, the claustrophobic atmosphere of Kensington, and the open atmosphere of Bloomsbury, see Nena Škrbic's 'Through the Realist Frame: "Phyllis and Rosamond" and the Masculine "I" ' in the *Virginia Woolf Bulletin*, 5 (September 2000), pp. 15-22.

11. 'Old Bloomsbury', p. 201.

12. *Mrs Dalloway* (New York: Harcourt Brace Jovanovich, 1981), p. 48. (First published Hogarth Press, 1925.)

13. 'Old Bloomsbury', p. 188; Quentin Bell, *Virginia Woolf* (London: Hogarth Press, 1972; New York: Harcourt Brace Jovanovich, 1972) Vol. I, pp. 496-7.

14. *The Letters of Virginia Woolf*, ed. Nigel Nicolson and Joanne Trautmann (London: Hogarth Press; New York: Harcourt Brace Jovanovich, 1975-1980) Vol. I, pp. 496-7.

15. *VW Letters* II, p. 6.

16. Leonard Woolf, *Beginning Again*: *An Autobiography of the Years 1911 to 1918* (New York: Harcourt Brace Jovanovich, 1964), p. 84.

17. *The Diary of Virginia Woolf*, ed. Anne Olivier Bell, assisted by Andrew McNeillie (London and New York: Harcourt Brace Jovanovich, 1977-1984), Vol. V, p. 17.

18. *VW Letters* II, p. 34.

19. Hermione Lee, *Virginia Woolf* (New York: Alfred A. Knopf, 1997), p. 322.

20. For accounts of Virginia Woolf's symptoms and medical treatment, see Leonard Woolf, *Beginning Again*, pp. 75-82; Hermione Lee, *Virginia Woolf*, pp. 171-93. Much has been written about the failures of Virginia Woolf's medical care, and Stephen Trombley analyses the medical assumptions of Woolf's doctors in a useful fashion in his *All That Summer She Was Mad*: *Virginia Woolf, Female Victim of Male Medicine* (New York: Continuum, 1982). Probably the best analysis of Woolf's illness appears in Thomas Caramagno's *The Flight of the Mind*: *Virginia Woolf's Art and Manic-Depressive Illness* (University of California Press, 1996). For the most recent book on the subject, see Peter Dally's *The Marriage of Heaven and Hell*: *Manic Depression and the Life of Virginia Woolf* (New York: St Martin's Press, 1999).

21. Leonard Woolf, *Downhill All the Way*: *An Autobiography of the Years 1919-1939* (New York and London: Harcourt Brace Jovanovich, 1967), p. 51.

22. *VW Diary* V, p. 183; *VW Diary* IV, p. 27.

23. *VW Diary* II, p. 283.

24. *VW Diary* II, p. 317.

25. *VW Diary* II, p. 290.
26. 'A Sketch of the Past', p. 81.
27. *VW Diary* II, p. 273.
28. *VW Diary* II, p. 48.
29. *VW Diary* III, pp. 62-3.
30. *VW Diary* III, p. 87.
31. *VW Diary* III, p. 30.
32. *VW Diary* II, p. 290.
33. *VW Diary* II, p. 323.
34. *VW Diary* III, p. 220.
35. 'Street Haunting: A London Adventure', in *Collected Essays*, ed. Leonard Woolf (New York: Harcourt, Brace, & World, 1967), Vol. IV, p. 156-7.
36. *VW Diary* II, p. 298.
37. *VW Diary* III, p. 186.
38. *The Letters of Vita Sackville-West to Virginia Woolf*, ed. Louise DeSalvo and Mitchell Leaska (New York: William Morrow and Co., 1985), p. 59.
39. *Mrs Dalloway*, p. 88.
40. *Mrs Dalloway*, p. 35.
41. *Mrs Dalloway*, p. 4.
42. *Mrs Dalloway*, p. 31.
43. *Mrs Dalloway*, p. 4.
44. *VW Diary* II, p. 273.
45. *Mrs Dalloway*, pp. 152-3.
46. *VW Diary* II, p. 290.
47. *Mrs Dalloway*, p. 9.
48. *Mrs Dalloway*, p. 63.
49. *Mrs Dalloway*, p. 163.
50. *Mrs Dalloway*, p. 86.
51. *Mrs Dalloway*, pp. 22-3.
52. *Mrs Dalloway*, p. 68.
53 'A Sketch of the Past', p. 78.
54. *VW Diary* II, p. 248.
55. *Mrs Dalloway*, p. 149.
56. *Mrs Dalloway*, p. 184.
57. *Mrs Dalloway*, pp. 185-6.
58. *Mrs Dalloway*, p. 186.
59. *Mrs Dalloway*, p. 193.
60. *Mrs Dalloway*, p. 194.
61. *VW Diary* II, p. 283.
62. *VW Diary* II, p. 272.
63. David Daiches and John Fowler, *Literary Landscapes of the British Isles*: A *Narrative Atlas* (New York and London: Paddington Press, 1979), p. 88; Jean Moorcroft Wilson, *Virginia Woolf, Life and London*: A *Biography of Place* (New York and London: W.W. Norton & Company, 1987), p. 196. Wilson suggests that Woolf saw the Barton Street house in 1923, but Stuart Clarke notes that Woolf's visit to Barton Street actually took place in 1915. See the Virginia Woolf Society of Great Britain's website at http://orlando.jp.org./vwsgb/dat/dwalk.html.
64. *Mrs Dalloway*, p. 4.
65. *Mrs Dalloway*, pp. 5-7.
66. *Mrs Dalloway*, p. 8.

67. *Mrs Dalloway*, p. 9.

68. *Mrs Dalloway*, ed. Morris Beja (Oxford: The Shakespeare Head Press, 1996), p. 148.

69. *Mrs Dalloway*, ed. David Bradshaw (Oxford: Oxford University Press, 2000), p. 168; *Mrs Dalloway*, ed. Beja, p. 148.

70. *Mrs Dalloway*, ed. Beja, p. 149; *Mrs Dalloway*, ed. Bradshaw, p. 169.

71. *Mrs Dalloway*, p. 12.

72. *Mrs Dalloway*, ed. Bradshaw, p. 170.

73. *Mrs Dalloway*, p. 14.

74 *Mrs Dalloway*, ed. Beja, p. 149.

75. *Mrs Dalloway*, p. 21.

76. *Mrs Dalloway*, pp. 24-5.

77. *Mrs Dalloway*, p. 24.

78. Michael Whitworth, ' "The Indian and His Cross" ' in *Mrs Dalloway*,' *The Virginia Woolf Miscellany*, Number 49 (Spring 1997), p. 4.

79. *Mrs Dalloway*, p. 25.

80. *Mrs Dalloway*, p. 26.

81. *Mrs Dalloway*, p. 83.

82. I am indebted to Jasmyne King-Leeder and Vanessa Curtis for information about the current interior arrangements of 22 Hyde Park Gate.

83. Leslie Stephen, *Sir Leslie Stephen's Mausoleum Book*, p. 43.

84. 'A Sketch of the Past', p. 116. Woolf may have exaggerated the number of maids living in the basement at 22 Hyde Park Gate. Stuart Clarke has recently researched census records and discovered that the 1891 census for 22 Hyde Park Gate lists a cook and four additional domestic servants. See Stuart Clarke, 'Pursuing Leslie Stephen Through the Censuses', *Virginia Woolf Bulletin*, 7 (May 2001), p. 65.

85. 'A Sketch of the Past', p. 118.

86. 'A Sketch of the Past', p. 118.

87. 'A Sketch of the Past', p. 158.

88. Stuart Clarke, 'Hyde Park Gate in 1894', *Virginia Woolf Bulletin*, 2 (July 1999): 46-7.

89 Leslie Stephen, *The Life of Sir James Fitzjames Stephen* (London: Smith, Elder, and Co., 1895), p. 66. I am grateful to Jasmyne King-Leeder for information about Broadwalk House.

90. 'A Sketch of the Past', p. 76.

91. 'A Sketch of the Past', p. 77.

92. *VW Letters* III, p. 247.

93. *Mrs Dalloway*, p. 184.

94. *VW Letters* I, p. 20.

95. *VW Letters* IV, p. 411.

96. *The Dictionary of National Biography*, ed. Leslie Stephen and Sidney Lee (New York: Oxford University Press, 1921-1922), Vol. XIX, p. 577.

97. *Survey of London*. Vol. XLII: Southern Kensington: Kensington Square to Earl's Court (London: The Athlone Press, 1986), p. 20; *Survey of London*. Vol. XXXVII: Northern Kensington (London: The Athlone Press, 1973), p. 72. I am indebted to Janet Newkirk, who trekked to the Kensington Library and uncovered this material for me. Thanks, Janet.

98. *A Passionate Apprentice: The Early Journals*, 1987-1909, ed. Mitchell Leaska (New York: Harcourt Brace Jovanovich, 1990), p. 68.

99. '22 Hyde Park Gate', p. 176.

100. '22 Hyde Park Gate', p. 176.

101. 'A Sketch of the Past', p. 87.

102. 'A Sketch of the Past', p. 87.

103. *Survey of London*, XXXVII, p. 126.

104. William Gaunt, *Victorian Olympus* (London: Jonathan Cape, 1952), p. 118-19.

105. '22 Hyde Park Gate', p. 176.

106. *VW Letters* I, p. 390.

107. 'Leslie Stephen' in *Collected Essays*, ed. Leonard Woolf (New York: Harcourt, Brace, & World, 1967), Vol. IV, p. 79.

108. *VW Letters* I, p. 390.

109. *VW Letters* I, p. 299.

110. *VW Diary* III, p. 267.

111. Frances Spalding, *Duncan Grant: A Biography* (London: Pimlico, 1998), p. 76.

112. Keynes, quoted in Robert Skidelsky, *John Maynard Keynes: A Biography* (New York: Viking, 1986), Vol. I, p. 256.

113. Fry, quoted in Frances Spalding, *Roger Fry: Art and Life* (Norwich: Black Dog Books, 1999), p. 165.

114. 'Old Bloomsbury', p. 199.

115. 'Old Bloomsbury', p. 199.

116. *Virginia Woolf & Lytton Strachey: Letters*, ed. Leonard Woolf and James Strachey (London: The Hogarth Press, 1969), p. 82.

117. *VW Letters* I, p. 167.

118. Frances Partridge, *Memories* (London: Phoenix, 1999), pp. 105-20.

119. 'A Sketch of the Past', p. 81.

120. Lee, *Virginia Woolf*, p. 301; Leonard Woolf, *Beginning Again*, p. 51.

121. 'Old Bloomsbury', p. 201.

122. *VW Letters* VI, p. 432.

123. *VW Diary* III, p. 80.

124. *A Room of One's Own* (New York: Harcourt, Brace and World, 1957), p. 26. (First published by the Hogarth Press, 1929.)

125. *Jacob's Room* (New York: Harcourt, Brace & World, 1959), p. 108. (First published Hogarth Press, 1922.)

126. Marjorie Caygill, *The British Museum Reading Room* (London: The Trustees of the British Museum, 2000), p. 13.

127. *Jacob's Room*, pp. 105-6.

128. My thanks to James Caira, Information Officer at the British Museum's Reading Room, for this information.

129. *Beginning Again*, p. 170.

130. *Beginning Again*, p. 172.

131. *Beginning Again*, pp. 172-3.

132. *VW Diary*, II, p. 283.

133. *VW Diary*, II, p. 283.

134. *VW Diary*, III, p. 132.

135. *Beginning Again*, pp. 172-3; *VW Diary*, II, p. 295.

136. 'Introduction' to *Victorian Photographs of Famous Men and Fair Women* (London: Hogarth Press, 1973), p. 19.

137. *Mrs Dalloway*, pp. 135-6.

138. *Mrs Dalloway*, p. 136.

139. *Beginning Again*, pp. 86-7. See also Stuart Clarke's description of 'Where Virginia Woolf Lived in London' on the website of the Virginia Woolf Society of Great Britain.

140. Curtis, 'Highgate Cemetery: The Restoration of the Stephen Graves in 2000', *Virginia Woolf Bulletin*, No. 5, September 2000, 48-52. See also Curtis' excellent account on the website of the Virginia Woolf Society of Great Britain.

Chapter Three   Vita, Virginia, Knole and Orlando

1. *The Diary of Virginia Woolf*, ed. Anne Olivier Bell, assisted by Andrew McNeillie (London and New York: Harcourt Brace Jovanovich, 1977-1984), Vol II, p. 216.
2. Victoria Glendinning's *Vita* (New York: Alfred A. Knopf, 1983) provides the definitive account of Vita Sackville-West's life and work. Kirkpatrick and Clarke's *A Bibliography of Virginia Woolf* (Oxford: Clarendon Press, 1997), p. 27, notes that approximately 3,200 copies of *Jacob's Room* were printed in 1922. But Willis notes a puzzling discrepancy: when Leonard Woolf closed the account books on *Jacob's Room* in March of 1924, his records indicated that 1,413 copies of the novel had been sold. See Jack Willis, *Leonard and Virginia Woolf as Publishers: The Hogarth Press, 1917-1941* (Charlottesville: The University of Virginia Press, 1992), p. 61.
3. Review quoted by Glendinning in *Vita*, p. 141.
4. *The Letters of Vita Sackville-West to Virginia Woolf*, ed. Louise DeSalvo and Mitchell Leaska (New York: William Morrow and Co., 1985), p. 165.
5. *The Letters of Virginia Woolf*, ed. Nigel Nicolson and Joanne Trautmann (London: Hogarth Press; New York: Harcourt Brace Jovanovich, 1975-1980), Vol. III, p. 150.
6. *VW Letters*, III, p. 381.
7. Leonard Woolf, *Downhill All the Way: An Autobiography of the Years 1919-1939* (New York and London: Harcourt Brace Jovanovich, 1967), pp. 158-9.
8. *VW Letters* III, p. 131.
9. *VW Letters* III, p. 198.
10. *VW Diary*, II, p. 217.
11. Leonard Woolf, *Downhill All the Way*, p. 112.
12. *VW Letters*, III, p. 150.
13. *VW Letters*, III, p. 85.
14. *Vita and Harold: The Letters of Vita Sackville-West and Harold Nicolson*, ed. Nigel Nicolson (New York: G.P. Putnam's Sons, 1992), p. 168.
15. *Vita and Harold*, p. 158.
16. Vita to Harold, 27 September 1928, in '*Orlando*: An Edition of the Manuscript', ed. Madeline Moore, *Twentieth Century Literature*, 25 (1979), p. 350.
17. *VW Diary*, III, p. 48.
18. *The Letters of Leonard Woolf*, ed. Frederic Spotts (New York: Harcourt Brace Jovanovich, 1989), p. 228.
19. *The Letters of Vita Sackville-West to Virginia Woolf*, p. 238.
20. *VW Letters*, III, p. 568.
21. *VW Diary*, III, pp. 51-2.
22. *The Letters of Vita Sackville-West to Virginia Woolf*, p. 88.
23. *The Letters of Vita Sackville-West to Virginia Woolf*, p. 89.
24. *VW Letters*, III, p. 233.
25. *VW Letters*, III, pp. 237, 243.
26. *VW Letters*, III, p. 233.
27. *The Letters of Vita Sackville-West to Virginia Woolf*, p. 94.
28. *The Letters of Vita Sackville-West to Virginia Woolf*, p. 110.
29. *VW Letters*, III, p. 232.
30. *VW Letters*, III, pp. 241, 249.

31. *VW Letters*, III p. 146.
32. *VW Diary*, III, p. 117.
33. *The Letters of Vita Sackville-West to Virginia Woolf*, p. 152.
34. *VW Diary*, II, pp. 306-7.
35. *VW Diary*, III, p. 125.
36. *VW Letters*, III, p. 307.
37. *The Letters of Vita Sackville-West to Virginia Woolf*, p. 161.
38. *The Letters of Vita Sackville-West to Virginia Woolf*, p. 163.
39. *VW Letters*, III, p. 321.
40. *VW Letters*, III, p. 328.
41. *VW Letters*, III, p. 342.
42. *VW Letters*, III, p. 325.
43. *VW Letters*, III, p. 331.
44. *The Letters of Vita Sackville-West to Virginia Woolf*, p. 169.
45. *VW Letters*, III, pp. 380, 377.
46. *VW Letters*, III, p. 390.
47 *The Letters of Vita Sackville-West to Virginia Woolf*, p. 209.
48. *VW Letters*, III, p. 391.
49. *Vita and Harold*, p. 159.
50. *Vita and Harold*, p. 175.
51. Harold Nicolson in *Portrait of a Marriage*, ed. Nigel Nicolson (New York: Atheneum, 1973), p. 206.
52. *The Letters of Vita Sackville-West to Virginia Woolf*, p. 213.
53. *VW Letters*, III, p. 344.
54. *VW Letters*, III, p. 302.
55. Glendinning, *Vita*, p. 176.
56. *VW Letters*, III, p. 395.
57. *VW Letters*, III, pp. 429-30.
58. *VW Letters*, III, pp. 429-30.
59. *VW Letters*, III, pp. 427-8.
60. *VW Letters*, III, p. 429.
61. *The Letters of Vita Sackville-West to Virginia Woolf*, p. 238.
62. *VW Letters*, III, 484, 488.
63. For a transcription and annotation of the first full draft of *Orlando*, see *Virginia Woolf's Orlando: The Holograph Draft*. Transcribed and edited by Stuart N. Clarke (London: S.N. Clarke, 1993).
64. *The Letters of Vita Sackville-West to Virginia Woolf*, p. 289.
65. *The Letters of Vita Sackville-West to Virginia Woolf*, p. 318.
66. *VW Letters*, IV, p. 29.
67. *VW Diary*, III, p. 187.
68. *VW Diary*, IV, p. 287.
69. *VW Letters*, III, p. 474.
70. *VW Letters*, III, p. 453.
71. *VW Letters*, III, p. 451.
72. Glendinning, *Vita*, pp. 189-90.
73. Glendinning, *Vita*, p. 188.
74. *Orlando* (New York: Harcourt Brace Jovanovich, 1973), p. 317. (First published Hogarth Press, 1928.)
75. *Orlando*, p. 15.
76. *Orlando*, p. 23.

77. *Orlando*, p. 15.

78. *Orlando*, pp. 185-6.

79. *Orlando*, p. 158.

80. *Orlando*, p. 264.

81. *Orlando*, p. 189.

82. *Orlando*, p. 168.

83. *Orlando*, p. 111.

84. *Orlando*, p. 317.

85. Vita Sackville-West, *The Land* in *The Land & The Garden* (Exeter, Devon: Webb and Bower, 1989), p. 79.

86. I am grateful to Nigel Nicolson for calling my attention to this section of *The Land*.

87. *Orlando*, pp. 18-19.

88. *Orlando*, p. 19.

89. *Orlando*, pp. 105-6.

90. *Orlando*, pp. 106-7.

91. *A Room of One's Own* (New York: Harcourt, Brace and World, 1957), p. 68. (First published Hogarth Press, 1929.)

92. Vita Sackville-West, *Knole and the Sackvilles* (London and Tonbridge, Kent: Ernest Benn, 1958), p. 119.

93. *VW Letters*, III, p. 469.

94. *Orlando*, pp. 314-15.

95. My discussion of the history of Knole and Knole Park is indebted to Robert Sackville-West's excellent scholarship in *Knole* (London: The National Trust, 1998).

96. *Orlando*, p. 14.

97. *Orlando*, p. 317.

98. *Orlando*, p. 313.

99. *Orlando*, p. 21.

100. Nigel Nicolson remembers standing head to head with the figure of Shakespeare as a child.

101. Vita Sackville-West, *Knole and the Sackvilles* 1958 ed., pp. 57-9.

102. *Knole and the Sackvilles*, 1923 ed., p. 13.

103. *Orlando*, p. 318.

104. *Orlando*, p. 171.

105. *Orlando*, p. 318.

106. *Knole and the Sackvilles*, 1923 ed., pp. 150-1.

107. *Knole and the Sackvilles*, 1958 ed., pp. 28-9.

108. *Knole and the Sackvilles*, 1923 ed., p. 16; Julia Briggs discusses Vita's revisions to *Knole and the Sackvilles* in 'Editing Woolf for the Nineties,' *Virginia Woolf International, A Special Issue of The South Carolina Review*, Vol. 29, Number 1 (Fall 1996), pp. 67-7. See especially pp. 73-4.

109. *Portrait of a Marriage*, p. 88.

110. *Knole and the Sackvilles*, 1923 ed., p. 16.

111. *Knole and the Sackvilles*, 1923 ed., pp. 15-16.

112. *Orlando*, p. 317.

113. *Orlando*, pp. 317-18.

114. *Knole and the Sackvilles*, 1923 ed., pp. 14-15.

115. *Knole and the Sackvilles*, 1923 ed., p. 11.

116. *Orlando*, p. 111.

117. *Knole and the Sackvilles*, 1923 ed., pp. 10-11.

118. *Orlando*, p. 318.

119. *Knole and the Sackvilles*, 1923 ed., p. 15.
120. *Knole and the Sackvilles*, 1958 ed., p. 30.
121. *Orlando*, pp. 108-9.
122. *Orlando*, p. 171.
123. *Orlando*, p. 318.
124. *Knole and the Sackvilles*, 1923 ed., p. 1.
125. I am grateful to Nigel Nicolson for this information about The Masthead.
126. *Knole and the Sackvilles*, 1923 ed., p. 17; 1958 ed., p. 32. See also Julia Briggs, pp. 73-4.
127. *Orlando*, p. 172.
128. *Orlando*, p. 262.
129. Nigel Nicolson provides a good account of life at Long Barn in his *Portrait of a Marriage*. See especially pp. 193-5.
130. Glendinning, *Vita*, pp. 79-80.
131. Glendinning, *Vita*, p. 162.
132. *Portrait of a Marriage*, p. 142.
133. 'Night: For Harold Nicolson', in *Collected Poems* (New York: Doubleday, 1934), pp. 144-6. 'Night' was originally published in Vita's *Orchard and Vineyard*, 1921.
134. *Knole and the Sackvilles*, 1958 ed., p. 80.
135. *Knole and the Sackvilles*, 1958 ed., p. 150.
136. See J.H. Willis, *Leonard and Virginia Woolf as Publishers: The Hogarth Press, 1917-1941* (Charlottesville: The University of Virginia Press, 1992), pp. 143-4.
137. Nigel Nicolson provides a delightful account of the Nicolsons at Sissinghurst in *Portrait of a Marriage*, pp. 222-33.
138. *The Letters of Vita Sackville-West to Virginia Woolf*, p. 39.
139. *Portrait of a Marriage*, p. 224.
140. See, for example, Suzanne Raitt, *Vita and Virginia: The Work and Friendship of V. Sackville-West and Virginia Woolf* (Oxford: Clarendon Press, 1993), pp. 117-18.
141. Glendinning, *Vita*, p. 206.
142. *VW Diary*, IV, p. 87.
143. Glendinning, *Vita*, p. 380.
144. *VW Diary*, IV, p. 287.
145. *VW Letters*, VI, p. 424.
146. *Portrait of a Marriage*, p. 224.
147. Glendinning, *Vita*, 235.
148. Nigel Nicolson, *Sissinghurst Castle Garden* (London: The National Trust, 1994), p. 21.
149. Glendinning, *Vita*, 247.
150. *Sissinghurst Castle Garden*, p. 31.
151. Glendinning, *Vita*, p. 278.

Chapter Four   *Cambridge and* **A Room of One's Own**

1. The best account of Leslie Stephen's life and work is Noel Annan's *Leslie Stephen: The Godless Victorian* (New York: Random House: 1984).
2. *The Letters of Virginia Woolf*, ed. Nigel Nicolson and Joanne Trautmann (London: Hogarth Press; New York: Harcourt Brace Jovanovich, 1975-1980), Vol. III, p. 247.
3. *A Passionate Apprentice: The Early Journals*, 1987-1909, ed. Mitchell Leaska (New York: Harcourt Brace Jovanovich, 1990), p. 87.

4. Good accounts of the 1897 vote on admitting women to Cambridge degrees can be found in Rita Tullberg's *Women at Cambridge* (Cambridge: Cambridge University Press, 1998), Felicity Hunt and Carol Barker's *Women at Cambridge: A Brief History* (Cambridge: The Press and Publications Office, University of Cambridge, 1998), and in Christopher Brooke's *A History of the University of Cambridge*, Vol. IV 1870-1990 (Cambridge: Cambridge University Press, 1993).

5. *VW Letters*, I, p. 77.

6. Leonard Woolf, *Sowing: An Autobiography of the Years 1880-1904* (New York: Harcourt Brace Jovanovich, 1975), pp. 183-4.

7. G.E. Moore, *Principia Ethica* (Cambridge: Cambridge University Press, 1978), p. 188.

8. *VW Letters*, I, p. 145.

9. For a good account of Caroline Emelia Stephen's life and work, see Robert Tod's unpublished 1978 essay entitled *Caroline Emelia Stephen, 1834-1909*. For various readings of Caroline Emelia Stephen's importance to Virginia Woolf's thinking, see the work of Jane Marcus, and in particular *Virginia Woolf, Cambridge, and A Room of One's Own* (London: Cecil Woolf, 1996); 'The Niece of a Nun: Virginia Woolf, Caroline Stephen, and the Cloistered Imagination' in *Virginia Woolf: A Feminist Slant*, ed. Jane Marcus (Lincoln: University of Nebraska Press, 1983), pp. 7-36; and 'Thinking Back through Our Mothers' in *New Feminist Essays on Virginia Woolf*, ed. Jane Marcus (Lincoln: University of Nebraska Press, 1981), pp. 1-30. The author is grateful to Sheila Wilkinson, who kindly made her copy of Tod's essay available.

10. *VW Letters*, I, p. 146.

11. *VW Letters*, I, p. 144.

12. *VW Letters*, I, p. 229.

13. *VW Letters*, I, p. 285.

14. 'Old Bloomsbury', in *Moments of Being*, ed. Jeanne Schulkind (New York and London: Harcourt Brace Jovanovich, 1985), p. 186.

15. 'Old Bloomsbury', p. 186.

16. 'Old Bloomsbury', pp. 189-90.

17. 'Old Bloomsbury', p. 186.

18. Vanessa Curtis makes this point about Headlam, Julia Stephen, and Stella Duckworth in her *Virginia and Stella An Unfinished Sisterhood* (London: Cecil Woolf Publishers, 2001), p. 14.

19. *VW Letters*, I, p. 470.

20. See Hermione Lee's interpretation of Waterlow in her *Virginia Woolf* (New York: Alfred A. Knopf, 1997), p. 243. See also Woolf's letter to Waterlow, *VW Letters*, I, pp. 485-6.

21. *VW Letters*, I, pp. 485-6.

22. The best account of Strachey's life and work is Michael Holroyd's *Lytton Strachey* (New York: Holt, Rinehart and Winston, 1968). For the letters Strachey wrote to Leonard Woolf about his proposal to Virginia Stephen, see *The Letters of Leonard Woolf*, ed. Frederic Spotts (New York: Harcourt Brace Jovanovich, 1989), p. 147.

23. For good accounts of Brooke's Cambridge years, see Christopher Hassall's *Rupert Brooke* (New York: Harcourt, Brace and World, 1964) and Graham Chainey's *A Literary History of Cambridge* (Cambridge: Cambridge University Press, 1995).

24. For various versions of this incident, see Leonard Woolf, *Beginning Again* (New York: Harcourt Brace Jovanovich), p. 19 and Virginia Woolf, 'Rupert Brooke', in *The Essays of Virginia Woolf*, ed. Andrew McNeillie (New York: Harcourt Brace Jovanovich, 1987), II, pp. 277-84. See also Lee, p. 291 and Quentin Bell's *Virginia*

Woolf: A Biography (London: Hogarth Press, 1972; New York: Harcourt Brace Jovanovich, 1972) Vol. I, p. 174.

25. Quoted in Lee, p. 291. Charleston Papers, University of Sussex.

26. 'Rupert Brooke', p. 279.

27. *The Diary of Virginia Woolf*, ed. Anne Olivier Bell, assisted by Andrew McNeillie (London and New York: Harcourt Brace Jovanovich, 1977-1984), Vol. I, p. 103.

28. *VW Letters*, II, p. 292.

29. *VW Diary*, III, p. 16.

30. *VW Diary* II, p. 98.

31. *VW Letters*, III, p. 555.

32. Quoted in Lee, p. 587.

33. *VW Letters* IV, p. 230.

34. *VW Letters*, II, p. 303.

35. *VW Letters*, IV, p. 327.

36. *VW Letters*, IV, p. 327.

37. *VW Letters*, VI, p. 20.

38. See Lee, p. 146; *VW Letters*, VI, p. 419.

39. *VW Letters*, VI, pp. 467-8.

40. *VW Letters*, VI, p. 468.

41. *VW Letters*, V, pp. 34-5.

42. *VW Letters*, IV, p. 106.

43. See Lady Barbara Stephen, *Emily Davies and Girton College* (Westport, CT: Hyperion Reprint, 1976), p. 332.

44. Accounts of the turmoil surrounding the 1921 vote on admitting women to degrees at Cambridge can be found in Brooke, *A History of the University of Cambridge*, p. 326; Ann Phillips, ed. *A Newnham Anthology* (Cambridge: Newnham College, 1988), p. 150; J.J. Thomson *Recollections and Reflections* (London: G. Bell and Sons, 1936), p. 88.

45. *Three Guineas* (New York: Harcourt, Brace and World, 1966), pp. 29-30. (First published Hogarth Press, 1938.)

46. *VW Diary*, III, p. 200.

47. *VW Diary*, IV, 79. For an excellent discussion of Trinity College's decision to offer Woolf the Clark lectures, see S.P. Rosenbaum, 'Virginia Woolf and the Clark Lectures', *The Charleston Magazine*, Issue 22, Autumn/ Winter 2000, pp. 5-10. The vote was apparently contentious enough that it was discussed and adjourned three times before the decision was finally made.

48. *VW Diary*, IV, p. 177.

49. *VW Diary*, IV, p. 298.

50. In February of 1936, Pernel Strachey had written to Woolf asking her to join a Committee of Patrons to launch Newnham's first public appeal for funds. Woolf accepted Strachey's invitation, and also pasted Strachey's letter into the reading notebooks associated with *Three Guineas*. See Brenda Silver, *Virginia Woolf's Reading Notebooks* (Princeton: Princeton University Press, 1983), p. 280. For Woolf's reply, see *VW Letters*, VI, p. 15.

51. In 1932, Queenie Leavis had published the influential *Fiction and the Reading Public*. Eventually, Leavis helped to establish the study of English literature at universities as a discipline in its own right.

52. For various firsthand accounts of Woolf's lectures to the women of Newnham and Girton, see *A Newnham Anthology*, pp. 172-5; Lee, pp. 556-7; Rosenbaum's introduction to *Women & Fiction: The Manuscript Versions of A Room of One's Own*,

Transcribed and Edited by S.P. Rosenbaum (Oxford: Shakespeare Head Press/ Blackwell Publishers, 1992), pp. xv-xvi.

53. *VW Diary*, III, p. 203.

54. *A Room of One's Own* (New York: Harcourt, Brace and World, 1957), p. 6. (First published Hogarth Press, 1929.)

55. *A Room of One's Own*, pp. 7-8.

56. *A Room of One's Own*, p. 8.

57. *A Room of One's Own*, p. 9.

58. See Rosenbaum's introduction to *Women & Fiction*, p. xvi; see also *Recollections of Virginia Woolf*, ed. and with an introduction by Joan Russell Noble (New York: W. Morrow, 1972), p. 144.

59. *A Room of One's Own*, pp. 10-11.

60. *A Room of One's Own*, p. 15.

61. *VW Diary* III, p. 16.

62. *A Room of One's Own*, pp. 17-18.

63. *A Room of One's Own*, p. 18.

64. *A Room of One's Own*, pp. 20-1.

65. *A Newnham Anthology*, p. 174.

66. Rosenbaum, introduction to *Women & Fiction*, p. xviii.

67. See Hunt and Baker, pp. 20-1.

68. *A Room of One's Own*, p. 26.

69. *A Room of One's Own*, pp. 33-5.

70. *A Room of One's Own*, p. 55.

71. Chainey, p. 180.

72. Chainey, p. 190.

73. *A Room of One's Own*, p. 38.

74. *A Room of One's Own*, p. 38.

75. *A Room of One's Own*, pp. 69-70.

76. *Emily Davies and Girton College*, p. 176.

77. *A Newnham Anthology*, p. 174.

78. *The Pargiters: The Novel-Essay Portion of The Years*, ed. Mitchell Leaska (New York: Harcourt Brace Jovanovich, 1977), p. 28.

79. *The Years* (New York: Harcourt Brace Jovanovich, 1965), p. 65. (First published Hogarth Press, 1937.)

80. *The Years*, p. 57.

81. *The Years*, p. 66.

82. *Three Guineas*, p. 21.

83. *VW Diary*, V, pp. 149-50.

84. *Three Guineas*, pp. 4-5.

85. *Three Guineas*, p. 5.

86. *VW Letters*, I, p. 77.

87. *Three Guineas*, p. 37.

88. *Three Guineas*, pp. 38-9.

89. *Three Guineas*, p. 39.

90. *Three Guineas*, pp. 33-4.

91. *Three Guineas*, pp. 35-6.

92. *Three Guineas*, pp. 36-7.

93. *Three Guineas*, p. 105.

94. *Three Guineas*, pp. 108-9.

95. Bell, II, p. 205.

96. Q.D. Leavis, 'Caterpillars of the Commonwealth Unite!' in Eric Bentley, ed. *The Importance of Scrutiny* (New York: G.W. Stewart, 1948), pp. 384, 386.

97. *VW Letters*, I, p. 498.

98. *A Room of One's Own*, p. 5.

99. *A Room of One's Own*, pp. 7-8. This information about regulations for visiting Wren Library in Woolf's day was discovered by Sheila Wilkinson, who also kindly lent the author her copy of *A Concise Guide to the Town and University of Cambridge*, written by John Willis Clark (Cambridge: Bowes and Bowes, 1929). Mrs Wilkinson also corresponded with the librarian at Trinity about regulations regarding the entry of women into Wren Library through the years, and confirmed that women were never specifically barred. I am grateful to Mrs Wilkinson for generously making this information available to me.

100. *A Room of One's Own*, pp. 9-10.

101. *VW Diary*, II, p. 300.

102. Jane Hill, *The Art of Dora Carrington* (London: Thames and Hudson, 1994), pp. 126-7.

103. *A Room of One's Own*, p. 55.

104. Chainey, p. 190.

105. E.M. Forster, *The Longest Journey* (New York: Random House, 1962), pp. 2-3.

106. The best source for information on John Maynard Keynes is Robert Skidelsky's definitive, multi-volume biography, *John Maynard Keynes*.

107. For an excellent account of this incident, see Chainey, pp. 230-2. See also Frances Spalding's *Duncan Grant: A Biography* (London: Pimlico, 1998), p. 169.

108. Lawrence, D.H., *The Letters of D.H. Lawrence*, general editor James T. Boulton (New York and London: Cambridge University Press, 1981-1998), II, pp. 320-1.

109. *The Letters of D.H. Lawrence*, II, p. 321.

110. *The Letters of D.H. Lawrence*, II, p. 319.

111. *VW Diary*, II, p. 231.

112. Spalding, *Duncan Grant*, pp. 231-2.

113. Frances Spalding, *Roger Fry: Art and Life* (London: Black Dog Books, 1999), p. 16. Spalding's biography of Fry is the best source for information on his life and work.

114. Virginia Woolf, 'Mr Bennett and Mrs Brown', in *Collected Essays*, ed. Leonard Woolf (New York: Harcourt, Brace & World, 1967), I, p. 320. (First published 1923).

115. *A Room of One's Own*, p. 13.

116. See Spalding, *Roger Fry*, p. 28.

117. *A Room of One's Own*, p. 9.

118. *A Room of One's Own*, pp. 15-16.

119. *VW Diary*, III, p. 16.

120. *A Room of One's Own*, p. 17.

121. *A Room of One's Own*, pp. 16-17.

122. *A Room of One's Own*, p. 17.

123. *VW Diary*, III, p. 181. For an excellent account of the life and career of Jane Harrison, see Mary Beard's *The Invention of Jane Harrison* (Cambridge, Massachusetts and London: Harvard University Press, 2000).

124. 'A Woman's College from Outside', in *The Complete Shorter Fiction of Virginia Woolf*, ed. Susan Dick (London: The Hogarth Press, 1985), pp. 139-41.

125. Leslie Stephen, *Sketches from Cambridge by a Don* (London and Cambridge: Macmillan and Co., 1865), pp. 4-5. For additional material on Trinity Hall, see Charles

Crowley's *Trinity Hall: The History of a Cambridge College, 1350-1992* (Cambridge: The Master and Fellows of Trinity Hall, 1992).

126. *Sowing*, p. 180.

127. *Sowing*, pp. 180-2.

128. *Jacob's Room* (New York: Harcourt, Brace & World, 1959), p. 38. (First published Hogarth Press, 1922.)

129. *Jacob's Room*, p. 43 ff.

130. *VW Diary*, III, p. 114. Sheila Wilkinson generously brought some of the sites mentioned in this section to my attention.

131. For material on Brooke, his life, and his work, see Christopher Hassall, *Rupert Brooke* (New York: Harcourt, Brace and World, 1964).

132. Rupert Brooke, 'Grantchester', in *The Poetical Works of Rupert Brooke*, Ed. Geoffrey Keynes (London: Faber and Faber, 1970), p. 70.

133. *VW Letters*, III, p. 178.

134. *The Letters of Rupert Brooke*, ed. Geoffrey Keynes (New York: Harcourt Brace and World, 1968), pp. 172-3.

135. *The Letters of Rupert Brooke*, pp. 185-6.

136. Chainey, pp. 123, 144.

137. 'Grantchester', pp. 68-9.

138. Robert Tod provides a good account of Caroline Emelia Stephen's life in Cambridge. Alister Raby has researched the history of Caroline Stephen's search for the right house in Cambridge, and provided accounts in two spots: in 'The Porch, Cambridge' (*Virginia Woolf Bulletin*, Issue No. 1, January 1999), pp. 36-8 and in his talk 'The Porch', presented on 4 September 2000, during the Virginia Woolf Society of Great Britain's 'Virginia in Cambridge' conference.

139. Herbert's 'The Church Porch' was the most frequently anthologised of Herbert's poems during the eighteenth and nineteenth centuries. I am grateful to Edmund Miller for bringing this fact to my attention.

140. *VW Letters*, I, p. 145.

141. 'Divine Guidance', in Caroline Emelia Stephen's *The Vision of Faith. (With Memoirs by her niece Katharine Stephen, Principal of Newnham College, and Dr. T. Hodgkin)* (Cambridge: W. Heffer and Sons, 1910), pp. 48-9.

142. Raby, Cambridge talk, 4 September 2000. See also *VW Letters*, I, p. 391.

Chapter Five   Monk's House, Rodmell and Between the Acts

1. *The Diary of Virginia Woolf*, ed. Anne Olivier Bell, assisted by Andrew McNeillie (London and New York: Harcourt Brace Jovanovich, 1977-1984), Vol. I, p. 286.

2. *VW Diary*, I, pp. 286-7.

3. *The Letters of Virginia Woolf*, ed. Nigel Nicolson and joanne Trautmann (London: Hogarth Press; New York: Harcourt Brace Jovanovich, 1975-1980) Vol. II, p. 382.

4. Leonard Woolf, *Beginning Again: An Autobiography of the Years 1911 to 1918* (New York: Harcourt Brace Jovanovich, 1964), pp. 61-2; Leonard Woolf, *Downhill All the Way: An Autobiography of the Years 1919-1939* (New York and London: Harcourt Brace Jovanovich, 1967), pp. 12-13. As Sarah Bird Wright points out, the earliest deed Leonard Woolf could find for Monk's House dated to 1707. Her further research indicates the possibility of an earlier ecclesiastical connection. See *Staying at Monk's House: Echoes of the Woolfs* (London: Cecil Woolf Publishers, 1995).

5. *VW Diary*, II, p. 3.

6. *Vita and Harold: The Letters of Vita Sackville-West and Harold Nicolson*, ed. Nigel Nicolson (New York: G.P. Putnam's Sons, 1992), p. 146.

7. *VW Diary*, III, p. 89.

8. *VW Diary*, II, p. 43.

9. *VW Diary* I, p. 287.

10. *VW Diary*, I, p. 298.

11. *VW Diary*, V, p. 274.

12. *VW Diary*, IV, p. 109.

13. *Downhill All the Way*, p. 52. Leonard Woolf describes Virginia's desk at Tavistock Square in this way.

14. Hermione Lee, *Virginia Woolf* (New York: Alfred A. Knopf, 1997), p. 816, n.55; *VW Diary*, III, pp. 192-3.

15. *VW Diary*, III, p. 114.

16. *VW Diary* III, p. 196.

17. *Downhill All the Way*, pp. 15-16.

18. *VW Diary*, III, p. 197.

19. *VW Diary*, IV, p. 338.

20. Leonard Woolf, *The Journey Not the Arrival Matters:An Autobiography of the Years 1939-1969* (New York and London: Harcourt Brace Jovanovich, 1969), p. 55. See also Virginia's account of the Dunkirk evacuation in *VW Diary*, V, p. 294.

21. Lee, *Virginia Woolf*, p. 856, n.51.

22. *VW Diary*, V, p. 292.

23. *VW Diary*, V, p. 284.

24. *VW Diary*, V, p. 292.

25. *VW Diary*, V, p. 288. For the 1938 Rectory Fête, Rodmell villagers had performed *Twelfth Night*. Annie Thomsett Penfold, who had been the Woolfs' cook until 1934, was part of the cast. (I am grateful to Sheila Wilkinson for this information; Sheila has recently inspected documents belonging to the Women's Institute.)

26. *VW Diary*, V, p. 313.

27. *VW Diary*, V, p. 311.

28. *VW Diary*, V, p. 300.

29. *VW Diary*, V, p. 314.

30. *VW Letters*, VI, p. 424.

31. *VW Diary*, V, p. 324.

32. *VW Diary*, V, p. 326.

33. *VW Diary*, V, p. 354.

34. *VW Diary*, V, p. 356.

35. Harold Nicolson, *Diaries and Letters*, ed. Nigel Nicolson (New York: Atheneum, 1966-1968), II, p. 138.

36. *VW Letters*, VI, p. 486.

37. *VW Diary*, V, p. 357.

38. *VW Diary*, V, p. 355.

39. Vanessa Bell, quoted in *VW Letters*, VI, p. 485.

40. *VW Letters*, VI, p. 481.

41. *The Waves* (New York and London: Harcourt Brace Jovanovich, 1959), p. 297. (First published Hogarth Press, 1931.)

42. *Between the Acts* (New York: Harcourt Brace Jovanovich, 1969), p. 16. (First published Hogarth Press, 1941.)

43. *Between the Acts*, p. 7.

44. *Between the Acts*, pp. 14, 20.

45. *Between the Acts*, pp. 53-4.
46. *Between the Acts*, p. 60.
47. *Between the Acts*, p. 41.
48. *Between the Acts*, p. 110.
49. *Between the Acts*, p. 99.
50. *Between the Acts*, p. 9.
51. *Between the Acts*, p. 25.
52. *Between the Acts*, p. 175.
53. *Between the Acts*, p. 71.
54. *Between the Acts*, p. 73.
55. *Between the Acts*, pp. 8-9.
56. *VW Diary*, V, p. 274.
57. *Between the Acts*, p. 108.
58. *VW Letters*, IV, p. 83.
59. *Between the Acts*, pp. 204-5.
60. *Between the Acts*, pp. 57, 153.
61. *Between the Acts*, p. 31.
62. *Between the Acts*, p. 75.
63. *VW Diary*, III, p. 197.
64. Lee, *Virginia Woolf*, p. 717.
65. *Between the Acts*, p. 140.
66. *Between the Acts*, p. 180.
67. *Between the Acts*, p. 181.
68. *Between the Acts*, p. 188.
69. *Between the Acts*, p. 189.
70. *Between the Acts*, p. 192.
71. *Between the Acts*, p. 193.
72. *Between the Acts*, p. 219.
73. *VW Diary*, III, p. 89.
74. *VW Letters*, IV, p. 159.
75. *VW Letters*, III, p. 273.
76. George Spater and Ian Parsons, *A Marriage of True Minds: An Intimate Portrait of Leonard and Virginia Woolf* (New York: Harcourt Brace Jovanovich, 1977), p. 163.
77. *VW Letters*, II, p. 384.
78. *Between the Acts*, pp. 36-7.
79. I am grateful to Sheila Wilkinson for this information – and for the chance to see her photos and hear other firsthand details of the upper rooms at Monk's House.
80. *VW Diary*, III, pp. 219-20.
81. *VW Diary*, IV, p. 180.
82. 'The Fascination of the Pool', in *The Complete Shorter Fiction of Virginia Woolf*, ed. Susan Dick (London: The Hogarth Press, 1985), p. 220
83. 'The Fascination of the Pool', pp. 220-1.
84. *VW Diary*, I, p. 286.
85. *VW Lettters*, IV, p. 83.
86. 'In the Orchard', in *The Complete Shorter Fiction of Virginia Woolf*, ed. Susan Dick (London: The Hogarth Press, 1985), pp. 143-5.
87. *Downhill All the Way*, p. 52.
88. *VW Letters*, II, p. 549.
89. *VW Diary*, IV, p. 249.
90. *VW Diary*, II, p. 59. For a history of the Abergavenny Arms, see Judy Moore's

Rodmell, A Downland Village (Seaford, E. Sussex: S.B. Publications, 1999), p. 36. Using Rodmell election registers for 1921, Sheila Wilkinson has verified that the Abergavenny Arms was owned by Mr Malthouse when the Woolfs lived in Rodmell.

91. *Between the Acts*, p. 212.

92. 'Old Mrs Grey', in *Collected Essays*, ed. Leonard Woolf (New York: Harcourt, Brace & World, 1967), Vol. 4, p. 150. Maire McQueeney's *Virginia Woolf's Rodmell* contains additional information on the structures in Rodmell, as well as excellent maps.

93. See 'The Widow and the Parrot: A True Story', in *The Complete Shorter Fiction of Virginia Woolf*, ed. Susan Dick (London: The Hogarth Press, 1985), pp. 156-63.

94. Richard Shone, 'Asheham House: An Outline History', *The Charleston Magazine*, Issue 9, Spring/ Summer 1994, p. 36.

95. *Beginning Again*, p. 57.

96. *Beginning Again*, p. 57.

97. 'A Haunted House', in *The Complete Shorter Fiction of Virginia Woolf*, ed. Susan Dick (London: The Hogarth Press, 1985), p. 117.

98. Quentin Bell, *Virginia Woolf: A Biography* (London: Hogarth Press, 1972; New York: Harcourt Brace Jovanovich, Inc., 1972) Vol. II, p. 169.

99. *VW Letters*, V, p. 41.

100. *VW Letters*, V, p. 10.

101. Mark Hussey, *Virginia Woolf A to Z* (New York: Oxford University Press, 1995), p. 9. For a full account of the destruction of Asheham – as well as an account of the mysterious 'spirit' of the property – see Carol Hansen's *The Life and Death of Asham* (London: Cecil Woolf, 2000).

102. *VW Letters*, I, p. 476.

103. *VW Letters*, I, p. 451.

104. *VW Letters*, II, p. 95.

105. *VW Letters*, II, p. 355.

106. 'A Sketch of the Past', in *Moments of Being*, ed. Jeanne Schulkind (New York and London: Harcourt Brace Jovanovich, 1985), p. 91.

107. Quentin Bell and Virginia Nicholson give an excellent account of Charleston and its furnishings in *Charleston: A Bloomsbury House and Garden*.

108. See Quentin Bell's memoir 'A Cézanne in the Hedge' in *A Cézanne in the Hedge and Other Memories of Charleston and Bloomsbury*, ed. Hugh Lee (Chicago: University of Chicago Press, 1992), p. 136.

109. *VW Diary*, I, pp. 287-88.

110. My thanks to Sheila Wilkinson, who has researched Lewes sites associated with Woolf and who provided me with this information.

111. *VW Letters*, II, p. 367.

112. *VW Diary*, I, p. 279.

113. *VW Letters*, II, p. 369.

114. *VW Diary*, I, p. 286.

115. *VW Letters*, I, p. 449.

116. *VW Letters*, I, p. 446.

117. *Between the Acts*, pp. 6-7.

118. *VW Diary*, II, p. 4.

119. *VW Diary*, III, p. 107.

120. *VW Letters*, II, p. 415.

121. *VW Diary*, IV, p. 124.

122. *VW Letters*, II, p. 415.

123. I am grateful to Stephen Barkway and David Wilkinson – both of whom are avid walkers and experts when it comes to reading maps – for advice on the details of this walk. I am also grateful to Malcolm Sherman and Teri Gower for sharing details of Firle Estates' soon-to-be published *Firle Walks* pamphlet with me.

Works Consulted

WORKS BY VIRGINIA WOOLF

FICTION

Between the Acts. (First published Hogarth Press, 1941.) New York: Harcourt Brace Jovanovich, 1969.

The Complete Shorter Fiction of Virginia Woolf. Ed. Susan Dick. London: The Hogarth Press, 1985.

Jacob's Room. (First published Hogarth Press, 1922.) New York: Harcourt, Brace & World, 1959.

Mrs Dalloway. (First published Hogarth Press, 1925.) New York: Harcourt Brace Jovanovich, 1981.

———. *Mrs Dalloway.* Ed. Morris Beja. Oxford: The Shakespeare Head Press, 1996.

———. *Mrs Dalloway.* Ed. David Bradshaw. Oxford: Oxford University Press, 2000.

Night and Day. (First published Duckworth, 1919.) Penguin, 1992.

Orlando: A Biography. (First published Hogarth Press, 1928.) New York: Harcourt Brace Jovanovich, 1973.

———. 'Orlando: An Edition of the Manuscript.' Ed. Madeline Moore. *Twentieth Century Literature*, 25 (1979), 303-55.

———. *Orlando.* Ed. Brenda Lyons. London: Penguin Books, 1993. (With extensive notes, and annotations by Nigel Nicolson.)

———. *Orlando: The Holograph Draft.* Transcribed and edited by Stuart N. Clarke. London: S.N. Clarke, 1993.

The Pargiters: The Novel-Essay Portion of The Years. Ed. Mitchell Leaska. New York: Harcourt Brace Jovanovich, 1977.

To the Lighthouse. (First published Hogarth Press, 1927.) New York: Harcourt Brace Jovanovich, 1981.

The Voyage Out. (First published Duckworth, 1915.) Penguin, 1992.

The Waves. (First published Hogarth Press, 1931). New York and London: Harcourt Brace Jovanovich, 1959.

The Years. (First published Hogarth Press, 1937.) New York: Harcourt Brace Jovanovich, 1965.

AUTOBIOGRAPHY, LETTERS, DIARIES

The Diary of Virginia Woolf. Ed. Anne Olivier Bell, assisted by Andrew McNeillie. 5 Vols. New York: Harcourt Brace Jovanovich, 1977-1984.

The Letters of Virginia Woolf. Ed. Nigel Nicolson and Joanne Trautmann. 6 Vols. New York: Harcourt Brace Jovanovich, 1975-1980.

'Old Bloomsbury.' In *Moments of Being*. Edited by Jeanne Schulkind. New York and London: Harcourt Brace Jovanovich, 1985, 179-201.

A Passionate Apprentice: The Early Journals, 1987-1909. Ed. Mitchell Leaska. New York: Harcourt Brace Jovanovich, 1990.

'A Sketch of the Past.' In *Moments of Being*. Edited by Jeanne Schulkind. New York and London: Harcourt Brace Jovanovich, 1985, 61-159.

'22 Hyde Park Gate.' In *Moments of Being*. Edited by Jeanne Schulkind. New York and London: Harcourt Brace Jovanovich, 1985, 162-77.

Virginia Woolf & Lytton Strachey: Letters. Ed. Leonard Woolf and James Strachey. London: The Hogarth Press, 1969.

ESSAYS

Collected Essays. Ed. Leonard Woolf, 4 vols. New York: Harcourt, Brace & World, 1967.

The Essays of Virginia Woolf. Ed. Andrew McNeillie. 6 Vols. (projected) New York: Harcourt Brace Jovanovich, 1986-1988.

'Introduction' to *Victorian Photographs of Famous Men and Fair Women*. (First published Hogarth Press, 1926.) London: Hogarth Press, 1973.

The London Scene: Five Essays by Virginia Woolf. London: Hogarth Press, 1982.

A Room of One's Own. (First published Hogarth Press, 1929.) New York: Harcourt, Brace and World, 1957.

Three Guineas. (First published Hogarth Press, 1938.) New York: Harcourt Brace Jovanovich, 1966.

Women & Fiction: The Manuscript Versions of A Room of One's Own. Transcribed and Edited by S.P. Rosenbaum. Oxford: Shakespeare Head Press/Blackwell Publishers, 1992.

OTHER WORKS CONSULTED

Annan, Noel. *Leslie Stephen: The Godless Victorian*. New York, Random House, 1984.

Beard, Mary. *The Invention of Jane Harrison*. Cambridge, Massachusetts and London: Harvard University Press, 2000.

Bell, Quentin. *Virginia Woolf: A Biography*. 2 Vols. London: Hogarth Press, 1972; New York: Harcourt Brace Jovanovich Inc., 1972.

Bell, Quentin and Virginia Nicholson. *Charleston: A Bloomsbury House and Garden*. New York: Henry Holt and Company, 1997.

Brewster, Dorothy. *Virginia Woolf's London*. New York: New York University Press, 1960.

Briggs, Julia. 'Editing Woolf for the Nineties,' *The South Carolina Review*, Vol. 29, No. 1 (*Virginia Woolf International* issue, Fall 1996), 67-77.

Brooke, Christopher. *A History of the University of Cambridge, 1870-1990*. Vol. IV. Cambridge: Cambridge University Press, 1993.

Brooke, Rupert. *The Poetical Works of Rupert Brooke*. Ed. Geoffrey Keynes. London: Faber & Faber, 1970.

——. *The Letters of Rupert Brooke*. Ed. Geoffrey Keynes. New York: Harcourt, Brace & World, 1968.

Caramagno, Thomas. *The Flight of the Mind: Virginia Woolf's Art and Manic-Depressive*

Illness. University of California Press, 1996.

Caygill, Marjorie. *The British Museum Reading Room*. London: The Trustees of the British Museum, 2000.

Chainey, Graham. *A Literary History of Cambridge*. Cambridge: Cambridge University Press, 1995.

Clark, John Willis. *A Concise Guide to the Town and University of Cambridge*. Cambridge: Bowes and Bowes, 1929.

Clarke, Stuart N. 'Hyde Park Gate in 1894.' *Virginia Woolf Bulletin*, 2 (July 1999): 46-7.

———. 'Pursuing Leslie Stephen through the Censuses.' *Virginia Woolf Bulletin*, 7 (May 2001):63-5.

Crowley, Charles. *Trinity Hall: The History of a Cambridge College, 1350-1992*. Cambridge: The Master and Fellows of Trinity Hall, 1992.

Curtis, Vanessa. 'Highgate Cemetery: The Restoration of the Stephen Graves in 2000,' *The Virginia Woolf Bulletin*, No. 5, September 2000, 48-52.

———. *Virginia and Stella: An Unfinished Sisterhood*. London: Cecil Woolf Publishers, 2001.

Daiches, David and John Flower. *Literary Landscapes of the British Isles*: A Narrative *Atlas*. New York and London: Paddington Press, 1979.

Dally, Peter. *The Marriage of Heaven and Hell*: Manic Depression and the Life of Virginia *Woolf*. New York: St. Martin's Press, 1999.

Delany, Paul. *D.H. Lawrence's Nightmare*: The Writer and His Circle in the Years of the *Great War*. New York: Basic Books, 1978.

Dell, Marion. *Peering Through the Escallonia*: Virginia Woolf, Talland House and St Ives. London: Cecil Woolf, 1999.

Forster, E.M. *The Longest Journey*. New York: Random House, 1962. (First published 1907.)

Gaunt, William. *Victorian Olympus*. London: Jonathan Cape, 1952.

Gayford, Martin. 'Still Winding and Wonderful: Zennor's Literary and Artistic Connections', *The Charleston Magazine*, Issue 19, Spring/ Summer 1999, 5-14.

Glendinning, Victoria. *Vita*. New York: Alfred A. Knopf, 1983.

Hansen, Carol. *The Life and Death of Asham*: Leonard & Virginia Woolf's Haunted *House*. London: Cecil Woolf, 2000.

Hardyment, Christina. *Literary Trails*: Writers in Their Landscapes. London: The National Trust, 2000.

Hassall, Christopher. *Rupert Brooke*. New York: Harcourt, Brace and World, 1964.

Hill, Jane. *The Art of Dora Carrington*. London: Thames and Hudson, 1994.

Holroyd, Michael. *Lytton Strachey*: A Critical Biography. 2 Vols. New York: Holt, Rinehart, and Winston, 1968.

Hunt, Felicity and Barker, Carol. *Women at Cambridge*: A Brief History. Cambridge: The Press and Publications Office, University of Cambridge, 1998.

Hussey, Mark. *Virginia Woolf A to Z*. New York: Oxford University Press, 1995.

Kirkpatrick, B.J. and Clarke, Stuart N. *A Bibliography of Virginia* Woolf. 4th ed. Oxford: Clarendon Press, 1997.

Lawrence, D.H. *The Letters of D.H. Lawrence*. General editor James T. Boulton. 8 Vols. New York and London: Cambridge University Press, 1981-1998.

Leavis, Q.D. 'Caterpillars of the Commonwealth Unite!' In Eric Bentley, ed. *The Importance of Scrutiny*. New York: G.W. Stewart, 1948.

Lee, Hermione. *Virginia Woolf*. New York: Alfred A. Knopf, 1997. (First published London: Chatto and Windus, 1996.)

315

Lee, Hugh, ed. *A Cézanne in the Hedge and Other Memories of Charleston and Bloomsbury*. Chicago: University of Chicago Press, 1992.

Marcus, Jane. *Virginia Woolf, Cambridge, and A Room of One's Own* London: Cecil Woolf, 1996.

———. 'The Niece of a Nun: Virginia Woolf, Caroline Stephen, and the Cloistered Imagination.' In *Virginia Woolf: A Feminist Slant*. Ed. Jane Marcus. Lincoln: University of Nebraska Press, 1983, 7-36.

———. 'Thinking Back through Our Mothers.' In *New Feminist Essays on Virginia Woolf*. Ed. Jane Marcus. Lincoln: University of Nebraska Press, 1981, 1-30.

McQueeney, Maire. *Virginia Woolf's Rodmell*. Rodmell, E. Sussex: Rodmell Village Press, 1991.

Moore, G.E. *Principia Ethica*. Cambridge: Cambridge University Press, 1978.

Moore, Judy. *Rodmell, A Downland Village*. Seaford, E. Sussex: S.B. Publications, 1999.

Nicolson, Harold. *Diaries and Letters*. Ed. Nigel Nicolson. 3 Vols. New York: Atheneum, 1966-1968.

Nicolson, Nigel. *Portrait of a Marriage*. New York: Atheneum, 1973.

——— *Sissinghurst Castle Garden*. London: The National Trust, 1994.

Noble, Joan Russell, ed. *Recollections of Virginia Woolf*. New York: W. Morrow, 1972.

Partridge, Frances. *Memories*. London: Phoenix, 1999.

Phillips, Ann, ed. *A Newnham Anthology*. Cambridge: Newnham College, 1988.

Raby, Alister. 'The Porch.' Conference: Virginia Woolf in Cambridge. Cambridge, 4 September 2000.

———. ' 'The Porch', Cambridge.' *Virginia Woolf Bulletin*, 1 (January 1999), 36-8.

Raitt, Suzanne. Vita and Virginia: *The Work and Friendship of V. Sackville-West and Virginia Woolf*. Oxford: Clarendon Press, 1993.

Rosenbaum, S.P. 'Virginia Woolf and the Clark Lectures', *The Charleston Magazine*. Issue 22, Autumn/ Winter 2000, 5-10.

Sackville-West, Robert. *Knole*. London: The National Trust, 1998.

Sackville-West, Vita. *Collected Poems*. New York: Doubleday, 1934.

———. *Knole and the Sackvilles*. London: William Heinemann, 1923. Revised 1948; reprinted London and Tonbridge, Kent: Ernest Benn, 1958. (First published 1922.)

——— *The Land* in *The Land & The Garden*. Exeter, Devon: Webb and Bower, 1989. (First published 1927.)

——— *The Letters of Vita Sackville-West to Virginia Woolf*. Ed. Louise DeSalvo and Mitchell Leaska. New York: William Morrow and Co., 1985.

——— and Nicolson, Harold. *Vita and Harold: The Letters of Vita Sackville-West and Harold Nicolson*. Ed. Nigel Nicolson. New York: G.P. Putnam's Sons, 1992.

Shone, Richard. 'Asheham House: An Outline History', *The Charleston Magazine*, Issue 9, Spring/Summer 1994, 36-40.

Silver, Brenda. *Virginia Woolf's Reading Notebooks*. Princeton: Princeton University Press, 1983.

Skidelsky, Robert. *John Maynard Keynes: A Biography*. Vol. I New York: Viking, 1986; Vol. II New York: The Penguin Press, 1994.

Škrbic, Nena. 'Through the Realist Frame: "Phyllis and Rosamund" and the Masculine "I"'. *Virginia Woolf Bulletin*, 5 (September 2000), 15-22.

Spalding, Frances. *Duncan Grant: A Biography* London: Pimlico, 1998.

———. *Roger Fry: Art and Life*. Norwich: Black Dog Books, 1999.

———. *Vanessa Bell*. New York: Tichnor & Fields, 1983.

Spater, George and Ian Parsons. *A Marriage of True Minds: An Intimate Portrait of Leonard and Virginia Woolf*. New York: Harcourt Brace Jovanovich, 1977.

Squier, Susan. *Virginia Woolf and London: The Sexual Politics of the City*. Chapel Hill and London: The University of North Carolina Press, 1985.

Stephen, Lady Barbara. *Emily Davies and Girton College*. Westport, CT: Hyperion Reprint, 1976.

Stephen, Caroline Emelia. *The Vision of Faith*. (*With Memoirs by her niece Katharine Stephen, Principal of Newnham College, and Dr. T. Hodgkin*). Cambridge: W. Heffer and Sons, 1910.

Stephen, Leslie. *The Dictionary of National Biography*. Ed. Leslie Stephen and Sidney Lee. New York: Oxford University Press, 1921-1922.

———. *The Life of Sir James Fitzjames Stephen*. London: Smith, Elder, and Co., 1895.

———. *Sir Leslie Stephen's Mausoleum Book*. Ed. and with an introduction by Alan Bell. Oxford: Clarendon Press, 1977.

———. *Sketches from Cambridge*. London and Cambridge: Macmillan and Co., 1865.

Survey of London. Vol. XXXVII: Northern Kensington. London: The Athlone Press, 1973.

Survey of London. Vol. XLII: Southern Kensington: Kensington Square to Earl's Court. London: The Athlone Press, 1986.

Thomas, Antony Charles. *'To the Lighthouse': The Story of Godrevy Light*. Redruth, Cornwall: Penwith Books, 1973.

Thomson, J.J. *Recollections and Reflections*. London: G. Bell and Sons, 1936.

Tod, Robert. *Caroline Emelia Stephen, 1834-1909*. Unpublished essay, 1978.

Tomalin, Claire. *Katherine Mansfield: A Secret Life*. New York: Alfred A. Knopf, 1988.

Trombley, Stephen. *All That Summer She Was Mad: Virginia Woolf, Female Victim of Male Medicine*. New York: Continuum, 1982.

Tullberg, Rita. *Women at Cambridge*. Cambridge: Cambridge University Press, 1998.

Whitworth, Michael. ''The Indian and His Cross' in *Mrs. Dalloway*.' *The Virginia Woolf Miscellany*, Number 49 (Spring 1997).

Whybrow, Marion. *St. Ives, 1883-1993: Portrait of an Art Colony*. Woodbridge, Suffolk: The Antique Collectors' Club, 1994.

Willis, J.H. *Leonard and Virginia Woolf as Publishers: The Hogarth Press, 1917-1941*. Charlottesville: The University of Virginia Press, 1992.

Wilson, Jean Moorcraft. *Virginia Woolf, Life and London: A Biography of Place*. New York and London: W.W. Norton, 1987.

Woolf, Leonard. *Beginning Again: An Autobiography of the Years 1911 to 1918*. New York: Harcourt Brace Jovanovich, 1964.

———. *Downhill All the Way: An Autobiography of the Years 1919-1939*. New York and London: Harcourt Brace Jovanovich, 1967.

———. *The Journey Not the Arrival Matters: An Autobiography of the Years 1939-1969*. New York and London: Harcourt Brace Jovanovich, 1969.

———. *Sowing: An Autobiography of the Years 1880-1904*. New York and London: Harcourt Brace Jovanovich, 1975.

———. *The Letters of Leonard Woolf*. Ed. Frederic Spotts. New York: Harcourt Brace Jovanovich, 1989.

Wright, Sarah Bird. *Staying at Monk's House: Echoes of the Woolfs*. London: Cecil Woolf Publishers, 1995.

Index